Volume 1
METHODS IN
PSYCHOBIOLOGY

Volume 1

METHODS IN PSYCHOBIOLOGY

Laboratory Techniques in Neuropsychology and Neurobiology

EDITED BY

R. D. MYERS

*Laboratory of Neuropsychology
Purdue University, Lafayette, Indiana, U.S.A.*

1971

ACADEMIC PRESS

London and New York

ACADEMIC PRESS INC. (LONDON) LTD
24-28 Oval Road
London, NW1, 7DD

U.S. Edition published by
ACADEMIC PRESS INC.
111 Fifth Avenue
New York, New York 10003

Copyright © 1971 By ACADEMIC PRESS INC. (LONDON) LTD

All Rights Reserved
No part of this book may be reproduced in any form by photostat, microfilm, or any other means, without written permission from the publishers

Library of Congress Catalog Card Number: 76–153535
ISBN: 0–12–587050–7

Made in Great Britain at the Pitman Press, Bath

LIST OF CONTRIBUTORS

A. J. CUSHMAN, *Department of Psychology, University of Waterloo, Waterloo, Ontario, Canada (p. 67).*

R. COOPER, *Burden Neurological Institute Research Unit, Stoke Lane, Stapleton, Bristol, BS16 1QT, England (p. 156).*

F. R. ERVIN, *Harvard Medical School, Stanley Cobb Laboratory, Massachusetts General Hospital, Boston, Massachusetts, U.S.A. (p. 207).*

J. L. FALK, *Department of Psychology, Rutgers University, New Brunswick, New Jersey 08903, U.S.A. (p. 301).*

G. J. KENNEY, *Stanley Cobb Laboratory, Massachusetts General Hospital, Boston, Massachusetts, U.S.A. (p. 207).*

D. R. MEYER, *Laboratory of Comparative and Physiological Psychology, Department of Psychology, Ohio State University, Columbus, Ohio 43212, U.S.A. (p. 92).*

P. MEYER, *Laboratory of Comparative and Physiological Psychology, Department of Psychology, Ohio State University, Columbus, Ohio 43212, U.S.A. (p. 92).*

R. D. MYERS, *Laboratory of Neuropsychology, Purdue University, Lafayette, Indiana 47907, U.S.A. (p. 27, p. 247).*

L. PELLEGRINO, *Department of Psychology, Middlebury College, Middlebury, Vermont, U.S.A. (p. 67).*

R. THOMPSON, *Department of Psychology, Louisiana State University, Baton Rouge, Louisiana 70803, U.S.A. (p. 131).*

M. J. WAYNER, *Brain Research Laboratory, 601 University Avenue, Syracuse University, Syracuse, New York, U.S.A. (p. 1).*

*G. WOLF, *Department of Anatomy, Mount Sinai School of Medicine, New York, New York, U.S.A. (p. 281).*

* Present Address: State University of New York, Purchase, New York 10577, U.S.A.

PREFACE

For many years, the need has existed for a unified collection of information pertaining to the basic laboratory methods used in experiments which relate the brain to behavior. The prodigious amount of technical knowledge and the resulting improvements and advances in laboratory procedures have made it imperative for the behavioral scientist interested in the function of the brain to adopt some relatively specialized techniques. In fact, the rapid developments in biochemistry, neurophysiology and neuropharmacology have already led to a situation whereby the psychologist is forced either to re-structure his theoretical and practical thinking or to lapse into an otherwise traditional rather than modern approach to experimental investigation.

Volume 1 of this series is intended for the beginning "student," of which there are several kinds: the undergraduate, who is exposed for the first time to a laboratory experience in which a specific aspect of brain function is introduced; the advanced undergraduate, who may require one or more of the methods presented here for a senior honors project or a course itself; the first-year graduate student who is majoring in (or reading) Physiological, Neuro-, or Bio-psychology (or whatever name one wishes to call this field), and who must know well all of these techniques as part of his basic training; the post-doctoral fellow, who has a concentration of technical understanding within his own field of endeavor, but who may wish to employ other unique methods so as to extend the scope of his investigative ability; and lastly, the established scientist who wishes to switch from his "main-line" of research onto a new spur in his scholarly career, by embarking on one of the intriguing aspects of the brain-behavior problem.

This volume was originally conceived of as a "how-to" book containing "cook-book" instructions for each method or technique. Although this concept has been upheld in most instances, the contributors could not help bringing forth some of the issues of theoretical importance associated with a given topic, and rightfully so. As a result, the rationale, advantages and limitations of a particular method are also discussed.

The authors who were selected to contribute to the "Methods in Psychobiology" series are scientists, currently working in the laboratory who are recognized within their own area of specialization or even outside of their field. Each individual has been involved in some way with a development or refinement of a specific technique, which underscores the precept that an infinite number of modifications of an established method can be made on an individual basis, often by trial, by error and by tears. Thus, every experimenter develops his own characteristic style of utilizing a procedure that suits him best. One important point that should not be overlooked is the fact that even within the covers of this single volume, there may not be total agreement on every facet of a given method. For this reason and for the purpose of emphasis, a certain detail may be repeated or duplicated in different chapters. Finally, in the context of furthering one's own skill, it is certainly most helpful if the sections on apparatus notes, technical notes or brief communications are consulted regularly in such periodicals as: *Physiology and Behavior, Journal of Applied Physiology, Journal of Physiology* (Demonstrations), *Electroencephalography and Clinical Neurophysiology, Psychological Reports*, and the *Journal of Experimental Analysis of Behavior*.

The Editor is indebted to a great many individuals for making Volume 1 possible: Marjorie A. Myers, Editor for the Purdue Laboratory of Neuropsychology, who supervised the mechanics of the Volume and succeeded so admirably in solving the formidable problems related to this arduous task; Peter Curzon, Head Technician of the Purdue Laboratory of Neuropsychology, who resolved many of the photographic and other difficulties; Sandra Toman, who typed indefatigably large portions of the manuscript; and our proof-readers, Jan Baker, Sue Sears, Linda Smith and Patricia Leedy. Finally, the Editor acknowledges with great pleasure the help and patience of the Academic Press, who contributed in so many ways to the final version of this volume.

Lafayette, Indiana R. D. MYERS
August, 1971

CONTENTS

List of Contributors v
Preface vii

Chapter 1
PRINCIPLES OF RESEARCH IN PHYSIOLOGICAL PSYCHOLOGY
Matthew J. Wayner

I. Physiological Psychology Defined 1
II. Scientific Observation and Measurement 3
III. Measurement, Statistics and Probability 13
References 25

Chapter 2
GENERAL LABORATORY PROCEDURES
R. D. Myers

I. Introduction 27
II. Care and Treatment of Animals 29
III. Methods of Drug Administration 35
IV. Calculation of Pharmacological Doses 40
V. Procedures for Inducing Anesthesia 43
VI. Laboratory Diseases 49
VII. Euthanasia 60
Acknowledgement 60
References 60
Appendix A 62
Appendix B 63
Appendix C 65

Chapter 3
USE OF STEREOTAXIC TECHNIQUE
Louis J. Pellegrino and Anna J. Cushman

I. Introduction 67
II. Stereotaxic Instruments 69
III. Stereotaxic Atlases 73
IV. How to Use the Stereotaxic Instrument 78
V. Histological Verification of Stereotaxic Placements . . 84
Acknowledgements 86
References 86
Appendix A: Stereotaxic Atlases 87
Appendix B: Manufacturers and Distributors of Stereotaxic Instruments 90

Chapter 4

NEUROSURGICAL PROCEDURES WITH SPECIAL REFERENCE TO ASPIRATION LESIONS
Patricia M. Meyer and Donald R. Meyer

I. Introduction	92
II. Neocortical Ablations in Rats	92
III. Maintenance of Hemostasis	108
IV. Sterile Surgical Techniques and Procedures	110
V. Techniques of Aspiration in Large Species	120
VI. Epilogue	128
References	130

Chapter 5

INTRODUCING SUBCORTICAL LESIONS BY ELECTROLYTIC METHODS
Robert Thompson

I. Introduction	131
II. Electrolytic Lesions	133
III. Electrolytic vs. Thermocoagulative Lesions	136
IV. How to Make Electrolytic Lesions	136
V. How to Control the Size of the Lesion	142
VI. One-stage vs. Two-stage Lesions	143
VII. Ways to Increase Accuracy of Lesion Placements	143
VIII. Verification of Lesion Placements—Some Rapid Techniques	146
IX. An Evaluation of the Lesion Method	150
References	152
Appendix	154

Chapter 6

RECORDING CHANGES IN ELECTRICAL PROPERTIES IN THE BRAIN: THE EEG
Ray Cooper

I. Historical Introduction	156
II. Origins of Brain Activity	157
III. Applications of Implanted Electrode for Encephalography	158
IV. The Electrodes	161
V. The Recording	181
VI. Interpretation of the Records	185
References	201
Appendix A: Commercially Available Recording Instruments and Apparatus	204
Appendix B: Wire Tables	205

Chapter 7

ELECTRICAL STIMULATION OF THE BRAIN
F. R. Ervin and G. J. Kenney

I. Introduction	207
II. Types of Electrodes	212

III. Electrode Construction	215
IV. Implantation Procedures	220
V. The Electrochemical Interface and Problems of Polarization	230
VI. Interpretation	238
VII. Conclusion	242
References	243
Appendix	245

Chapter 8
METHODS FOR CHEMICAL STIMULATION OF THE BRAIN
R. D. Myers

I. Introduction	247
II. Construction of an Intracerebral Cannula	250
III. Implanting the Cannula into Brain Tissue	259
IV. Methods of Applying a Chemical	260
V. Interpretation of Data	270
Acknowledgements	278
References	278
Appendix	280

Chapter 9
ELEMENTARY HISTOLOGY FOR NEUROPSYCHOLOGISTS
George Wolf

I. Introduction and Historical Background	281
II. Preparation of Sections	283
III. Preparation of Slides	287
IV. Introduction to Staining	290
V. Staining Recipes	292
VI. Analysis of Brain Sections	297
References	299
Appendix	300

Chapter 10
DETERMINING CHANGES IN VITAL FUNCTIONS: INGESTION
J. L. Falk

I. Introduction	301
II. Mechanical Arrangements for Presenting Foods and Fluids	305
III. Special Diets	313
IV. Spatio-Temporal Arrangements: Their Influence on Intake and Choice	316
V. Extraneous Environmental Variables	319
VI. Acceptance, Rejection and Preference	320
VII. Analysis and Interpretation of Food and Fluid Intake Patterns	323
References	327
Appendix	330
AUTHOR INDEX	333
SUBJECT INDEX	339

Chapter 1

Principles of Research in Physiological Psychology[1]

MATTHEW J. WAYNER

*Brain Research Laboratory, Syracuse University,
Syracuse, New York, U.S.A.*

I. Physiological Psychology Defined 1
II. Scientific Observation and Measurement 3
   A. Observation 3
   B. Measurement 5
III. Measurement, Statistics and Probability 13
   A. Validity and Indeterminacy 13
   B. Errors of Measurement and Reliability 14
   C. Probability 20
   D. The Experiment 23
References 25

I. Physiological Psychology Defined

BEHAVIOR, what an organism does, the total of its overt activity at any moment, can be scrutinized from a variety of points of view. Behavior can be studied by a psychologist, a physiologist, a physicist or, as a matter of fact, by anyone. Psychologists are, however, those people who *concentrate* their efforts on the study of behavior. Behavior is a continuous stream of activity. Usually an attempt is made to limit the examination to some particular aspect of the process. The choice seems to be determined primarily by the investigator's interest at the moment and available instrumentation. Almost any type of method or technique is legitimate and permitted provided the human

---

[1] Supported in part by NSF Grant GB-18414X and NIMH, USPHS Grants 15473 and 16640. The author wishes to express his appreciation to the students working in the Brain Research Laboratory who helped in the preparation of this manuscript.

subject's life or liberties are not endangered and no unnecessary cruelty is imposed upon experimental animals.

The spectrum of behavior is very broad and, although the extremes can be defined, has been divided into subdisciplines almost without limitation. Physiological psychology or biopsychology represents one end of the spectrum. Biopsychology is the study of the biological determinants of the relations between the interactions of an organism with its environment. Environment includes both the external world and the internal structures of the individual. Physiological psychology is more concerned with complex organisms such as man and other primates, carnivores and rodents and the more obvious interactions with the external environment involved in certain vital adjustments necessary for survival. Behavior in these species and under these conditions can be defined as muscular activity and how muscular activity is modulated when the conditions change. For example, physiological psychology is concerned with the mechanisms of action in muscular movements, that is, exactly how the organism does something and the conditions which produce the changes. Such a point of view contrasts sharply with behavioristic psychology, which is somewhere close to the other end of the behavior continuum, and is concerned mainly with the effects an organism has on its environment, including other individuals. In the latter context, the effects are the products of muscular movements, for example, speech sounds or something as simple as closing a switch. Frequently, the products of muscular movements result in permanent alterations in the organism's environment. From a behavioristic point of view the contingencies and the other relations are of prime importance and the actual changes in the environment are considered to be less interesting. It is also possible to ignore the organism almost completely and place the major emphasis on environmental variables.

Psychology has been defined as the scientific study of behavior, and physiological psychology as a major subdivision is also alluded to as a science. What makes a study scientific? What differentiates scientific inquiry from other human activities? Science is factual and many people believe it is unequivocal and precise. Science is an organized body of knowledge which must be readily accessible to the international community. Knowledge is the accumulation of evidence in answer to specific questions as a result of the application of a variety of methods. Science is, therefore, both a body of knowledge, and some rules concerning how the information should have been collected. Science is a product of human activity and fraught with many of the same failings which limit other endeavors.

II. Scientific Observation and Measurement

Science begins with facts. A scientific fact is an accurately described observation which is also verifiable. An observation can be any sensory event; usually visual or auditory but other sense modalities can also be used. Most scientific observations are indirect and specialized devices must be employed to extend the capacities of the human senses. The electron microscope is a very complicated extension of the eye and produces photographs of objects not directly observable. Science is characterized by measurement, a subject which will be examined later in greater detail.

Measurement and the study of physics are intimately related in the history of mankind, and for most practical purposes measurement and physics are almost synonymous. It is interesting that physics began with a detailed examination of obvious characteristics of various objects and naturally occurring events and has advanced to the point today where theoretical physics is concerned with relations and interactions so complex that reality in terms of sensory events completely eludes the naïve observer. At this level, the scientific rigor is almost pure mathematics and logic. As one progresses from mathematics and physics into other disciplines such as chemistry, biology, psychology and sociology, the rigor of mathematical precision decreases, the phenomena appear to be more complex, descriptions are less quantitative, investigators rely more on intuition, and both the object and objectives of the study are more obvious and more easily verified by direct observation. As a matter of fact, psychology has been referred to in the philosophical literature as a study of the obvious. Human behavior is relatively obvious and overt, easy to describe, and not very difficult to understand.

A. Observation

There are two types or classes of scientific observation. Naturalistic observation refers to a description of an object or event under natural conditions, and it is based upon the assumption that the process of observation does not affect the object or phenomenon being observed. The observation is limited, however, by the sensory capacity of the individual and the available scientific instruments; for example, the light-gathering power of the large reflecting mirror telescopes or the diameter of the largest radio-telescope. Descriptive astronomy is an excellent example of naturalistic observation because most of the events being observed occurred many light years away and long before the existence of mankind began. Many other examples can be found in the geological study of natural rock formations, marine and terrestrial ecology, ethology and in many studies of human and animal behavior based only upon direct observation. In physiological psychology, the student should be advised to observe the commonly available experimental animals under natural laboratory living conditions. If possible, the student should also be encouraged to observe the same or similar species in their natural habitats. The direct observation of animal behavior under natural conditions can be very informative.

Controlled observation usually takes place in the laboratory, a relatively permanent physical structure which makes possible the production of unusual conditions under which the observation will be made. In the laboratory the observer or experimenter makes a special attempt to control or change the conditions under which the observation occurs. A horticulturist might discover some unusual exotic fruit-bearing plant and, in terms of his knowledge about terrain, soil chemistry and climate, predict unusual growth under different conditions. Only by moving the plant to a greenhouse can the conditions be altered rapidly and sufficiently enough to change effectively the growth rate or other characteristics of the fruit. Every known critical condition such as soil composition and chemistry, temperature, type of illumination and many others can be varied independently, and the effects on some desirable characteristics of the plant can be determined. In the laboratory, it is also possible to create substances such as plastics which do not occur naturally. Unfortunately, in studies of human behavior it is difficult, if not impossible, to transplant people even for apparent worthwhile purposes. Therefore, every serious attempt to study human behavior results in a compromise in methodology, some conditions can be changed but others cannot, and one must rely on naturalistic observation and uncontrolled changes in conditions. Verbal discussion, the interviewing technique and logical persuasion are interesting limited methods which have been employed successfully in the study of human behavior. In the physical sciences and biology, controlled observations can also be limited by legal restrictions; however, such studies which employ dangerous radioactivity, highly infectious viruses, potent poisonous and other pernicious substances or forms of life and chemical or nuclear explosives usually represent a relatively small percentage of the basic research effort. When for purposes of national security and prevention of disease such research must be conducted, it should be carried out only if sufficient precautions can be guaranteed to the entire population.

Research can therefore be dangerous. Because of man's attempt to accomplish everything which is technologically possible and to exploit his natural resources, he has failed to assess the long-range detrimental effects of such abuse on both himself and the environment. Consequently, one of the major problems facing science today is a reorientation in terms of applications to correct the undesirable and harmful effects which its applications have already produced. Physiological psychology, brain research, psychopharmacology and the experimental control of behavior in general are all potentially perilous to the individual and hazardous to society as well as tremendously beneficial. The discovery of new drugs, drug addiction, emotional disturbances resulting from brain surgery and stimulation, persuasion, propaganda and prejudice induced through mass media are efficient instruments of destruction which society can use against itself. Can science be restrained? Science is the product of the human brain, available knowledge and the instrumentation to obtain new information. New ideas will continue to emerge and discoveries will be made as long as man has the free time to pursue them. Can society protect itself against the advancements of science? Society must prepare itself to decide between the alternatives which science will produce. Does science have a purpose? No. However, science can make it possible for man to define a realistic purpose for himself and provide the means to achieve it within a reasonable length of time. By limiting the population, increasing the amount of food, eliminating strenuous labor, and reducing injury and disease, science can provide man with more time to learn and to develop more effective methods for the control and management of his own affairs.

The spirit of scientific inquiry is to formulate and ask questions, to challenge established beliefs, to evaluate critically and to seek the fundamental basis, either logic or data, for a particular assertion or contention. In science the assumptions which scientists accept and use on an everyday basis are usually difficult for the student to discover, but it is important that the assumptions be continuously examined and re-evaluated in terms of new discoveries and data. Many times it is the student who must take a fresh and novel approach to an old problem and discover a new solution.

B. *Measurement*

Physiological psychology is to a large extent semiquantitative and relies upon naturalistic observation and a considerable amount of useful anecdotal material which has been collected. A major difficulty in the study of behavior is to determine what aspects or property of behavior is measurable. When two substances or events differ, they are different with respect to some property of the substance or process.

The statements which scientists make concerning these differences fall into one or both of the following classifications—qualitative or quantitative.

Quantitative statements are based upon measurements. For example, a laboratory rat was deprived of water and its general locomotor activity increased, and the animal moved about its environment, explored, and eventually discovered a familiar reservoir of water. The animal drank continuously for four minutes and ingested 8·0 milliliters (ml) of water. The observations and statements that "the animal moved about its environment", "general locomotor activity increased", "discovered a familiar reservoir of water" are qualitative. The fact that the animal drank 8·0 ml of water is quantitative and is expressed in commonly accepted units of volume. The rate of drinking, 2·0 ml per minute, although it was not observed directly, is also quantitative. Since behavior is usually observed directly with the unaided senses, much of the data are qualitative or semiquantitative. In many studies of the effects of electrical stimulation of the brain in both normal, awake humans and laboratory animals, statements such as ". . . unidirectional rectangular electric pulses 0·3 milliseconds in duration, 3·9 volts intensity, were delivered at the rate of 60 per second for 1·5 seconds to the cerebral motor cortex of the right brain hemisphere at the point indicated and labeled M in Figure 15 . . . the stimulation evoked a rapid, jerky movement of the forearm . . ." are found. What is required is a more precise method for measuring fundamental characteristics of properties of movements.

Measurement is difficult to define exactly. Norman Campbell, a physicist, in 1921 published a monograph entitled "What is Science?" in which he explains some fundamental features of measurement. Measurement is the expression of certain properties of objects and events in terms of numbers. Why are only some properties measurable? Measurable properties change in a predictable manner when the objects or events are combined in certain ways. Weight or mass is an excellent example. Consider two cages each containing five rats and each animal weighing 300 g. The total weight in each cage is 1500 g. Each rat is also a member of a special genetically inbred strain of rats referred to as the Wistar strain. If all the animals are placed in one cage the total weight of rats in the combined cage has increased to 3000 g. If each cost $1·00, the cost for the total number of animals is $10·00. Both the weight and cost or price of the animals changed as new combinations of the animals were formed and are therefore considered to be measurable properties of rats. Units of weight and cost are determined arbitrarily and standard units exist by unanimous agreement within the scientific community. The fact that each animal is a member of the same genetic strain, which does not change when we consider new combinations of rats, means that it is a non-measurable property of animals. The difference is a somewhat crude definition, but nonetheless it represents the beginning of a powerful set of ideas.

What is the meaning of number? The term is confusing because it has been used to denote two distinctly different meanings—a name, a word or a symbol and sometimes a property of an object or event. Therefore, the collections of animals in our previous example have another property—the number of rats in each cage and the number is just as much a property of the animals as their weight or cost. When a number is employed to designate the "number of . . . ", it is not itself a property of the object but a symbol or name which represents the property. When measurement is defined as the representation of properties by number, it is the representation of properties other than number by the symbols which are used to represent number. The symbols are referred to as numerals. Number is the property of an object or event which is always represented by numerals. These considerations emphasize an important point. Measurable properties of an object must resemble in some special way the property of number. Since they can be represented by the same symbols, they must have some fundamental quality common with number. What is it?

The number of animals in a cage is determined by the process of counting. Numerals and counting are intimately related and apparently evolved early in history in order to answer the question "How many?". Such a need undoubtedly gave rise to the development of natural numbers or positive integers 1, 2, 3, 4, etc. The process of division of quantities led naturally to the introduction of positive rational fractions, $\frac{1}{2}$, $\frac{3}{4}$, etc. and they developed to help answer the question "How much?". The concept of zero must have occurred when a positive integer was subtracted from itself, when quantities of a substance were exhausted (the absence of a quantity) and when quantity could be indicated in two opposite senses which suggests negative numbers and a zero point. Early number systems were crude and awkward to use and the decimal system which corresponds to true life operations evolved. Common arithmetic operations were therefore based on the number ten, probably, because man has five digits on each hand and employed his fingers in the process of counting. Ten has no other special properties and any base can be used. Because of the recent advent of digital electronic computers, many students and scientists are learning to count in different number systems such as the hexadecimal, octal, and binary systems. There are many other fascinating and significant properties of numbers which will not be discussed here. However, there are several rules for counting which will be described.

Rules of counting are so obvious that they tend to be overlooked. First, if two sets of objects are counted against a third set and have the same number as the third set, then when counted against each other they will have the same number. This rule permits one to determine if two sets of objects have the same number without bringing them together. Second, by starting with a set containing a single object and continually adding other single objects (one at a time), it is possible to construct a standard series of sets such that any given set of the series will contain one object more than the preceding set. Any other observed set may then be compared to this standard series of sets, and there will be one member set of the series having exactly the same number as the observed set. This rule suggests that one set should not be counted against another but against a standard series. In the standard series each set is included in the next larger one. Numerals are therefore distinguishable objects with which a standard series of sets is constructed by adding them in turn to previous numbers of the series. By an ingenious convention, the set of the series which has the name number as a set counted against it can be described by quoting the last numeral in the set of the standard series. These two rules are necessary to explain the "number of . . ." and how that number is ascertained. The third and final rule is that equals added to equals must produce equal sums. If A and B represent sets or collections of objects which have the same number and the same is true of C and D, then $A + B$ must equal $C + D$; that is, both combined sets must have the same number.

Measurable properties are similar to numerals and must follow equivalent rules. First, if two objects are identical with respect to some property of a third subject, they are indistinguishable from each other with respect to that property. Second, by adding objects successively, a standard series can be constructed such that some one member will always be identical with respect to this property as any other object to be measured. Third, equals added to equals produce equal sums. In order for a property to be measurable, some method of judging equality and of adding objects together must be found such that these rules are true. The weight or mass of an object meets these requirements. Weight is therefore a measurable property of an object. If a balance is available and if object A balances object B and B balances C, then A will balance C. By placing an object in one pan of the balance and continually adding others to it, collections of objects can be built up which will balance any other object placed in the other pan. The operation will be successful only if the first object selected has a smaller weight than any other object to be weighed and it is possible to add objects which are fractions and multiples of the first object. If object A balances object B, and C balances D, then A and C in the same pan will balance B and D in the other pan.

It is because of these rules that measurable properties of objects are so similar to their conceptual counterparts in numbers. Any property which meets these requirements would represent a fundamental measurement. Weight and volume are fundamental properties of any quantity. By agreement, the unit in which weight is measured is the kilogram and length is measured in terms of the meter. Standards exist for these and other units; for example, the volt (a unit of electrical potential) and the candle (a unit of light intensity). Originally the meter was intended to be one ten millionth of the distance measured on a meridian of the earth from the equator to the pole. Actually, it is the distance between two lines on a platinum iridium bar kept at the International Bureau of Weights and Measures at Sevres, near Paris. Because of the difficulty in standardizing other bars, the wavelength of fluorescing krypton, which is equal to the distance on the bar divided by 1650, 763·73 is used for precise measurement. The cubic meter, volume of a cube one meter on an edge, is the standard unit of volume. Another standard unit of volume is the liter, the volume of 1000 g of water at 4°C. The liter is equal to 1000·027 cc. However, for many practical purposes, one cubic centimeter is considered equal to one milliliter. The basic unit of mass or weight is the gram—the weight of a platinum iridium cylinder at the International Bureau of Weights and Measures. Many countries maintain their own national bureau of standards which manufacture and sell calibrated electrical cells, lamps and weights.

Other properties of objects can be derived from the fundamental ones. One can refer to these as derived properties. The density d of a substance is defined as the mass or weight w of the substance per unit volume v.

$$d = \frac{w}{v}$$

The units are usually defined arbitrarily and relative to some substance of general interest such as water, for a standard set of conditions, to which other solutions are compared. Density is a derived magnitude and a mathematical function, and it is not possible to add densities of different substances together in a meaningful physical sense. Velocity, distance traveled per unit time, is another example. Most measurements or magnitudes are the derived type and they are defined as mathematical expressions. By definition, density is equal to weight divided by volume and for a given volume of a substance then the weight is proportional to its density.

If we consider an easy-to-compress substance such as a gas, then the density of a gas is proportional to the pressure upon it, and, therefore, the weight of a given volume of any gas is proportional to the pressure upon it. Also pressure must be defined, and some means must be developed for its measurement. Therefore, the basic assumption concerning fundamental measurable properties of objects is that the magnitudes can be added in a physical sense which corresponds to mathematical additivity. These basic properties give rise to the derived mathematical functions of these fundamental magnitudes. Sometimes these functions are referred to as numerical laws.

Another important consideration in these relations are the constants in the equations and the constants in a real sense. For example π is a very useful and practical number or constant which is dimensionless and requires no experimental proof; $\pi = C/D$ where C is the circumference of a circle and D is its diameter; also, $e^{\pi i} + 1 = 0$, where e is $2 \cdot 718$ and $i = \sqrt{-1}$. Other constants such as the velocity of light are commensurable quantities and are subject to experimental determination.

It is important for the physiological psychologist to consider some practical aspects of measurement. First of all there is usually some reason or need for the measurement—to verify a previous measurement, to select some quantity of a substance, or to produce something according to predetermined specification. In order to determine the effect of some drug on the performance of a rat in a given behavioral test situation, it is necessary to adjust the amount administered for the body weight of the animal—a larger animal should receive proportionately more drug than a smaller one. Therefore, it is necessary to weigh the animal before the amount of the drug to be administered is determined. The weight will be determined by means of a calibrated balance. The animal will be placed in the weighing pan. In place of a pan to hold weights for balancing the object being weighed, the balance has three parallel beams, and by adjusting the positions of three weights, one on each beam, it is possible to determine the weight of an object to $0 \cdot 1$ g. The final adjustment of the triple beam balance is made by moving the smallest weight on the third beam until the entire beam balances. The scale on this beam is graduated into millimeters (mm) and each mm corresponds to $0 \cdot 1$ g. After balancing, the three weights line up on each beam in the following way: 0–500 g scale, 200 g; 0–100 g scale, 50 g; 0–10 g scale 4·3 g. However, the slide on the third beam actually came to rest somewhere between 4·3 and 4·4 g (see Fig. 1). Under these conditions, the observer must interpolate between the two subdivisions of the scale and estimate the proportion of the interval cut off by the edge of the slider. A more exact reading would be 4·36 g for a total weight of 254·36 g. The last digit 6 is significant, because it is fixed between 4·3 and 4·4, and should

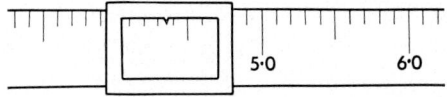

FIG. 1. A portion of the scale, 0–10, on a triple beam balance. Pointer indicates 4·36.

enter into further computations. Actually the fifth digit is non-significant in terms of the accuracy required to calculate the amount of drug administered. The number can be rounded to 254·4 g. If the recommended dose for this particular drug is 35 mg/kg of body weight, the difference in amount of drug administered is approximately 1/1000 of a milligram. For an extremely potent or toxic substance, such a small difference might be significant. The significance of a difference in this context requires prior knowledge or an experimental test.

The example illustrates two other important considerations about measurement. In counting, the basic mathematical process involves integer arithmetic and several simple fractions. Counted values are exact numbers; whereas, in actual measurements the results can rarely be expressed as whole or exact numbers. Experimental numbers raise the question of significant figures which depend upon the ability of the observer and the precision of the measuring instrument. The weight of the animal in the previous example can easily be determined to 0·001 g; however, this degree of precision is not required. Significant figures are those which result from direct observation. Figures which are not significant appear in combining experimental numbers by addition, subtraction, multiplication and division. The numbers which result from calculations must be eliminated because they indicate a greater degree of precision than are actually employed in the measurements and are probably incorrect. Bilateral radio frequency lesions are made in the lateral hypothalamus of five rats and their 24 hr food intakes were measured following the surgery. On the second day following the surgery the following intakes were measured: 19·10,

0·050, 21·41, 7·001, and 14·3 g. The total intake for all five animals is by simple addition 61·861. The total should be reported as 61·9 g. The smallest intake of 0·050 g contributes little to the total and is smaller than the possible error in one of the other intakes. The number of significant figures in the total is determined by the least precise number to be added, and is, therefore, related to the position of the decimal point. Even though the least precise number contained only one figure to the right of the decimal point, all figures in the next column for the more precise numbers should be retained in the addition process. If the sum of those figures is greater than 5, it will contribute to the last significant figure. The number has been rounded to the last significant figure. The other non-significant figures are dropped. A sum therefore can contain no significant figures to the right of the last significant figure relative to the decimal point of any of the experimental numbers to be added. The same rule applies to subtraction. The sum in our example is therefore 61·9 g. The average or mean intake for the five animals is therefore 61·9 divided by five or 12·38 g which should be rounded to 12·4 g. The quotient of two numbers can have no more significant figures than either the divisor or the dividend. The same rule applies to a product which has the same number of significant figures as the multiplier with the least number. These rules are somewhat arbitrary and should not be applied indiscriminately. Zero can be confusing when it is employed only to fix the decimal point and has no effect on the manipulation of the digits in the calculation.

A direct measurement need not be made with the maximum precision. The degree of precision or the tolerance which can be accepted in a measurement is usually specified before the measurement is made. In the previous example, body weight is commonly expressed in tenths of grams by digits. What is acceptable depends upon the possible applications of the information and prior experience in the use of such information. The degree of precision required today might be inadequate in the future as more knowledge accumulates and measuring instruments are improved.

In general, an experiment in physiological psychology does not require the great precision or narrow tolerances expected for analytical chemistry, construction of missiles for space travel and many other fields, except when similar methods are employed. Some physiological psychologists are actually engaged in analytical brain biochemistry. Others have spent a considerable amount of time in the design and construction of electronic equipment for special application to problems of behavior. In routine stereotaxic implantation of electrodes and ablation studies, an overall error of ±0·2 mm can be expected in the placement of the electrode tip into the predetermined structure. Therefore, in the design of a stereotaxic instrument tolerances to 0·01 mm during construction would be adequate, and it should be possible to read the graduated scales to 0·1 mm. Consequently, most available instruments are equipped with millimeter scales with verniers which permit accurate readings to 0·1 mm.

III. Measurement, Statistics and Probability

A. Validity and Indeterminacy

When a scientist is reasonably certain that he knows what he is measuring and can convince other scientists of his conviction, he has established the validity of his observations. Validity appears to be implicit in the measurement of fundamental physical entities of length, weight, volume, time, voltage and resistance, and the closely related derived properties of velocity, density, current, ionic conductance and many others. It never arises as a question in counting. However, there is an inconsistency here, and the measurement and number basis for an exact science can break down. As A. S. Eddington emphasized many years ago ". . . in digging deeper and deeper into that which lies at the base of physical phenomena we must be prepared to come to entities which, like many things in our conscious experience, are not measurable by numbers in any way; and further it suggests how exact science, that is to say the science of phenomena correlated to measure-numbers, can be founded on such a basis." He was commenting on Dirac's treatment of quantum mechanics and the q-numbers. His comments are also related to the fact that even in physics, some phenomena are indeterminate in a number sense.

Heisenberg's Principle of Uncertainty states that a particle may have position or it may have velocity, but it cannot in any exact sense have both. In determining the position of a particle very precisely, the determination itself decreases the precision with which the velocity or momentum can be determined. The particle must interact with some part of the universe before a scientist can indirectly observe it. Therefore, in observing its position its momentum must have changed. The uncertainty principle is sometimes referred to as the principle of indeterminacy.

Many things in science are indeterminate. In the study of muscle movements, prior knowledge giving the exact lengths of all muscle fibers would seem to be invaluable in the determination of how a change in position is produced. However, the exact value is indeterminate. In order to measure the required information the muscle would have to be partially destroyed. Therefore, the methods of science interact with the observed phenomena and to a certain extent determine what the methods reveal.

Each method or experimental technique can be considered a colored window through which we observe a particular phenomenon. Only when some phenomenon is examined in great detail by a variety of different methods does a clear picture begin to emerge, the greater detail and increasing complexity resulting in greater clarity and understanding. Therefore, the validity of a single observation can never be determined. Multiple criteria must be involved. Even rare astronomical events must occur at least twice. P. A. M. Dirac once stated that "The main object of physical science is not the provision of pictures, but the formulation of laws governing phenomena and the application of these laws to the discovery of new phenomena." An interesting paradox is that science creates pictures in order to discover which pictures do not represent reality. Theories are pictures in a sense, as they tend to fill gaps in our knowledge. Any worthwhile theory must, therefore, be difficult to develop because it is a fabrication of knowledge which is not readily available or immediately and directly observable. A theory is testable then in the sense that it leads to the discovery of new information.

B. Errors of Measurement and Reliability

Measurement implies two fundamental concepts; validity which is enigmatic and can be paradoxical, and reliability which is usually easier to define. An observation is reliable if, when replicated under the same conditions, will produce identical results. However, measurements are not exact. One of the assumptions in measurement theory is that any number which results from an observation has two components—the true value, T, plus some error, E. When the error is small, repeated observations on the substance or process should produce similar results. When the error is large, the outcomes will vary and depend upon the type of error. In a previous example, the weight of an animal based upon a single determination was 254·4 g. A single observation can be misleading.

In science, observations are repeated in order to establish the reliability of the measurement. If, for some unknown reason, the weighing pan for the balance had been interchanged with another that was heavier by 5 g, each measurement would overestimate the weight of the animal by a constant amount. Repeated observations would, in this case, produce similar but incorrect results. Such an error is referred to as a constant error. Constant errors can be very difficult to detect but relatively easy to correct. Any scientific instrument must be calibrated and checked periodically. The calibration procedure can employ a standard set of weights or, if these are not readily available, a method based upon standard volumes can be developed. If some means are available for measuring volumes precisely, then 100 ml of water at room temperature will weigh approximately 100 g. Once a constant error has been detected, the measurements can usually be corrected easily by the addition or subtraction of a constant to the observed value.

If the animal had been weighed many times by a single individual, or if many individuals had each weighed the animal once, the outcome could have differed in a more obvious respect; that is, the same number would not have occurred every time. Some of the numbers would be different. Actually, the numbers would differ more for ten individuals, each making one determination, than for those obtained from the same individual making all ten determinations. With one individual, prior knowledge would be a factor and the measurements would not be independent of one another. If the individual made an error in the initial determination, he would notice the difference in the second determination and balance the scales again in an attempt to correct the error. Except for gross errors of judgment, it is better for the individual to attempt to make independent observations and to accept a certain amount of variability in the results, than to impose what might be some personal bias and introduce a constant error into the data. Some individuals tend to overestimate, and others underestimate when reading scales. Errors of this type occur frequently when the indicator of a scale falls between two graduation marks (as in Fig. 1) and the individual has to interpolate or estimate the value. Every measurement contains some error, and it is necessary to repeat the observation in order to estimate the magnitude of the error.

When a measurement is repeated many times, many numbers result and many of them will be identical in value. The numbers are usually arranged into classes which are mutually exclusive and exhaustive such that each observation falls into one and only one class. The various classes are usually arranged in some meaningful order, and each class is paired with its frequency number, the number of measurements which can be included in that category. A list of the classes and their frequencies is called a frequency distribution. There are many different ways in which this basic information can be displayed—an exact listing of class and frequency pairs, graphically, or the statement of a mathematical rule for pairing a class of observations with its frequency.

If M represents the measured number, T the true desired value and E the error in the measurement which is not a constant error, then:

$$M = T + E$$

and if T is a constant, the nature of the frequency distribution will be determined primarily by how E varies. A simple model for considering how E might vary is the following. Assume that E is itself a sum:

$$E = e_1 + e_2 + e_3 + \ldots$$

Where e_1 is a random variable which can have only two values $e_1 = 1$ when some factor is operating and $e_1 = -1$ when the factor is not operating. Assume that there are many other random errors $e_2, e_3, \ldots$ which result from as many other different factors and also take on only the values of 1 or -1. Assume that the determining factors operate independently of one another, and that for each factor the probability of occurrence is 0·5. Then $e_1, e_2, e_3 \ldots$ behave somewhat as coins and the proportion of time that 5 heads will occur or five factors will operate if N coins are tossed simultaneously or N factors are expected to operate at the moment can be determined from the binomial expansion. The limiting form of the binomial distribution, as N becomes very large ($N \rightarrow \infty$) for $p = 0·5$ is the normal distribution. Therefore, the expected frequency distribution for M is normal, as illustrated in Fig. 2, with a mean of m when a large number of uncontrolled factors are contributing to the error. Also, if any factor is just as likely to operate as not to operate when M is observed, then the probability of occurrence $=0·5$ and as $N \rightarrow \infty$ the occurrences of $+1$ should begin to equal the occurrences of -1, the factors will tend to cancel one another, and the error will approach zero.

Since many frequency distributions are normal, the normal distribution can be employed to illustrate most of the important points concerning reliability. From a logical point of view, it is important and convenient to assume that a frequency distribution underlies any measurement and that it has been compiled from a relatively large number, N, of independent observations. Is any one value a better representation of the distribution than other values? The most frequently occurring value, which is called the mode, might be suitable. The median, that calculated value above and below which 50% of all the other values lie, might be adequate. The mean or average of all

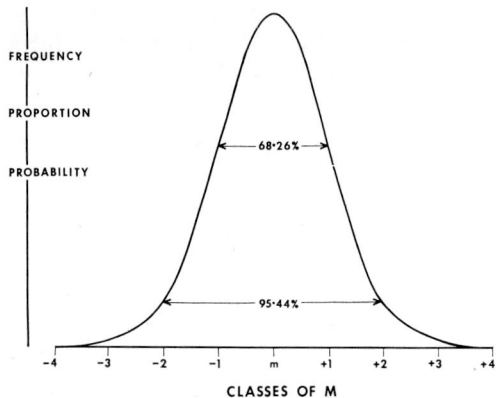

Fig. 2. A normal distribution in which the frequency, proportion or probability associated with each class of some measurement is presented. In a plot of the frequencies per class interval the abscissa is divided into units which are positive or negative multiples of the standard deviation, s. The point m, on the abscissa, indicates the location of the mean.

the measurements in a distribution is the most commonly used value. All three of these characteristics of a frequency distribution are descriptive statistics and in the normal distribution have the same value. The normal distribution is symmetrical about the mean. The mean, m, is obtained by adding together all the measurements and dividing the sum by N:

$$\frac{1}{N} \sum_i M_i$$

The mean provides an estimate of the true value T. In mathematical statistics the observed frequency distribution is called the sample distribution, and its mean is an estimate of the mean of the population distribution which, in a practical sense, is another frequency distribution based upon a very large but finite N. The population distribution is usually described mathematically. The mean of such a mathematical distribution is called the true value and is a parameter of the population.

Another important characteristic of the frequency distribution is variability, how much the values differ from one another. An obvious indication of the variability is the range, the difference between the largest and smallest value in the distribution. However, the range is not very representative, because it is based upon only two values in the distribution. The variability will depend upon the degree of precision required by the observer and the accuracy of the measuring instrument. In the construction of a house, an error of several millimeters can be tolerated in measuring and cutting the length of a wooden beam; whereas in the manufacture of an optical diffraction grating, the tolerance must be less than one thousandth of a millimeter. Therefore, it is important to express variability in terms of the actual units of measurement. Two different frequency distributions are depicted in Fig. 3 which differ from one another only with respect

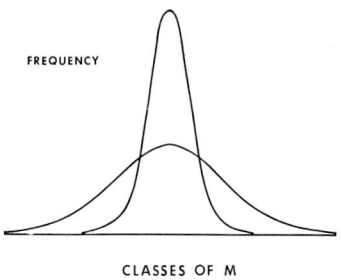

Fig. 3. Two normal frequency distributions containing equal numbers of observations N, identical means, and different standard deviations. The wide distribution has an $s = 1$ and the narrow distribution an $s = 0\cdot 4$.

to variability. Both distributions are based upon the same number of observations and have the same mean and range. They differ in variability. Variability can be defined as the average dispersion of the actual values about the mean m. Every measurement M can be expressed as a deviation d from the mean m:

$$d = M - m$$

The algebraic sum of the deviations about the mean in any distribution is equal to zero. However, if each deviation is squared, the algebraic sign is eliminated, and the average or mean squared deviation is then:

$$\frac{1}{N} \sum_i d_i^2$$

This quantity is called the variance v and is expressed in the squared units of measurement. In order to recover the original units of measurement, it is necessary to take the square root of the quantity, which is then referred to as the standard deviation s. The variance and s are descriptive statistics and represent the variability in a frequency distribution:

$$s^2 = v$$

If a set of observations is reliable, then when the observations are repeated, the means of the various sample distributions should agree with one another very closely. Each sample distribution will contribute one mean to a new distribution made up of all the sample distribution means. The new distribution is called a sampling distribution of the mean, and its mathematical form depends upon the specific population distribution. In order to measure reliability precisely, the variability of the sampling distribution of the mean must be determined. If it is small, the reliability is greater than when the dispersion is greater. It can be obtained empirically by repeating the original set of observations until the mean of the sampling distribution approaches some stable value. However, such a course of action will be costly.

A reasonable estimate of how much the sampling distribution of the mean will be expected to vary can be determined by statistical inference from the original sample or frequency distribution. The variance $\hat{v}$ of the sampling distribution can be estimated from the sample distribution. If each sample or frequency distribution is based upon a large N, then each sample mean will be more representative of the population mean, and the means in the sampling distribution will vary less and $\hat{v}$ will be small. Therefore $\hat{v}$ is expected to be inversely related to N:

$$\text{(a)} \quad \hat{v} \propto \frac{1}{N}$$

If the sample or frequency distribution v is small, then the variability $\hat{v}$ of the sampling distribution is expected to be small. Therefore $\hat{v}$ will be directly related to v:

$$\text{(b)} \quad \hat{v} \propto v$$

By combining (a) and (b):

$$\hat{v} = \frac{v}{N}$$

Since $s^2 = v$, the original units of measurement can be recovered by taking the square root:

$$\hat{s} = \frac{s}{\sqrt{N}}$$

and s is a biased estimate of the standard error of the mean. In measurement theory $\hat{s}$ has been referred to as the standard error of measurement. As $s/\sqrt{N}$ is a biased estimator and if N is small, $\hat{s}$ should be corrected by substituting $N-1$ for N. The standard error of measurement is an estimate of the standard deviation of the distribution formed by all sample means were it possible to obtain all samples and calculate all sample means. The means of this hypothetical sampling distribution of means is the same as the population mean or the true value. Therefore if $\hat{s}$ is small, more confidence can be placed in the assumption that the sample mean is close to the true value.

Again, if a large number of random factors contribute to the error in the measurements, then the expected sampling distribution will be normal, as illustrated in Fig. 2. Since the $\hat{s}$ is expressed in the units of measurement, it can be located exactly on the abscissa and if positive, will be to the right of m. In a normal distribution, approximately 68·26% of all the observations will have values between the $m \pm 1\,\hat{s}$, 95·44% between the $m \pm 2\,\hat{s}$, and 99·73% between $m \pm 3\,\hat{s}$.

C. Probability

A sampling distribution is a theoretical frequency distribution in which the various values of some sample statistic, such as the mean obtained from all possible samples of a given size, are related to their probability of occurrence given a specific population distribution. Each frequency, f, must be considered in relation to the total number, N, of values in the distribution. A frequency ratio (f/N) can be considered to be an estimate of a probability.

Probability p is defined as follows. If an event can happen in a certain number of distinguishable ways, and if some of the ways can be considered favorable, then the ratio of the number of favorable ways to the total number of ways is called the probability of the event occurring favorably, provided the total number of ways of occurrence are independent and equally likely. Favor does not imply a bias but is chosen only because of interest. For example, in tossing a single coin with a head and tail, the p of obtaining a head is $\frac{1}{2}$ or 0·50. In rolling a die, the p of obtaining one dot is $\frac{1}{6}$, p of two dots is $\frac{1}{6}$, etc. A cube has six faces which represent the total number of ways in which the event can occur. The p of not obtaining one dot is $1 - p$ or $\frac{5}{6}$. By definition, the p of any event is between zero and one; that is, $0 \leq p \leq 1$.

Probability depends upon being able to count the number of distinguishable events which can occur, and the total probability of all possible events in any situation is 1·00. To calculate the total probability of all the independent alternate events, the p of the two or more alternate events is the sum of the probabilities of the separate events. The p of tossing a head is $\frac{1}{2}$ and a tail is $\frac{1}{2}$, and either a head or tail is $\frac{1}{2} + \frac{1}{2}$ or 1·00. The p of obtaining either one dot or two dots when rolling a die is $\frac{1}{6} + \frac{1}{6}$ or $\frac{2}{6} = \frac{1}{3}$. In order to find the probability of a repeated or combined event, the independent probabilities of the single events are multiplied together. If a single coin is tossed twice, what is the p of obtaining two heads? It is $\frac{1}{2} \times \frac{1}{2}$ or $\frac{1}{4}$. If the coin is tossed three times, then the p of obtaining three successive heads is $\frac{1}{2} \times \frac{1}{2} \times \frac{1}{2}$ or $\frac{1}{8}$. In tossing two coins simultaneously, what is the p of obtaining one head and one tail? The two desirable outcomes are HT or TH, the other unfavorable ways are HH and TT. Therefore, there are two favorable ways out of four possible ways or $\frac{2}{4} = \frac{1}{2}$. In tossing three coins, the p for $2H$ and $1T$ is $\frac{3}{8}$. In tossing four coins the p of $2H$ and $2T$ is $\frac{6}{16}$. In all these fractions, the total number of possible outcomes is 2^n where n is the number of coins. When the case of two heads is called for, the numerator depends upon the number of combinations, C, of two heads that can be found among three or four coins. The number of n objects (coins) taken r (in this case 2) at a time can be calculated from:

$$_nC_r = \frac{n!}{r!(n-r)!}$$

If n = three coins, then $n!$ (factorial) = $1 \times 2 \times 3 = 6$. Therefore, the numerator can always be determined by $_nC_r$ and the denominator for any number n of coins = 2^n. The same information can be obtained from the binomial expansion $(p + q)^n$ where p is the probability that the particular event will occur and $q = 1 - p$. In the most simple case of tossing two coins simultaneously, then $(p + q)^2 = p^2 + 2pq + q^2$ or $(\frac{1}{2} + \frac{1}{2})^2 = \frac{1}{4} + \frac{2}{4} + \frac{1}{4}$ where the values of each successive term in the expansion represent the p of obtaining 0, 1 and 2 heads.

When coins are actually tossed in an experiment, the outcomes do not match the *a priori* theoretical probabilities. The theoretical p is calculated assuming that ideal instruments are involved in the game and that each toss is independent of every other toss. In this model, the individual game is called an experiment, the instruments display no bias, and each trial or toss is an independent event. As a matter of fact, in the ideal situation, the outcome by definition is determined by chance. The actual outcomes will vary just as any observation varies with respect to some ideal or true value. Each event or outcome, if examined by itself, appears to be part of a random series, very irregular, and difficult to interpret. A random series is one in which it is impossible to predict the next successive value with any degree of success. However, in spite of the irregular behavior of individual results, the average results of long sequences of random experiments display a striking statistical regularity. In a long series of repeated random observations carried out under uniform conditions, the frequency, f, or frequency ratio, f/N, of a fixed event ξ will show a tendency to become more or less constant for large values of N. In an experiment a coin was tossed, 1, 2, 5, 10, 20, 50 and 100 times. The proportion of times heads occurred is plotted in Fig. 4 against the

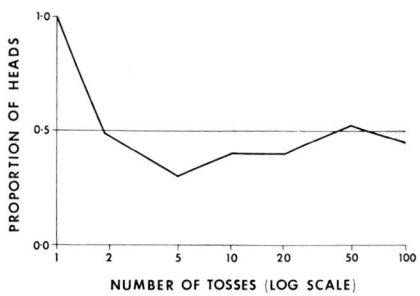

FIG. 4. A coin was tossed 1, 2, 5, 10, 20, 50 and 100 times. The proportion of heads which occurred in each experiment is plotted as a function of the number of tosses. A logarithmic scale was used for convenience.

number of tosses. The logarithmic scale is used for convenience. Therefore, any frequency ratio, f/N, in a long series of repetitions will approximate some number p which is called the probability of that event occurring under those conditions. The principle was first formulated as a theorem and proved by James Bernoulli in the eighteenth century. A more precise statement of Bernoulli's theorem is: the probability that the frequency ratio, f/N, differs from its mean value p by a quantity at least equal to x approaches zero as $N \to \infty$, however small $x > 0$ is chosen. The statement forms the basis for a frequency interpretation of probability. The probability number p is introduced as a conceptual counterpart of an empirical frequency ratio (a number associated with that event) and is similar to other fundamental properties discussed previously.

The sampling distribution is a theoretical probability distribution which relates various values or intervals of values of some sample statistic to their probabilities of occurrence over all possible samples of a given size. The standard error of the mean can be used also in a probability statement concerning the expected value of the next sample mean if the experiment were to be repeated. For example, if some observed mean is 100 units and the standard error is one unit, then the observed mean would be expected to lie between the mean $\pm 3\ \hat{s}$, that is between 97 and 103, at least ninety-nine times out of a hundred, if the experiment were repeated that many times. The probability that the mean would be less than some value m' is the cumulative sum of the probabilities associated with all smaller values of the mean.

If an experiment is properly designed and executed, the results will tend to be reliable. To each observation or measurement it should be possible to assign some number, the probability that such an event will recur, if the conditions remain unchanged and are repeated. Therefore, every scientist should have a working knowledge of the fundamental ideas of measurement, statistics and probability. Even though the concepts may be self-evident and axiomatic, they are difficult to discover and understand, almost impossible to explain, but fortunately easy to use.

D. The Experiment

An experiment is a controlled set of observations or measurements. A definite attempt is made to control the conditions under which the measurement is carried out. An experiment is an organizing concept in scientific thinking. Scientific thinking represents the strategies in doing research, and the experiment is the plan of action. Scientific knowledge, thinking, and theorizing produce the options or alternatives which confront the scientist; results of experiments enable him to assign probabilities to the various options and to order the alternatives, and in the final analysis, he must decide between them as an informed person. An experiment is a continuous ever-changing process in a laboratory with new tactics being developed as new instrumentation becomes available and as minor technical problems arise. The strategy will also be changed as new data and knowledge become available. The feedback in the process is a necessary condition to amplify the significant developments and to reduce the noise or error. The purpose of science is usually defined as the search for truth; however, it is just as much a search for error. Only by discovering and eliminating or minimizing errors of measurement will it be possible to understand what is really there!

Many people believe that the experimental study of behavior requires some special methodology and techniques because human behavior in particular defies physical measurement. However, such an assumption in science would be presumptuous, at least until other proven methods had failed. As a matter of fact, the study of human behavior, as compared to animal behavior in general, is facilitated by language. But therein lies the difficulty. Because of man's ability to use language very effectively, he has set himself apart from the rest of nature and has consistently failed to view himself objectively as a subject of scientific inquiry. Common sense has generated many interesting concepts such as mind and consciousness which do not qualify as scientific entities. In a sense, they are answers and science has been asked to find the questions. To accept such a challenge can only lead to an imponderable course of action. It is extremely difficult for an individual to regard his own behavior with complete objectivity, as he would the performance of a complex electronic circuit, some complex interaction between particles in some particular atom, or a digital computer. In the study of behavior, many of the terms and concepts are a product of the language which defines them; that is, they exist in the vernacular. When carried over into the scientific process of thinking they become very confusing, since they did not result from a particular logical system. The existence of a God is axiomatic in religion and self-evident to a religious person. The mind is axiomatic in mentalism and self-evident to a mentalist. When science is asked to prove or disprove such entities, the required task is impossible. Pure theory belongs entirely to a conceptual world, and although many conceptual objects can be tested by experience and can be regarded as practically certain, many other objects of such a realm will never involve properties which are perceptual things in experience. Mathematical arguments are therefore fundamentally incapable of proving physical facts. It is not surprising that when A. S. Eddington followed a very intricate and profound physico-mathematical pathway into the inner recesses of the atom, and when in passing from physics into pure mathematics, he looked inside and found nothing there.

Sometimes in the study of physiological psychology it is useful to adopt a systems approach to some problem. The organism is considered to be a structurally empty entity at the particular level of examination. The system is characterized by its capacity or ability to respond to certain inputs or specified stimuli. Many neurophysiologists have studied the cat eye in great detail. From the results of many experiments, it was established that the photoreceptors and other nerve cells of the retina which innervate them display a differential sensitivity to the spectral hue or colour of the light stimulus. It is possible in the anesthetized cat to record from a single nerve axon in the optic nerve when a very small pin point of light is used to illuminate the retina of the eye. If the light stimulus falls within the receptive field of the particular axon under study, a burst of activity in the form of repetitive nerve discharges will result. The burst of activity will vary in frequency as a function of both the intensity and hue of the stimulus. Some particular discharge frequency is carefully selected to serve as a response measure, sometimes referred to as an indicator response or criterion response. Assume that 10 discharges per second will be adequate and that stimuli can be selected from six different hues: red, orange-red, yellow, yellow-green, green and blue, each corresponding to a specific wave-length of light. The problem is to determine the spectral sensitivity of the cat retina. The six different spectral hues can also be varied in intensity. Therefore, if some intensity I_R is found for the red hue which produces the criterion response of 10 discharges/sec, and I_{OR} for the orange-red hue and if I_{OR} is greater than I_R, then the retinal unit is less sensitive to orange-red than to red. By continuing this procedure of examining each wave-length (different spectral hues) and determining the energy (intensity) required to produce the criterion response, it is possible to determine the spectral sensitivity of any one or more functional units of the retina and indirectly the spectral sensitivity of the eye. Actual results demonstrate that the cat eye is capable of hue discrimination. Does the cat utilize this capacity in foraging for food? Can some muscular movement such as lifting a forepaw and depressing a manipulandum be utilized as a criterion response in a hue discrimination experiment?

In studying behavior, many different types of responses can and should be utilized. In traditional human psychophysics, the "yes" by which the subject indicates that the stimulus has been perceived is the criterion response. Under certain conditions some responses are unreliable or cannot be used at all. In very young children and in the mentally deficient, verbal behavior is lacking or unreliable and in place of speech sounds, some distinguishing feature of the electrical potential recorded across the eyeball, breathing movements, changes in blood pressure, heart rate and other overt muscular movements can be utilized to assess the presence and effectiveness of stimulation. Therefore, studies of animal behavior can be informative and helpful in the development of non-verbal methods and techniques which can be utilized in the investigation of human capacities and performance.

REFERENCES

Anderson, Barry F. (1966). "The Psychology Experiment. An Introduction to the Scientific Method." Wadsworth Publishing Co., Inc., Belmont, California.

Campbell, Norman R. (1921). "What is Science?" Methuen and Co., Ltd., London.

Eddington, A. S. (1928). "The Nature of the Physical World." The MacMillan Co., New York.

Hays, William L. (1963). "Statistics for Psychologists." Holt, Rinehart, and Winston, Inc., New York.

Newman, James R. (1956). "The World of Mathematics." (J. R. Newman, ed.), Vol. 3. Simon and Schuster, Inc., New York.

Riggs, Douglas S. (1970). "The Mathematical Approach to Physiological Problems." First M.I.T. Press paperback edition. Cambridge, Mass.

Stevens, S. S. (1951). *In* "Handbook of Experimental Psychology." (S. S. Stevens, ed.), pp. 1–49. John Wiley and Sons, Inc., New York and Chichester.

Chapter 2

General Laboratory Procedures

R. D. MYERS

*Laboratory of Neuropsychology, Purdue University,
Lafayette, Indiana, U.S.A.*

I.	Introduction	27
II.	Care and Treatment of Animals	29
	A. The Arrival of New Animals	29
	B. Daily Care of the Animal	31
	C. Restraint and Handling of the Animal	32
III.	Methods of Drug Administration	35
	A. Oral or Gastro-Intestinal Route of Administration	36
	B. Parenteral Injections	37
IV.	Calculation of Pharmacological Doses	40
	A. Variations in the Response to a Drug	40
	B. Important Considerations for the Use of a Drug	41
V.	Procedures for Inducing Anesthesia	43
	A. Volatile (Inhalation) Anesthetics	43
	B. Administration of Volatile Anesthetics	44
	C. Barbiturates Given by Injection	45
	D. Pre-Anesthetics	47
	E. Special Problems	48
VI.	Laboratory Diseases	49
VII.	Euthanasia	60
Acknowledgement		60
References		60
Appendix A		62
Appendix B		63
Appendix C		65

I. Introduction

ALTHOUGH experiments with animals have been performed since ancient times, the earliest accounts of these procedures have been lost in antiquity. In the second century A.D., Galen carried out some of the original medical experiments, and among other observations, he verified his belief that blood rather than air occupies the arterial spaces.

With the advent of chemical anesthetics in the middle of the nineteenth century, research in brain as well as in general physiology has increased at an enormous rate, and the monumental advances of the last decade are common knowledge to us all. Nevertheless, there are a few individuals who express their violent opposition to the use of animals for experiments which have provided obvious benefits to all of mankind. The unequivocal fact cannot be denied that the gradual understanding of man's brain as well as his other vital organs is due almost entirely to the results of imaginative experiments of diligent scientists working with animals. The development of antibiotics, the discovery of vaccines for virile diseases, the extraordinary advances in transplant and other surgical techniques, the synthesis of compounds which miraculously soothe the disturbed mind of a disordered personality—all of these have been brought about directly through careful research with animals. In actuality, the future of neuropsychology or psychobiology rests in the hands of each laboratory scientist, young or old, who is striving to establish one basic relationship or another between the brain and behavior.

The purpose of this chapter is to present, in summary form, selected information which is essential for carrying out well-controlled experiments in the area of physiological psychology or neuropsychology. Certain critical knowledge about the care and treatment of animals, both pre- and post-operatively, as well as the general techniques of injecting chemical agents and drugs is essential for nearly every investigation in the field of neuropsychology. In considering the problem of general anesthesia, information is also required for administering an anesthetic as well as about the variety and properties of anesthetics that are available today for use with species commonly employed in the physiological psychology laboratory.

As a starting point for basic techniques in this field, every laboratory should have a "library shelf" containing a small set of volumes easily accessible to every worker in the facility. The following ones are recommended to be included in the selection:

1. The UFAW Handbook, "The Care and Management of Laboratory Animals" (1967).
2. "The IAT Manual of Animal Practices and Techniques" (Short, D. J. and Woodnott, D. P., 1969).
3. "Small Animal Anesthesia" (Lumb, W. V., 1963).
4. "Methods of Animal Experimentation," Vol. I. (Gay, W. I., 1965).
5. "Fundamentals of Small Animal Surgery" (Leonard, E. P., 1968).
6. "Experimental Surgery" (Markowitz *et al.*, 1964).
7. "The Pharmacological Basis of Therapeutics" (Goodman, L. S. and Gilman, A., 1965).

(See reference list for complete details.)

The Ethicon Company has published a booklet of great help to the beginning "surgeon" entitled, "Manual of Operative Procedure and

Surgical Knots", which can be obtained free by writing to the Company. *The Animal Care Panel* and *Animal Welfare Institute* publish a large amount of material on the use of animals in research. For a current directory of commercially available experimental animals, laboratory equipment, cages and feed, a booklet published by the Institute of Laboratory Animal Resources, National Academy of Sciences, provides the names, addresses, and telephone numbers of suppliers of laboratory equipment, animals and materials.

II. Care and Treatment of Animals

The success of any experiment in the field of neuropsychology depends largely, if not exclusively, on the health of each animal. For this reason, cleanliness in every facet of the laboratory endeavor is absolutely mandatory. In our laboratory, all work surfaces, tables, benches and sinks are wiped down with a disinfectant or cleaning solution daily, and the floors are likewise kept spotless. These kinds of precautions help to reduce the all too prevalent incidences of vermin, such as fleas, roaches and ticks, as well as the devastating bacterial infestations considered in detail in Section VI.

A. *The Arrival of New Animals*

All newly acquired animals should be isolated, preferably in individual cages, from animals already in residence. The fur of cats, monkeys and other large animals should be treated with commercial tick and flea powder or parasite spray according to the directions. Ordinarily, the animals should remain in isolation for 2-to-6 weeks, depending on the species, for a period of acclimation and observation. On arrival, cats are usually given a prophylactic injection of feline enteritis antiserum, and monkeys are screened for tuberculosis by P.P.D. (protein purified derivative of mammalian tuberculin) injected into the eye-lid. The palpebral region of a positive reactor will become reddened and edematous, and it is advisable to dispose of this animal at once.

During the acclimation period, certain animals, such as mice and rats, can be bred, and the offspring can be introduced to the permanent stock if the breeders are free of disease. If any signs of sickness arise in the new animals during the regular routine examinations, the individual in question should be isolated for further observation, treatment, or possible disposal. If a particular animal species is going to be used for the first time in the laboratory, it is always advisable to refer to the "UFAW Handbook on the Care and Management of

Laboratory Animals" (1967). This volume considers in great detail the nature, maintenance and handling of all sorts of species of experimental animals including earth worms, molluscs, insects, reptiles, birds, rodents, carnivores and primates.

Determining the sex of the commonly used laboratory animal is relatively straightforward if the animal is an adult. If infant rats are acquired, or perhaps bred in the laboratory, they can be sexed quite easily by determining the distance between the anus and the genital papilla or protuberance. Generally, this so-called anogenital space is twice as great in the male rat; Table I presents the average anogenital separation in young rats at five age levels.

TABLE I

Anogenital distance in young albino rats of various ages

Age	Average anogenital distance (mm)	
	Male	Female[1]
Newborn	2·8	1·2
7 days	5·2	2·7
14 days	8·2	4·9
20 days	12·0	7·0
42–50 days	21·0	13·0

[1] Females lack nipples at birth, but show six pairs when they are from 8 to 15 days old.

For identification of laboratory rodents, ear punching or staining the fur is practiced routinely. Although marking the fur with carbol-fuchsin (red) or picric acid (yellow) or other biological stain is perhaps the most convenient way of identifying an animal, re-marking is required after several weeks. The arrival of all incoming animals should be recorded in the colony stock booklet. In our laboratory, each of the large animals such as the cat or monkey is assigned its own experimental folder. The number of the animal (designated arbitrarily), its weight, food consumption, water intake, all experimental data and protocol sheets are retained in this folder. In this way, every piece of information pertinent to an experiment is recorded, and the history of the animal is maintained in continuity until the experiments with the animal are terminated. It is perpetually surprising how some sort of remote or ostensibly trivial detail, noted down in systematically and accurately kept records, will suddenly disclose at a later date the reason for a peculiar behavioral or physiological response of a given animal in a given experiment.

A point which should be obvious to every student scientist, but which is sometimes neglected to the point of serious detriment, is the collection of interval data precisely at the same time every day. Procedures such as daily weighing, recording of food or water intakes at 12 or 24-hour periods, monitoring body temperature at given intervals, testing an animal in a behavioral apparatus, or administering by injection an experimental compound or therapeutic drug must be carried out with scrupulous punctuality. To disregard this not only contributes to the "error variance" of an experiment but because of unknown variables can lead to the ultimate uselessness of the data collected.

B. Daily Care of the Animal

The living conditions under which an experimental animal is maintained can have a direct effect on the outcome of an investigation. The cage itself should be sufficiently large enough to provide space for exercise. Guidelines for the cage size for several different species have been set down by governmental agencies in various countries including the United States, Canada, and Great Britain. Most of the commercial cages available today for rodents, cats, monkeys and other species have been designed for the comfort of the animal, convenience and ease of cleaning, accessibility of litter pans, and resistance to corrosion with repeated washings or sterilization. If the purchase of cages is contemplated, these factors should be considered carefully.

Generally, the environment of the animal room should be held constant with respect to all variables. Ambient temperature should be maintained at approximately 70–74°F for most species, although slightly higher or lower temperatures are acceptable. Humidity levels should range between 40 and 60%. Adequate sunlight and ventilation are desirable, but care must be taken that the animals are not exposed to drafts.

Sawdust, wood shavings or commercial litter products (such as Sterolite) are placed in pans to absorb the excreta of animals. Litter should be changed (or renewed) a minimum of three times a week for small laboratory animals and each day for a large animal. Bedding is supplied to nesting animals, and should be renewed at least once a week. Hay and shredded paper are highly satisfactory as the bedding material to absorb moisture and for the comfort of the animal.

Every animal should have free access to food and water at all times unless deprivation or some special dietary restriction is required by the experiment. Most animals will prosper on commercially available food in cubed or pelleted forms (see Chapter 10), but daily supplements of green foods such as lettuce or cabbage for rats, and fruit or other sources of Vitamin C for primates should be given. The drinking bottles should be filled with fresh water at least once a day, because stale water can, of course, act as a culture medium for certain bacteria. To prevent the possibility of cross-infection or cross contamination, each water bottle should be returned to the same cage from which it was taken. Larger animals such as monkeys should be given food and water twice a day, early in the morning and late in the afternoon. Animals which are recovering from surgery often must be fed particularly palatable foods: a monkey can be tempted to eat by offering small bite-sized pieces of banana, orange, raisin or brown bread; lumps of tuna fish or liver will usually be devoured by an otherwise recalcitrant or "finicky" cat.

Food hoppers or dispensers should be fixed outside the cage in a position where the food can be reached easily by the animal but cannot be contaminated with excreta. Once a week, all water bottles, food dishes and fittings should be sterilized as described in Section VI of this chapter. Richter tubes or special watering devices are washed once per week in Micro, Alconex or other standard biological detergent.

For determining the body weight of a smaller laboratory animal, a top-loading pan or other commercial balance will suffice. For cats and monkeys, it is best if the experimenter stands on a floor scale, takes his own weight while holding the animal, and again without the animal in hand. The difference in the reading, of course, represents the animal's weight; this is required for calculations of drug and anesthetic dosages as well as for the record of the animal's weight gain taken daily or weekly as required.

C. Restraint and Handling of the Animal

Some animals seem to be quick to detect apprehension in the human handler. Therefore, anyone who uses an animal for repeated behavioral observations must learn to overcome his reservations so that the animal can be picked up without hesitation. In general, an animal is never placed on a slippery surface. Once the animal has been grasped in an appropriate region, one should never "let go" of the animal regardless of its obstinacy. If the grip on an untame animal is once lost and it begins to struggle free, the probability of being bitten increases sharply. The following procedures describe ways of handling several species:

(1) *Mouse*

The mouse is grasped initially by the base of its tail close to the body, only for short periods, for the purpose of sorting or sexing. For an injection, the mouse can be held by the "scruff" or loose skin at the back of its neck using the thumb and index finger while the third and fourth fingers restrain the tail.

(2) *Rat*

The rat is *never* picked up by its tail, but rather it is restrained under its shoulders by placing the palm of the hand over the back and then closing together the thumb and index finger so that the head is immobilized. Animal gloves should not be worn unless the rat is unusually wild or vicious. If the rat should attempt to bite, pressure from the thumb, as shown in Fig. 1, will prevent it from doing so. A

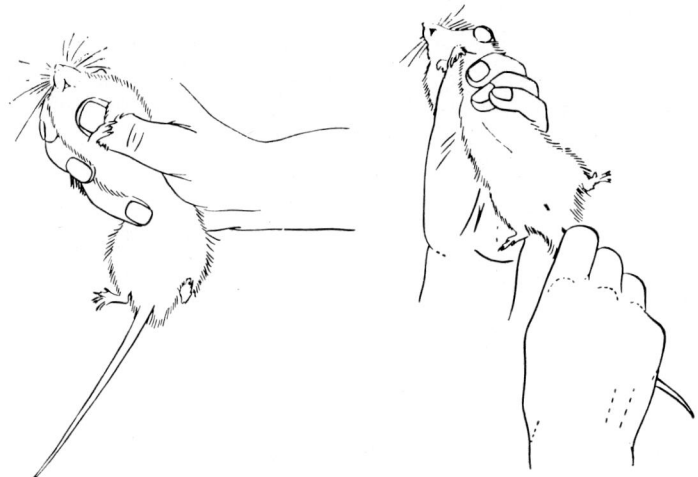

FIG. 1. Position of fingers when a mouse or rat is grasped. Note how the thumb is held. (From Short and Woodnott, 1969.)

turkish towel folded over the rat, rolled and fastened with safety pins, so that the legs are secure, is an acceptable means of restraint for a long interval during which there is no harm done to the animal (Lumb, 1963). Commercial restrainers or chambers are also available for holding a rat in position for a long period of time. If an unruly rat is going to be used for any extended length of time in a behavioral or physiological experiment, the animal should be gentled, at least to some degree. This can be accomplished by placing the rat on the arm of one's laboratory coat and rubbing the fur on the head and neck for short periods several times a day. Again, picking up a rat by its tail will only serve to enhance its wildness and the tendency to bite.

(3) Rabbit

A rabbit can be picked up by the loose skin on the back of its neck or by its ears but it should never be held solely by its ears. To carry a rabbit, the index finger is placed between the ears so that the other fingers and thumb can thus control the head. The body of the animal is supported by placing the free hand under the animal's hind quarters. An assistant or restraining box is usually required to hold the entire animal when an injection is given in one of the ear veins (Lumb, 1963; UFAW Handbook, 1967).

(4) Cat

To lift up a domesticated cat and retain complete control over it is usually a very easy task. For an untame cat, the same principle is applied as that employed by a mother cat in picking up her kitten. A firm hold is obtained by grasping the fur at the nape of the neck at a position high enough to control the head. In this position, the cat cannot possibly bite the handler, particularly if the forearm is kept in line with the cat's spine. One's free hand is used to grasp the two hind legs for, let us say, some sort of treatment or injection. In the case of an untame cat, a muzzle or restraining apparatus such as stocks may also be necessary. A venous puncture can be done single handedly but it is better to have an assistant hold the cat, so that a fore- or hind-limb can be more easily presented.

(5) Monkey

To catch a large primate, a folding net (Gay, 1960) or a noose at the end of a metal or wooden stick is used most satisfactorily. If the monkey is housed in a Kirshner or other cage containing a moveable back panel which can be brought forward, the animal can be forced to the front of the cage. Then, a limb is easily withdrawn from the cage so that the entire animal can be grasped, or an injection of a sedative or tranquilizing agent can be given in the femoral or other muscle accessible through the cage. Whenever the animal is handled directly, special heavy gloves must be worn, and complete control of the monkey must be maintained. Each of the experimenter's hands is used to grasp each of the arms, which are retracted behind the animal's back as shown in Fig. 2. The monkey can also be moved by means of a restraining or transport cage, held up to the door of its home cage, in which a banana or other fruit is used to entice the primate into the portable cage.

For long-term experiments, restraining chairs of various kinds are readily available from a number of suppliers. Since the rhesus monkey sleeps in an upright position, this species is particularly well-suited for long-term experiments in which continual monitoring of behavioral and physiological parameters is required. In these situations, the restraining chair is essential and the danger of bites and scratches is reduced considerably.

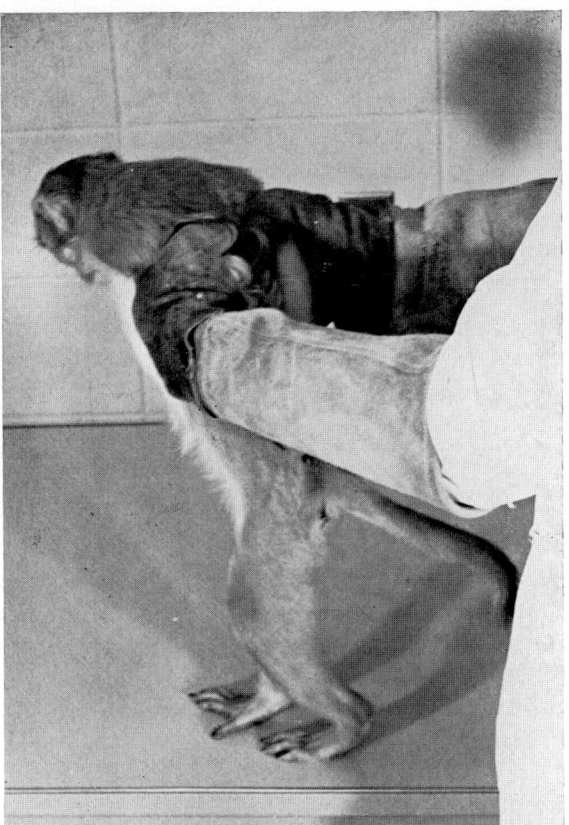

FIG. 2. Restraint of a rhesus monkey by grasping arms in the biceps region and retracting them behind the animal's back.

III. Methods of Drug Administration

In investigations in neuropsychology and physiological psychology, drugs and chemical substances are used for many reasons ranging from the desire to deplete or increase the level of certain endogenous substances in the brain such as RNA or acetylcholine, or the need for anesthetizing an animal for a neurosurgical procedure.

There are several different routes by which a substance can be introduced into the animal's body: (1) *inhalation* of a drug in vapor form;

(2) *intrathecal*, whereby the injection of the chemical is made into the cerebrospinal fluid; (3) *rectal*, whereby a fluid is introduced very slowly via a flexible catheter into the rectum or colon; (4) *topical*, whereby the substance is applied in ointment form on the surface of the skin on an area which must be kept from the animal's reach until absorption has occurred; (5) *intradermal*, in which a short syringe needle must be inserted into the shaved skin at an angle parallel to the surface; (6) *intramuscular*, in which a drug is given in the femoral, gluteal or other large muscle after the syringe plunger has been aspirated to ensure that a blood vessel has not been punctured; and two routes which will be considered in more detail: the (7) *oral*, and (8) *parenteral*.

A. Oral or Gastro-Intestinal Route of Administration

A drug can be administered precisely if given in tablet, pill or capsule form. Most animals will accept and swallow a pill or capsule if it is placed far back on the tongue, after the mouth is forced open and the head is tilted in a vertical position. A drug can also be mixed with the animal's food, and the dose can be accurately estimated if the animal consumes all of its food.

Intragastric intubation is also a commonly used technique for introducing, rapidly into the stomach, a compound which the animal might otherwise refuse to accept, such as a solution of alcohol. For an animal such as a rat, an intragastric tube is cut from polyvinylchloride (PVC) tubing of appropriate diameter (usually 2 mm o.d.) and length (7-to-8 cm) and connected by friction fit to a blunted hypodermic needle. When the rat is held as described in the previous section, thumb-forceps or a large Kelly-Crile hemostat is placed between the rat's teeth to hold open its jaws. After the tubing is attached to a syringe filled with the solution to be injected, it is then threaded over the tongue and down into the esophagus. In our laboratory the rat is grasped by the nape of the neck, as with a cat, and the head is held so that the oral cavity-esophagus is in a vertical plane as shown in Fig. 3. After the intragastric tube is placed into the mouth, it is gently rotated until the stomach is reached. The contents of the syringe are than discharged.

In several recent studies, we have found that if the rat is lightly sedated by exposure to a mixture of ethyl chloride and ether soaked in cotton padding in a desiccator jar, the intubation procedure is rapid, non-injurious and without trauma (Myers and Veale, 1968; 1970). However, when examining the effects of a drug on behavior, it is essential that the control animals are also sedated by the same agents in the same manner and for the same duration.

B. Parenteral injections

When an injection of a solution is made into the body by a route other than the alimentary canal, it is often referred to as parenteral or "non-intestinal". The parenteral administration of a drug prevents its destruction in the digestive tract.

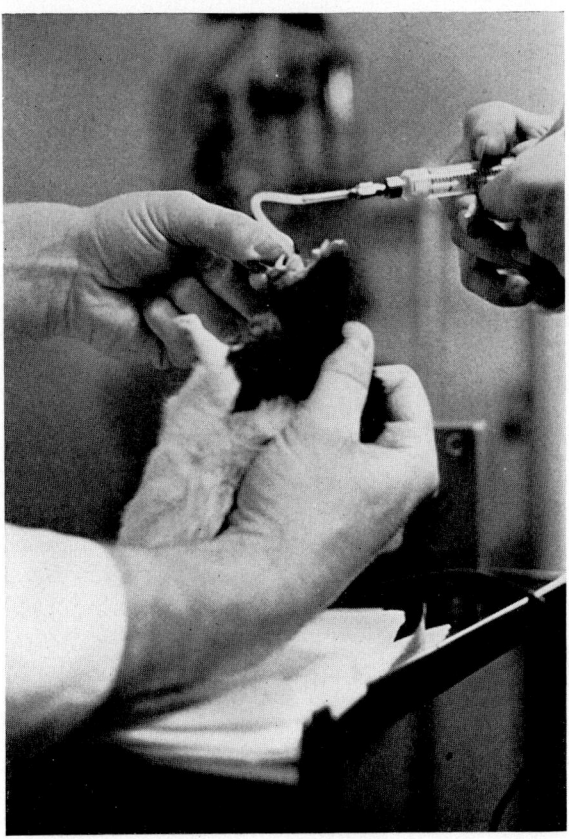

Fig. 3. Intragastric intubation of rat lightly sedated with ether-ethyl chloride mixture. The soft PVC tubing is gently rotated as it is passed into the esophagus, after the jaws are held open by thumb forceps.

Before making any kind of injection, a needle and syringe of proper size must be selected and prepared carefully. In small animals such as the mouse, a 25 to 27 gauge $\frac{1}{2}$ to $\frac{3}{4}$ in needle and a 1 ml syringe are used. For the rat, 22 to 24 gauge needles are satisfactory, and 20 to 22 gauge needles may be used in still larger animals. Since the point of the needle must be sharp, disposable needles are certainly recommended. Similarly, plastic disposable syringes which are pre-sterilized and available in volumes from 1 to 50 ml are most convenient. Since a large syringe is not necessary for a small volume, a syringe of a size corresponding to the volume of the dose is generally preferred. When an anesthetic is injected in smaller animals, the drug is often diluted with sterile water to make a 50% solution.

(1) *Intravenous injection*

The intravenous route is preferred perhaps because it is the most reliable means of injecting a drug. With this route, the guesswork concerning the amount to be given, and the rate of systemic absorption is removed. Moreover, an anesthetic can be given intravenously "to effect". The cephalic vein on the anterior part of the forelimb, the saphenous vein on the lateral surface of the hind limb, or the femoral vein on the medial surface of the thigh are the vessels most commonly used for intravenous injection in large animals (refer to Fig. 11 of Chapter 4). An intravenous injection in the mouse or rat is normally given in the lateral vein of the tail after the tail has been placed in warm water, so as to facilitate visualization and puncture of the vessel (Barrow, 1968). For making an intravenous injection, the animal is restrained and the hair over the vein is removed by means of clippers or a depilatory. The area overlying the vein is cleansed with an antiseptic solution such as 70% ethyl alcohol. The pressure point proximal to the site of injection is occluded. The vein is then distended by "pumping up" (increasing) the local pressure, either by stroking the thumb over the vein in a distal to proximal direction or by a rapid flexion of the limb.

After it is filled with the drug, the syringe is held between the thumb and middle finger and balanced by the forefinger. The needle is placed bevel-side-up at a point on the skin medial to the midline of the vein and then "threaded" up into the vein until the hub is at the site of the venipuncture. The scale-side of the syringe barrel should always face outward so that the volume given can be accurately determined. As soon as blood appears in the barrel of the syringe or after the plunger is withdrawn slightly until the fluid appears, the injection is begun. A cotton sponge saturated with 70% alcohol is then placed directly on the site of the venipuncture, and gentle pressure is applied primarily on the distal side of the puncture until the bleeding from the vein has ceased. If sub-dermal swelling due to local hemorrhage of the puncture occurs, the distal portion of the vein must be gently occluded until all signs of bleeding have disappeared. If by accident part of the solution is deposited outside the vein, the area should be massaged gently after the syringe needle has been removed.

(2) Intraperitoneal injections

Relatively large quantities of fluid can be injected into the peritoneal spaces. Although absorption by this route is fairly rapid, a major disadvantage of this kind of injection is the lack of accurate control over the dose as one does have with an intravenous injection. Also, an unusually high proportion of error, estimated to be as high as 20%, surprisingly occurs even when skilled or experienced workers give an intraperitoneal injection. More often than expected, the injections are actually made intra-intestinally, retroperitoneally, subcutaneously or intracystically (Lewis et al., 1966; Hamilton et al., 1967).

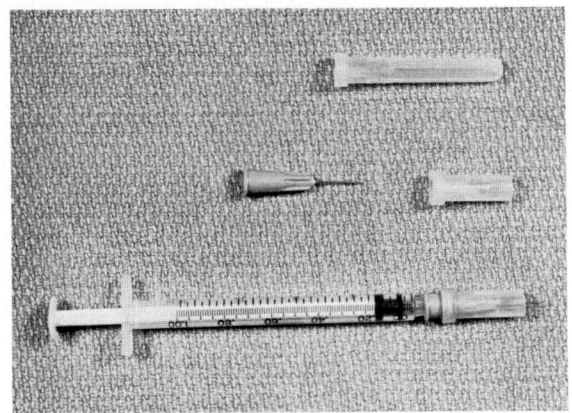

Fig. 4. Needle stop, for intraperitoneal injection, cut from the dust cap of a sterile disposable syringe needle. When placed over the syringe needle, the stop prevents the needle from entering too deeply into the intraperitoneal cavity and provides consistent and reliable injections from animal to animal.

After the animal is restrained, an area just lateral to the midline (in a larger animal) is shaved, and a suitable antiseptic agent is applied. In the rat, this is not necessary. A $\frac{1}{2}$ to $\frac{1}{4}$ in needle is inserted just lateral to the midline in the left caudal quadrant of the ventral abdomen. The stomach and spleen are in the left cranial quadrant, the liver in the right cranial quadrant, and the major part of the cecum in the right caudal quadrant. Since there are no vital organs other than the intestine in the left caudal quadrant, an authentic intraperitoneal injection can be achieved if (a) the animal is held in the vertical position so that the intestinal mass is maximal, and (b) the plunger of the syringe is aspirated (withdrawn) twice to ensure that blood, urine or other fluid does not enter the syringe barrel.

A short needle "stop" which can be made from the protective needle sheath as shown in Fig. 4 (Hamilton *et al.*, 1967) will prevent the needle from entering the peritoneal cavity to a depth of more than 4 or 5 mm. Keeping the animal perfectly still during the injection may also help to reduce the error factor inherent in the intraperitoneal injection.

(3) Subcutaneous injection

For slow absorption, the easiest way to introduce a solution is by the subcutaneous route. In this case, the injection is made in the loose skin at the back of the neck, after the animal is grasped by the nape of the neck, and the syringe and needle of an appropriate size are held parallel to the animal's head. With the animal's feet planted firmly on a table, the fold of skin is lifted slightly with the thumb and index finger, and the needle is introduced from an anterior to posterior direction at the base of this fold of skin. Part of the fluid is discharged from the syringe and then the needle is backed up slightly, but not removed, and more fluid is discharged into a slightly different area.

IV. Calculation of Pharmacological Doses

The interaction of many factors is responsible for the marked variation from one animal to the next in the response to a standard dose of a drug or anesthetic. Further, extreme caution must be exercised when attempting to extrapolate a single dose from one species to another.

A. Variations in the Response to a Drug

Several variables affect the metabolic rate of an animal and will influence the rate of detoxification of an anesthetic, and the degradation or excretion of a drug. Among these variable are:

(1) Health

An animal in poor physical condition requires less anesthetic. For example, many diseases often affect the basal metabolism of an animal, in that fever increases the metabolic rate, whereas shock will decrease it.

(2) Sex

Females of some species may be more sensitive to drugs than males, and pregnancy and/or lactation also may alter the response to a compound. For instance, it is well known that a barbiturate is not nearly as potent an anesthetic when it is administered to a pregnant cat or other gravid animal.

(3) *Age*

A young animal is more susceptible to the action of a drug than an older animal, since the drug is taken up more rapidly. Generally, only two-thirds of the adult dose is given to a very young animal.

(4) *Activity and feeding*

Activity and/or a large meal may alter an animal's metabolic rate. Thus, an animal which is excited, exhibiting a fear reaction and very active must be given a larger dose of a drug such as an anesthetic. In these instances, the danger of an overdose is somewhat augmented, particularly if an anesthetic is given intravenously "to effect". Generally, an animal should be fasted before an anesthetic is administered.

(5) *Size*

The *weight* of an animal is the principal factor used in determining a dose, as it provides an index of the amount of drug required to raise the concentration of the agent to a given serum level. Larger animals ordinarily have a somewhat lower basal metabolic rate per kg of body weight; therefore, for an anesthetic, a large animal would require a lower dose per kg of body weight. An animal with large depositions of fat also does not need as much anesthetic, since adipose is a relatively inactive, non-metabolizing tissue.

When administering an anesthetic or drug to an animal which has been fasted, extra care must be taken, because drugs are absorbed relatively well in an animal with an "empty stomach". Further, certain drugs if given together will synergize in such a way that their action together is far greater than the sum of the responses of each drug given separately. Thus, the action of one drug may be potentiated remarkably when given in combination with another drug.

B. *Important Considerations for the Use of a Drug*

The purpose, dose and efficacy of each anesthetic or drug must be known thoroughly *before* its administration to an experimental animal. It is especially helpful to consult a veterinary or standard pharmacology text which contains pertinent information about the drug in question. The drug of choice for the treatment of a specific disorder, and its special properties, can be determined in that way. For example, once an antibiotic is administered, the therapy is ordinarily continued for 5 to 10 days so as to maintain the serum concentration at an adequate level; hence, it is rather pointless to give the animal a single dose of penicillin or other antibiotic. In addition, since most antibiotics do not pass through the blood brain barrier, a careful decision must be made before these compounds are used to treat a septic condition arising in the central nervous system after a neurosurgical procedure.

Several technical details should be remembered when administering a compound. In a large animal such as a cat or monkey, not more than 0·5 ml of a solution of a drug such as an antibiotic should be given intramuscularly. Also, the injection sites should be alternated from left to right and from femoral to gluteal to biceps muscles. Following an injection into it, the muscle should always be massaged gently. A sterile disposable syringe and needle is not used for more than one animal, because the danger of cross-infection increases drastically.

A given agent, such as an anesthetic, is usually administered on the basis of the dose (D) in milligrams per kilogram (K) of the animal's body weight (W) in grams. The amount of the drug (X) to be injected can be calculated by a simple formula:

$$\text{Dose (D)} \div \frac{\text{Kilogram (K)}}{\text{Weight (W)}} = \text{Amount (X)} \tag{1}$$

Using Nembutal (pentobarbitone sodium) anesthetic as an example, a dose of 33 to 36 mg per kg of body weight is frequently given by the intraperitoneal route to rats or by the intravenous route to cats and other animals. If a light level of anesthesia is desired for a 250 g rat, one could use a dose of 36 mg/kg. Substituting these values in the formula, one calculates the dose as follows:

$$36 \text{ mg} \div \frac{1000}{250} = 36 \text{ mg} \div 4 = 9\cdot0 \text{ mg} \tag{2}$$

Usually, Nembutal is dissolved in a solution having a concentration (C) of 50 mg per ml. The actual volume (V) to be injected is calculated by the formula:

$$\frac{\text{Amount (X)}}{\text{Concentration (C)}} \times 1 \text{ ml} = \text{Volume (V)} \tag{3}$$

For our 250 g rat in which 9·0 mg of Nembutal is the amount (X) required for anesthesia, the volume (V) is determined as follows:

$$\frac{9\cdot0}{50} \times 1\cdot0 = 0\cdot18 \text{ ml} \tag{4}$$

Thus, the tuberculin syringe would be filled with 0·18 ml of the Nembutal solution for the injection.

V. Procedures for Inducing Anesthesia

An anesthetic used to prevent an animal from feeling pain can be classified as local, regional or general. The general anesthetic is most extensively used in neuropsychology experiments and is administered by injection and/or inhalation (Strobel and Wollman, 1969). The type and method of induction depends on (a) the species of the animal, and (b) the kind of surgery to be carried out.

A. Volatile (Inhalation) Anesthetics

A variety of vapor anesthetics have been used by physiological psychologists for surgical procedures in the past. From the commonly used agents available today, we have not considered several including chloroform, trilene, and nitrous oxide because of their toxicity, difficulties in induction, or problems caused during the neurosurgical exercise.

(1) Ether, U.S.P. $(C_2H_5)_2O$

Ether is a very effective general anesthetic for most experimental animals; however, because of its irritating effect on the mucous lining of the respiratory tract, salivation increases. This may be ameliorated by pre-treatment with atropine sulfate or scopolamine hydrobromide. Ether can be administered from a nose-cone formed either from wire mesh or a 10 ml beaker, each filled with cotton saturated with ether (Ben et al., 1969). Although stable, relatively inexpensive, and easily administered with little equipment, it is nevertheless highly inflammable and explosive when mixed with oxygen. During induction, the vapor often evokes violent struggling and may cause nausea and vomiting. Perhaps its worst side effect is the increased bleeding, particularly from the calvarium, with continued inhalation during neurosurgery.

(2) Halothane (fluothane) $(CF_3CHClBr)$

This potent vapor anesthetic is suitable for all animals, and if a sedative is administered preoperatively, induction is fairly rapid, and an anesthesia of long duration can be achieved. Halothane is non-explosive and non-flammable, but because of its expense, the vapor should be administered in a closed metered system with a low-dead-space anesthetic mask, such as that designed for cats by Mann and Boretos (1968). The rate of recovery or emergence from halothane is more rapid than from ether, and it seldom produces nausea, vomiting or an irritation of the respiratory tract.

(3) *Methoxyflurane* (*Penthrane*) ($CHCl_2CF_2OCH_3$)

Methoxyflurane is a clear colorless liquid, which has been used successfully in rats by many neuropsychologists (see Chapter 4). Molello and Hawkins (1968) have described a multichamber anesthetic box whereby 10 rats can be maintained under anesthesia at one time. The lack of explosive capability, good muscle relaxation, and freedom from toxic side-effects are its principal advantages. The long induction time, of as much as 10 minutes, and a slow recovery period would seem to render its greatest utility as an adjunct to barbiturate anesthetic. Respiratory acidosis may develop if methoxyflurane anesthesia is maintained over a long period, and the classical eye signs cannot be used to determine the stages of anesthesia, since the pupils become fixed early. The concentration of methoxyflurane for induction is approximately 4% at 23°C, whereas a 2% concentration is necessary for the maintenance of surgical anesthesia.

(4) *Ethyl chloride* (C_2H_5Cl)

Ethyl chloride may be used in a restricted way for a very short period of anesthesia in kittens or adult cats. Although the loss of consciousness proceeds rapidly, ethyl chloride must be used in conjunction with ether, as it cannot be used to maintain anesthesia alone. Also, it is a substance of high toxicity to the heart and possesses adverse effects on circulation. Because of these and other disadvantages, its use as a general anesthetic is limited to minor surgical or experimental procedures such as catheterization of a blood vessel or intragastric intubation. Usually 5 ml and not more than 10 ml is sprayed onto the anesthetic mask.

B. *Administration of Volatile Anesthetics*

(1) *The open drop method*

A conical mask containing cotton batting covered by a patch of gauze is positioned over the animal's nose, and it is placed loosely enough so that the animal can freely exhale CO_2. Ether, methoxyflurane or other liquid anesthetic agent is dropped onto the gauze, and the depth of anesthesia is regulated by adding more drops onto the gauze, or simply by moving the mask away from the nostrils. The animal's nose and eyes should not be touched by the cotton within the mask, as contact with most vapor anesthetics will severely irritate the mucous membranes.

(2) *Covered chamber method*

A small animal such as a rat can be anesthetized in a desiccator jar or other container into which a layer of cotton batting saturated with a liquid anesthetic is placed. After the animal is lightly anesthetized, it is removed from the jar and the depth of anesthesia is maintained by the mask or by a 10 ml beaker containing cotton moistened with the inhalant.

(3) *Semi-closed system*

Oxygen and the anesthetic are administered simultaneously by means of an endotracheal tube. An expiratory valve allows CO_2 and excess gas to escape into the surrounding atmosphere. If the vapor is introduced via a small diameter tube directly into the trachea, exhalation can occur around the tube as long as the air-way is not occluded.

(4) *Closed-circuit method*

Although it is the most expensive procedure, the closed-circuit method is the most ideal for larger animals. In this system, oxygen and the anesthetic are delivered simultaneously to the animal either through a rubber mask or endotracheal catheter with an inflatable cuff. The CO_2 is removed by absorption in lime water, and the exhaled anesthetic is rebreathed since none is removed. The equipment needed for this method (see Appendix B for manufacturers) includes: an anesthetic container with regulators, canister of soda lime, flowmeters on either the compressed-air or oxygen tank, rebreathing bag, rebreathing valve, and an inflatable cuff on the intubation tube. A detailed description of the equipment used for administering inhalant anesthetics is given by Lumb (1963).

C. *Barbiturates Given by Injection*

Barbiturates have been used widely in behavioral studies to investigate the factors affecting learning, frustration or fear in certain avoidance situations. They are also widely used as hypnotics and general anesthetics, as a result of their interference with the transmission of nerve impulses within the cerebrum and the subsequent depression of the central nervous system. Although barbiturates can be classified into four groups according to their duration of action, those used for surgical anesthesia fall into the short and ultrashort categories.

(1) *Pentobarbitone sodium (Nembutal)*

Nembutal is perhaps the most widely used small-animal anesthetic, because it is especially suitable for procedures of 40 to 60 minute duration. The drug, a crystalline salt which is highly soluble in water, should be injected by the intravenous or intraperitoneal route (refer to Chapter 4). When administered by the intravenous route, the injection of approximately one-half of the volume is made rapidly so that the excitable stage is overcome. Then it is given slowly "to effect". The excitable action of Nembutal can be suppressed by a preanesthetic such as Meperidine (5 mg/kg in the cat) or Sernyl (5 mg/kg in the monkey). Table II gives suggested average doses in mg/kg body

TABLE II

Doses expressed in mg/kg for anesthetics and atropine

	Nembutal	Seconal	Pentothal	Atropine
Mouse				
IV	35	30	25	—
IP	60	60	—	—
O	80	—	—	—
IM	—	—	—	—
SC	—	70	—	0·05
Rat	Nembutal	Seconal	Pentothal	Atropine
IV	25	20	20	—
IP	30–50	40	40	—
O	50	65	70	—
IM	—	—	—	—
SC	—	60	—	0·05
Rabbit	Nembutal	Seconal	Pentothal	Atropine
IV	30	22	20	—
IP	40	30	—	—
O	45	—	—	—
IM	—	—	—	—
SC	—	50	—	0·05
Cat	Nembutal	Seconal	Pentothal	Atropine
IV	25–30	25	30	—
IP	33–36	35	60	—
O	50	—	—	—
IM	—	—	—	1.0
SC	—	—	—	0·05
Monkey	Nembutal	Seconal	Pentothal	Atropine
IV	25–35	18	15	—
IP	30	—	—	—
O	45	—	—	—
IM	—	—	—	—
SC	—	—	—	0·05

IV = Intravenous; IP = Intraperitoneal; O = Oral; I = Intramuscular; SC = Subcutaneous.

weight for Nembutal and two other barbiturate anesthetics as well as atropine for five species commonly used in neuropsychological experiments (Barnes and Eltherington, 1965).

(2) *Secobarbital sodium (Seconal)*

Seconal produces an anesthesia of short duration with the special features of quick onset and rapid recovery. Although it can depress respiration and circulation rather markedly, this compound may be used successfully alone or in combination with a muscle relaxant such as mephenesin. Myothesid is an ethical compound containing both 50 mg of Seconal and 30 mg of mephenesin per ml. Table II presents the average doses for several routes in different animals.

(3) *Thiopental sodium (Pentothal)*

As an analog of pentobarbital sodium, pentothal is a yellow crystal powder, which when dissolved in sterile saline is used as a general anesthetic for procedures which require a relatively short duration of 10 to 20 minutes. Since this anesthetic is a general irritant, it is best given by the intravenous route in a 2·5% solution administered in a dose of 12·5 to 25·0 mg/kg body weight, as shown in Table II. Because it is absorbed readily into fatty tissue and is thereby metabolized rather than excreted, the emergence phase may be quite prolonged.

D. *Pre-anesthetics*

A number of drugs may be used before an operation to (a) reduce anxiety and fear, (b) facilitate the induction or to potentiate the action of a general anesthetic, and (c) to inhibit salivation and emesis.

As a result of its anticholinergic action in the autonomic nervous system, atropine reduces secretions in the gastro-intestinal tract and controls the excessive amount of salivation caused by some anesthetics. Atropine is degraded quickly in the body, and may be given subcutaneously or intramuscularly as shown in Table II. In some laboratories, the use of atropine is considered mandatory particularly when vapor anesthetics such as ether are used either as a supplement to Nembutal or exclusively.

A tranquilizer such as a phenothiazine or a muscle relaxant such as mephenesin is also acceptable as a pre-anesthetic. Nembutal in a low-dose can be used as a pre-anesthetic for methoxyflurane or other vapor anesthetics, and the two compounds acting synergistically afford excellent control over the depth of anesthesia.

E. Special Problems

Probably the most common cause of operative or post-operative death in the animal surgery is hypothermia. Failure to keep the animal warm, by a heating pad or heat lamp, is absolutely foolhardy. For this reason, temperature should be monitored continuously by a YSI probe inserted into the colon of the rat (shown in Fig. 5), or other

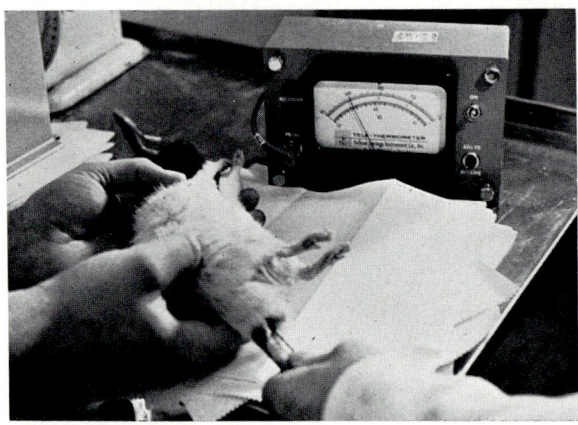

FIG. 5. Measuring the temperature of a rat with a thermistor probe inserted 3 cm into the colon, and held in place for 60 seconds. A telethermometer provides the temperature reading.

animal and taped to the base of the tail. Although we usually permit the animal's temperature to fall by as much as 2·0°C during neurosurgery, for purposes of hemostasis, the animal is warmed externally if its temperature declines below the level of 35°C. At temperatures of 34°C and below, the surgical shock is enhanced, and respiratory and cardiac rates decline rapidly. This hypothermic condition should be avoided at all costs.

Since every animal responds differently to an anesthetic, great care should be taken to avoid an overdose of the anesthetic agent. The principal sign of such an overdose is usually shallow and irregular breathing which, in the case of a volatile anesthetic, can be reversed by removal of the vapor and verifying the patency of the animal's trachea. Since cardiac function continues even after respiration has ceased, artificial respiration at a rate comparable to the normal rate will keep the animal alive until the anesthetic has lost its effect. If firm pressure is applied repeatedly on the rib cage in the region approximating the lower third of the sternum, the respiratory system will be stimulated.

A simple small-animal resuscitator should be close at hand for the emergency situation of respiratory arrest. A simple device for the rat (shown in Fig. 6) can be made from a rubber atomizer bulb (Fisher

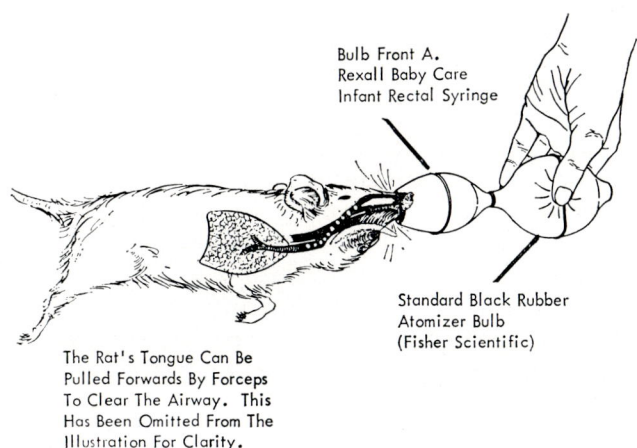

FIG. 6. A small animal resuscitator consisting of two rubber bulbs joined together. When the atomizer bulb is squeezed 60 to 80 times per minute, an animal which has received an overdose of either ether or other vapor anesthetic can be resuscitated. (From Ingall and Hasenpusch, 1966.)

Scientific) and an ordinary one ounce infant rectal syringe according to the design of Ingall (1966). The administration of 95% oxygen in combination with 5% CO_2 also provides an excellent stimulus for the chemoreceptors in the carotid and aortic bodies, which will cause a subsequent increase in the respiratory rate.

Following an overdose of a barbiturate, an intravenous or intraperitoneal injection of a stimulant such as Bemegide (10 mg/kg) or Leptazol (5 mg/kg) may help to stimulate respiration; however, these analeptics are in general not as effective in smaller animals as in the monkey or dog.

VI. Laboratory Diseases

An outbreak of a disease in an animal colony is not only costly in terms of the possible loss of an entire group of animals, but the physiological and behavioral consequences arising from certain infections may serve to complicate or even invalidate an experimental finding. The prevention and control of disease can be facilitated if the origins are considered. Diseases can originate from (1) a newly introduced animal carrying bacteria or viruses to the animals already present;

(2) a wild rat, wild mouse, cockroach or other pest; (3) a member of the laboratory staff or a visitor to the laboratory; (4) unsanitary cage conditions which facilitate the culture and growth of bacterial organisms.

If an animal should die, the reason for death should be determined if at all possible. Post-mortem examination of an animal must be done with the utmost caution and care. A monkey necropsy requires surgical gloves, mask, hat and gown, worn in the assumption that the animal could have succumbed from (or is a carrier of) a disease which is contagious to the human. Following necropsy, all instruments should be thoroughly sterilized; all objects, tables and apparatus which came into contact with the animal are decontaminated with surgical disinfectant and wiped thoroughly with 70% alcohol. The animal should be disposed of in two or more coverings of plastic wrap (bags) sealed to prevent leakage of body fluids. Electrodes, cannulae, pedestals, cranial platforms, thermistor connectors and other materials which may have been implanted into the brain or affixed to the skull should also be cleansed thoroughly in a biological disinfectant or detergent (Micro or Alconox), and then placed in zephiran or other suitable sterilizing solution. Usually, these devices are re-used in a second animal only if it is absolutely certain that every fragment of dead tissue from the first animal has been removed. We have witnessed an extraordinary inflammatory reaction followed by a septic response within cerebral tissue of an animal in which a used cannula-electrode was implanted which contained bits of tissue from another animal.

Recognition of a disease state may not always be easy for the beginner in physiological psychology, and appropriate clinical treatment can prove to be very difficult. Therefore, it is always best to consult with a veterinary specialist for a particular disease problem. For greater detail concerning the etiology, symptoms and treatment of a disease, the reader should also consult Farris (1957), Ruch (1959), Harris (1962), the UFAW Handbook (1967) and perhaps the most comprehensive of all, Short and Woodnott (1969).

After a diseased animal is removed from its cage, the cage and its litter pan, water bottle and associated materials must be sterilized. Cleaning with a jet of steam from a "steam gun" for 10 minutes, during which time the cage temperature reaches 212°F should be sufficient to kill most pathogenic organisms. This procedure will not, however, kill spore-forming bacteria. In an autoclave, the steam under 15 lb/sq in pressure raises the temperature at which the water boils to 250°F. If this temperature is held for 30 minutes, most forms of organisms, including spores, are killed.

Common diseases of the laboratory mouse

Major category	Disease	Cause	Symptoms	Treatment
Viral	Chronic respiratory disease	Virus or pleuro-pneumonia-like-organisms (PPLO)	"Chattering," sniffing or carrying head in a tilted position	Sacrifice the diseased colony or any susceptible animals, and establish a pathogen-free colony by using Caesarian-derived breeders, and begin anew with healthy stock. The rooms, cages, equipment, etc., must be sterilized and/or disinfected
	Mouse pox	Ectromelia virus	Skin lesions and scabs. Tail and feet may become edematous	Inoculate with vaccinia virus; sacrifice animals with symptoms and sterilize as above
	Infantile diarrhea	Virus	Yellow diarrhea, dehydration, and high mortality	Special diets should control this disease; if the infection spreads, destroy susceptible animals. Sterilize cages, etc., as above
Bacterial	Mouse typhoid	*Salmonella* bacteria	Loss of weight; sometimes conjunctivitis and diarrhea	Eradication seems to be necessary as the only permanent solution. Sterilize cages and equipment
	Tyzzer's disease	Gram negative bacillus (*Bacillus piliformis*)	Loss of weight, diarrhea	Sacrifice infected animals and sterilize cages and equipment
	Arthritis	Gram negative bacillis (*Streptobacillus moniliformis*)	*Acute*: Loss of weight, palpebral fissures occluded, and conjunctivitis. *Chronic*: legs are arthritic and edematous. Inguinal and maxillary glands may be enlarged	Either sacrifice infected animals, or if an epidemic occurs, the whole colony may have to be destroyed. Sterilize cages and equipment
	Septicemia	Gram negative or Positive bacteria	Loss of weight, dyspnea and death	Infected animals should be sacrificed, as above

TABLE III—continued

Common diseases of the laboratory mouse

Major category	Disease	Cause	Symptoms	Treatment
Fungal	Ringworm	Fungus	Scaling, lesions, loss of hair. Spore sheaths can be seen microscopically if skin scrapings or hair are mounted in 10% potassium hydroxide	Infected animals should be sacrificed to prevent spread of infection. Sterilize cages and equipment
Ecto-parasites	Body mange	Mite	Loss of hair and inflammation of the skin	Dusting with or dipping the infected animals in malathion
	Neck–head mange	Mite	Inflammation and formation of scab	As above
	Ear–body mange	Mite	Occlusion of the ear with a waxy mass; skin pouches caused by mites burrowing under the skin. Mites can be seen microscopically	Do not remove wax. Put a large drop of dibutyl phthalate into the ear every 7 days. Topical application of 15% Aramide may be used to treat body mange
Helminths	Roundworm infestation	Nematodes	No observable symptoms, worms found on autopsy	Add piperazine acid citrate ($1\frac{1}{2}$ g/l) to drinking water for 7 days
	Cysticerosis	Cystic stage of cat tapeworm	No observable syndromes. Cysts found on autopsy.	Adequate sanitation and sterilization is best control

TABLE IV

Common diseases of the laboratory rat

Major Category	Disease	Cause	Symptoms	Treatment
Viral	E.M.P. (Epidemic murine pneumonia)	Virus	"Chattering," and snuffling. In prolonged infection there may be rales, emaciation and roughened hair	Sacrifice diseased colony or susceptible animals and establish a pathogen-free colony by using Caesarian-derived breeders or re-introduce healthy stock. The cages, equipment and rooms must be sterilized and/or disinfected. The drug tylocin may be used
Bacterial	Labyrinthitis	PPLO (pleuro-pneumonia organisms) and *Streptobacillus moniliformis*, a bacteria	Tilting the head and moving in a circular rather than straight line	Sacrifice animals with symptoms. Sterilize all cages, etc.
Protozoal	Coccidiosis	Coccidia	Diarrhea	Adequate nutrition and sanitation controls this disease
Ecto-parasites	Body mange	Mites	Irritation and inflammation of the skin. A microscopic examination of scrapings of hair and skin in 10% potassium hydroxide will reveal mites	Dusting with or dipping infected animals in malathion
Nutritional	Vitamin E deficiency	Lack of Vitamin E in diet	Infertility and abortion	Add Vitamin E to the diet

TABLE V

Common diseases of the laboratory rabbit

Major Category	Disease	Cause	Symptoms	Treatment
Viral	Myxomatosis	Virus	Lesions on the eyelids. Nose, lips and genitalia may become swollen	Vaccine prepared from Shope fibroma virus can give immunity for 6 months
	Rabbit pox	Virus	Inflammation of eyelid, pus-like discharge from the nose, rash on the ears and exposed areas of the skin	Vaccination with vaccinia virus will give immunity
Bacterial	Snuffles	Gram negative bacilli	Discharge from nose. Rabbits make "snuffling" noise and may sneeze	Adequate diet, sanitation and sterilization of cages prevent outbreaks. Diseased animal is sacrificed
	Pneumonia	Same as above	Usually disease is diagnosed only on autopsy	As above
	Syphilis	Bacteria	Ulcer-like lesions on the genitalia	Injection of penicillin or neosalvarsan
Fungal	Ringworm	Fungus	Bald spots. Scrapings mounted in 10% potassium hydroxide show spores	Most treatments are not effective. To prevent spread, sacrifice the animal and sterilize all bedding, cages, etc.
Protozoal	Coccidiosis (intestinal)	Parasitic protozoa	Diarrhea, loss of weight	Regular cleaning and sterilization of cages. Sulphadimidine or sulphaquinoxaline may be added to the drinking water
	Coccidiosis (hepatic)	Protozoa	Faulty metabolism, loss of weight, death	As above

TABLE V—*continued*

Common diseases of the laboratory rabbit

Major Category	Disease	Cause	Symptoms	Treatment
Ecto-parasites	Ear canker	Mites	Scratching of ears	Drop into the ear tetraethylthurium monosulphide in a 1:10 dilution with warm water
	Body canker	Mites	Loss of hair, irritation of skin	Wash infected part with an 0·05 per cent solution of gamma-benzene-hexachloride
Helminths	Bladder worms	Cystic stage of dog tapeworm	No serious ill effects	Sterilization and strict hygienic conditions

TABLE VI

Common diseases of the laboratory cat

Major Category	Disease	Cause	Symptoms	Treatment
Viral	Feline panleukopenia distemper/infectious feline enteritis	Virus	Sudden onset of aphagia, vomiting, diarrhea and high fever. Mortality as high as 60–90%. A low leucocyte count less than 2000/mm	Protective, inactivated vaccine is given to kitten at 6 weeks of age. Booster, two weeks later and once a year
	Feline pneumonitis	Virus	Loss of appetite, conjunctivitis, temperature rise, nasal discharge and sneezing	Topical application of antibiotics for secondary bacterial infection of the eyes and nose. Aureomycin 12·5 mg/lb given orally. Cats immunized with yolk-sac-virus-vaccine. Chlortetracycline to treat kittens
Bacterial	Septicemia	Various bacteria	Rise in temperature, loss of appetite, loss of weight	Broad-band antibiotics such as penicillin, terramycine, tetracycline administered parenterally
	Pneumonia	*Bordetella bronchiseptica*	Loss of appetite, loss of weight and dyspnea	Treat with antibiotics such as penicillin, terramycine, tetracycline or specific antiserum administered parenterally

TABLE VI—continued

Common diseases of the laboratory cat

Major Category	Disease	Cause	Symptoms	Treatment
Fungal	Ringworm	Fungi	Small or large bald areas, crustings, and skin lesions. Spores can be seen with microscopic examination	Isolate the infected animals, sterilize cages, etc. A systemic antimycotic, such as griseofulvin may be effective
Ecto-parasites	Mange	Mites	Lesions on the skin caused by the burrowing of the mites	Topical applications of benzyl benzoate emulsion or benzene hexachloride
	Ear canker	Mites	Dark-brown wax in the ear causes scratching and shaking of head	Use same preparation as above. Analgesics used to reduce the cat's discomfort
Helminths	Nematode infestation	Round worms	Severe loss of weight	Oral administration of piperazine acid citrate
	Tapeworm infestation	Flat worms	Loss of weight, vomiting and diarrhea	Arecoline hydrobromide, drocarbil or arecoline acetarsol (estimate dosages carefully!)
Miscellaneous	Flea and louse	Cat flea and louse	Scratching; inflammation of skin	Destroy infested bedding and spray and clean cages. Dust cat with pyrethrin dust (do not use DDT on cats)

TABLE VII

Common diseases of the laboratory monkey

Major Category	Disease	Cause	Symptoms	Treatment
Viral	B-virus	Herpes virus simiae	Ulcer-like lesions of the mouth area, lips, cheeks, tongue, hard and soft palate	Disease not dangerous to monkeys, but *fatal to man*. Suspect or newly acquired animal should be isolated for at least 14 days, during which time the monkey should become non-infective
Bacterial	Dysentery	Gram negative bacilli of *Shigella* or *Salmonella* genus	Loss of weight and diarrhea	Strict hygiene is imperative! House animals separately, and sterilize cages. Kaopectate 1 oz/day or chloromycetin 100 mg/kg may be used. *Note*: Dehydrated monkeys need extra fluids (i.e. 5% glucose in saline [150–300 ml])
	Pneumonia	Gram negative bacillus	Loss of appetite, respiratory distress and coughing, shivering, and rise in temperature	Treat with parenterally administered antibiotics such as penicillin, terramycin and tetracycline
	Tuberculosis	*Mycobacterium tuberculosis*	Loss of weight, apathy and respiratory problems such as coughing	Monkeys screened using PPD (purified protein derivative) test (injection into the eyelid). Eye of positive reactor becomes red and closed. Positive reactors are sacrificed.

TABLE VII—*continued*

Common diseases of the laboratory monkey

Major Category	Disease	Cause	Symptoms	Treatment
Helminths	Esophageal roundworm infestations	Nematode	No signs. In advanced cases, there may be loss of weight and diarrhea	Phenothiazine: 140 mg/kg, Piperazine hydrate or other oral anthelmintics. Good hygiene and cleanliness is essential
	Intestinal parasitic infestation	Strongylodes	Diarrhea with mucous; eggs and larvae in stools	"Gentian violet" 60 mg/kg may be used
Ecto-parasites	Pulmonary acariasis	Acari mites	Pulmonary distress. On autopsy, mites are found in the lungs	Dust animals with DDT

Equipment and supplies which would be damaged by steam or water can be sterilized by using dry heat, provided by a hot-air oven, which reaches all parts of the object. Dry sterilization requires a longer time (one to two hours) and a hotter temperature of 260°F. Irradiation and ethylene oxide machines are now being more widely used for sterilizing procedures. Commercial disinfectants of phenol or coal-tar origin are also suitable for removing bacteria from the surfaces of a cage, feeding-dish or other pieces of equipment. Germicidal ultraviolet irradiation can be used to prevent cross-infection between animals when a UV light is suspended in the animal colony room. (Lurie, 1944; Phillips et al., 1957).

VII. EUTHANASIA

There are several ways by which an animal can be sacrificed humanely at the end of an experiment. Since the emphasis here is entirely on the humane aspect, an anesthetic is certainly recommended. In addition to handling the animal carefully, a basic principle is that the animal should be removed from the colony and not killed in the presence of other animals (Short and Woodnott, 1969).

An overdose of Nembutal (60–90 mg/kg) given by the intraperitoneal route or inhalation of a volatile anesthetic are common procedures. Chloroform, although not recommended as an anesthetic, can be used for sacrificing a small animal if the liquid is dropped onto cotton batting placed on the bottom of a desiccator jar or a 3-pound coffee can with a removable plastic lid.

ACKNOWLEDGEMENT

The material presented in this chapter was compiled largely by my wife, Marjorie A. Myers, to whom it is a pleasure to acknowledge my deep indebtedness.

REFERENCES

Barnes, C. D. and Eltherington, L. G. (1965). "Drug Dosage in Laboratory Animals." University of California Press, Berkeley, California.
Barrow, M. V. (1968). *Laboratory Animal Care* 18, 570–571.
Ben, M., Dixon, R. L. and Adamson, R. H. (1969). *Fedn. Proc.* 28, 1522–1527.
Farris, E. J. (1957). "The Care and Breeding of Laboratory Animals." John Wiley & Sons, Ltd., New York and Chichester.
Gay, W. I. (1960). *Proc. Animal Care* 10, 75–78.
Gay, W. I. (1965). "Methods of Animal Experimentation, Vol. I." Academic Press, Inc., New York and London.
Goodman, L. S. and Gilman, A. (1970). "The Pharmacological Basis of Therapeutics" (4th Ed.). MacMillan Co., New York.
Hamilton, P. B., Boegli, G. and Rutledge, J. H. (1967). *Laboratory Animal Care* 17, 251–252.

Hamilton, P. B., Rutledge, J. H. and Boegli, G. (1967). *Laboratory Animal Care* **17**, 362–364.
Harris, R. J. C. (1962). "The Problems of Laboratory Animal Disease." Academic Press, New York and London.
Ingall, J. R. F. and Hasenpusch, P. H. (1966). *Laboratory Animal Care* **16**, 82–83.
Leonard, E. P. (1968). "Fundamentals of Small Animal Surgery," W. B. Saunders Co., Philadelphia.
Lewis, R. E., Kunz, A. L. and Bell, R. E. (1966). *Laboratory Animal Care* **16**, 505–509.
Lumb, W. V. (1963). "Small Animal Anesthesia." Lea and Febiger, Philadelphia.
Lurie, M. B. (1944). *J. Exp. Med.* **79**, 559–572.
Mann, P. E. G. and Boretos, J. W. (1968). *Laboratory Animal Care* **18**, 657–659.
Markowitz, J., Archibald, J. and Downie, H. G. (1964). "Experimental Surgery," 5th Edition, The Williams and Wilkins Co., Baltimore.
Molello, J. A. and Hawkins, K. (1968). *Laboratory Animal Care* **18**, 581–583.
Myers, R. D. and Veale, W. L. (1968). *Science, N.Y.* **160**, 1469–1471.
Myers, R. D. and Veale, W. L. (1970). *Neuropharmacology* **9**, 317–326.
Phillips, G. B., Reitman, M., Mullican, C. L. and Gardner, G. D., Jr. (1957). *Animal Care Panel* **7**, 235–244.
Ruch, T. C. (1959). "Diseases of Laboratory Primates." W. B. Saunders Co., Philadelphia.
Short, D. J. and Woodnott, D. P. (1969). "The I.A.T. Manual of Laboratory Animal Practice and Techniques" (2nd Ed.). Crosby Lockwood & Son, Ltd; London.
Strobel, G. E. and Wollman, H. (1969). *Fedn Proc.* **28**, 1386–1403.
UFAW Handbook, "The Care and Management of Laboratory Animals" (1967). (W. Lane-Petter, A. N. Warden, B. F. Hill, J. S. Paterson and H. G. Vevers, eds), E. & S. Livingstone, Ltd; Edinburgh and London.

Appendix A

In addition to those Journals and Books cited in the Reference list, the following publications and periodicals will be of use to the beginning student:

CARE OF ANIMALS AND GENERAL LABORATORY KNOWLEDGE
"Manual for Laboratory Animal Technicians"
published by: American Association for Laboratory Animal Science
    Box 10
    Juliet, Illinois 60434
    U.S.A.
"Laboratory Animal Care" (6 volumes/year)
published by: American Association for Laboratory Animal Science
    P.O. Box 10
    Juliet, Illinois 60434
    U.S.A.
"Journal of the Institute of Animal Technicians" (4 volumes/year)
published by: Institute of Animal Technicians
    21 Glebe Road
    Welwyn, Hertfordshire
    England.
"Guide for Laboratory Animal Facilities"
order from: Superintendent of Documents
    U.S. Government Printing Office
    Washington, D.C. 20402
    U.S.A.

SOURCES FOR COMMERCIALLY AVAILABLE LABORATORY ANIMALS, EQUIPMENT, CAGES AND FEED
"Animals for Research" (7th Ed., revised July, 1968, publication 1678)
order from: Institute of Laboratory Animal Science
    National Academy of Science Printing and Publication Office
    2101 Constitution Avenue, N.W.
    Washington, D.C. 20418

SURGERY
"Manual of Operative Procedure on Surgical Knots"
published by: Ethicon, Inc.
    Sommerville, New Jersey, U.S.A.

Appendix B

Some suppliers of common drugs and equipment

DRUGS

Atropine Sulfate	Moore Kirk Laboratories, Inc. Worcester 1, Massachusetts, U.S.A.
Chloroform	Merck, Sharpe, and Dohme Philadelphia, Pennsylvania, U.S.A.
Ether	E. R. Squibb & Sons 745 5th Avenue New York, New York 10022, U.S.A.
Ethyl Chloride	Gebauer Chemical Co. Cleveland, Ohio, U.S.A.
Halothane	Ayerst Laboratories 685 3rd Avenue New York, New York 10017, U.S.A.
Methoxyflurane (Penthrane)	Abbott Laboratories North Chicago, Illinois, U.S.A.
Pentobarbital Sodium (Nembutal)	As above
Thiopental Sodium (Pentothal)	As above
Secobarbital Sodium (Seconal)	Eli Lilly & Company Indianapolis, Indiana, U.S.A.

ANESTHESIA EQUIPMENT

Professional Veterinary Services Inc.
2855 East 11th Avenue
Hialeah, Florida, U.S.A.

Ethical Veterinary Supply Co.
34 31st Street
Long Island 6, New York, U.S.A.

Fort Dodge Laboratories
Fort Dodge, Iowa

CAGES

Wahmann Manufacturing Co.
P.O. Box 6883
Baltimore, Maryland 21204, U.S.A.

Porter-Mathews Scientific Co.
U.S. Route 1
Princeton, New Jersey 08540, U.S.A.

Kirshner Manufacturing Co.
Vashon, Washington, U.S.A.

Unifab Corporation
5260 Lover's Lane
Kalamazoo, Michigan 49002, U.S.A.

Acme Metal Products, Inc.
5500 Muddy Creek Road
Cincinnati, Ohio 42238, U.S.A.

GENERAL EQUIPMENT

Fisher Scientific
711 Forbes Avenue

Lapine Scientific Co.
6001 South Knox Avenue

Pittsburg, Pennsylvania 15219, U.S.A.
Arthur H. Thomas Co.
Vine Street at Third
P.O. Box 779
Philadelphia, Pennsylvania 19105, U.S.A.

Chicago, Illinois 60629, U.S.A.
American Hospital Supply
2020 Ridge Avenue
Evanston, Illinois 60201, U.S.A.

STERILIZERS

American Sterilizer Co.
2424 W. 23rd Street
Erie, Pennsylvania 16512, U.S.A.

THERMISTORS

Yellow Springs Instrument Co., Inc.
Yellow Springs, Ohio, U.S.A.

Appendix C

Physiological Solutions

Salt	Saline	Ringer (Summer)	Ringer (Winter)	Locke	Tyrode	Krebs	Artificial CSF†
			(g/l)				
NaCl	9·00	7·00	6·75	9·00	8·00	6·90	7·46
KCl	—	0·14	0·15	0·42	0·20	0·35	0·19
$CaCl_2$*	—	0·13	0·40	0·19	0·20	0·28	0·14
$MgCl_2.6H_2O$	—	—	—	—	0·02	—	0·19
$MgSO_4.7H_2O$	—	—	—	—	—	0·29	—
$NaHCO_3$	—	0·20	0·20	0·15	1·00	2·10	1·76
Na_2HPO_4	—	—	—	—	—	—	0·18
NaH_2PO_4	—	—	—	—	0·05	—	—
KH_2PO_4	—	—	—	—	—	0·16	—
Glucose	—	—	—	2·00	1·00	1·00	0·61

* Anhydrous.
† Based on the standard Merlis CSF modified for the monkey.
N.B.—Always dissolve PO_4 salts and HCO_3 salts *separately*, add to $\frac{9}{10}$ of the final solution and bring up to 1 liter with distilled H_2O.

Chapter 3

Use of the Stereotaxic Technique

LOUIS J. PELLEGRINO

*Department of Psychology, Middlebury College,
Middlebury, Vermont, U.S.A.*

and

ANNA J. CUSHMAN

*Department of Psychology, University of Waterloo,
Waterloo, Ontario, Canada*

I.	Introduction	67
II.	Stereotaxic Instruments	69
III.	Stereotaxic Atlases	73
IV.	How to Use the Stereotaxic Instrument	78
	A. Pre-operative Calibration of the Implanted Device	78
	B. Determination of Instrument Zero	79
	C. Arbitrary Horizontal Zero	79
	D. Calculation of Final Instrument Coordinates	79
	E. An Alternative Stereotaxic Technique	81
	F. How to Place the Animal in the Instrument	82
V.	Histological Verification of Stereotaxic Placements	84
Acknowledgements		86
References		86
Appendix A. Stereotaxic Atlases		87
Appendix B. Manufacturers and Distributors of Stereotaxic Instruments		90

I. INTRODUCTION

THE stereotaxic method had its birth in the study of neuroanatomy. With the development of methods for fixing and staining tissue from the central nervous system, neuroanatomists began to trace the intricate connections within and between brain areas. The procedure employed in these studies was to destroy an area in the brain of an experimental animal, and then sacrifice it a few days later. After the brain had been adequately fixed, the anatomist would study very thin sections of tissue and trace the course of the degenerating fibers leading away from the lesioned area. In order for these data to be reproduced, it became necessary to devise a method by which lesions could be precisely and repeatedly placed within deep structures of the brain with a minimum amount of damage to overlying areas.

Sir Victor Horsley and his co-worker, R. H. Clarke, were attempting to study the connections of the cerebellum in the rhesus monkey (*Macaca mulatta*) when they felt that it was imperative to develop a method for making discrete lesions in various cerebellar nuclei (Clarke and Horsley, 1906; Horsley and Clarke, 1908). The brain was divided into three planes—horizontal plane, sagittal plane, and frontal plane—and a three-dimensional coordinate system was derived. Clarke designed an instrument which would hold the animal's head solidly within this coordinate system. With the stereotaxic instrument and a bone-sectioning device, also designed by Clarke (Horsley and Clarke, 1908), called a macrotome, they were able to construct brain charts showing the location of brain structures relative to each other and the outer surface of the skull. With the brain charts and the stereotaxic apparatus, Horsley and Clarke were able to make measurements on the animal's skull, then drill a hole in the bone just large enough to permit them to introduce the lesion electrode. Besides permitting the accurate placement of the probe, this method resulted in minimal damage to overlying brain areas as well as a minimum amount of bone defect. The methods of stereotaxic surgery as they are employed today are essentially the same as those developed by Horsley and Clarke and will be discussed in detail later in the chapter.

The value of stereotaxic surgery to neuropsychology is patently obvious. The use of stereotaxic techniques permits the neuroscientist to place electrodes accurately for stimulation of discrete brain areas (e.g. specific nuclei of the hypothalamus), or to destroy the cells in selected areas and study the effects on the behavior of the animal. The methods of stereotaxis also allow for the implantation of a very small tube or cannula so that substances such as chemicals, drugs or hormones may be injected directly into the brain.

To depart from the experimental value of stereotaxic surgery, it is important to consider briefly the applied significance of these techniques. Although the stereotaxic instrument was developed in the early part of this century, it was not until 1947 that a similar apparatus was designed for use in human brain operations (Spiegel *et al.*, 1947). Human stereotaxic surgery has now come into its own in the last twenty years and its major application has been in the alleviation of the symptoms of motor disorders, especially Parkinson's syndrome (Levy, 1967; Van Manen, 1967).

The correct use of the stereotaxic instrument is probably one of the most valuable techniques employed by the neuropsychologist. However, as with any technique, the *correct use* must be stressed. The first concern of the investigator as he prepares for stereotaxic surgery is that the instrument be in good repair with all scales clearly and accurately marked, and all moving parts working smoothly. The second consideration, and probably more important, is that the experimental animal be of the same size and species as the animals used in preparing the selected atlas. For example, Snider and Niemer's (1961) atlas for the cat (*Felis domesticus*) was prepared for animals weighing 2·0 to 3·5 kg. A cat which is much heavier (or lighter) than this weight, is not a suitable subject for stereotaxic procedures if the Snider and Niemer atlas is to be used when determining the coordinates for the structure selected for investigation. A more detailed examination of coordinate systems follows.

II. Stereotaxic Instruments

The major consideration when selecting a stereotaxic apparatus is that it be rigid and that the scales be accurately and clearly marked. Stereotaxic instruments vary considerably in versatility; some are limited to one species, others can be adapted for use with many different animals (see Appendix B for a list of manufacturers and distributors). The versatility of an apparatus which can accommodate many species is convenient, but certainly not essential. Figure 1 shows a drawing of a rat mounted in a small-animal stereotaxic instrument (Hart, 1969). This type of instrument is suitable for mice, rats, chickens and other small animals. With a different type of mount for the frame and appropriate adaptors this apparatus is wide enough to accommodate cats, rabbits and squirrel monkeys.

One disadvantage of the above type of stereotaxic instrument is that there is only one electrode carrier. If there is more than one electrode to be implanted, this limitation can greatly increase the length of the surgical procedure and therefore increase the risk to the animal. In recent years, the trend in the manufacture of stereotaxic instruments has been to construct a rigid frame with two parallel bars extending back from a crosspiece. Most of these devices are suitable for both large and small animals by simply changing the ear bars and the mouth adaptors.

Figures 2 to 5 show both large and small animals mounted in the same stereotaxic instrument (#1204, David Kopf Instruments). This type of instrument does not have the single electrode limitation of the smaller apparatus. Many carriers may be mounted on the bars and

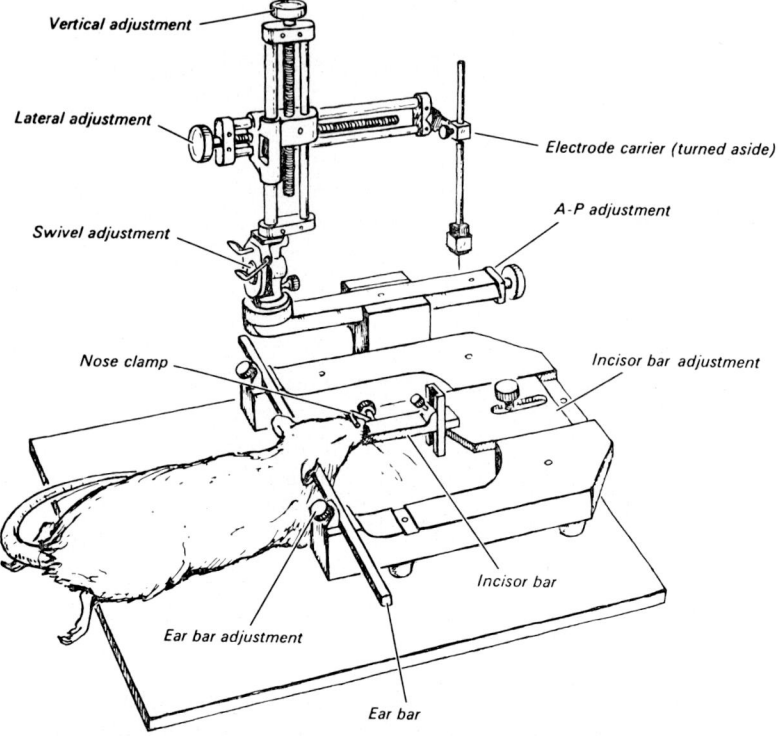

Fig. 1. Diagram of a rat properly positioned in a small stereotaxic instrument. Reproduced with permission from Hart (1969).

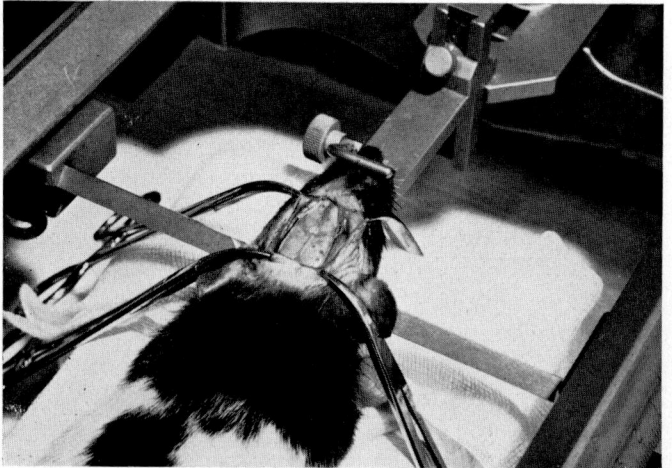

Fig. 2. Rat correctly mounted in a stereotaxic instrument with a midline incision exposing the skull for surgery. Bregma and lambda can be seen at the anterior and posterior intersections of the sagittal and coronal sutures. (With permission from P. Meyer and D. R. Meyer.)

3 Use of the Stereotaxic Technique

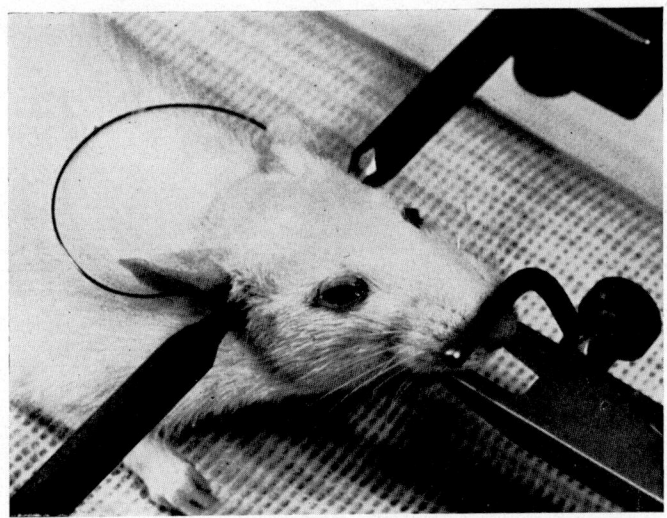

FIG. 3. Close-up view of rat correctly mounted in a stereotaxic instrument.

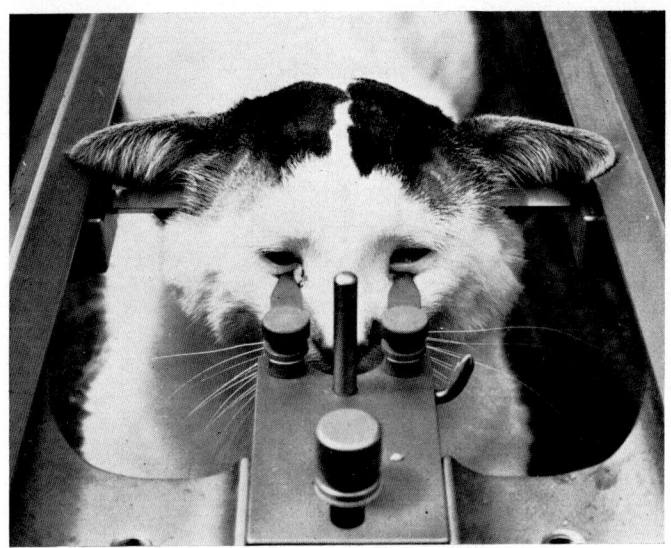

FIG. 4. Cat correctly mounted in a stereotaxic instrument with eye bars resting on infraorbital ridge.

the probes lowered almost simultaneously. When using the larger apparatus with small animals such as mice or rats, it is necessary to support the animal's body either with a wooden platform or a sling suspended from the bars of the frame.

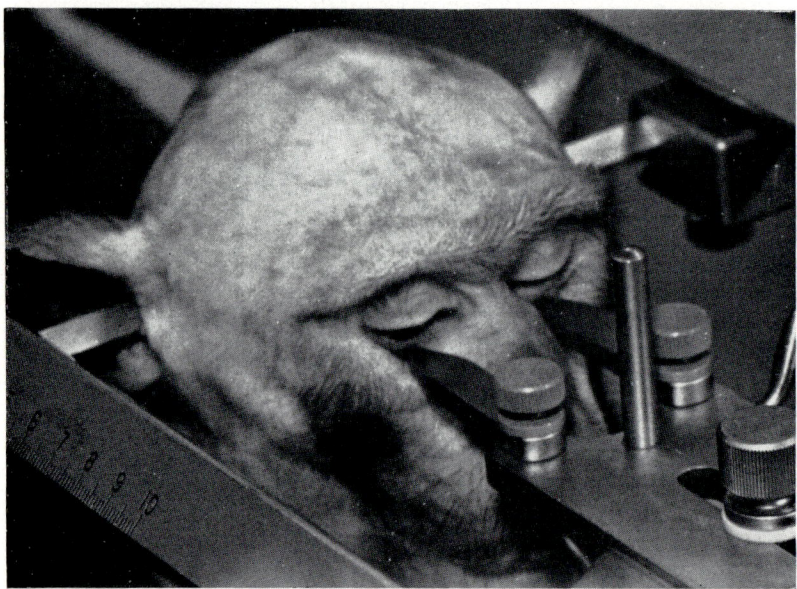

FIG. 5. Rhesus monkey correctly mounted in a stereotaxic instrument with eye bars resting on infraorbital ridge.

There are many varieties of electrode holders available, all of which fit on the carriers supplied with the stereotaxic frame. Among these holders, there is an attachment available which is specifically designed for the insertion of cannulae. The student or researcher should select the style of holder which best suits the design of his electrode and also which takes into account the number of probes to be implanted into the animal.

Many experimenters find it desirable to insert electrodes into the brain at an angle other than perpendicular to the horizontal zero plane in order to avoid penetrating certain structures with the electrode. If such angular insertion is desired, the electrode carrier must have an angle adjust mechanism. It is extremely important that this angle adjustment be accurate and that when locked in position it does not slip. A useful device for angular insertion of electrodes is an electrode angle calibrator. This device makes it possible to insert electrodes at any angle without actually computing the number of degrees off vertical at which the electrode should be inserted. If an electrode angle calibrator is not available, the necessary angle can be computed simply by using elementary trigonometry.

Various modifications of the standard stereotaxic instrument are available for more specialized research. These include one with an extremely rigid frame for recording the electrical activity from within a single cell. The electrode carrier driving mechanism for these instruments is graduated more finely than those supplied for gross work, and hydraulic micro-manipulators are also available. For those primarily interested in investigating the visual system, there are instruments available which make it possible to present stimuli to the eye while the animal is in the apparatus. There are also instruments available which permit stereotaxic surgery on the spinal cord as well as the brain.

It is important to stress again that the major requirements for a stereotaxic instrument are rigidity and accuracy.

III. Stereotaxic Atlases

A variety of stereotaxic atlases are readily available for the mouse, rat, cat, dog and various primates (see Appendix A). Although many stereotaxic atlases of the brain of the rat, the most common laboratory animal, have been published the most detailed ones available to date are by de Groot (1959); König and Klippel (1963); and Pellegrino and Cushman (1967). The latter two atlases consist of photomicrographs of serial histological sections of the rat brain accompanied by labelled line drawings delineating the major structures in each section. The de Groot (1959) atlas does not provide photomicrographs of actual histological sections, but simply unilateral line drawings. Figures 6 to 8(B) present examples of sections from each atlas chosen to be at equivalent anterior-posterior levels of the hypothalamus.

One major difference that can be seen in these three figures is that although the three atlases agree fairly closely in the ventral half of the sections, there are considerable differences between the atlases in the structures shown in the dorsal halves of the sections. This discrepancy is due to different "stereotaxic angles": the angle at which the rat's head is placed in the stereotaxic instrument and consequently the plane at which the above coronal sections are cut. In the actual implantation procedure, an error in the angular position would, of course, destroy the accuracy of the placement. In the de Groot and Pellegrino and Cushman atlases, the head is placed into the stereotaxic instrument so that the upper incisor bar (UIB) is 5·0 mm above the interaural line (IAL) produced by the ear bars. In the König and

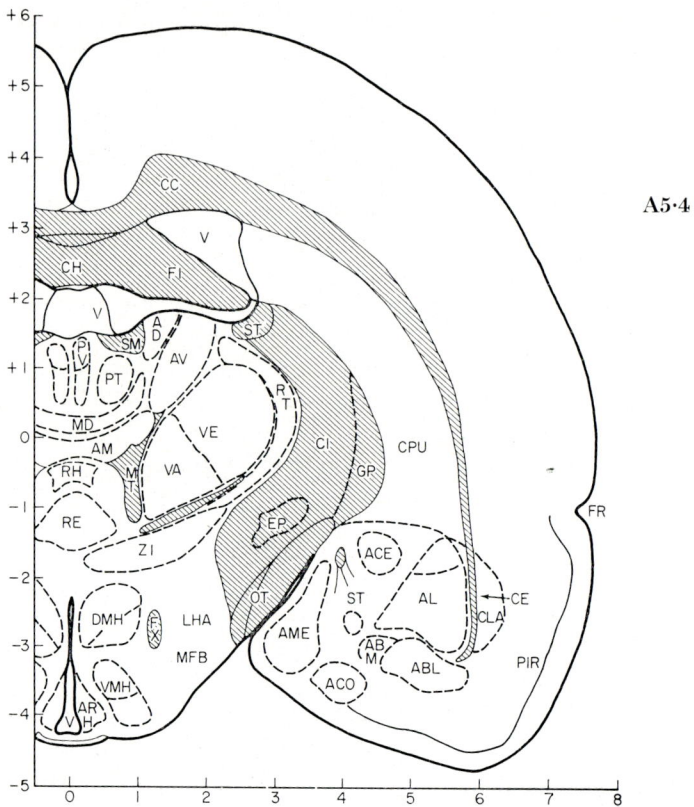

Fig. 6. Schematic drawing of a rat brain section from the de Groot (1959) atlas. Number in the upper right corner (A 5·4) is the anterior-posterior coordinate. Reproduced with permission.

Klippel atlas the upper incisor bar (I) is 2·4 mm below the interaural line (A).

Each of the three atlases most commonly used have their advantages and disadvantages. The de Groot atlas was produced for 200–300 g albino rats but has also been successfully used with hooded rats. However, there are two disadvantages to this atlas. It does not provide the photomicrographs of actual stained sections which can make verification of electrode or lesion placements less difficult (see below). Secondly, this atlas does not contain drawings of the extreme anterior or posterior regions of the rat brain.

The König and Klippel (1963) atlas was constructed from the brains of 150g female albino rats. Although it does not suffer from the deficiencies noted above in the de Groot atlas, it has one peculiarity all

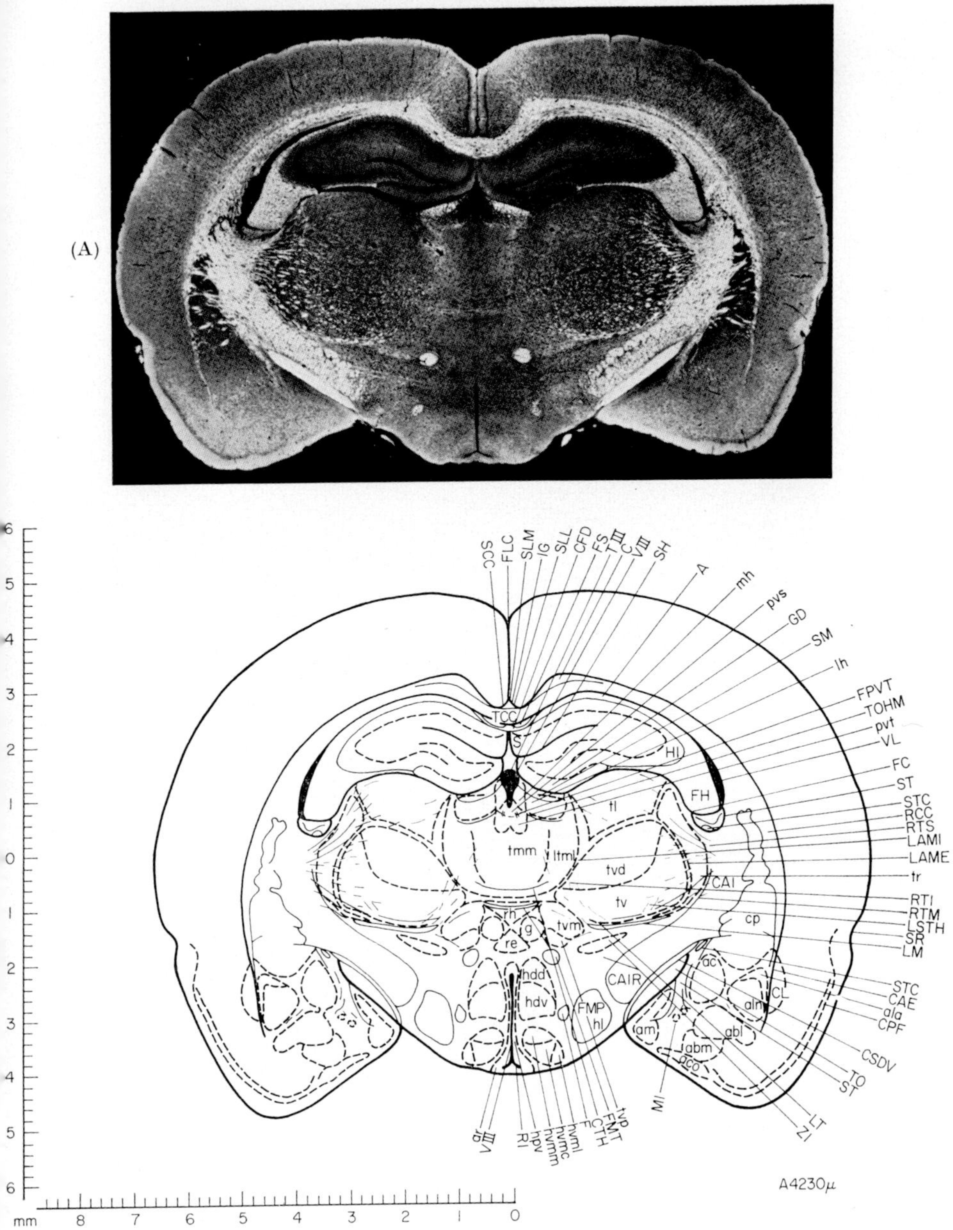

3 Use of the Stereotaxic Technique

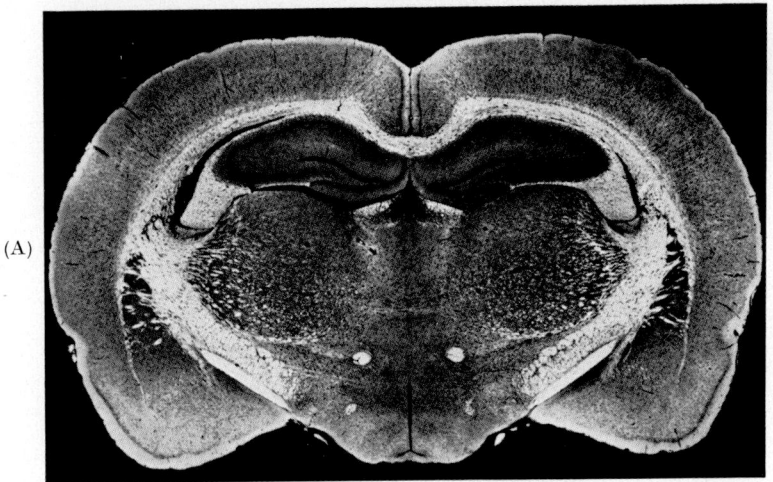

FIG. 7. (A) Photomicrograph of a stained section of the rat brain. (B) Schematic drawing of the major structures in Fig. 7(A) with stereotaxic coordinates. Reproduced with permission from König and Klippel (1963).

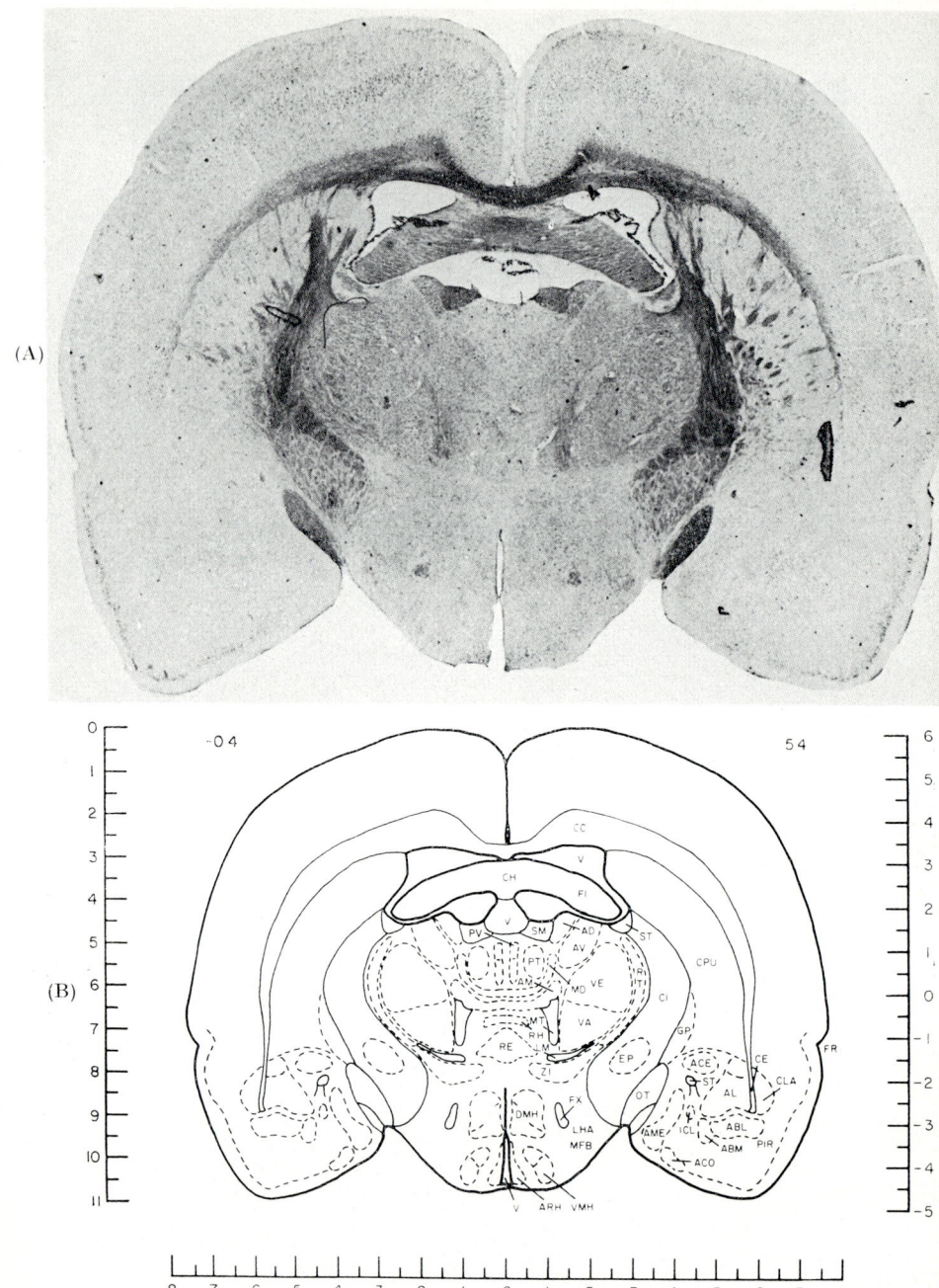

Fig. 8. (A) Photomicrograph of a stained section of the rat brain. (B) Schematic drawing of the major structures in Fig. 8(A). Reproduced with permission from the Pellegrino and Cushman (1967) atlas.

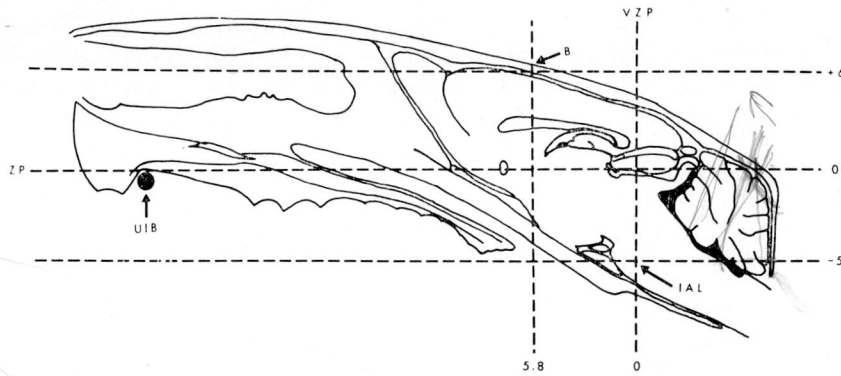

Fig. 9. Mid-sagittal section through the head of a rat illustrating the position of the head in the stereotaxic instrument when either the de Groot (1959) or Pellegrino and Cushman (1967) coordinate system is used. Abbreviations—B: bregma; HZP: horizontal zero plane; IAL: interaural line; UIB: upper incisor bar; VZP: vertical zero plane. Reproduced with permission from König and Klippel (1963).

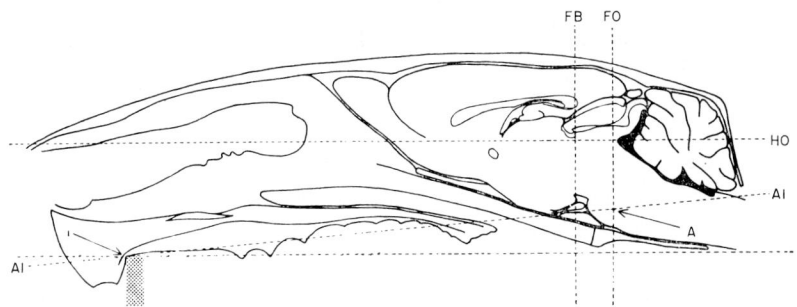

Fig. 10. Mid-sagittal section through the head of a rat illustrating the position of the head in the stereotaxic instrument when the König and Klippel (1963) coordinate system is used. Abbreviations—HO: horizontal zero plane; FO: frontal zero plane; AI: plane through the interaural line (A) and parallel through the rostral edge of the upper incisor bar (I); FB: frontal base plane. Reproduced with permission from König and Klippel (1963).

its own. The plates in the atlas are not regularly spaced throughout the brain. In some regions the sections are 80 μ apart, but in others they are as far as 670 μ apart.

The Pellegrino and Cushman (1967) atlas was constructed from the brains of 300 g male hooded rats, but has also been used successfully with the albino rat. It was specifically designed to overcome the shortcomings of the other two atlases mentioned above. It provides regularly spaced sections (200 μ apart) from the frontal poles through the rostral one-third of the cerebellum. It also provides two alternative stereotaxic coordinate systems commonly used with the rat (see below). This atlas, however, does not provide the sagittal sections or drawings that are available in the de Groot and König and Klippel atlases.

IV. How to Use the Stereotaxic Instrument

Since most investigators initially learn stereotaxic techniques with the rat and these techniques are readily extended to other species, the focus of this section will be on the stereotaxic technique with the rat.

A. Pre-operative Calibration of the Implanted Device

Electrodes for implantation are frequently made from twisted wire insulated with Formvar or Teflon. These may or may not be perfectly straight when first placed into the stereotaxic electrode holder. The first step is to be certain that the electrode is straight. This can easily be done by setting the ear bars of the instrument so that they are separated by 1 to 2 mm at their tips and then tightening the set-screws on the ear bars. Then the electrode is fastened to the instrument's electrode holder and is carefully lowered until its tip is midway between the tips of the ear bars. If the electrode is perfectly straight, then continuing to lower it beyond this point as far as possible should not alter the distance between either ear bar tip and the electrode. If on lowering the electrode its position relative to the ear bars does change, the electrode must be gently bent until it *is* straight and can be lowered between the two ear-bar tips without changing its position relative to them.

When this adjustment in the lateral plane has been completed, the electrode must then be checked to see if it is bent in the anterior-posterior plane. This is done again by centering the electrode tip between the two ear-bar tips while sighting down one of the ear bars and then lowering the electrode as far as possible, making certain that the electrode remains in the center of the two ear-bar tips throughout its full excursion in the vertical direction. If it does not, it must be adjusted by bending it gently until it does. Once this step is completed, it is wise to go back and check the first adjustment in the lateral direction. When the electrode can be lowered its full excursion without any variation in either the anterior-posterior direction *or* the lateral direction simultaneously, then one can be certain that the electrode is straight.

B. Determination of Instrument Zero

Once the above step has been completed, it is then possible to determine stereotaxic zero. For the most commonly used atlases of the rat brain described above, this is defined as the midpoint between the two ear-bar tips when they have both been centered. Stereotaxic zero can be determined by setting the ear bars so that the scale on each reads 1·0 mm and then clamping them in this position. This will leave a 2·0 mm distance between the ear-bar tips. Then the electrode, which has previously been checked for straightness, is lowered until its tip is exactly in the middle of the space between the two ear-bar tips. It now rests at stereotaxic zero and all three vernier scales[1] (anterior-posterior [A-P], lateral [L], and horizontal [H]) on the stereotaxic instrument should be read and recorded. A typical reading on a Kopf instrument might be the following: A-P: 44·4, L: 36·1, H: 18·8. These three coordinates will later be used in determining the instrument coordinates for the final resting site of the electrode tip within the animal's brain.

C. Arbitrary Horizontal Zero

Each of the three atlases has an arbitrary horizontal zero plane which differs from the empirically determined horizontal plane of the stereotaxic zero described above. In the de Groot and Pellegrino and Cushman atlases, this imaginary plane passes through the anterior and posterior commissures which lie 5·0 mm above the interaural line (instrument horizontal zero), which is the imaginary line between the center of each ear bar. Further, this plane also requires that the animal's head is positioned in the instrument with the upper incisor bar adjusted to be 5·0 mm *above the interaural line* (see Fig. 9). In the König and Klippel atlas the arbitrary horizontal zero plane is 4·9 mm above the interaural line (instrument horizontal zero) when the instrument is adjusted so that the upper incisor bar is 2·4 mm *below the interaural line* (see Fig. 10).

D. Calculation of Final Instrument Coordinates

The calculation of final instrument coordinates is accomplished with the following general formula: Atlas Coordinate ± Instrument Zero Coordinate = Final Instrument Coordinate. The easiest way to explain how to calculate the stereotaxic coordinates for a particular

---

[1] A discussion of the use of vernier scales can be found in any of the following sources: Bernard (1964) and Cenco Selective Experiments in Physics #110 and #111, available from Central Scientific Company, Chicago, Ill., $0·10 each.

structure is probably with an example. Suppose an investigator wished to place an electrode in the fornix[2] at a rostral-caudal (A-P) point which conveniently corresponds to the illustrations above from the de Groot, König and Klippel, and Pellegrino and Cushman atlases (see Figs 6, 7B and 8B). The procedure he would follow would be first to determine the atlas coordinates for this structure (see Table I).

TABLE I

Atlas coordinates (mm) for the fornix

Plane	de Groot	König and Klippel	Pellegrino and Cushman
Anterior-posterior (A-P)	5·4	4·2	5·4
Lateral (L)	1·2	1·0	1·2
Horizontal (H)	−3·0[a]	−3·0	−3·0

[a] Minus sign indicates that the structure is located below the arbitrary horizontal zero plane.

The final instrument coordinates are determined by: (1) adding the atlas A-P coordinates to the stereotaxic zero A-P figure obtained earlier; (2) adding (and subtracting in the case where bilaterally symmetrical placement of lesions or electrodes is intended) the atlas L coordinate to the stereotaxic zero lateral coordinate also obtained earlier; and (3) adding 5·0 mm to the stereotaxic zero H coordinate for the de Groot and Pellegrino and Cushman atlases (4·9 mm for the König and Klippel atlas) and then subtracting 3·0 mm for the distance the fornix is from the horizontal zero plane in all three atlases. The final stereotaxic instrument coordinates[3] are given in Table II.

TABLE II

Final instrument coordinates (mm) for the fornix

Plane	de Groot	König and Klippel	Pellegrino and Cushman
Anterior-posterior (A-P)	49·8	48·6	49·8
Lateral (L)	37·3	37·1	37·3
Horizontal (H)	20·8	20·7	20·8

[2] Abbreviated FX in the de Groot and Pellegrino and Cushman atlases and F in the König and Klippel atlas.

[3] Calculated with reference to the hypothetical stereotaxic zero mentioned in Section B above.

These are the numbers that the three vernier scales on the stereotaxic instrument should read when the electrode has been lowered into the fornix.

E. An Alternative Stereotaxic Technique

In recent years many investigators have been using a simpler stereotaxic technique than the one described above. This technique uses the skull landmark called the *bregma*, which is the intersection of the coronal and sagittal sutures on the surface of the skull, as the zero reference point rather than the midpoint of the interaural line. Since both the de Groot and Pellegrino and Cushman atlases provide the A-P coordinates of bregma (5·8 to 5·9 mm anterior to the vertical zero plane), it is possible to implant devices stereotaxically by using the bregma as a reference point.

Using our earlier example of implanting an electrode in the fornix, the procedure would be first to determine the atlas coordinates of the structure with reference to the bregma (see Table III).

TABLE III

Alternate atlas coordinates (mm) for the fornix

Plane	de Groot	Pellegrino and Cushman
Anterior-posterior (A-P)	−0·5	−0·4
Lateral (L)	1·2	1·2
Horizontal (H)	8·5	8·7

The A-P coordinate indicates the distance from the bregma, with the negative sign signifying that the direction is posterior to the bregma. The H coordinate indicates the depth the electrode should be lowered from the dura. If one wishes to measure from the surface of the skull, the usual procedure is to add 0·5 to 1·0 mm to the H coordinate to account for the thickness of the skull. However, measuring from the surface of the skull may entail some error since the skull is not uniformly thick in all places nor in all rats. Therefore, it is recommended that the dura always be used as the horizontal zero reference point.

From this point the procedure is basically the same as the one described above that uses the midpoint of the interaural line as the zero reference. The instrument zero is now determined *after* the animal has been placed in the instrument and the skull has been exposed revealing the location of its bregma. When the landmark has been located, the electrode is then lowered until it touches the bregma and the "zero" readings on the A-P and L scales are recorded. The H zero reading is determined later when the electrode hole has been drilled and the dura is exposed. To these A-P and L "zero" readings adjustments are made according to the atlas coordinates (-0.4 to the A-P figure and ± 1.2 to the L figure) to determine the final instrument coordinates when the tip of the implanted device is resting in its intended site in the brain, the fornix in our example.

Some questions have been raised as to the accuracy of this method. Some investigators feel that it is difficult to identify precisely the position of bregma. Yet other investigators maintain that they have been able to use this method reliably. Perhaps the best advice which we can offer to you, the reader, is to try both methods and to adopt the one that proves empirically to be more successful.

F. How to Place the Animal in the Instrument

(1). Adjustment of upper incisor bar

Prior to placing the animal into the instrument the nose bar or upper incisor bar must be adjusted to correspond to the stereotaxic atlas being used. If the König and Klippel (1963) atlas is being used, the upper incisor bar should be adjusted so that it is 2·4 mm *below* the interaural line, that is the imaginary line passing through the center of the two ear bars. If either the de Groot (1959) or Pellegrino and Cushman (1967) atlas is being used, the upper incisor bar should be adjusted to be 5·0 mm *above* the interaural line.

Some stereotaxic instruments (e.g. Kopf) provide a millimeter scale on the upper incisor bar making this adjustment routine. However, if the instrument being used does not provide such a scale, the upper incisor bar can be calibrated by the following procedure: (1) measure the distance from the interaural line to the base plate of the stereotaxic instrument; (2) measure the distance from the upper surface of the upper incisor bar to the base plate of the stereotaxic instrument; (3) adjust the upper incisor bar until the figure obtained in step 2 is either 5·0 mm more (if either the de Groot or Pellegrino and Cushman atlas is being used) or 2·4 mm less (if the König and Klippel atlas is being used) than the figure obtained in step 1.

(2). Insertion of ear bars and plugs

Some stereotaxic instruments such as the Kopf and Stoelting provide a separate pair of ear plugs connected by a short hemicircle of stiff wire. These plugs have tips which are more blunt than the instrument's ear bars, and thus the risk of damage to the tympanic membrane is reduced when they are inserted into the external auditory meatus. However, with care, it is possible to use the ear bars without the ear plugs and not damage the ear drum.

Proper insertion of the ear bars or plugs is probably one of the most difficult of the manual skills that one must learn in stereotaxic surgery. If one is using ear plugs, they are generally inserted by placing them between the thumb and forefinger, with the wire in the arch between these fingers. Then they are carefully inserted into each ear until they are in the external auditory meatus (see Fig. 11). Perhaps one of the

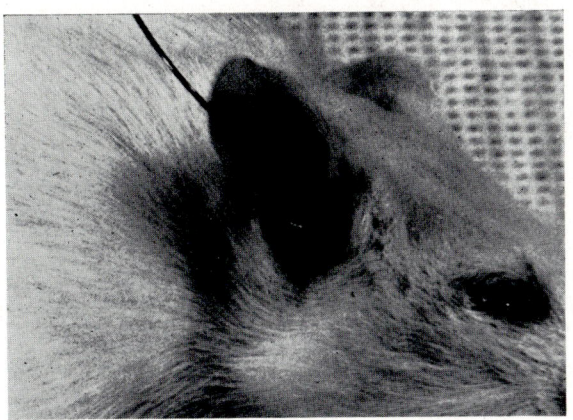

Fig. 11. Close-up of ear plugs properly positioned in the external auditory meatus of a rat.

most difficult steps of all is deciding when they are properly inserted. This is a skill that one acquires a "feel for" only after much practice. Often, however, the animal may provide some helpful cues as to when the plugs are in the canal. Frequently the rat may blink reflexively or twitch the ipsilateral eye as the plug enters the canal.

Once the plugs are inserted, the animal is then carefully placed onto the ear bars of the stereotaxic instrument. This is done by gently lifting the animal close to one ear bar which has been clamped tightly to the instrument (the other ear bar is retracted and kept unclamped until needed). Then the finger which is holding the ear plug is slowly withdrawn from the center of the ear plug to the edge of the outer surface of the ear plug. As soon as the hollowed-out portion is visible, it is placed over the tip of the clamped ear bar and the finger is retracted completely. Next, the retracted ear bar is brought close to the rat's ear, inserted in the hollowed-out part of the ear plug, and clamped in place.

If the ear plugs and ear bars have been properly inserted, the animal's head will pivot freely in a vertical direction about the ear bars but will not move in a horizontal direction. This can be easily tested by grasping the rat's nose and gently attempting first to move it up and down, and then from side to side. It should freely move up and down but it should not move at all from side to side. If this is not the case, then remove the ear bars and begin the process again. Secondly, when the ear bars are properly inserted and one examines the animal's head from the front of the instrument, the head should appear straight (that is, the midline of the head should be perpendicular to the line formed by the two ear bars). If the animal's head is not properly placed into the instrument, often one eye will appear to bulge or one eye will be closed.

If ear plugs are not provided or one wishes not to use them, the procedure is to clamp one ear bar in place and retract the other ear bar as described above. The tip of the clamped ear bar is first inserted into one ear canal and then the other ear bar is inserted into the contralateral ear canal and clamped into place. Although the procedure is simpler and may require less manual dexterity than the one described above with the ear plugs, the risk of damaging the ear drum is much greater and consequently greater care must be taken when using it.

Once you are convinced that the ear plugs or bars are properly inserted, the entire head must be centered in the instrument. This is done by sliding both ear bars until their millimeter scales both have identical readings. Although this generally requires two people to prevent the ear bars or plugs from slipping out of the canals, it can be done by one person in the following manner: loosen the ear-bar set screws $\frac{1}{4}-\frac{1}{2}$ turn and place the palms of each hand against the ends of the ear bars and then gently slide both ear bars simultaneously in the direction necessary for centering. When this is completed the final step is to place the animal's upper teeth over the upper incisor bar and *gently* push down on the nose until the top surface of the upper incisor bar rests on the upper surface of the rat's mouth just behind his upper incisors (see Fig. 3). Then gently pull the nose bar forward until the incisor bar fits tightly against the animal's teeth. Finally, the nose clamp is placed over the rat's nose and gently tightened.

V. Histological Verification of Stereotaxic Placements

Histological verification of electrode, cannula or lesion placements is an essential step in the interpretation of the behavioral effects of these placements. A detailed description of histological methods appears elsewhere in this book (see Chapter IX). Stereotaxic atlases are an essential tool not only in the original placement of electrodes, cannulas and lesions but also in the determination of the exact site of placement. After the stained histological sections have been obtained, they can be correlated with the sections or drawings of a stereotaxic atlas and the precise location of the implanted device or lesion can be determined.

The correlation of an actual stained section with an atlas section is usually done by matching some distinctive anatomical landmark on the sections being studied. Some examples of convenient landmarks are the hippocampus and the corpus callosum with their unique shapes, or the decussation of the anterior commissure. The selection of a landmark for identifying a particular section is complicated by the fact that it is frequently difficult to cut brain tissue in precisely the same plane as those cut in a stereotaxic atlas. Generally, this means that while the structures in the ventral half of a stained section match the atlas section very closely, the structures in the dorsal half may not correspond well at all. Conversely, if the dorsal structures match well, the ventral structures do not. An example of such a discrepancy can actually be seen in the plates from the three atlases presented

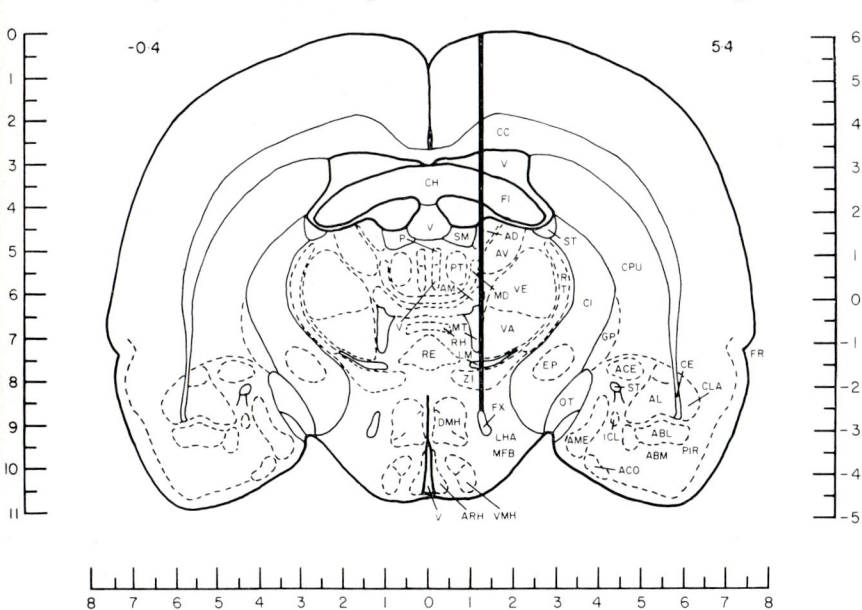

FIG. 12. Schematic drawing showing electrode placement. Reproduced with permission from Pellegrino and Cushman (1967).

earlier in this chapter (Figs 6–8B). Although the three sections agree reasonably well in their ventral halves, there is considerable disagreement in their dorsal halves. This, of course, is due to the different angles at which they were sliced.

The discrepancy between actual stained sections and atlas sections is dealt with by selecting a landmark for correlating the sections which is at approximately the same dorsal-ventral level as the structure being studied. In our example of an electrode in the fornix, a good landmark would be the optic tract and its distinct shape and position.

Once one has determined which atlas section corresponds best to the actual stained section from the animal, the remaining task is to describe the site of the placement. This can be done in several ways. First, one can simply describe the placement anatomically, that is, by describing surrounding structures that are distinctively different at this particular A-P level than at other levels. Alternatively, one can give the atlas coordinates of the placement (e.g. A-P: 5·4; L: 1·2; H: −3·0 in the Pellegrino and Cushman atlas). Finally, one can reproduce the atlas section with the electrode drawn in as shown in Fig. 12.

ACKNOWLEDGEMENTS

The authors wish to acknowledge the assistance of J. M. Cornell, A. H. Ewell, A. S. Pellegrino and D. Weening in the preparation of this chapter.

REFERENCES

Bernard, C. H. (1964). "Laboratory Experiments in College Physics." Blaisdell Publishing Co., Waltham, Mass., U.S.A.

Clarke, R. H. and Horsley, V. (1906). *Br. Med. J.* **2**, 1799–1800.

de Groot, J. (1959). The Rat Forebrain in Stereotaxic Coordinates. *Verh. koninklijke Nederlandse Akademie van Wetenschappen, Afd. Natuurkunde*. N. V. Noord-Hollandsche Uitgevers Maatschappij, Amsterdam.

Hart, B. L. (1969). "Experimental Neuropsychology: A Laboratory Manual." W. H. Freeman, San Francisco.

Horsley, V. and Clarke, R. H. (1908). *Brain* **31**, 45–124.

König, J. F. R. and Klippel, R. A. (1963). "The Rat Brain: A Stereotaxic Atlas of the Forebrain and Lower Parts of the Brain Stem." Williams and Wilkins, Baltimore, Md., U.S.A.

Levy, A. (1967). *Confina Neurologica*, No. **29**, (Suppl.).

Pellegrino, L. J. and Cushman, A. J. (1967). "A Stereotaxic Atlas of the Rat Brain." Appleton-Century-Crofts, New York.

Snider, R. S. and Niemer, W. T. (1961). "Stereotaxic Atlas of the Cat Brain." University of Chicago Press, Chicago.

Spiegel, E. A., Wycis, H. T., Marks, M. and Lee, A. J. (1947). *Science, N.Y.* **106**, 349–350.

Van Manen, J. (1967). "Stereotaxic Methods and Their Applications in Disorders of the Motor System." Royal Van Gorcum, Assen, The Netherlands.

Appendix A
Stereotaxic Atlases

Primates

Davis, R. and Huffman, R. D. (1968). "Stereotaxic Atlas of the Brain of the Baboon (*Papio*)." University of Texas Press, Austin, Texas, U.S.A.

DeLucchi, M. R., Dennis, B. J. and Adey, W. R. (1965). "Stereotaxic Atlas of the Chimpanzee Brain (*Pan satyrus*)." University of California Press, Berkeley, Calif., U.S.A.

Eidelberg, E. and Saladias, C. A. (1960). A stereotaxic atlas for cebus monkeys. *J. Comp. Neurol.* 115, 103–123.

Emmers, R. and Akert, K. (1963). "Stereotaxic Atlas of the Brain of the Squirrel Monkey (*Saimiri sciureus*)." University of Wisconsin Press, Madison, Wisconsin, U.S.A.

Gergen, J. A. and MacLean, P. D. (1962). "A Stereotaxic Atlas of the Squirrel Monkey's Brain (*Saimiri sciureus*)." U.S. Department of Health, Education and Welfare, Bethesda, Maryland, U.S.A.

Manocha, S. L., Shantha, T. R. and Bourne, G. H. (1968). "A Stereotaxic Atlas of the Brain of the Cebus Monkey (*Cebus apella*)." Oxford University Press, New York.

Olszewski, J. (1952). "The Thalamus of the *Macaca mulatta*; An Atlas for Use with the Stereotaxic Instrument." Karger, Basel, Switzerland.

Pecci Saavedra, J. and Mazzuchelli, A. L. (1969). A stereotaxic atlas of the brain of the marmoset (*Hapale jacchus*). *J. Hirnforsch.* 2, 105–122.

Russell, G. V. (1961). Hypothalamic, preoptic and septal regions of the monkey. *In* "Electrical Stimulation of the Brain" (D. E. Sheer, ed.), pp. 232–250. University of Texas Press, Austin, Texas, U.S.A.

Shantha, T. R., Manocha, S. L. and Bourne, G. H. (1968). "Stereotaxic Atlas of the Java Monkey Brain." Williams and Wilkins, Baltimore, Maryland, U.S.A.

Snider, R. S. and Lee, J. C. (1961). "Stereotaxic Atlas of the Monkey Brain (*Macaca mulatta*)." University of Chicago Press, Chicago, Illinois, U.S.A.

Tigges, J. W. and Shantha, T. R. (1968). "Stereotaxic Atlas of the Tree Shrew Brain (*Tupaia glis*)." Williams and Wilkins, Baltimore, Maryland, U.S.A.

Toshio, K. (in press). "Stereotaxic Atlas of the Brain of *Macaca fuscata*." University Park Press, Baltimore, Maryland, U.S.A.

Winters, W. D., Kado, R. T. and Adey, W. R. (1969). "Stereotaxic Brain Atlas for *Macaca nemistrina*." University of California Press, Berkeley, California, U.S.A.

Cat and Dog

Berman, A. L. (1968). "Brain Stem of the Cat: A Cytoarchitectonic Atlas with Stereotaxic Coordinates." University of Wisconsin Press, Madison, Winconsin, U.S.A.

Bleier, R. (1961). "The Hypothalamus of the Cat. A Cytoarchitectonic Atlas in the Horsley-Clarke Co-ordinate System." Johns Hopkins Press, Baltimore, Maryland, U.S.A.

Dau-Sharma, S., Kamal, N. and Jacobs, H. L. (1971). "The Canine Brain in Stereotaxic Coordinates." Massachusetts Institute of Technology Press, Cambridge, Massachusetts, U.S.A.

Jasper, H. H. and Ajmone-Marsan, C. (1961). Diencephalon of the cat. In "Electrical Stimulation of the Brain" (D. E. Sheer, ed.), pp. 203–231. University of Texas Press, Austin, Texas, U.S.A.

Jimenez-Castellanos, J. (1949). Thalamus of the cat in Horsley-Clarke coordinates. J. comp. Neurol. 91, 307–330.

Lim, R. K., Chan-Nao, L. and Moffett, R. L. (1960). "Stereotaxic Atlas of the Dog's Brain." Charles Thomas, Springfield, Illinois, U.S.A.

Singer, M. (1962). "Brain of the Dog in Section." Saunders, Philadelphia, Pennsylvania, U.S.A.

Snider, R. S. and Niemer, W. T. (1961). "Stereotaxic Atlas of the Cat Brain." University of Chicago Press, Chicago, Illinois, U.S.A.

Verhaart, W. J. C. (1964). "Stereotaxic Atlas of the Brainstem of the Cat." Davis Co., Philadelphia, Pennsylvania, U.S.A.

See also Fifkova and Marsala (1967), listed under other species.

Rodents

Albe-Fessard, D., Stutinsky, F. and Libouban, S. (1966). "Atlas Stéréotaxique du Diencéphale du Rat Blanc." Éditions CNRS, Paris, France.

Bernardis, L. L. and Skelton, F. R. (1965). Stereotaxic localization of supraoptic, ventromedial and mammillary nuclei in the hypothalamus of weanling and mature rats. Am. J. Anat. 116, 69–74.

de Groot, J. (1959). "The Rat Forebrain in Stereotaxic Coordinates." Verhandelingen der koninklijke Nederlandse Akademie van Wetenschappen, Afd. Natuurkunde. N. V. Noord-Hollandsche Uitgevers Maatschappij, Amsterdam, The Netherlands.

Eleftheriou, B. E. and Zolovick, A. J. (1965). The forebrain of the deermouse in stereotaxic coordinates. Bull. Agric. Exp. Station, Kansas State University of Agriculture and Applied Science, Technical Bulletin No. 146.

Hudspeth, W. J. and Herz, M. J. (in preparation). "Stereotaxic Atlas of the Mouse Brain." W. H. Freeman, San Francisco, California, U.S.A.

König, J. F. R. and Klippel, R. A. (1963). "The Rat Brain: A Stereotaxic Atlas of the Forebrain and Lower Parts of the Brain Stem." Williams and Wilkins, Baltimore, Maryland, U.S.A.

Krieg, W. J. S. (1946). Accurate placement of minute lesions in the brain of the albino rat. Quart. Bull. Northwestern Univ. Med. School 20, 199–208.

Massopust, L. C. (1961). Diencephalon of the rat. In "Electrical Stimulation of the Brain" (D. E. Sheer, ed.), pp. 182–202. University of Texas Press, Austin, Texas, U.S.A.

Pellegrino, L. J. and Cushman, A. J. (1967). "A Stereotaxic Atlas of the Rat Brain." Appleton-Century-Crofts, New York, New York, U.S.A.

Slotnick, B. M., Essman, W. B. and Morgane, P. J. (in preparation). "A Stereotaxic Atlas of the Mouse Brain."

Sherwood, N. M. (1970). "A Stereotaxic Atlas of the Developing Rat Brain." University of California Press, Berkeley, California, U.S.A.

Sidman, R. L., Angevin, J. B. and Pierce, E. T. (1971). "Atlas of the Mouse Brain and Spinal Cord." Harvard University Press, Cambridge, Massachusetts, U.S.A.

See also Fifkova and Marsala (1967) below.

Other Species

Blobel, R., Gonzalo, L. and Schuckardt, E. (1960). Stereotaktisches Vefahren zur Lokalisation der Zwischenhirnkerne beim Meerschweinchen. *Endokrinol.* 167–172.

Fifkova, E. and Marsala, J. (1967). Stereotaxic atlases for the cat, rabbit, and rat. In "Electrophysiological Methods in Biological Research" (J. Bureš, M. Petráň and J. Zachar, eds.), pp. 653–731. Academic Press, New York and London.

Karten, H. J. and Hodos, W. (1967). "Stereotaxic Atlas of the Brain of the Pigeon (*Colomba livia*)." Johns Hopkins Press, Baltimore, Maryland, U.S.A.

Kemali, M. and Braitenberg, V. (1969). "Atlas of the Frog's Brain." Springer-Verlag, New York, New York, U.S.A.

Luparello, T. J. (1967). "Stereotaxic Atlas of the Forebrain of the Guinea Pig." Williams and Wilkins, Baltimore, Maryland, U.S.A.

Luparello, T. J., Stein, M. and Park C. D. (1964). A stereotaxic atlas of the hypothalamus of the guinea pig. *J. comp. Neurol.* 122, 202–218.

McBride, R. L. and Klemm, W. R. (1968). Stereotaxic atlas of the rabbit brain, based on the rapid method of photography of frozen, unstained sections. *Commun. Behav. Biol.* 2, 179–215.

Messen, H. and Olszewski, J. (1949). "A Cytoarchitectonic Atlas of the Rhombencephalon of the Rabbit." Karger, New York, New York, U.S.A.

Monnier, M. and Gangloff, H. (1961). "Atlas for Stereotaxic Brain Research on the Conscious Rabbit." Elsevier, Amsterdam, The Netherlands.

Oswaldo-Cruz, E. and Rocha-Miranda, C. E. (1968). "The Brain of the Opossum (*Didelphis marsupialis*)." Williams and Wilkins, Baltimore, Maryland, U.S.A.

Salinas, M. E., Zeballos, G. A. and Wang, M.B. (1971). A Stereotaxic atlas of the opposum brain. *Brain Behav. Evol.*, 4, 114–150.

Sawyer, C. H., Everett, J. W. and Green, J. D. (1954). The rabbit diencephalon in stereotaxic coordinates. *J. comp. Neur.* 101, 801–824.

Smith, O. A. and Bodemer, Ch. N. (1963). A stereotaxic atlas of the brain of the golden hamster (*Mesocricetus auratus*). *J. comp. Neurol.* 120, 53–64.

Tienhoven, A. van and Juhasz, L. P. (1962). The chicken telencephalon, diencephalon and mesencephalon in stereotaxic coordinates. *J. comp. Neurol.* 118, 185–198.

Tindal, J. S. (1965). The forebrain of the guinea-pig in stereotaxic coordinates. *J. comp. Neurol.* 124, 259-266.

Tindal, J. S., Knaggs, G. S. and Turvey, A. (1968). The forebrain of the goat in stereotaxic coordinates. *J. Anat.* 103, 457–469.

Appendix B
Manufacturers and Distributors of Stereotaxic Instruments

Baltimore Instrument Co.
716 W. Redwood Street
Baltimore, Maryland, U.S.A.

David Kopf Instruments
7324 Elmo Street
Tujunga, California 91042, U.S.A.

Lab-Tronics
H. Neuman and Co.
8136 N. Lawndale Avenue
Skokie, Illinois 60076, U.S.A.

Lehigh Valley Electronics
Box 125
Fogelsville, Pennsylvania, 18051,
U.S.A.

Scientific Prototype Manufacturing
 Corp.
615 W. 131st Street
New York, N.Y., 10027, U.S.A.

C. H. Stoelting Co.
424 N. Homan Avenue
Chicago, Illinois, 60624, U.S.A.

Mechanical Developments Co.
Trent H. Wells, Jr.
8120 Otis Street
South Gate
California, 90280, U.S.A.

Chapter 4

Neurosurgical Procedures with Special Reference to Aspiration Lesions[1]

PATRICIA M. MEYER[2] and DONALD R. MEYER

The Ohio State University[3,4], *Columbus, Ohio, U.S.A.*

I.	Introduction	92
II.	Neocortical Ablations in Rats	92
	A. Types of Headholders	93
	B. Surgical Materials	94
	C. Care of Surgical Instruments	95
	D. Preparing the Animal	95
	E. Placing the Rat in the Headholder	97
	F. Surgical Procedures	99
	G. Localized Extirpation of Neocortex	103
	H. Closure of the Wound	104
	I. Complete Extirpation of Neocortex	106
III.	Maintenance of Hemostasis	108
IV.	Sterile Surgical Techniques and Procedures	110
	A. Sterilization Procedures	110
	B. Preparing the Animal	113
	C. Placing the Animal in the Headholder	115
	D. Surgical "Scrub-in", Gowning and Gloving	116
	E. Positioning the Instruments	117
V.	Techniques of Aspiration in Large Species	120
	A. Craniotomy	122
	B. Turning a Bone Flap	123
	C. The Dura Mater Flap	124
	D. Aspiration of Neocortex	125
	E. Closure of the Wound	127
VI.	Epilogue	128
	References	130

[1] Preparation of this report was supported by Grants MH-02035 and MH-06211 from the National Institutes of Mental Health.

[2] Research Scientist Development Investigator, National Institutes of Mental Health Grant 5-K2-MH-12,747.

[3] Laboratory of Comparative and Physiological Psychology.

[4] Mr. Richard Arnold, Department of Photography, The Ohio State University, prepared the majority of the illustrations in this chapter.

I. Introduction

ABLATION of the cerebral cortex is a method which has been employed in neuropsychological research since the early decades of the nineteenth century. The techniques involved in the production of a lesion have changed very greatly in that time. However, the procedures featured in this chapter, which are termed sub-pial aspirations, are still carried out in essentially the same manner as they were when they were first devised by Clinton Woolsey some thirty years ago. The techniques can also be employed for the removal of certain other tissues of the body, but have proved most useful for experiments concerned with the effects of circumscribed destructions of the various subregions of the brain's outer surface.

Both of us consider surgery to be a craft that must be learned from a preceptor. Thus, in no sense do we consider the instructions contained within this chapter to be a substitute for a neurosurgical apprenticeship. They are meant, instead, to save a teaching surgeon's time by giving his beginner some materials to be studied between the all-important operating sessions which the two of them will have together.

Not everybody who would like to be a surgeon is personally suited to the work. A successful operator must, above all, be able to keep cool in an emergency. Emergencies are generally of two related kinds, namely, anesthesia and bleeding. A man who is capable of handling hemorrhages with skill and dispatch as they occur has relatively few of the problems encountered in maintenance of proper anesthesia which others attribute to poor luck or a lack of vigor of his animal subjects. The late Paul H. Settlage, who developed the urea treatment for cerebral edema, served as our model of this most important trait of surgical unflappability.

The skills of neurosurgery are not unlike the skills required in building light-weight model airplanes. Thus, in either instance, the product can be spoiled at any time by heavy-handed actions, and how well the several parts of either preparation fit or re-fit when they have been put together depends upon the care that is taken in the execution of each step in the procedure. Speed is important in neurosurgery, but rushing always spells catastrophe; meticulousness takes time, but much less time than is required for patching up the outcome of an error.

II. Neocortical Ablations in Rats

Not only is the skill of the surgeon and his assistants crucial for successful surgery, but also the equipment must be in perfect condition, and the room must be clean, neat and orderly. Figure 1(A) illustrates a typical operating-room set up for neocortical surgery on rats. Included is a vacuum pump, which provides the negative pressure for removing the cortex, a waste basin, and an instrument tray. On top of the operating table is a headholder for positioning the rat.

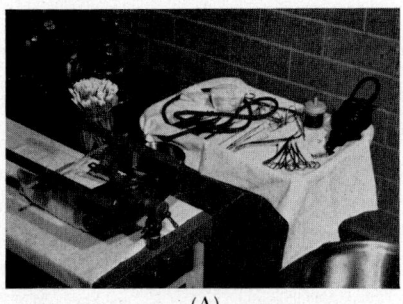 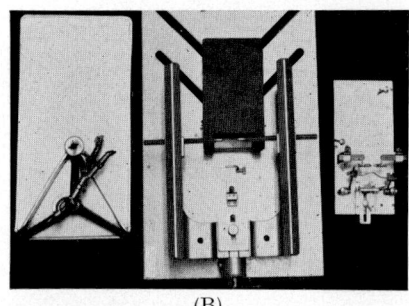

(A) (B)

Fig. 1. (A) Operating-room set up for neocortical surgery on rats. (B) Three types of rat headholders.

A. Types of Headholders

Three types of headholders that have been used at our Laboratory are shown in Fig. 1(B); naturally, each has its own advantages and disadvantages. The first one, the most primitive of the three, is homemade, and thereby has the distinct advantage of being inexpensive. Basically, it is constructed from a block of wood covered with Formica. At one end is a ring stand with a shortened pole, to which a burette clamp is attached. The rubber tip of the clamp has been removed, and the metal jaws have been trimmed to fit the snout of a rat. Inside the lower jaw of the clamp is a lump of dental acrylic cement molded to fit the roof of the rat's mouth, and immediately anterior to it, a hole has been punctured to accommodate a rat's upper incisors. Thus, when the rat's front teeth are put into this hole and the screw of the clamp is turned, the upper jaw of the clamp forces the roof of the rat's mouth tight against the acrylic mold. This headholder is adequate, and is particularly advantageous for the young investigator with limited funds, but it does not hold the animal's head absolutely firm.

The other two headholders, which are made commercially, are constructed such that the roof of the animal's mouth rests on a mouth bar, and two ear bars are inserted into the external auditory meatuses. A nose clamp is swung down on top of the snout, and the rat's head is held firmly in the apparatus. The third apparatus in Fig. 1(B) is superior for maintaining head rigidity, but we prefer the second headholder for stereotaxic procedures.

B. Surgical Materials

Two equipment trays are set up for rat neurosurgery, a preparation tray and an instrument tray. The former, which is illustrated in Fig. 2(A), contains the equipment necessary for procedures carried out prior to surgery.

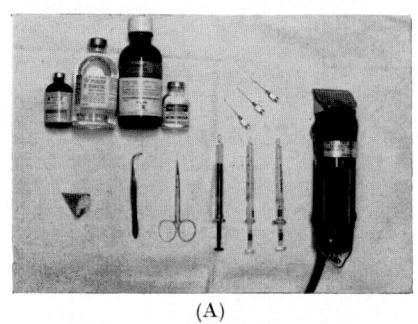 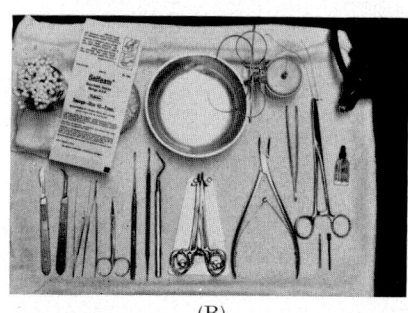

(A) (B)

FIG. 2. (A) On the top row of the rat preparation tray, left to right, are: atropine sulphate (0·4 mg, 1/150 g/cc); veterinary sodium pentobarbitol (60 mg/ml); veterinary methoxyflurane; long-acting bicillin; and three 1 in #22 hypodermic needles. On the bottom row, left to right, are: one rat nose cone containing a few dental pellets; one pair of 4 in curved forceps with teeth; 4 in straight, sharp-on-sharp iris scissors, three 1 cc tuberculin syringes; and a pair of animal clippers. (B) On the top row of the rat instrument tray, left to right are: cotton swabs, 2×2 in gauze sponges; #4 dental pellets; gelfoam; normal saline in a stainless-steel bowl; binocular loupes; #3-0 suture silk; $4\frac{1}{2}$ in dressing forceps with serrated jaws; 6 in needle holders with scissors holding #7 half-circle cutting-edge surgeon's needle; 5% boric acid opthalmic ointment; and an electric drill. On the bottom row, left to right, are: #3 knife handle with #10 blade; #3 knife handle with #12 blade; 6 in slender dressing forceps with serrated jaws; 6 in slender tissue forceps with serrated jaws and teeth; 4 in straight, sharp-on-sharp iris scissors; an elevator; a dental tool used as a muscle retractor; a dental ejector; four 5 in curved mosquito forceps with serrated jaws and box locks; Lempert rongeur forceps with slender curved jaws; a #2 trephine; and a dental bur.

Figure 2(B) illustrates the items most frequently used for removing neocortical tissue in the rat. Not shown in the photograph are a slightly curved House-Rosen needle and two glass aspirators. The latter two items are illustrated on the bottom row in Fig. 9(D), and the needle is shown in Fig. 9(C).

The items in Figs. 2(A) and (B) can be purchased at drugstores and at surgical, dental and veterinary supply houses. Before discussing the applications of these instruments, their care and maintainance will be considered.

C. Care of Surgical Instruments

Surgical tools are accurately-crafted instruments, and students must learn not only how and when to use them, but also how to maintain them. Scissors, except for special ones such as bandage scissors, are used *only* for cutting tissue. Scissors attached to needle-holders are used for cutting silk thread. We highly recommend this latter instrument for research laboratories with surgical instruments common to all personnel. When it is necessary to cut cloth, bandage scissors are ideal. The jaws of rongeurs are never pressed together; only bone is inserted between those jaws. When any of the instruments with joints, such as scissors or mosquito forceps, become stiff and difficult to manipulate, they should be oiled with a special lubricant for surgical instruments. When the instruments become dull, throw them away if they are inexpensive, or have them sharpened by a professional surgical instrument maker. Dull instruments can have fatal consequences because the surgeon becomes adapted to his dull equipment. After he finally does sharpen them, or reaches for a new knife blade, he is apt to apply too much pressure with the unwanted outcome of cutting too far or too deep.

To clean the instruments, soak them in warm water that contains a surgical soap powder with ingredients for dissolving blood. Wash them carefully to remove all blood stains from difficult crevices such as serrated jaws. A soft toothbrush is handy for this purpose. After the instruments are rinsed and dried thoroughly, store them in a dustfree cabinet. Instruments with box locks should be stored locked.

D. Preparing the Animal

The adult male hooded rat, 90 to 120 days old, is prepared for surgery in a room separate from the operating room to avoid cluttering and contaminating the surgery. The preparation tray in Fig. 2(A) illustrates all the surgical equipment necessary to carry out the following preoperative procedures.

First, the rat is weighed on a surgical scales, and is then given either one of two anesthetics. A short intermediate-acting anesthetic commonly used at our laboratory is a barbiturate, sodium pentobarbital. It is advisable to use male subjects if this anesthetic is selected, because the lethal dosage for female rats approaches the anesthetic dose. For males, the dosage is 60 mg/kg of veterinary sodium pentobarbital, which is easily remembered because it transposes to 0·1 cc per 100 g of body weight. Thus, if a rat weighed 300 g, it would receive 0·3 cc of the anesthetic.

Sodium pentobarbital is injected intraperitoneally as shown in Fig.

3(A). The animal's front legs are crossed under its chin so that it cannot bite. The rear legs are pressed against the table, and the back slightly arched so that the peritoneal area is readily accessible. With a quick, jab-like motion, insert the 1 in #22 needle approximately $\frac{1}{2}$ in into the belly. Before injecting the drug, pull back on the plunger

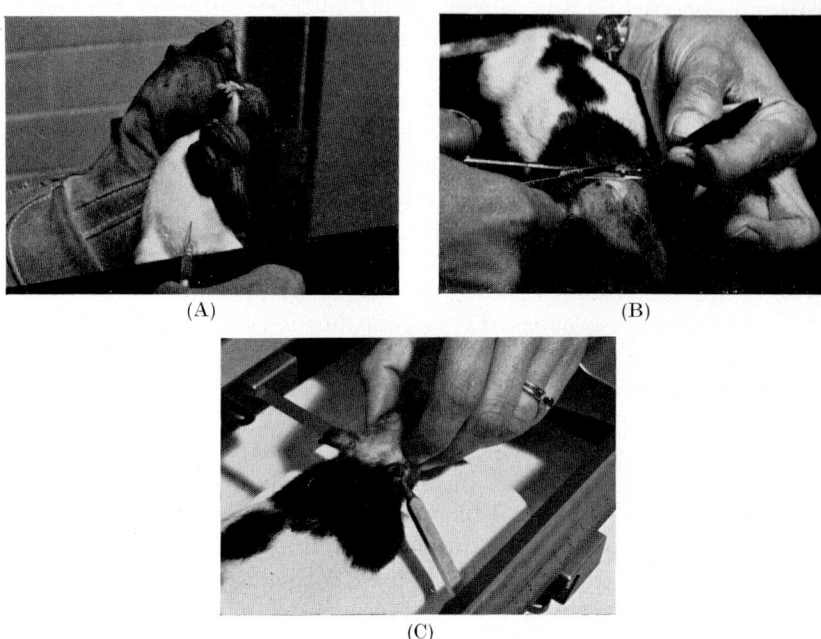

FIG. 3. (A) Technique for intraperitoneal injection in the rat. (B) Removal of cartilage from the rat's ear. (C) The surgeon, holding the head from above, has just positioned one ear bar and is ready to insert the second one.

of the syringe. If blood is detected, extract the needle and insert it into another area. If a rather large hypodermic needle is used, it will tend to push an organ aside, rather than puncture it. The surgical stage of anesthesia is reached in 5 to 10 min, and is maintained for approximately 45 to 60 min. If additional time is needed to complete the operation, we recommend methoxyflurane, for death following supplemental doses of sodium pentobarbital is not uncommon.

An important point about the use of a syringe is that air bubbles must be forced out through the needle before an injection is given. This is done by holding the needle straight up so that all bubbles rise to the top of the syringe, and then pushing the plunger until a drop of the fluid to be injected appears at the end of the needle. If air bubbles get into a blood vessel, they function as emboli and sometimes kill the preparation.

Methoxyflurane is a short-acting, inhalation anesthetic, which is highly desirable because it is virtually impossible to overdose the patient. It can be administered safely to both males and females. However, methoxyflurane does have a slow induction time, which necessitates first injecting the rat with half the anesthetic dosage of sodium pentobarbital (0·5 cc per 100 g of body weight). This amount is enough to make the animal drowsy so that after 5 to 10 min has elapsed, the animal's snout can easily be held in the nose cone that contains about 0·5 cc of methoxyflurane-soaked cotton pellets. It has been our experience that one minute's administration of the inhalant maintains anesthesia for approximately 10 min. Supplemental doses during the course of surgery are safely and easily given by placing a few of the anesthetic-soaked pellets under the rat's nose.

We do not recommend ether anesthesia because its administration causes the blood vessels in the meninges and the brain to dilate. Not only is more blood lost, but it becomes virtually impossible to see and work in the surgical field.

Following the anesthetic injection, 0·2 cc of atropine sulfate is injected intraperitoneally. This drug inhibits secretions in the nose, mouth, throat and lungs. Hence an anesthetized animal which has inactive swallowing and coughing reflexes, is less likely to be drowned by its own saliva.

Next the head is shaved with the animal clippers, starting at the base of the neck and continuing to the tip of the nose. This removal includes the whiskers and hair on the dorsal surface of the head, cheeks and under the ears. All loose hairs must be brushed off the animal before it is transported to the surgery.

E. Placing the Rat in the Headholder

Preparation of the rat's ears for mounting in the headholder, if ear bars are to be used, involves removal of the cartilage just ventral to the pinna so that each external auditory meatus is better exposed. The tip of the ear is held with the left hand, and, with the right hand, an incision approximately 4 mm long is made through the skin with the iris scissors. In Fig. 3(B) this procedure has been done, and the surgeon is grasping the cartilage with the curved forceps, ready to extract it with the iris scissors. In the vicinity of this incision is the posterior facial vein, which, if punctured, can easily be stopped from bleeding by continuous pressure with a cotton swab for a few minutes. Some surgeons feel that removing the cartilage is unnecessary, but it does permit one, particularly the beginner, to insert the ear bars into the meatuses easily.

After preparations for surgery are complete, the next step is to place the animal's head into the headholder. Reference to the second headholder in Fig. 1(B) will help the reader understand this procedure. The rat's upper incisors are placed in the hole of the headholder's tooth plate, and the animal is lined up by sliding the headholder such that the external auditory meati are approximately in the vicinity of the ear bars. One of the ear bars is removed, and the other one is locked in the apparatus. The animal's head is then grasped from above with the thumb and the first two fingers of the left hand. The rat must not be held under the throat for it can be choked easily. The ear bar is positioned in the meatus by moving the head towards the bar. After the earbar is seated, continuous but gentle pressure is applied with the left hand against the locked ear bar. The surgeon next sights the other meatus, inserts the ear bar into it, and locks it in place. Figure 3(C) illustrates this procedure.

If the animal is positioned properly, its head will be straight and held firm. Also, its ears will be perked sideways rather than drooping. If these criteria are not met, remove both ear bars and try again.

Once the rat's head is firm and square in the appartus, the ear bars are loosened slightly, and the head is centered by moving both ear bars in the same direction until the mm values on each of them read the same. Slight pressure must be exerted on both ear bars as they are centered, or the bars will become dislodged from the external meati. Finally, both ear bars are locked.

The rat adapter headholder, which has been unlocked throughout this procedure, is pulled forward until some resistance is met from the upper incisors. Next, the headholder is locked and the nose clamp is swung over the snout and locked.

For purposes of illustration, we shall describe how to remove the posterior neocortex in the rat brain. The black area in Fig. 4 indicates the amount of cortex to be aspirated. This region includes visual as well as auditory and some somatosensory neocortex. Refer once again to Figs. 1(A) and 2(B) for the equipment and instruments used to perform this operation.

To remove all loose hair, the animal's head in washed with saline using a 2×2 in sponge. No foreign objects like hair or bone chips should fall into the wound and remain there. An infection would be certain to occur, and would probably culminate in the death of the animal.

The rat's eyes are covered with boric-acid ophthalmic ointment to prevent solutions from dripping into them. Although rats are resistant to many infections and sterile surgical procedures are often not necessary (in the view of most, but not all experimenters), clean precautions should always be taken. This involves, first, a thorough scrubbing of one's hands with an antiseptic skin detergent. Particular attention

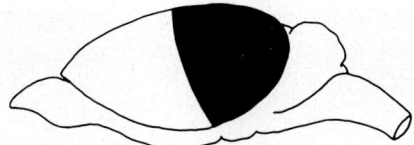

FIG. 4. Diagram of the amount of posterior neocortex removed (darkened area) in the brain of a rat.

should be given to fingernails, which should be scraped and, if necessary, brushed so that no foreign matter remains beneath them. If the surgeon has sores or scratches on his hands, they should be washed as thoroughly as possible and then covered by surgical gloves via techniques to be described below.

Next, the rat's head is washed in an anterior to posterior direction with a 2 × 2 in gauze sponge that is moistened with 70% alcohol. To be certain that the area just washed will not become contaminated, only one stroke is taken with each sponge, and it is then thrown away. Repeat the washing procedure about three times.

F. Surgical Procedures

Typically, the novice surgeon works over the surgical field with his elbows high in the air as though afraid to touch anything. From the beginning he should be encouraged to brace his working arm against the apparatus, and his other arm on the table. Not only will he become less fatigued, but he will also be more accurate in the execution of the techniques.

The next step is to make a midline scalp incision as the first procedure in exposure of the brain. The skin immediately behind the ears is first retracted with the left thumb and middle finger until it is taut. Then, with the flat part of the #10 knife blade, the skin is cut through on the midline at ear level until the resistance of the skull is felt. The knife is pulled forward, along the midline, approximately to eye level. If the incision needs to be larger, iris scissors should be used to enlarge the cut. It is better to have an opening that is too large rather than too small. Small incisions not only impede vision, but also lead the surgeon to put unnecessary pressure upon the brain at times. Bleeding as a consequence of the skin incision is almost always insignificant.

The next procedure is to remove the fascia beneath the scalp. This is done as shown in Fig. 5(A). The surgeon retracts the edge of the skin incision with the 4½ in dressing forceps in his left hand. The underlying fascia is then cut away laterally, anteriorly, and posteriorly with the iris scissors. This permits easy retraction of the skin.

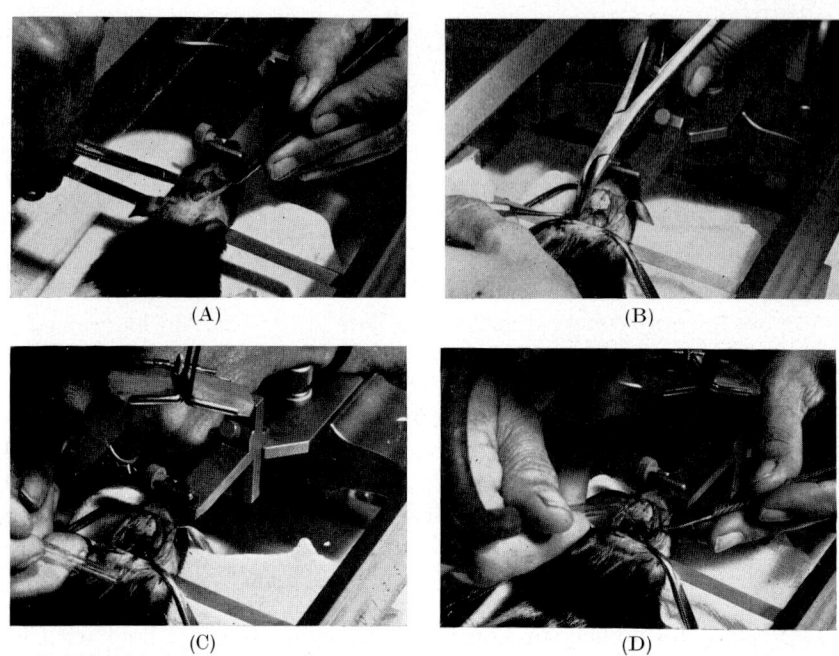

Fig. 5. (A) The surgeon is removing the fascia beneath the scalp. (B) The size of the bone defect and the placement of the rongeur jaws prior to cutting. Note attachment of the mosquito forceps. (C) The pipette is held parallel to the brain for neocortical ablation. The dura and pia-arachnoid and most of the neocortex have been removed in the right hemisphere. The left hemisphere has not been invaded. (D) The surgeon is retracting the temporal muscle and aspirating the lateral neocortex by moving the pipette in a dorsal to ventral direction.

Skin retraction can be accomplished by either one of two methods. For surgery not requiring a large incision, an eye speculum, which is a small spring retractor, can be pressed together, and the edges of the skin inserted into its jaws. The jaws are then released, and the skin is retracted. For surgery requiring extensive work laterally and ventrally the attachment of 4 curved mosquito forceps exposes a wider working field. Figure 5(B) shows their position. The surgeon takes the dressing forceps in the left hand, elevates the skin, and attaches and locks the mosquito forcep to the subcutaneous tissue. The point of attachment is important. If the forceps is attached to the outer layer of the skin, the pressure from its jaws interrupts the skin's blood circulation and kills the surrounding area. Then, if the dead skin is not removed prior to suturing, the incision will not heal at these points.

The fascia covering the bony skull is now exposed. It is next removed over the area of the intended bone removal or craniectomy, which covers the parietal bone posterior to the coronal suture. The lambda and bregma are the posterior and anterior intersections of the skull (see Fig. 2, Chapter 3). Part of the fascia is removed by scraping it away with the end of a #10 knife blade. The remainder is easily scraped away with cotton swabs and, in the process, oozing of blood from small blood vessels is arrested.

Next, the temporal muscle is retracted. It inserts upon the lateral bony ridge of the frontal and parietal bones. With the aid of a cotton swab, the fascia is cleared away from the medial edge of the ridge. Through the use of the point of the dental ejector, the temporal muscle is freed from its insertion without damage to its fibers. The dental ejector is rolled over the bony ridge in such a manner that continuous pressure is applied medially toward the skull and not laterally toward the muscle. The tool is moved anteriorly and posteriorly along the skull until the muscle has been retracted. Since the muscle is attached only to the bony ridge, it is not necessary to insert the dental ejector very far ventrally.

During all stages of the operation, all exposed soft tissue and bone must be kept moist with physiological saline. Dried tissues generally become debris which interferes with the process of postoperative healing. But moistening is not the same as flooding, and too much saline also has its undesirable effects. A thin covering of the saline that does not run is ideal for the tissues.

The bone covering the posterior neocortex is now ready for removal. The size of the defect is dictated by the size of the neocortical ablation. Thus, in this case, the craniectomy includes parts of the parietal and squamosal bones, and should be shaped like the example in Fig. 5(B). A hobby motor tool or dental drill with bur or trephine attachments is convenient for penetrating the skull. If a bur is used, a round tipped-type about 2 mm is diameter gives good results. The surgeon repeatedly outlines the area to be removed until the bur pierces the bone, whereupon the shelf is lifted out with forceps. Care must be taken in this procedure not to get the skull too hot, which will happen if the bur dwells too long at any one point.

If a trephine is used, two holes about 2 mm in diameter are drilled in the parietal bone on either side of the midline just posterior to the coronal sucture. The drill is held perpendicular to the skull so that all sides of the defect are cut through simultaneously. The progress of the drill can be checked at any time by prying on one side of the bone chip with the dental ejector. Just as the trephine breaks through the skull, the surgeon will feel a slight "give". At that moment, the drill is lifted and the bone chip extracted. Should bleeding be encountered, it is usually advisable to finish trephining so that the source of the hemorrhage can be determined. More than likely, in the rat, the bleeding is not from bone, but from damaged blood vessels beneath it. Techniques for maintaining hemostasis will be discussed in a later section.

After the first plaque of bone has been removed, the defect is enlarged with rongeurs. Figure 5(B) demonstrates this technique. The lower jaw of the rongeur is slipped between the brain and the bone. If undue pressure upon the brain is to be avoided, the rongeur must not be inserted very far. As the dorsal jaw of the rongeur is closed to cut the bone, the instrument is rotated outward and away from the brain. Snipping the bone without this wrist action or with an inward rotation toward the cortex are techniques which cause undue pressure on the brain and also tend to start bleeding points.

When the bone defect is completed, it extends anteriorly to the coronal suture and ventrolaterally to the area where the squamosal bone flares out laterally. Posteriorly, it usually is enlarged behind the transverse suture. However, this boundary is defined by the appearance of the transverse sinus, at which point the caudal expansion is terminated. A thin ridge of bone is left along the sagittal suture on the midline to protect the superior sagittal sinus. After the bone defect has been shaped, all rough bone edges are smoothed with the rongeurs, and all stray bone chips are carefully searched for and removed. Finally, the area is covered with saline-soaked cotton pellets while the defect on the opposite side is prepared.

When both bone defects are completed, the dura mater on one side is turned back or reflected. Next, the pia-arachnoid membrane covering the lesion site is removed. From now until the skin incision is sutured, binocular loupes or magnifiers are worn so that the surgeon has a better view for the more delicate aspects of the surgery. The dura is punctured in the center of the exposed field with the #12 knife blade, and approximately 4 pie-shaped wedges are cut in it and retracted with forceps. This procedure can be carried out without damaging the underlying neural tissue by holding the knife laterally and parallel to the brain surface while cutting. The surgical field is then covered with saline-soaked cotton pellets while the same procedures are carried out on the opposite side of the head.

The pia-arachnoid membrane, which is now in view, contains the superficial cerebral blood vessels. It is a much thinner membrane than the dura and adheres very closely to the brain. Consequently, it is teased away or peeled off in strips of uneven sizes with the House-Rosen needle. Some surgeons prefer to aspirate it away as they ablate the neocortex. It has been our experience, however, that this latter procedure yields lesions that are often more extensive than intended.

G. Localized Extirpation of Neocortex

Finally, the posterior neocortex is ready to be extirpated. Two essential instruments are the suction pump and the glass aspirator. The pump can be purchased from any surgical supply house, but the aspirators are home-made and are shaped from glass tubing held over a hot flame. The internal diameter of the tip of the pipette for cortical removals in rats is approximately $\frac{1}{2}$ mm, and the external diameter is about 1 mm. The transparency of glass has several advantages. The surgeon can see the amount of neural tissue being taken out as it passes through the pipette; this is important because he may not be removing any cortex at a given moment due to the pipette's gliding over some unremoved pia. However, if he watches the aspirator, this error can be readily corrected. The surgeon can also estimate the amount of blood that is being sucked away inadvertently. It is essential for bleeding to be stopped as it occurs, and for as little blood as possible to be lost by the rat.

Glass also has the advantage in that the pipette can be shaped in any fashion the surgeon desires. For cortical ablations in the rat, we prefer the "L" shape, particularly because the pipette can be held like a pencil parallel to the surface of the brain as shown in Fig. 5(C). The heel of a pipette with a more obtuse angle tends to push against the cortex. Also these latter pipettes tend to cause more damage than expected because the tips are angled toward the cortex rather than lying parallel with it when the barrel of the pipette is held in a comfortable position.

Six to seven lb/sq in of negative pressure from the vacuum pump is adequate for aspirating rat neocortex. However, the amount of negative pressure to be used depends upon the size of the pipette's tip and the efficiency of the pump. The adjustment of the suction in conjunction with the manipulation of the pipette must be such that only neocortex is ablated. The underlying white matter should remain intact so that fibers of passage will not be destroyed, and this is possible in principle because the fibrous matter of the brain is mechanically stronger than the cellular matter. Experience and knowledge of histological results are the best teachers of this point.

The dorsal surface of the neocortex is removed by holding the aspirator parallel to the brain, and moving it in an anterior to posterior direction. The pipette should be flushed out periodically with saline. As shown in Fig. 5(C), adjacent rows of furrows are aspirated until the entire dorsal surface is extirpated. The same photograph also gives a comparison between an intact and a partially ablated area.

To remove the lateral surface of the posterior neocortex, the surgeon retracts the temporal muscle and glides the pipette in a dorsal to ventral direction until all visible cortex has been ablated. Figure 50 illustrates this technique.

The posterior dorsal, posterior-ventral-lateral cortex and the neocortex just dorsal to the rhinal fissure are hidden under bone. To remove these regions, the tip of the aspirator is inserted between the bone and the brain, beneath the pia-arachnoid. Pressure on the pipette should be applied toward the bone and away from the nervous tissue. To ablate the cortex dorsal to the rhinal fissure, the pipette is inserted until resistance is felt from underlying bone. The tip is then withdrawn, and the surgeon proceeds to make adjacent dorsoventral furrows beneath the bone. Placement of the aspirator under the pia not only ensures that the cortex will, indeed, be suctioned, but it is also a safety measure. In particular, the possibility of puncturing the transverse sinus in the posterior-dorsal and posterior-ventral-lateral regions by the pipette tip is significantly diminished if this technique is accurately executed.

If, following histological analysis, the cortical removal is found not to be as extensive as had been intended, the aspirator was probably: (a) gliding over the top of the pia, or (b) the regions hidden by bone were not successfully removed. On the other hand, if too much neural tissue was extirpated, (a) the pressure might have been too great, (b) the pipette tip might have been too large, or (c) the surgeon might have aspirated over the same region several times.

H. Closure of the Wound

The rat is now ready to be sutured. All bleeding must be stopped before the head wound is closed, and bone chips and cotton pellets must all be extracted. If connective tissue or skin has died because of insufficient blood supply or failure to keep the area moist with saline, the necrotic areas must be cut away. In the rat, only the skin is sutured. The dura and pia are too thin to sew, and the temporal muscle is forced to its former position as the scalp is closed.

When suturing the skin, the surgeon stands to one side of the animal and grasps the skin firmly on the far side at the anterior portion of the incision with the $4\frac{1}{2}$ in dressing forceps in the left hand. The threaded needle is held with the locked holder in the right hand. With the forceps, the skin is forced halfway on the needle. Subsequently, the forceps are laid down and the suture needle is freed from the needle holder. With the latter instrument, the needle is pulled through the skin. This procedure, shown in Fig. 6(A), is repeated for the skin on

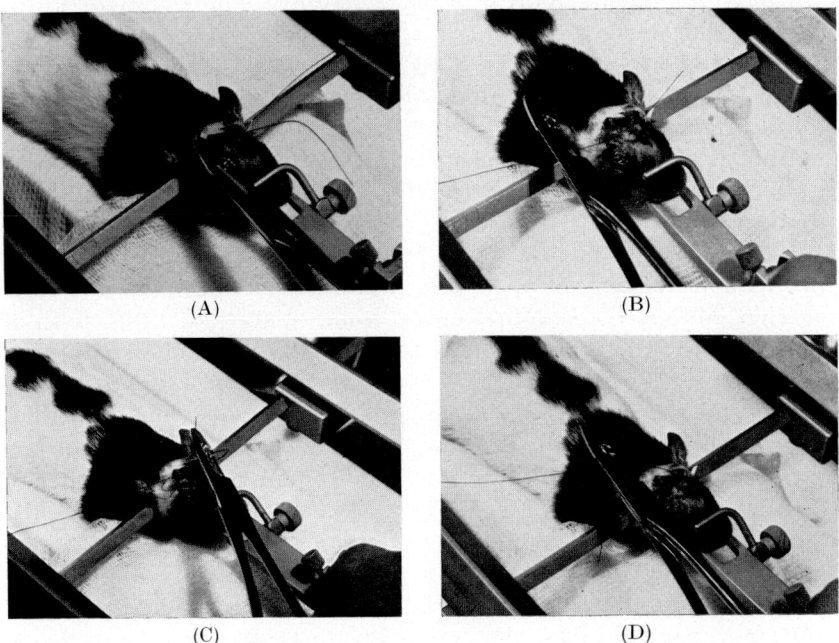

FIG. 6. (A) The suture needle is completely through the far side of the incision and part-way through the near side. (B) This photograph shows the one-inch tying end and the needle holder laid on top of the thread. (C) The thread is looped around the needle holder which is grasping the one-inch typing end. (D) The needle holder is positioned under the thread.

the near side of the surgeon. Except for the tying end which is $\frac{1}{2}$ to 1 in long, the suture thread is pulled through the near and far holes punctured by the suture needle, and then the needle holder is placed on top of the thread as shown in Fig. 6(B). With the left hand, the thread is next looped around the needle holder, and the one inch tying-end is grasped with the needle holder jaws as illustrated in Fig. 6(C). With the suture needle held in the left hand, the thread is now pulled toward the surgeon's left shoulder. This movement closes the loop of thread at the end of the needle holder and draws the skin incision together. The needle holder clamping the $\frac{1}{2}$ in thread is held stationary during this latter procedure. Next, the needle holder is again laid on top of the thread; the thread is looped around the needle holder; the thread remnant is grasped with the needle holder; and the thread is pulled through the loop. These two ties complete a granny knot, which can be slipped and hence tightened. When the two edges of the incision are drawn together, they are approximated. Do not pull together too tightly or the blood supply will be interrupted, and the incised area will not heal.

Next, a square knot is tied atop the granny knot so that the final suture will not slip. The needle holder is placed *under* the thread as shown in Fig. 6(D), and the thread is looped around the instrument; the thread remnant is grasped with the needle holder, and the thread is pulled through the loop. Both ends of the suture thread are pulled tightly and are then cut with the scissors on the needle holder. The knots are spaced about 3–4 mm apart, or just enough to close the skin without leaving an open gap. Placement of the knots too close together puckers the skin and makes unnecessary punctures, both of which increase the likelihood of a postoperative infection.

The rat's head is next lightly washed with saline using a 2×2 in sponge and the animal is given a prophylactic injection of bicillin. The bicillin is injected into the large muscle behind the femur of one hind leg, which is squeezed between the thumb and middle finger of the left hand as shown in Fig. 7. The dose of 0·25 cc bicillin is administered with a 22 gauge hypodermic needle.

The animal is next removed from the ear bars and placed on a cloth in warm surroundings. When its reflexes become brisk and it initiates some movement on its own, it is ready to be returned to its home cage. However, no food or water should be given until the rat has completely recovered from the anesthesia. This protects the animal from vomiting and choking to death before all of its reflexes are functioning properly.

I. Complete Extirpation of Neocortex

The aspiration technique just described is ideal for removing localized portions of the cerebral cortex. To remove the entire neocortex, though, Professor Woolsey has developed a much more facile method. After the brain has been exposed in the usual manner, the pia-arachnoid is incised near the midline, picked up with the forceps, and

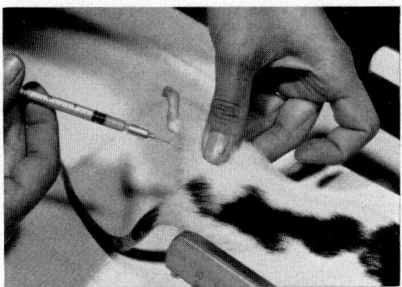

Fig. 7. Technique for intramuscular injection of bicillin in the rat.

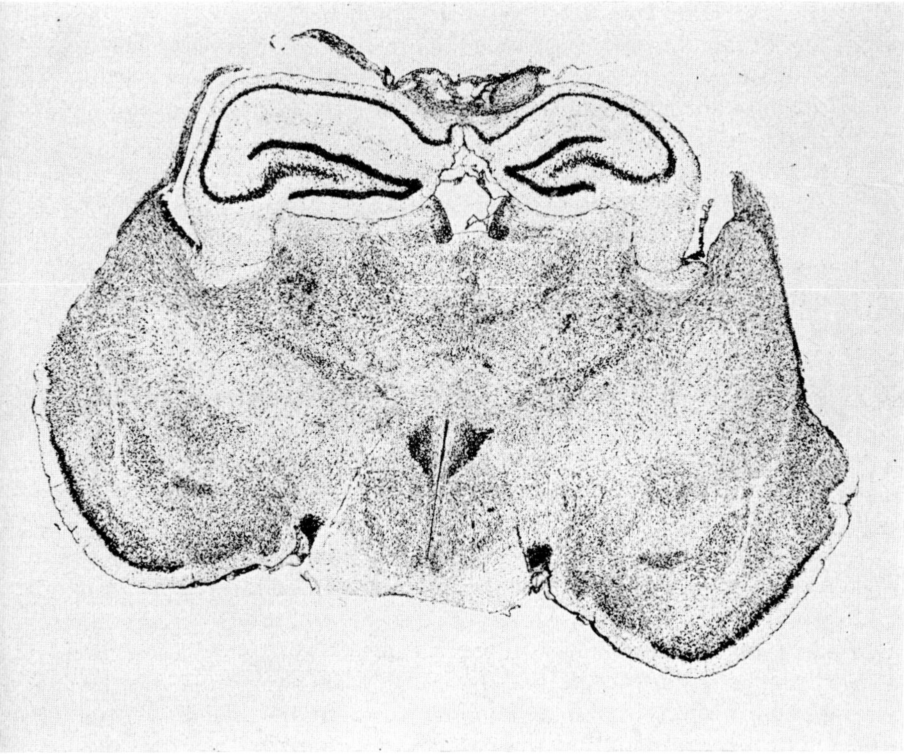

Fig. 8. A transverse section of a rat brain showing the absence of neocortex. This removal was accomplished merely by interrupting the blood supply. Reproduced with permission from Woolsey (1970).

stripped laterally as far as the rhinal sulcus. Thus, interrupting the blood supply to the neocortex leads to cortical necrosis. Medially, he suggests that the cortex of the most medial surface of the hemisphere be aspirated by pipette. Figure 8 shows a transverse section of a rat brain which was neo-decorticated by this technique. This section passes through the caudal part of the optic chiasm below and the habenula above. The mediodorsal nucleus appears centrally above surrounded laterally by the intralaminar nuclei and still more laterally by the reticular nucleus. There are clumps of neuroglia in degenerated parts of the ventrobasal complex between the intralaminar and the reticular nuclei.

III. Maintenance of Hemostasis

The importance of maintaining hemostasis and preventing hemorrhage cannot be stressed strongly enough. One mark of a fine surgeon is the ease and completeness with which he can arrest the flow or oozing of blood from a large or small blood vessel. Surgeons who ignore the latter type of hemorrhage, particularly if it is not within the immediate surgical field, overlook a major reason for losing animals from one of several possible complications which attend blood loss.

In the rat and in the cat, the scalp incision is usually on the midline in an anterior to posterior direction. Bleeding is minimal and presents no problem. In the monkey, bleeding can be easily controlled by continuous pressure applied to the edge of the cut with 4×4 in sponges. If a small bleeder persists, a mosquito forceps and the cloth or sponge used to reflect the skin flap can be attached to maintain hemostasis.

In the cat or monkey, bone wax can be packed into the rongeured edge of the bone defect when it bleeds. For bone wax to be effective, though, the site must be dried with a sponge or cotton swab, and the wax immediately rubbed into the site before the blood begins to flow again. Care should be taken not to leave scraps of bone wax in the field.

Oxyacel, which is a cotton-like coagulant, can also be used when bone bleeding is profuse and the area cannot be cleared fast enough to apply the bone wax. However, oxyacel is fibrous, and its subsequent removal from bone is difficult especially if the edge is rough.

Bleeding from bone is not a serious problem in rats and can be stopped by applying continuous pressure to the bleeding point. It occurs most commonly during rongeuring between the parietal and intraparietal bones. A piece of gelfoam, which is a sponge-like absorbable material, cut and shaped to cover the area will stop the bleeding. Some surgeons prefer to soak gelfoam in saline before application. In either event, the problem area must be temporarily cleared of blood or the gelfoam will not adhere. Even though gelfoam, as well as oxyacel, is absorbed after some time it is wise to remove it, if it is possible to do so, before closing the wound.

Another technique that can be used on all three species involves special manipulation of the rongeurs. In cases where the bone is slowly hemorrhaging, one can crush the bone, in a pinching fashion as opposed to snipping it, and this procedure will tend to inhibit the bleeding. Pressure is never applied inward toward the brain. The wrist is always rotated outward away from the brain as described in the previous section. When hemorrhage occurs from either skin or bone, continuous pressure can be employed with safety to facilitate coagulation. But this is not so when it becomes necessary to arrest bleeding near the brain. Extreme care must be taken to avoid trauma that might lead to edema or excessive tissue destruction.

As described above, the rolling of cotton pellets gently over the brain with the tip of the aspirator not only clears the surgical field of blood, but sometimes stops bleeding. This procedure works as well with cats and monkeys as it does with rats, and is superior to using a cotton swab applied directly on the brain. Cotton swabs, however, are ideal for absorbing blood that has seeped down from the brain. Blood-soaked cotton pellets should be saved and laid to one side, for they now contain thrombin, which is of great help in maintaining hemostasis. Gelfoam, oxyacel and small strips of muscle are other materials that can be laid upon the brain to stop hemorrhage. Cotton pellets soaked in topical thrombin or powdered thrombin are also excellent for control of oozing bleeding points.

In monkeys, bleeding can sometimes be prevented or stopped by the tying or crushing of large blood vessels. For example, if a large blood vessel is in the path of an intended dural cut, two knots can be tied around it with 5–0 suture approximately 2 to 3 mm apart, and the vessel can be safely severed between the two ties. Smaller vessels can be merely crushed with mosquito forceps and then cut in two at that area without the use of knots.

If a large blood vessel has been damaged unintentionally, the cut end should be grasped shut with a mosquito forceps for a minute or two. However, before the mosquito forceps is attached, the bleeding area must first be cleared so that the exact location of the torn vessel can be identified. Once this is done, the forceps must be attached quickly but gently. This requires skill, and it is common for novices to panic when the task first confronts them. Unless one can learn to keep cool at such times, he has no business doing surgery.

At our laboratory, we do not use electrocautery during experimental neurosurgery. The techniques described above have been satisfactory in maintaining hemostasis for the types of operations we perform, and we do not want to risk the possibility of injuring other areas because of excessive heat. Electrocautery is very useful in the making of acute preparations of the kind employed by neurophysiologists, but it leaves small patches of dead tissue which retard postoperative healing in chronic preparation.

IV. Sterile Surgical Techniques and Procedures

After the student has mastered the skills of rat neurosurgery, he is ready to be trained in sterile surgical procedures. At our laboratory, this transition usually involves, first, watching an operation on a cat or monkey, then learning the duties of the circulating nurse or technician, then assisting the surgeon, and finally, performing the surgery. Some techniques are common to both sterile and nonsterile surgeries. However, the procedures which were elaborated upon earlier in the chapter, but which are also applicable in sterile surgery, will not be repeated in this section.

The following outline will familiarize the student with the sequence of events during sterile surgery before the minute details of the various procedures are discussed.

After the animal is weighed, anesthetized and shaved, it is carried into the operating room and placed into a headholder. The surgeon and his assistant scrub-in while the circulating nurse dons cap, mask and sterile gloves before scrubbing the animal's head. The circulating nurse then helps the assistant surgeon into his gown and gloves. Once dressed, the assistant is ready to open the sterile packs containing some of the instruments. In the meantime, the circulating nurse is free to dress the surgeon. Subsequently, the circulating nurse is offered and accepts the sterile utility forceps and forceps jar from the assistant surgeon so that he can list the instruments that have been sterilized in solution onto the surgical trays.

Both surgeons arrange the instruments and equipment before an incision is made. After the surgeon and his assistant place the sterile drapes upon the animal, the scalp is incised. Throughout the operation, the circulating nurse keeps records of the animal's condition. When the surgery is completed, the animal is removed to an incubator until it has recovered from the anesthesia. Rigid aseptic precautions must be taken during cat or monkey operations to prevent infection. The surgeon's clothing as well as the instruments and equipment are sterilized either in solution or by autoclaving.

A. Sterilization Procedures

Instruments with cutting edges are disinfected in a solution, such as C.R.I. or zephiran chloride of the type used for instruments, because the heat from autoclaving affects the temper of the metal, leaving the tool permanently dull. C.R.I. will sterilize tools in 10 min, but zephiran chloride requires 24 hrs. Figures 9(A), (B) and (C) illustrate the instruments with cutting edges which are typically used during neocortical extirpations. Instruments such as scissors are placed in solution with their blades open. Duplication of tools is prudent, for one of them might become contaminated while the operation is in progress.

Cloth and instruments with no cutting edges are sterilized by autoclaving. The equipment is assembled on Mayo trays, and then wrapped in a sheet of at least double thickness, secured with masking tape, labeled and sterilized. Two instrument packs, shown in Figs. 9(D) and (E) have been stripped of their wrappings, and the tools have been arranged for photographic purposes less compactly than is usual.

There should also be an anesthesia pack which contains two 1 cc syringes, two 5 cc syringes, four #22 needles, and a few 2 × 2 in and 4 × 4 in sponges. If sterile disposable syringes are used, the glass syringes can be left out of the pack.

The scrub pack should hold two stainless-steel bowls, three surgical scrub brushes, and 30 to 35 4 × 4 in sponges.

In the gown pack there are 3 stainless-steel Mayo trays and 4 surgical gowns, two for each surgeon. On top of each gown is a towel for drying hands. Since the assistant surgeon is dressed first, his gown is placed on top of the surgeon's gown. To prevent their contamination during dressing, the gowns are folded in a particular way. The gown is spread out upon a table, front side up. As shown in Fig. 10(A), each lengthwise side is folded over the midline or center of the gown. Next, the gown is folded "accordion-style" by grasping the wrong-side-out shoulder area as illustrated in Fig. 10(B).

All of the packs are autoclaved at 250°F for 30 min, and dried for 20 min. All packs must be thoroughly dry before they are removed from the autoclave, or contamination will occur.

Items which we purchase from drugstores and surgical, dental and veterinary supply houses that are already sterilized are: surgical gloves in packs of various sizes, pre-powdered, and ready to open according to directions; a 20 ml vial of saline for mixing the thrombin solution; a 20 ml vial of thrombin; oxyacel; bone wax, gelfoam, bicillin antibiotic; 250 ml saline, pentobarbital sodium; atropine sulfate; #10 and #12 knife blades; 3–0 suture thread; and 6–0 suture thread with half-circle non-cutting-edge needle attached.

The remaining equipment, which needs no sterilization, can be arranged in the surgery in a convenient and easily accessible location: boric acid ophthalmic ointment; an antiseptic skin detergent such as

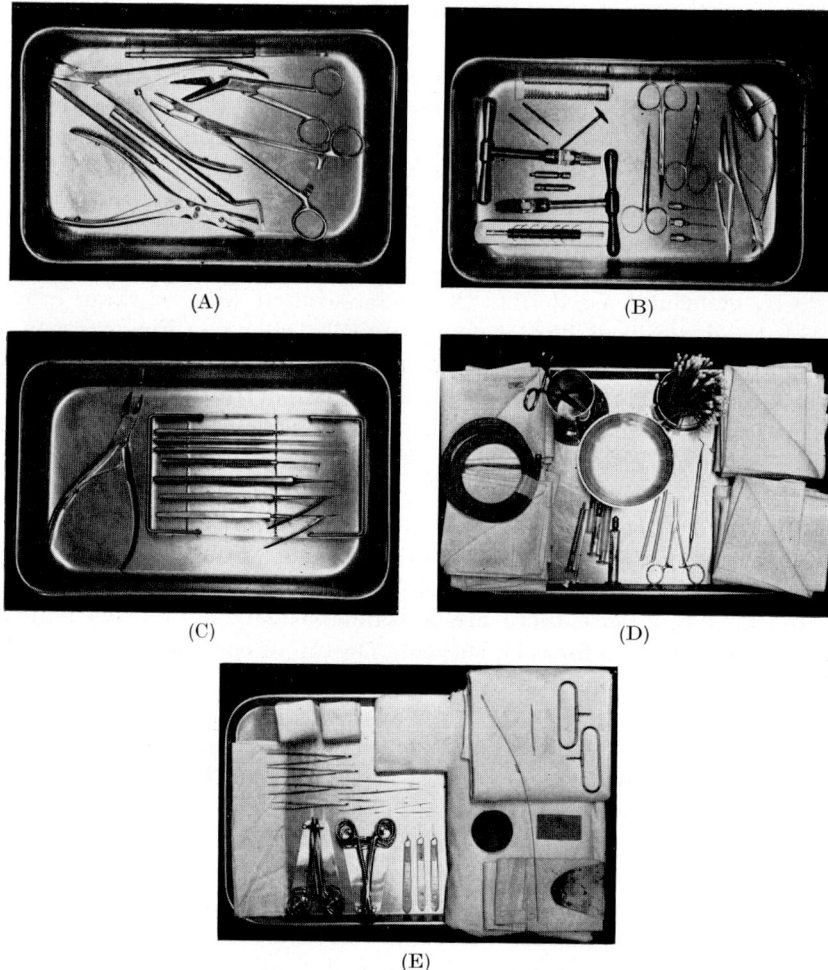

Fig. 9. (A) Some of the instruments with cutting edges that are disinfected in solution are the bone chisel, the single-action rongeurs, the bandage scissors, the needle holder, the dental ejector, the elevator and the double-action rongeurs. (B) This photograph displays the wound clips, burs and a saw, two skull trephines with removable centering points, #6 or #7 half-circle cutting-edge suture needles, two straight sharp-and-sharp iris scissors, one slightly curved sharp-and-blunt iris scissors, three #22 one inch hypodermic needles, suture-clip-applying forceps, suture-clip-applying-and-removing forceps and the binocular loupes. (C) Some of the more delicate instruments sterilized in solution are a dura hook, two slightly curved House-Rosen needles, a 4 mm ruler, a Wullstein fine knife, two pairs of iridocapsulotomy scissors, and a pair of diagonal cutters. (D) This instrument pack contains towels

Hexa-germ or Phisohex; a germicide such as tincture of zephiran chloride; a respiration detector; masking tape; an infant airway to place in animal's mouth to aid breathing; surgical caps; and surgical masks.

B. Preparing the Animal

Food and water are removed from the animal's cage 24 hours before surgery. This routine tends to minimize vomiting or excessive secretions in the animal's mouth and throat during surgery which could lead to asphyxiation.

The monkey or cat is first weighed and then injected intraperitoneally with veterinary sodium pentobarbital. The dosage for monkeys and for cats is 30 mg/kg and $\frac{1}{2}$ the dosage for rats. Induction time for both species is 10 to 15 min. Atropine sulfate is usually given to cats about $\frac{1}{2}$ hour before the anesthesia to allow time for it to take effect. However, in the monkey, it is given simultaneously with the anesthesia because the animals are not easily captured.

Cats that are tractable receive the anesthesia intravenously. After determining the dosage and measuring the sodium pentobarbital into a syringe, an equal volume of sterile saline is added to dilute the anesthetic. Dilution tends to reduce the chances of respiratory arrest during the administration. The advantage of the intravenous procedure is that induction time is rapid, and the anesthetic can be given "to effect"; i.e. the correct amount can more nearly be determined for each individual animal by noting the disappearance of several reflexes.

In the intravenous anesthetic technique, the inside of the forelimb is shaved and washed with 70% alcohol. The assistant wraps his thumb

folded "accordion style" with a turned flap, a suction hose, a pair of utility forceps in a forceps jar, cotton swabs, a stainless-steel basin for saline, an assortment of syringes, two glass aspirators (which should be wrapped in 4×4 sponges to prevent breakage), a fine needle holder for sewing dura, and a dural elevator. A container of #4 dental pellets and a small glass container for thrombin solution should also be included in this pack. (E) On this Mayo tray are four 3×8 in muslin strips, a dozen 5 in curved mosquito forceps, a dozen 5 in towel clamps, three #3 knife handles, an assortment of forceps, two packages of 2×2 in sponges (only a few illustrated in photograph), one package of 4×4 in sponges (only a few illustrated in photograph), and a sheet for covering the animal. On top of the sheet are: a towel with an incision hole, two gigli saw handles, tantalum wire, a gigli saw guide, #60 or #80 stainless-steel wire mesh cloth, and a sock to cover the electric drill. The towel clamps and the mosquito forceps are unlocked while being sterilized, but they are stored in a locked position.

and fingers around the limb above the elbow, and rotates the leg laterally as shown in Fig. 11. Thus, the hand is used as a tourniquet to raise the cephalic vein. The anesthetist places his left thumb adjacent to the vessel to immobilize it. Then the 1 in #22 needle, with bevel up, is inserted through the skin quickly. After the needle is under the skin, it is next inserted, with a quick and gentle thrust, into the lateral side of the vein and parallel to it so that both walls

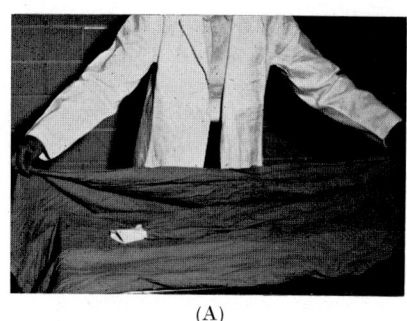 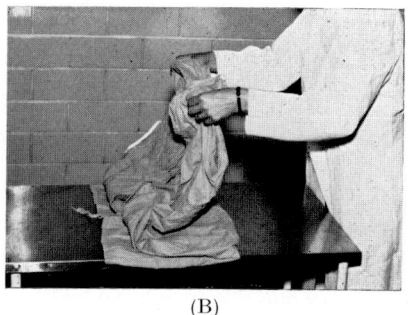

(A) (B)

Fig. 10. (A) Folding the surgical gown lengthwise. (B) Folding the surgical gown "accordion style".

are not punctured. Blood entering the syringe indicates that the needle is in the lumen of the vessel. At that moment, the assistant removes the pressure on the cephalic vein by raising his thumb, and the anesthetist injects approximately $\frac{3}{4}$ of the anesthetic. Usually this is enough to traverse the delirious or excitable stage of anesthesia into the anesthetic stage. The injection should then be discontinued for 1 to 2 min and the palpebral, corneal and flexor reflexes should be checked to determine when they become sluggish and disappear. Approximately 0·2 cc of the anesthetic and saline mixture should be administered if the reflexes are still brisk. Another 2 min then should intervene before more is injected if necessary. Respiration should be abdominal and there should be about 15 to 18 respirations per min. If the reflexes are sluggish and still present, but the respirations become shallow and slower, the anesthetic should be terminated. If the animal is overdosed, 4 mg/kg of metrazol is administered intravenously to reverse the narcosis.

The animal's head is next shaved, and a hair-remover is rubbed onto the scalp to remove whatever hair the razor missed. The animal is now ready for surgery. Some surgeons clean off the excess loose hair on the animal's body with a vacuum cleaner before taking them into the operating room.

A circulating nurse with foresight, one who can accurately predict the needs of the surgeon and his assistant, is a sheer delight. Since his performance is crucial for a smooth and successful surgery, his duties will be described in some detail. The nurse keeps a written record of the surgical proceedings beginning with the administration of the anesthetic and ending after the last knot has been tied. Respiration rate,

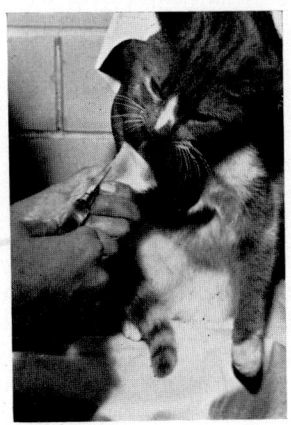

FIG. 11. Intravenous injection of the anesthetic in a cat.

blood pressure, heart rate, additional anesthesia, time of skin incision, and any notes the surgeon might wish to record are included in the ledger. The animal's respiration and other vital signs should be checked frequently. However, it has been our experience that the frequency and type of respiration (shallow or deep) is the best indicator of the condition of the animal.

C. Placing the Animal in the Headholder

The nurse assists in putting the animal into the headholder (see Chapter 3). The monkey's head is placed on the mouth bar, and the ear bars are inserted into the external auditory meatus with relative ease. Usually the nurse and the assistant surgeon work together, each positioning one of the ear bars.

Inserting ear bars into a cat's ears is somewhat more difficult than in the monkey. The nurse positions one side and the assistant positions the other. The tip of the cat's ear is pulled upward with the left hand, and the ear bar is placed into the ear in the vicinity of the auditory meatus so that it stands free and firm and does not fall out. Next, the assistant and the nurse simultaneously push the ear bars inward toward the skull and lift the cat's head with the ear bars into the ear-bar holders.

Another method of positioning the cat's ear bars is first to rest its head on the mouth bar, and then pull the tip of the ear backwards parallel to the top of the head. Next the ear bar is inserted into the ear until the bony ridge surrounding the meatus in the skull is felt with the ear bar (it feels like running into a bump). When the ear bar is slipped below the ridge, it falls into the external auditory meatus.

The same criteria described for the rat will indicate whether the ear bars are positioned properly.

The final steps for securing the animal in the headholder are the same for both cats and monkeys. After the ear bars have been fixed, the head is centered, and the bars are locked. The infraorbital ridgeposts are placed over the animal's infraorbital ridge and then locked. Finally, the mouth bar is raised up against the roof of the mouth until resistance is met, and it is locked.

The procedure just described for securing the animal into the headholder is only one of several available methods. In fact, during some operations, such as temporal lobe surgery, the head may be merely taped or lying free upon the table. Whenever possible, however, we prefer a rigidly-held head, particularly during drilling and rongeuring procedures.

The scalp is now ready to be scrubbed. The circulating nurse applies boric-acid ointment in the eyes to protect them from the cleaning solutions, and then inserts the infant airway. He then puts on a cap and mask before opening the scrub pack. Two stainless-steel bowls are removed from the pack, and the antiseptic skin detergent is poured into one, and tincture of zephiran chloride is poured into the other. After slipping on a pair of sterile surgical gloves, the nurse dips a sterile 4 × 4 sponge into the zephiran chloride, and scrubs the head, anteriorly and posteriorly, from the supraorbital ridge to the base of the neck. Another sterile sponge, this time dipped into the detergent, is used to wash the head over the same area previously cleaned with zephiran chloride. The combination of zephiran chloride and the detergent is repeated five times over the same area before scrubbing another portion of the head. To prevent contamination of an area just cleansed, the sponge used to scrub it is never used to retrace the washed region. After one anterior to posterior stroke, the sponge is thrown away.

D. Surgical "Scrub-in", Gowning and Gloving

After the animal is scrubbed, the circulating nurse removes the sterile gloves, and assists the surgeons as they "scrub in" by supplying skin detergent as they call for it. First, though, the surgeons remove their jewelry, clean their finger nails, and don surgical caps and masks.

When scrubbing in, the surgeons bend their arms at the elbow and keep hands pointed toward the ceiling. In this position, washing and rinsing of the hands, forearms, and the region immediately above the elbow can take place without soiled water running over and thus contaminating regions that have just been washed. Between moves, the surgeons maintain this position throughout the operation to avoid breaking sterile technique. If at any time, a glove, gown or instrument becomes contaminated, it must be discarded and replaced.

After the hands and arms are washed and then scrubbed with the sterile brush from the scrub pack, the nurse pours 70% alcohol over them. While the surgeons are scrubbing in, which takes 4 or 5 min, the nurse carefully opens the gown and instrument packs without touching their contents or the side of the pack sheet next to the equipment.

The nurse next dresses the assistant surgeon. The sterile gown is picked up by the inside shoulder seams and allowed to unfold so that nothing touches it. Since the sterile outside front of the gown is facing the nurse, he must be careful not to bump into it. Holding the gown by the inside shoulder seams, the nurse extends it at arm's length so that the surgeon can place his arms halfway into the sleeves. The nurse then moves behind the surgeon to pull the gown on the rest of the way by the inside seams. Lastly the neck- and waist-bands are tied.

The nurse next opens the sterile pre-powdered surgical gloves according to the instructions on the package, and the assistant surgeon puts them on. The gloving technique used at our laboratory is shown in Figs 12(A), (B), (C) and (D).

The circulating nurse next dresses the surgeon, and the assistant-surgeon places two of the stainless-steel Mayo trays from the gown pack onto the Mayo stand. Without breaking sterile technique, he rests one end of the tray onto one rim of the stand, and permits the opposite side of the tray to drop into place. The assistant places two sterile towels upon each Mayo tray and then arranges the instruments from the pack onto the trays as illustrated in Fig. 13. During the operation, he keeps the trays orderly and supplies the instruments as they are needed.

E. Positioning the Instruments

After the nurse has dressed and gloved the surgeon, he accepts the forceps jar and utility forceps from the assistant surgeon. The nurse grasps the bottom of the jar containing the forceps to avoid touching the assistant, and fills it with cold-sterilization solution. The nurse next opens #10 and #12 knife blades because these are the first tools

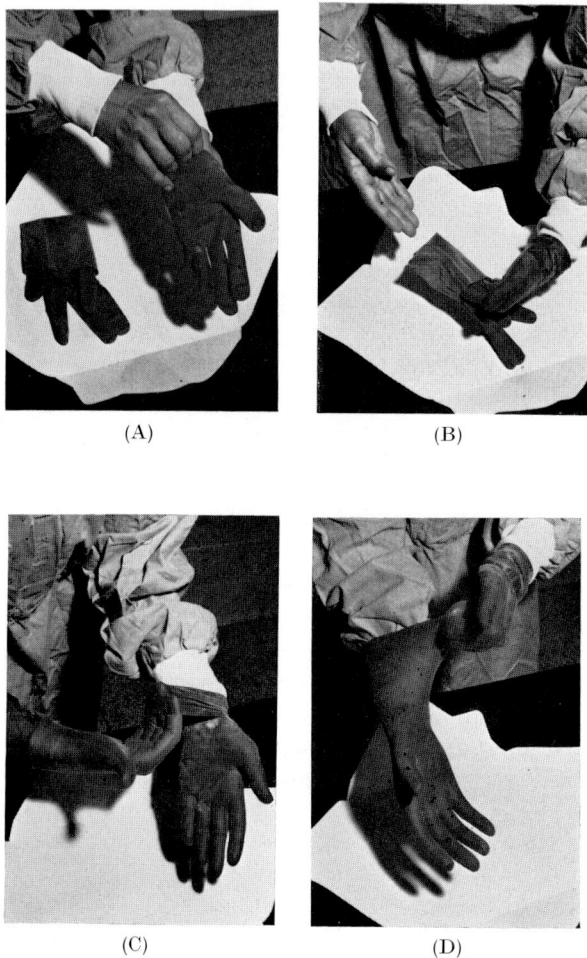

Fig. 12. (A) Since the cuffs of the gloves are turned down, and thus, wrong-side-out, the left glove can be picked up and pulled on by the folded cuff. Without touching the gown or unfolding the cuff, the glove is permitted to snap into place against the wrist. (B) Using the gloved left hand, which is now sterile, the right glove is picked up by inserting the fingers under the turned-down cuff of the right glove. (C) As the glove is pulled on, the cuff simultaneously is folded so that it snaps around the wrist and covers any exposed skin between the sleeve of the gown and the top of the glove. (D) To unfold the cuff of the left glove, the fingers of the right hand are slipped under the cuff. The right thumb must be raised up so that it does not touch the previously contaminated folded cuff of the left glove. Finally the left cuff is unfolded and snapped around the wrist.

the surgeon will use. The assistant-surgeon removes the blades from the sterile packages with a pair of dressing forceps and attaches them to knife handles.

The nurse next uses the utility forceps to transfer the cutting-edge instruments from the cold-sterilization trays to the Mayo stand as they are needed by the surgeon. When doing this, the nurse must be careful not to hit the sides of the instrument trays where they are not covered by the solution.

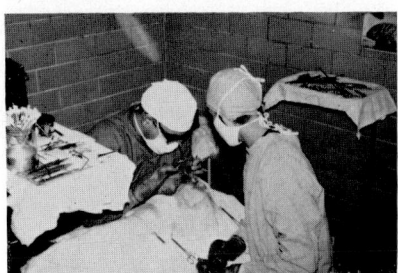

FIG. 13. Sterile surgical procedures.

After the instruments and equipment have been put in order, the surgeon and the assistant are prepared to drape the animal. The draping procedure is for a midline incision. A sterile towel is folded about $\frac{1}{4}$ of its length and laid upon the head with the folded side down in an anterior to posterior direction just lateral to the midline. The purpose of the fold is merely to obtain a smooth, even edge. A second towel is similarly folded and laid just dorsal to both supraorbital ridges. If necessary, the assistant-surgeon holds them in place while the surgeon clips a towel clamp through them and the underlying skin at the corner formed by the two towels. The technique of doing this is shown in Fig. 14(A). If a towel slips, the area should not be contaminated by repositioning it. Rather, it should be discarded and replaced with another sterile towel. Similarly, if the towel clamp does not fasten simultaneously both the towels and the skin, another sterile clamp should be substituted.

To complete the draping, two more towels are unfolded. One is placed anteriorly to posteriorly on the other side of the midline, and the other horizontally to the posterior extent of the intended incision. Towel clamps are attached at the remaining three corners. Finally, the entire animal is draped with a sterile sheet of double thickness. The preparation and the table are then completely covered with sterile cloth except for a small, clean, rectangular region of the scalp.

Before the incision, all of the materials and equipment essential for maintaining hemostasis are prepared. The circulating nurse opens a container of sterile saline, pours a small amount over the lip of the bottle into a waste-basket, and then into a stainless-steel bowl held by one of the surgeons. The assistant-surgeon withdraws the appropriate amount of physiological saline with a syringe and injects the

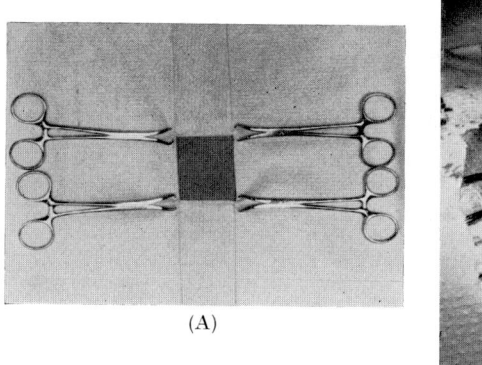
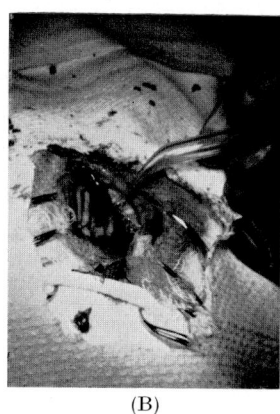

FIG. 14. (A) Draping technique. (B) Neurosurgical techniques.

fluid into the vial containing powdered thrombin. The nurse, who holds the nonsterile bottle, also shakes the container to mix the thrombin solution, and then the surgeon withdraws the mixture and injects it into the small glass container. The nurse also opens the sterile packets containing gelfoam, bone wax and oxyacel, all of which are accepted by the assistant-surgeon by means of dressing forceps.

Throughout the surgery, the circulating nurse aids the surgeons in various ways. He adjusts the lighting; puts the binocular loupes on the surgeon; makes up additional packs for autoclaving, if necessary; empties waste basins; maintains an orderly room; and performs any duties to facilitate the operation.

V. Techniques of Aspiration in Large Species

Since there are many similarities between cat and monkey neurosurgery, the procedures detailed in this section are appropriate for both species unless otherwise specified.

Prior to making the incision, the surgeon may wish to outline the area of the skin incision with sterile ink. With monkeys, the size and shape of the skin flap will vary depending upon the type of surgery to be performed. With cats, a midline incision is suitable for most neocortical ablations. Once the incision has been made and hemostasis obtained, the subcutaneous fascia is cut with iris scissors so that the skin flap can be turned.

One method of retracting the scalp is shown in Fig. 14(B). The ventral layer of the skin is attached to 4×4 sponges by means of the curved mosquito forceps. This figure also serves to illustrate what is meant by a break in sterile technique. In the foreground of the photograph, one mosquito forcep has become detached, and a portion of the skin is exposed. After the incision is completed, all skin should be covered by sterile cloth. Thus, another mosquito forcep should have been used to replace the detached one.

Another technique for scalp retraction involves the use of wound clips and muslin strips. We prefer this method for midline incisions because the skin remains moist and in good condition even throughout long operations. The muslin strips are folded just enough to obtain a smooth, even edge. The surgeon, standing on one side of the animal and lateral to the skin incision, lays the strip, folded-side up, adjacent to the skin flap farthest from him. The assistant, using a pair of forceps, offers the wound clips to the surgeon, and the surgeon attaches them to the scalp and muslin strip with the suture-clip-applying forceps along the entire incision. Then the muslin cloth is flipped over and the edge of the incision, as well as the wound clips are neatly concealed. The other side of the scalp is retracted in the same manner. More wound clips are added if any portion of the skin is exposed. Instead of wound clips, slightly curved $5\frac{1}{2}$ in Mayo hemostats can be used.

After the scalp has been retracted, a towel with a hole the size of the incision is placed over the surgical field.

The next step is to retract the muscle covering the site of the intended bone defect. Preferably, it is detached from the skull at its insertion. An ideal tool for prying the muscle's fascia from the bone is the end of a #3 knife handle. In resistant areas, the elevator or bone chisel are also helpful. As a general policy, one should avoid cutting muscle. However, some surgeries, such as temporal lobe operations, require it. If such procedures are called for, the cut should be made parallel to the muscle fibers, as this damages the muscle least and cuts through the fewest blood vessels. Once the muscle is pulled free, it is retracted only when necessary. Two #3 knife handles serve as excellent retractors.

Throughout the entire operation, the assistant surgeon must keep the skin, muscle and bone moist with saline.

A. Craniotomy

The skull is now exposed, and the bone defect is ready to be formed. Since the techniques are somewhat different for cats and monkeys, several procedures will be described. Generally, though, the cranium of the cat is opened by trephination and rongeuring, and following cortical extirpation the defect is covered by the temporal muscle. In the monkey, either a bone flap can be turned, or the skull can be trephined and rongeured with the brain being subsequently covered by stainless-steel wire mesh.

First, we shall discuss the method of trephination and rongeuring. The whitest area within the proposed defect is selected for making the trephine hole because the least bleeding is usually at that site. After the area is thoroughly dried with a sponge, the surgeon inserts the centering point into the hand trephine, and rotates the instrument clockwise and counterclockwise upon the skull. Firm pressure is applied, and the instrument must be held perpendicular to the skull to assure an even penetration. Once the circular edge of the trephine has imprinted the bone circumferentially, the centering point is removed and the trephining is continued. The dental ejector can be used to check the progress of trephining, and during that time the assistant can clear the field of the many small bone fragments. The trephine first passes through the superficial layer of bone, then into the spongy and porous diploic tissue before passing through the final inner bone. It is not uncommon for the beginner to assume that he has completely penetrated the bone, whereas, actually, he still has to cut through the lower bone table. If bleeding occurs during trephination, the bone disc should be removed quickly but carefully, so that the source of bleeding can be determined and rapidly controlled.

The trephine opening is enlarged with rongeurs and shaped to the contour of the intended ablation. To avoid unnecessary trauma to the brain, the rongeurs are used in the manner previously described, and the rough bony edges are trimmed off when the defect is completed. During this procedure, the assistant should be alert for bone chips, and should assist the surgeon in maintaining hemostasis by having the hemostatic agents ready for immediate use. Seldom, in the cat, does the dura adhere to the skull. If this should happen, it is necessary to separate the dura from the bone with a dural elevator before rongeuring. Nevertheless, when rongeuring over the sagittal sinus, to remove, for example, the striate cortex, one should search for dural adhesions by running the dural elevator under the bone before proceeding boldly.

When performing prefrontal operations in the cat, we usually plug up the frontal sinuses with dental acrylic before the wound is closed in order to reduce the possibility of infection. For acrylic to adhere, the bone must be very dry.

B. Turning a Bone Flap

In the monkey, the bone defect is made in the same manner as described for the cat if the surgeon closes the opening with stainless-steel wire mesh. If, however, the surgeon decides to turn a bone flap, the following procedures are undertaken. To turn a flap, the surgeon must make trephine holes at strategic locations and saw between all but two of them; here the bone will be broken so that the flap can be raised to expose the brain. As much of the muscle as possible should be left attached to the bone flap to continue a supply of blood to the flap. If, however, the bone flap becomes detached from the muscle the bone flap can be wrapped in a 4 × 4 sponge and placed in saline with no serious consequences.

For purposes of illustration, a bone flap for a dorsolateral frontal operation will be described. Figure 15 shows the location on the skull of trephine holes, linear cuts, and wire holes for this particular flap. The temporal muscle is detached above the two most dorsal trephine holes and retracted only enough to accommodate the holes and the saw-cuts. Also, the muscle is severed parallel to its fibers for the anterior and posterior saw-cuts. After the muscle has been cut with the #10 knife blade, the assistant-surgeon should be prepared to apply steady pressure with 4 × 4 sponges to maintain hemostasis.

Next, four trephine holes are drilled into the skull with a hand trephine. Two are placed ventrally and two are placed on the midline over the sagittal suture. Saline-moistened cotton pellets are loosely packed into each opening following removal of the bone plug.

After trephining, the bone is sawed in three places between the holes with a gigli saw or a small, circular saw run by an electric hand-drill as shown in Fig. 15. If a gigli saw is used, all dural adhesions in the vicinity of the openings must be disconnected from the bone in the vicinity of the trephine holes. The surgeon then slides the dural protector under the bone from one hole to the other, and the gigli saw-guide with the saw attached is slipped between the holes. After the guide is pulled out, the surgeon, grasping both ends of the wire-like saw, cuts the bone between the holes by applying steady upward and alternating pressure on the handles.

Cutting with the gigli saw stresses the skull at all points where it is secured in the headholder; therefore, we prefer to use the electric saw. To prevent contamination of the surgeon, the circulating nurse, with help from the assistant-surgeon, dangles the electric drill into the sterile sock. The surgeon then inserts one of the circular-saw blades into the chuck of the drill. All dural adhesions are detached from the skull before slipping the dural protector between two of the trephine holes. As the surgeon cuts through the bone, he tilts the saw in such a way that an inward-slanting bevel is formed on the edge of the bone flap to assure a matched and firm fit when the bone flap is replaced.

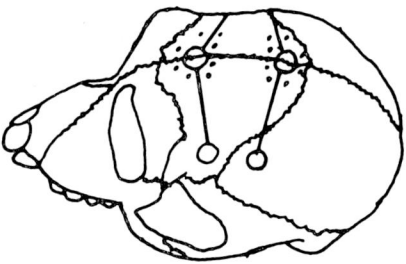

Fig. 15. Bone flap for dorsolateral frontal operation in monkeys.

After all three cuts have been made, the surgeon lifts the flap at the dorsal cut with either his fingers or a dural elevator, and cracks the bone between the two ventral trephine holes while the assistant applies pressure with his fingers in the vicinity of the break. Care must be taken neither to detach the temporal muscle from the flap, nor the flap from the skull.

The surgeon next removes the saw blade from the drill and replaces it with a #26 or #27 surgical bone bur so that he can drill small holes in the flap and in the adjacent bone as indicated in Fig. 15. These holes will accommodate tantalum wire for securing the flap after the lesion is complete. Before drilling, the holes are lined up and the dural protector is inserted beneath the bone. Lastly, the flap is wrapped in saline-soaked 4 × 4 sponges. The brain also is kept moist with 4 × 4 sponges, but the saline is never applied directly upon the brain. The surgical team is now ready to turn the flap on the opposite hemisphere.

C. The Dura Mater Flap

After the cranium has been opened, the dura is incised and retracted. The circulating nurse helps the surgeon put on the binocular loupes, and the assistant-surgeon removes the tools used for entering the brain and replaces them with the instruments for the following more delicate procedures. Also, the assistant-surgeon and the circulating nurse attach the sterile aspirator hose to the vacuum pump. A towel clamp attached through a fold in the drape arranged around the hose prevents the hose from falling off the table.

For many operations, the shape of the dural flap described previously is adequate. In the center of the surgical field, the assistant-surgeon carefully lifts the dura with a dura hook or a pair of tissue forceps with slightly curved jaws with teeth and elevates the dura so that the surgeon can readily incise it without damaging the underlying brain. As the surgeon cuts the pie-shaped wedges with either the #12 knife blade or the slightly curved sharp-and-blunt iris scissors, the assistant continues to raise the dura, thus enabling the surgeon to make the incision under visual control. This also diminishes accidental damage to underlying blood vessels. Occasionally, however, blood vessels are in the path of the incision, or they traverse from the pia-arachnoid through the dura and become continuous with it. These vessels must be clamped or tied and severed as discussed in the hemostasis section. After the dura has been incised, the wedge-like sections are retracted and kept moist with saline-soaked pellets or sponges.

If a differently shaped dural incision is made so that the cut is near the edge of the bone, several suture threads about 3 inches long can be tied in the dura. Then, when the dura is ready to be closed, the surgeon has easy access to it, even if the dura has receded beneath the bone. This almost always happens.

After the dura has been retracted, the gyri of the brain, which are covered by the pia-arachnoid membranes, are in full view in the region of the intended extirpation. These membranes contain the cerebral blood supply and should be preserved if possible during the operation. Otherwise, areas adjacent to the lesion which are nourished by the same blood vessels, are destroyed. Also, indiscriminate destruction of the blood vessels leads to unnecessary hemorrhaging.

D. Aspiration of Neocortex

The neocortex is removed one gyrus at a time. Usually, we ablate the cortex from the most lateral gyrus of the lesioned area followed by the next most medial one. This sequence of ablating usually assures a clear surgical field and allows the surgeons to operate under good visual conditions. The procedure of working laterally to medially reduces the possibility that blood will have obscured the details of a gyrus containing neocortex which has not yet been removed.

To gain access to the cortex, two transverse knife cuts are made in the pia-arachnoid approximately 6 to 8 mm apart with a Wullstein knife or a #12 knife blade. The actual distance between the two incisions is controlled by the blood vessel pattern and the length of the pipette shaft. In general, blood vessels large enough to see should not be severed, and the thick part of the pipette shaft must not be pushed beneath the membrane. Cerebrospinal fluid will escape from the wounds, but cotton pellets gently rolled across the brain surface readily absorb the fluid.

In aspiration of the gray matter between the two knife cuts in the pia-arachnoid, the tip of the pipette is inserted beneath the incised membrane. For the reasons already explained, we prefer a right-angled pipette made from glass. The neocortex is removed with approximately 7 pounds of negative pressure and is gradually excavated from the gyrus until the second incision is reached. Jamming or forcing the shaft immediately from one cut to the next almost always results in severe bleeding and edema, and must be avoided. The white matter, which appears as glistening and whitish under the neocortex, should be left intact to preserve fibers of passage to other cortical regions. Figure 14(B) illustrates the bruised appearance of a gyrus after its cortex has been removed.

After the neocortex on top of the gyrus has been extirpated, the gray matter from both sides of the gyrus are ablated. If the two cuts in the pia-arachnoid are not very far apart, entry to the cortex on the sides of the gyrus can be accomplished through the same cuts used for the dorsal removal. Sometimes, however, due to the blood-vessel pattern, additional longitudinal cuts must be made in the membrane so that the most ventral neocortex of the gyrus can be removed.

Although the surgeon should be cognisant of the approximate depth of the sulcus he is operating upon, subtle cues, such as the amount of resistance encountered by the pipette as the floor of the sulcus is approached, will be learned with experience. When the sides of the gyrus are being cleared, the surgeon should keep in mind the general principle that a relatively large artery and vein will be found both above the sulcus and also at the floor of the sulcus. If either of these pairs is severed accidentally, the usual consequence is a loss of tissue outside the area of intent.

The neocortex of each gyrus is progressively removed by making the pia-arachnoid incisions just before each segment of the gyrus is ablated. Hemostasis must be achieved before each new segment is removed. If severe bleeding occurs before the cortex has been entirely removed in one gyrus, it is advisable to stop the bleeding there, complete the operation on another gyrus, and then return to the problem area. However, the surgeon should report to the circulating nurse that the area is still intact so that the nurse can remind him to complete the lesion before the wound is closed.

At times, it is absolutely necessary to apply pressure upon the brain by gently retracting a gyrus with a cotton swab to gain access, for example, to some of the most medial gyri tucked within the longitudinal fissure. In general, however, unnecessary pressure and retraction must be avoided to decrease the possibility of unwanted damage and/or edema.

E. Closure of the Wound

Before the wound is closed, according to the anatomical layers, the circulating nurse reminds the surgeon where such foreign objects as cotton pellets and bone chips are located so that they can be removed. If muscle or fascia has died, the necrotic material should be cut away. Finally, it is imperative that all bleeding points are controlled before the dura and, eventually, the bone flap and scalp are closed.

The reflected dura is next carefully replaced over the brain and sewed together with a pair of fine needle holders containing 6-0 suture thread and a half-circle noncutting-edge needle. Interrupted knots are tied as has been described previously. The edges of the dura are approximated, but are not pulled together tightly. If the edges do not meet, they are loosely tied together to avoid unnecessary pressure on the brain. This latter problem arises when the surgeons fail to keep the dura moist during the operation and/or it may result from an edematous brain.

If a bone flap has been turned, it is replaced next. Strands of tantalum wire are threaded through the small bur holes adjacent to the flap, and as the flap is lowered to its former position the wire is run through the bur holes in the flap. The wire is twisted, and cut off with diagonal cutters before it is smoothed down upon the skull. No rough edges should be exposed.

In replacing the muscle, knots approximately 1 in apart are tied across the midline between the two temporal muscles. The muscles are not stretched together with the sutures, but merely approximated to their previous insertion. In the case of the monkey, the muscle is also tied where it was cut to make the bone flap.

The drape with the center hole is next removed, and the wound clips are retracted from the edge of the scalp with the suture-clip-removing forceps. In the case of the cat, the skin is approximated and tied with interrupted knots in the same way that the rats' scalps are closed. However, in the monkey, a buried continuous stitch is used so that the animal will not disturb the sutures postoperatively. A #6 or #7 half-circle cutting-edge suture needle and a single strand of either 3-0 or 2-0 suture thread are required. The surgeon faces the longitudinal side of the incision, and, working from the right to the left side, passes the needle into the subcutaneous tissue of the incision on the far side. After the thread is pulled through, a knot is tied. The surgeon then passes the needle through the subcutaneous tissue of the incision on the near side. The procedure of alternately sewing the far side and then the near side without cutting the thread is repeated until the last stitch is ready to be placed. To make the final knot, the surgeon enters the needle into the subcutaneous tissue on the near side of the incision, but this time a double loop of thread about 2 in long is left and not pulled through. Next, the needle is passed through the far side, and a knot is tied with that strand of thread and the looped thread. Finally, the thread is cut, and the knot is tucked under the incision. It is important that the knot be completely buried and that no part of the thread is visible so that the animal cannot pull its scalp wound open.

Before the monkey is taken from the headholder, it is injected intramuscularly with 1,200,000 units of bicillin. Its head is bandaged so that it cannot pick directly at the wound. By the time the incision has healed, the animal will have managed to remove the dressing. It has been our experience that cats recover just as well without having their heads bandaged. However, their stitches must be removed approximately one week postoperatively.

Following surgery, the animals should be placed in a warm human-infant incubator which is padded with cloth to prevent head injury as it recovers from the anesthetic. It should be watched carefully and turned frequently. If the animal becomes congested, the mucus must be aspirated from its air passages with a plastic tube connected to the vacuum pump. Usually about 12 to 15 lb/sq in of vacuum is sufficient. If the depth of anesthesia increases alarmingly, the animal should be stimulated by pinching its ears or tail until its respirations increase and become regular. A respirator, if available, is helpful in reversing the anesthesia.

VI. Epilogue

We have tried in this chapter to concentrate upon the first things that novices in surgery must learn. We suspect that most accomplished surgeons who chance to read it will think that there are much better ways to carry out at least some of the methods we describe. Surgeons, like artists, commonly discover that certain tools are better in their hands than are other tools which are the favorites of perhaps the majority of other operators. They also find, like businessmen, that organizations which permit them to do a proper job are not necessarily the kinds of arrangements they encounter in other people's shops. We thus feel sure that anyone who starts with the techniques described in this discussion will soon be changing them to suit his own style and will only then be happy in his work.

The method of ablation is most commonly employed as a means of identifying or defining the integrative systems of the brain. Changes in behavior produced by ablations have classically supplied us with suggestions as to where one might profitably implant an electrode in order to have a fair chance of detecting events within the brain which mediate a given kind of conduct or behavior. The same kinds of outcomes have often indicated likely sites of placements for electrodes or cannulae in studies concerned with effects of artificial stimulation of the nervous system. Also, the outcomes of experiments in which a portion of the brain has been destroyed have hinted at places where histologists and chemists might look for signs of changes in the properties of neurons associated with the learning process.

It has equally been true that information derived from recording and stimulation methods has had its effects upon the conduct of studies which involve ablative interventions. Thus, for example, the evoked-potential method has revealed sensory-system duplication, and ablative studies have since been directed toward the question as to what the functional significance of such duplication could be. Similarly, neuroanatomical discoveries are continuously suggesting new targets for studies which combine ablative methods with methods of analysis of animal behavior.

Ablative methods have their limitations. Thus it has been shown that there are integrative systems which are interdigitated in the brain, but can be teased apart if one applies different kinds of stimulating agents to the same site within the nervous system. It has also been shown that subregions of the cortex are supplied with many different kinds of inputs, and this is a story that has largely been uncovered through the use of stimulation and recording. Hence our current notions of the way in which the brain is organized have come from many sources, and stable facts about it have, in general, been established by several complementary techniques.

Increasingly, the method of cortical ablation is being used in combination with at least two other methods of obtaining information with respect to brain-behavior problems. Thus, for example, in our own laboratory, we are interested in changes in behavior produced by combinations of cortical lesions and lesions of limbic structures which have been produced by stereotaxic procedures. Other investigators presently are looking at neuroanatomical changes which can be induced by cortical ablations and which appear to serve as bases for subsequent recoveries of behavioral functions. We find such approaches exciting and rewarding, and commend them to young investigators; the brain is not likely to yield completely to them, but at least it is likely to be bent.

REFERENCES

Bromiley, R. B. (1948). *J. comp. physiol. Psychol.* **41**, 102–110.
Goodman, D. C. and Horel, J. A. (1966). *J. comp. Neurol.* **127**, 71–88.
Gurdjian, E. S. (1934). "Operative Neurosurgery." Williams and Wilkins, Baltimore.
Horel, J. A., Bettinger, L. A., Royce, G. J. and Meyer, D. R. (1966). *J. comp. physiol. Psychol.* **61**, 66–78.
Meyer, P. M., Johnson, D. and Vaughn, D. (1970). *Brain Research* **22**, 113–120.
Rose, J. E. and Woolsey, C. N. (1943). *Bull. J. Hopkins Hosp.* **73**, 65–128.
Rose, J. E. and Woolsey, C. N. (1958). *In* "Biological and Biochemical Bases of Behavior" (H. F. Harlow and C. N. Woolsey, eds), pp. 127–150, University of Wisconsin Press, Madison, Wisconsin, U.S.A.

Chapter 5

Introducing Subcortical Lesions by Electrolytic Methods

ROBERT THOMPSON

Louisiana State University, Baton Rouge, Louisiana, U.S.A.

I.	Introduction	131
II.	Electrolytic Lesions	133
III.	Electrolytic *vs* Thermocoagulative Lesions	136
IV.	How to Make Electrolytic Lesions	136
	A. Lesion-makers	136
	B. Electrode Construction	137
	C. Electrode Carrier Adjustments	139
	D. Surgical Instruments, Supplies and General Procedures	140
V.	How to Control the Size of the Lesion	142
	A. Test Lesions	142
VI.	One-stage *vs* Two-stage Lesions	143
VII.	Ways to Increase Accuracy of Lesion Placements	143
	A. Uniform Weight of the Subjects	143
	B. Correct Orientation within the Headholder	144
	C. Use of the Superior Sagittal Sinus	144
	D. Making Reference to Bregma and Lambda	145
	E. Know the Depth of the Structure to be Lesioned	146
VIII.	Verification of Lesion Placements—Some Rapid Techniques	146
	A. Equipment and Supplies	146
	B. Obtaining the Brain Sections	147
	C. Photographing Brain Sections	148
	D. Sketching Brain Sections	149
	E. Use of Worksheets in Mapping Lesions	150
IX.	An Evaluation of the Lesion Method	150
References		152
Appendix		154

I. Introduction

THE study of the behavior of animals or humans having specific portions of the central nervous system destroyed is one of the oldest and most widely used methods in neuropsychology. In its simplest laboratory application, part of the brain of a "normal" animal is first damaged. Subsequently, we observe what behavioral deficits have occurred. The function of the structure damaged is then inferred from the nature of the ensuing behavioral changes. While there are many pitfalls in making such an inference in the absence of other relevant data (see the last section of this chapter), this approach to the study of brain-behavior relationships has nevertheless been very profitable. It was by this means that Ferrier (1886) discovered the visual functions of the occipital cortex in the monkey, that Fulton and Jacobsen (1935) obtained compelling evidence of the affective functions of the prefrontal cortex in the chimpanzee, and that Hetherington and Ranson (1942) established that the ventromedial portion of the hypothalamus is implicated in the regulation of food intake in the rat.

This general approach in relating function to structure in animals is commonly referred to as the "lesion," "ablation," "extirpation," or "mutilation" method. A comparable approach using humans as subjects has long been available through the study of clinical cases with known neuropathology or with specific head injuries. In recent years, however, neurosurgical intervention in the treatment of Parkinsonism, psychosis, intractable pain, epilepsy and other disorders has afforded a unique opportunity to examine the functions of different parts of the human brain by the lesion method.

Prior to the development of the stereotaxic technique, the lesion method was, for the most part, limited to the study of the more superficial regions of the brain, such as the cerebral and cerebellar cortices. While some information bearing upon the possible functions of the deeper structures of the brain came from the study of clinical cases with subcortical neuropathology and from the observations of animals with massive ablations, such as decorticate and decerebrate preparations, there was a growing need for a technique of making discrete subcortical lesions without concomitantly damaging adjacent neural structures. Horsley and Clarke (1908) constructed the first stereotaxic instrument and demonstrated the technique of making localized lesions within the deep structures of the brain. By passing electric current through the tip of an electrode, virtually every nucleus and fiber tract of the central nervous system became potentially accessible to study by the lesion method.

Curiously, however, the usefulness of the Horsley-Clarke technique in producing localized lesions was not fully realized until the early 1930's when Ranson, Ingram, Hinsey, Magoun and others at the

Northwestern University Institute of Neurology reintroduced the method and made some important innovations with respect to the lesion-making device, electrode construction and brain charts.

With the availability of the stereotaxic technique, there has been considerable interest in determining the most efficient way of producing a neural lesion. Numerous procedures have been explored (see Carpenter and Whittier, 1952), including mechanically-induced lesions with the use of a probe, chemically-induced lesions obtained by injections of injurious substances through a cannula, and electrically-induced lesions. The latter procedure, by virtue of its simplicity and reliability, has become the most popular in the experimental laboratory for the production of localized subcortical lesions.

II. Electrolytic Lesions

According to Roussy (1907), Golsinger in 1895 was the first to make electrolytic lesions in the brain of a dog. Electrolytic lesions are customarily produced by passing anodal direct current through a monopolar electrode, a single metal wire or needle which is insulated except for the tip. The tip of the electrode is positioned into that part of the brain that is intended to be destroyed. One lead of the direct-current power source, usually the anode, is connected to the electrode, while the other lead, cathode, is either attached to a muscle or other subdermal tissue exposed by the incision across the cranium, clipped to the metal frame of the headholder, or inserted into the rectum.

Figures 1 and 2 show some typical electrolytic lesions made in various structures of the brain. Almost invariably, the lesion consists of an evacuolated area immediately surrounded by a narrow rim of severely coagulated tissue. Surrounding the latter may be a field of gliosis, a region of varying size in which there is heavy infiltration of glial cells. These two areas constitute the "central necrotic zone" of the lesion, and all cells and fiber systems within this area are destroyed or in a state of cytolysis. The gliotic area, on the other hand, may contain a significant proportion of "normal" functioning cells and fiber systems.

The process by which direct current causes cytolysis at the site of the electrode tip is not fully understood, but the two factors most likely responsible for the production of the neural lesion are (a) metallic ions and (b) gas bubbles (Reynolds, 1965). It is well known that the passage of direct current through metallic plates immersed into a saline bath will cause diffusion of metallic ions into the solution as well as the formation of gas bubbles on the surface of the metal. This process is called *electrolysis*. Since the brain has the properties of a saline bath, the tissue surrounding the electrode tip will be invaded by metallic ions and/or will be subject to mechanical deformation by the production of gas bubbles. The extent to which each factor partici-

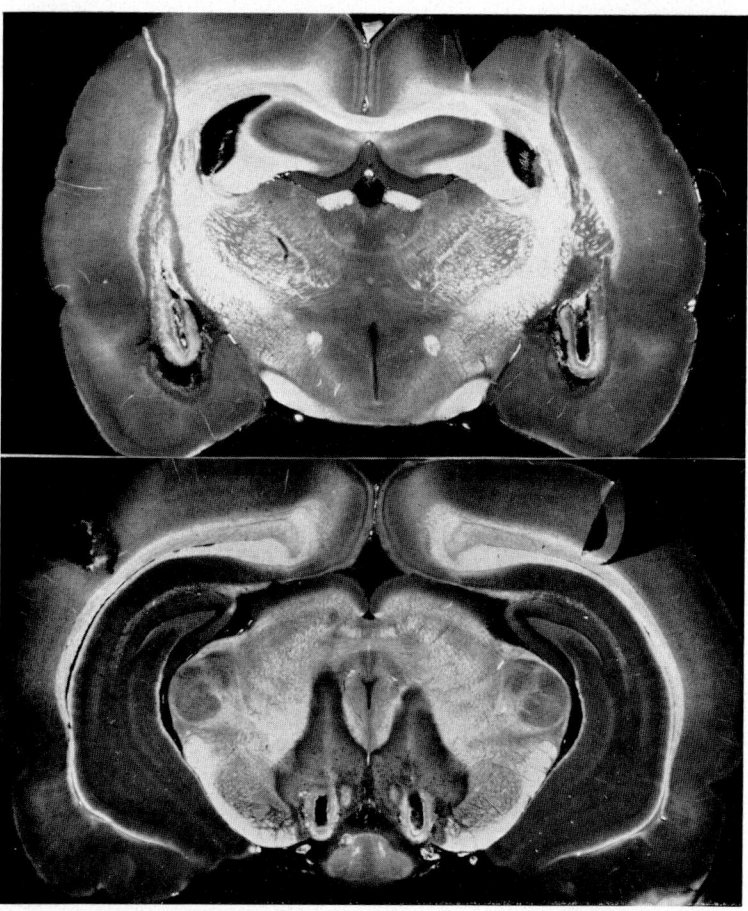

FIG. 1. Photographs of unstained sections derived from two albino rats showing bilaterally placed electrolytic lesions in the amygdaloid (top) and ventromedial midbrain (bottom) areas. Note the three zones of the lesion. Lesion parameters: 3·0 mA for 15 sec (top); 2·0 mA for 5 sec (bottom).

pates in the formation of a neural lesion depends upon the type of metal used in the construction of the electrode and whether or not anodal or cathodal current is applied to the electrode tip. Platinum electrodes apparently produce neural lesions mainly through the formation of gas bubbles, while iron or copper electrodes induce neural

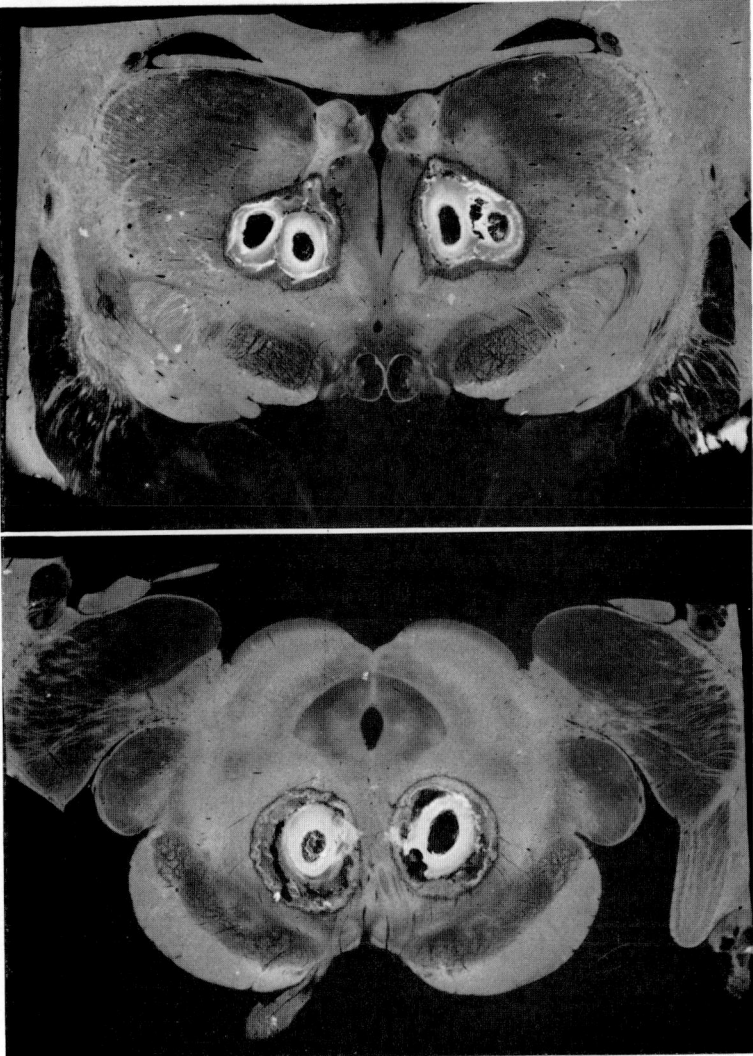

Fig. 2. Photographs of unstained sections derived from two rhesus monkeys showing bilaterally placed electrolytic lesions in the ventromedial thalamic (top) and rubral (bottom) areas. Note that the thalamic lesions involved two insertions of the electrode on either side of the brain. Lesion parameters: 10·0 mA for 15 sec (top); 10·0 mA for 30 sec (bottom).

lesions primarily through the diffusion of metallic ions. The use of cathodal current favors the production of gas bubbles at the site of the electrode tip.

III. ELECTROLYTIC vs THERMOCOAGULATIVE LESIONS

Two other methods involving the use of electric current have been investigated in relation to the development of neural lesions. One employs an electrosurgical spark-gap cautery (Bovie) machine, whereas the other makes use of a radio-frequency current generator (Aronow, 1960). In both cases, the lesions are produced by generation of heat at the electrode tip. The former has not led to encouraging results because the lesion size is erratic, but the latter has been found to produce well-controlled destruction of neural tissue surrounding the electrode tip (Sweet et al., 1960).

In recent years, there has been some concern as to whether lesions produced by different procedures will yield the same deficits in behavior. This concern reached its peak following a study by Reynolds (1965) who presented data suggesting that hypothalamic hyperphagia is readily obtained following direct current (electrolytic) lesions of the ventromedial hypothalamus, but is rarely observed following radio-frequency (thermocoagulative) lesions of the same area. This very interesting finding, however, has been seriously questioned (Herrero, 1969; Hoebel, 1965; Pool, 1964, 1967). Although the data of Reynolds cannot be entirely ignored, the overall results of lesion research on various parts of the brain strongly suggest that the behavioral effects of electrolytic lesions are not decidedly different from those of thermocoagulative, mechanical, chemical or suction lesions.[1]

IV. HOW TO MAKE ELECTROLYTIC LESIONS

The essential materials and apparatus needed to produce electrolytic lesions include lesion-maker, the electrode, electrode carrier and surgical instruments and supplies.

A. Lesion-makers

Direct-current lesion-makers can be purchased for a little over $100 (Lehigh Valley Electronics, C. H. Stoelting Co.). However, it is possible to build an electrolytic lesion-maker for under $30. The necessary items include two "B" batteries (45 volts each), a 50,000 ohm potentiometer, a 1500 ohm resister, an ammeter (0–5·0 mA scale),

---

[1] The region of the nucleus posterior thalami has repeatedly been found to be critically involved in the normal performance of visual discrimination habits in the albino rat (Breen, 1965; McNew and Thompson, 1966; Peters and Cooper, 1969; Thompson and Rich, 1961). I have damaged the nucleus posterior in rats either electrolytically, thermocoagulatively, mechanically, or by suction. The resulting deficits in visual discrimination performance were not markedly different in any of the cases (unpublished findings).

and an on-off switch. These items are connected together in a manner shown in Fig. 3. Calibration of current to be used to produce the lesion involves joining the positive and negative leads and adjusting the potentiometer until the desired reading is given on the milliammeter.

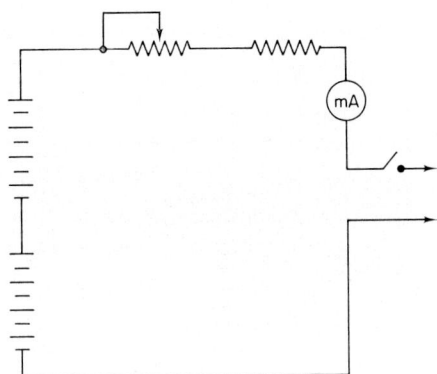

FIG. 3. Diagram of a battery-powered lesion maker. See text for description of the various components.

If thermocoagulative lesions are desired, a radio-frequency lesion-maker (Grass Instrument Co.) can be purchased for about the same price as a commercial direct-current lesion-maker.

B. Electrode Construction

Electrolytic lesions are made most effectively with a *monopolar electrode* (see Fig. 4). A stainless-steel needle is frequently used as an electrode and will provide an excellent lesion as illustrated in Fig. 1. For the rat and animals of comparable size, stainless-steel "insect pins" are quite satisfactory, are inexpensive, come in various diameters and are commercially obtainable (Clay-Adams, Inc.). For the production of small lesions of approximately 1·0 mm in diameter, a No. 4 needle is sufficient, having a diameter of 0·55 mm. The No. 5 needle is slightly larger and is better suited to make lesions of at least 2·0 mm in diameter. For the cat or monkey, metal shafts of greater length and rigidity are necessary. I have used stainless-steel stylets obtained from an 18 gauge, 2·5 in hypodermic needle assembly No. 1295 (Becton, Dickinson and Co.).

To make an electrode that will be used to produce subcortical lesions, it is first necessary to insulate the section of the needle that is to be inserted into the brain. One of the finest insulating materials is epoxyiite (Epoxylite Corp.) which must be baked on the needle.

While other insulating materials are available which do not require baking, such as Insl-x (Insl-x Products Corp.), epoxylite is durable and resistant to cracking, chipping, and "popping." I have used a single epoxylite-insulated electrode for lesions in as many as a dozen different animals.

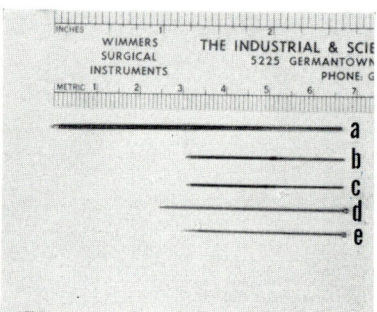

Fig. 4. Stainless-steel electrodes used to make electrolytic lesions. (a) Epoxylite-insulated stylet from hypodermic needle assembly No. 1295; (b) Epoxylite-insulated insect pin No. 6; (c) Epoxylite-insulated insect pin No. 4; (d) Uninsulated insect pin No. 6; (e) Uninsulated insect pin No. 4.

(1). *Insulating process*

(a) Pour epoxylite from the can into a small jar or test-tube that can be closed with an air-tight lid or stopper. Epoxylite will thicken rapidly if left uncovered. The jar should be deep enough so that the length of the needle requiring insulation can be completely immersed without touching the bottom.

(b) Before dipping the needle into the epoxylite, it should be cut to the desired length, the tip filed to a conical shape, and the shaft inspected for straightness and cleanliness. To make large lesions in the rat, a blunt tip is used. For larger animals, a conical tip is required in order to penetrate the dura and assure a vertical descent of the electrode.

(c) Clamp the base of the needle into the jaws of an alligator clip so that the needle can stand upright when the alligator clip is lying flat on a level surface. Using the clip as a handle, slowly immerse the needle into the insulating liquid. Be sure not to insulate that part of the needle which will fit into the chuck of the electrode carrier. *Slowly* withdraw the needle from the insulating liquid and then carefully lay the alligator clip on a level surface inside an oven. A dri-clave sterilizer or a home oven is satisfactory for this purpose. If several needles require insulation, it is convenient to

dip each needle and place all of them into the oven to be baked at the same time. Bake for approximately one hour at a temperature of at least 360°F.
(d) When cooled, repeat the dipping and baking process in order to apply *two coats of insulation.*
(e) Once the insulation is baked on, scrape the insulation off the tip of the electrode with a scalpel blade under low-power magnification. For small lesions, bare no more than 1·0 mm of the tip. If larger lesions are required, bare from 2·0 to 3·0 mm of the tip.
(f) Since there is gradual erosion of the electrode tip with repeated use, it is advisable to scrape the tip clean after each use. It may also be necessary to cut off the used tip and scrape off additional insulation in order to maintain a constant diameter of the electrode tip.

C. Electrode Carrier Adjustments

In most instances, electrolytic lesions are produced subcortically and, therefore, require the use of a stereotaxic instrument which contains an electrode carrier assembly. At the base of this assembly is the chuck into which the electrode is secured. The chuck is normally insulated from the remainder of the electrode carrier assembly.

Before putting the animal into the headholder, it will be necessary to adjust the electrode so that the position of the tip can be recorded with respect to stereotaxic zero. See Chapter 3 for complete details.

(a) Adjust the electrode carrier to zero on the anterior-posterior (A-P) scale. Do the same for the lateral (L) scale.
(b) Adjust the ear bars of the headholder so that there is no more than a 2·0 mm separation between the tips. Be sure that the reading on the scale of each ear bar is the same.
(c) Secure the needle electrode to the chuck. Then lower the electrode carrier assembly to the point where the electrode tip is exactly between the ear bars. The reading on the vertical scale will then constitute the zero in the horizontal (H) plane. In most stereotaxic atlases, horizontal zero is a fixed distance above the interaural line and must be taken into account to determine the stereotaxic coordinate for depth. Again, refer to Chapter 3.
(d) Advance the electrode carrier upward to its maximum position. Be sure that there will be sufficient clearance between the tip of the lesion needle and the head of the animal when placed into the headholder.

D. Surgical Instruments, Supplies and General Procedures

The surgical items and procedures required for an electrolytic lesion differ somewhat from one animal species to another. The following discussion will apply specifically to the rat.

Surgical items include: an anesthetic, hypodermic syringe and needles, electric hair-clippers, tincture of Merthiolate, scalpel handle and blades, gauze pads, an electric or hand drill, an assortment of forceps, wound clip applier, wound clips, and 3% Aureomycin ointment.

Before presenting details about the surgical procedures, a comment is worthwhile on the necessity of sterilizing the instruments and certain materials. The rat is generally resistant to infection as a result of a head wound, however, if a sterilizer is available, then it is certainly a good idea to operate under aseptic conditions. In spite of the fact that I have not used aseptic procedures in the rat for a number of years, I have not encountered a single case of an infection of the tissues *provided that a pencil is not used for marking the skull*. The precautions that I do observe are as follows: (a) wash the hands thoroughly; (b) paint the animal's shaven head with tincture of Merthiolate; (c) employ clean instruments; (d) *do not use a pencil* to mark the points on the skull where drill holes are to be located; (e) use new gauze pads, scalpel blades and wound clips, and (f) apply a generous coating of 3% Aureomycin ointment on the head wound following suturing of the skin.

(1). *Procedure for making an electrolytic lesion in the rat brain*

(a) The animal is first anesthetized, after it is deprived of water for about 24 hours prior to surgery; this minimizes the secretion of fluids which might otherwise block the respiratory passages. Of a number of different anesthetic agents used, chloral hydrate seems to be the most acceptable, as it acts quickly and yet is short-lasting; the animal usually comes out of the anesthetic state after about 60–90 min. Mix chloral hydrate crystals in water at a concentration of 50 mg/cc. For animals weighing at least 300 g, administer intraperitoneally 2·0 cc (100 mg) of chloral hydrate solution. If the animal is not anesthetized within about 5 minutes, inject an additional 1·0 cc. For smaller animals (between 150–250 g), start with about 1·5 cc and then administer an additional 0·5 cc, if needed, to anesthetize the animal fully.

(b) After the rat is anesthetized, the hair over the cranium should be shaved closely with the clippers.

(c) Check again that the needle tip has been zeroed between the ear bars of the stereotaxic instrument, and then position the head in the headholder. To facilitate positioning the ear bars in the auditory canals, use a scissors to make a 5 mm vertical slit of the skin flap which "hides" the canal.
(d) Paint the shaved portion of the head with tincture of Merthiolate.
(e) With the scalpel, make a longitudinal incision starting approximately at eye-level and proceeding caudally to the point where the neck muscles are attached to the occipital bone. Reflect the underlying tissues laterally with the handle end of the scalpel and use gauze pads generously to remove blood from the exposed surface of the skull. If bone bleeding continues, scrape the area with the scalpel blade. In some cases, forceps can be used to keep the skin flaps retracted, but this can be avoided by reflecting the muscles on either side of the occipital-parietal region.
(f) Mark the points of the skull, *using a rigid needle rather than a pencil*, where the lesion electrode will be inserted. If small holes in the skull are desired, it will be necessary to locate these points by adjusting the electrode carrier to those coordinates that will be used for the lateral (L) and frontal (AP) planes.
(g) Drill the holes in the skull, being *very careful not to puncture the dura* or penetrate the brain. This phase of the surgical procedure requires considerable skill which, of course, can only be obtained with practice. Fewer difficulties are encountered in the drilling process if a large cutting burr, 3 mm in diameter, is used rather than a small cutting burr. After drilling the holes, be sure to check that the dura has been exposed. This can be accomplished by palpating the area gently with the points of a forceps. If a thin sheet of bone remains, it can be picked out with forceps. The animal is now prepared for stereotaxic-placed lesions.
(h) Following placement of the lesion and after all bleeding has stopped, the skin must be sutured (see Chapter 4 for suturing procedure). A convenient procedure for closing the incision is to use wound clips. Appose the skin flaps with tissue forceps and clamp together with wound clips, spacing each clip no more than 5·0 mm apart.
(i) After the wound clips have been applied, spread Aureomycin ointment liberally over the wound.
(j) Remove the animal from the headholder, and place in a separate cage; food or water may be withheld until the following morning.
(k) Some surgical deaths can result from fluids blocking the respiratory passages. It is advisable to purchase a portable aspirator

(American Hospital Supply Corp.). An eye-dropper fitted into the end of the rubber suction tubing can serve as a nozzle. If the animal's breathing (e.g., wheezing sound) denotes fluid blockage during anesthesia, the fluids must be sucked out immediately. This is accomplished by grasping the tongue and lower jaw with tissue forceps and inserting the nozzle deep within the throat. Moving the nozzle in and out of the throat area will ensure retrieval of the fluids.

V. How to Control the Size of the Lesion

The size of the central necrotic zone of the electrolytic lesion will depend upon the length and diameter of the electrode tip, the intensity of current as expressed in milliamperes (mA), and the duration of the current. In general, adjusting the intensity of current is the most satisfactory way to control the size of the lesion.

Small lesions of about 1·0 mm in diameter in the rat can be obtained by using 1·0 mA applied for 5 sec through an electrode with no more than 1·0 mm of the tip exposed. Doubling the size of the lesions requires from 2·0–4·0 mA for 10 sec passed through an electrode tip of about 2·0 mm in length. If still larger lesions are required in a small animal, it is *far better to reposition the electrode* anteriorly, laterally and/or ventrally and make a second lesion rather than using a current strength above 5·0 mA. For the cat and monkey, the use of 5·0–10·0 mA for as long as 60 sec may be required to produce a central necrotic area of 2·0–3·0 mm in diameter. Multiple insertions again are advisable when larger lesions are to be investigated.

Certain brain structures seem to require more current than others for the production of lesions of equivalent size. In the rat, for example, a current of 2·0 mA applied for 10 sec will generally make a smaller lesion in the caudate nucleus or red nucleus than in the thalamus or hypothalamus. Undoubtedly, the density of heavy myelinated fibers is partially responsible for the differences in the size of the lesions.

A. Test Lesions

One way of determining the approximate size of a lesion prior to surgery is to use the albumen of a raw egg as a "test brain." Fill a small glass (1 oz) or 2·0 cc beaker (1 oz) with albumen and attach the cathodal lead to the side of the glass so that it makes contact with the albumen. Then lower the electrode into the albumen to a depth of about 5 mm. Apply the current. The reaction around the electrode tip is readily observable and its volume of involvement approximates the size of the lesion that will be induced within the brain. It is also instructive to note that the greatest reaction around the electrode tip occurs within the first few seconds after the onset of the current.

VI. One-stage vs Two-stage Lesions

When it is necessary to investigate the effects of extensive lesions to subcortical areas, there is a strong likelihood that the animal will not survive longer than a few days after the operation. Even lesions of moderate size to certain areas of the brain stem, such as the caudate nucleus, anteromedial or posterolateral hypothalamus, posterior thalamus, subcollicular area, ventromedial midbrain or inferior colliculus, may cause death for one reason or another within a day or two.

One way to increase the probability of survival is to make lesions in two or more stages with an inter-operative period of at least a week. As an example, an extensive lesion of the left inferior colliculus is done first and after one week, the same lesion is introduced in the right inferior colliculus. Although accuracy in the placement of two-stage lesions will be considerably reduced, the degree of imprecision in the placement of the second lesion can be minimized by a very simple procedure. Make identifying marks on the skull, using a sharp needle, during the first operation which indicate the anterior-posterior and lateral points of the first lesion. At the time of the second operation, reference to these marks will reduce the possibility of a gross error in the placement of the second lesion. In those instances where a medial structure is the target of a lesion, make the second lesion about 0·25–0·50 mm *more medial* than the first lesion. This will take into account the slight medial drifting of one side of the brain toward the side that was initially damaged.

VII. Ways to Increase Accuracy of Lesion Placements

Accurately placed lesions depend upon such variables as the precision and reliability of the stereotaxic instrument used, the exactness of the brain atlas used for the coordinates of the electrode needle tip, the rigidity of the electrode, as well as the care and skill of the surgeon. Certain measures can be taken which tend to decrease errors in the placement of lesions.

A. *Uniform Weight of the Subjects*

Virtually all brain atlases refer to the fact that an animal of a certain age and/or weight was used to construct the brain charts. In the case of the Massopust (1961) atlas, a 200 g rat was used, whereas monkeys weighing 2·4–4·5 kg were studied in the construction of the Snider and Lee (1961) atlas. Although it is not absolutely necessary to restrict the weight of an animal to be lesioned to that specified in a given atlas, it is important to employ animals within a comparatively small weight range. This reduces the variability in the lesion placements and will facilitate the "correction" of the coordinates for a lesion that is consistently off the mark.

B. Correct Orientation within the Headholder

It is of utmost importance that the animal be fitted into the headholder properly. The most common error occurs when the ear bars are not positioned correctly within the auditory canals. A lateral tilt in the animal's head or the dislodging of the animal from the ear bars by applying light pressure to the head reveals improper alignment. Special attention must always be given to this aspect of stereotaxic surgery before any attempt is made to proceed with the operation.

C. Use of the Superior Sagittal Sinus

In most experiments, animals with lesions that are misplaced serve as excellent "controls" *provided that the lesions are symmetrical*. The most common occurrence of asymmetry is in the lateral plane, i.e. the left lesion is more medial than the right lesion. This error may occur even though the animal may have been placed properly within the headholder. The frequency of this type of error is reduced simply by exposing the superior sagittal sinus at the plane where the electrode is to be inserted. This sinus then serves as the zero for the lateral plane. *Do not trust the longitudinal suture* of the skull as an approximation of zero since it may "wander" off mid-line by as much as 1·0 mm in the rat and 2·0–3·0 mm in the cat and monkey.

In the monkey, exposing the superior sagittal sinus without puncturing it offers no technical difficulties; although extreme care is required, a trephine can be used for this purpose. In the rat, however, drilling is necessary to expose the sinus and it requires special attention. The safest procedure is to drill through the skull on either side of the sinus and then, with a sweeping motion, drill over the sinus. Although penetration of the sinus may cause considerable bleeding for a few minutes, it can be stopped by a gelfoam sponge and pressure (see Chapter 4).

When lesioning certain midline structures, such as the interpeduncular nucleus, central tegmentum, midline thalamic nuclei, medial mammillary or medial septal nuclei, some investigators will tilt the electrode carrier laterally for the purpose of avoiding damage to the superior sagittal sinus. Such a procedure often leads to an error in both the lateral and horizontal planes. It is possible to penetrate the sinus with impunity.

5 Introducing Subcortical Lesions

D. Making Reference to Bregma and Lambda

As shown in Fig. 5, the bregma is the intersection of the coronal and longitudinal sutures, whereas lambda refers to the confluence of the transverse and longitudinal sutures. These landmarks on the skull are very useful for checking the stereotaxic coordinate reading of the frontal plane. With respect to the Massopust (1961) atlas, for example,

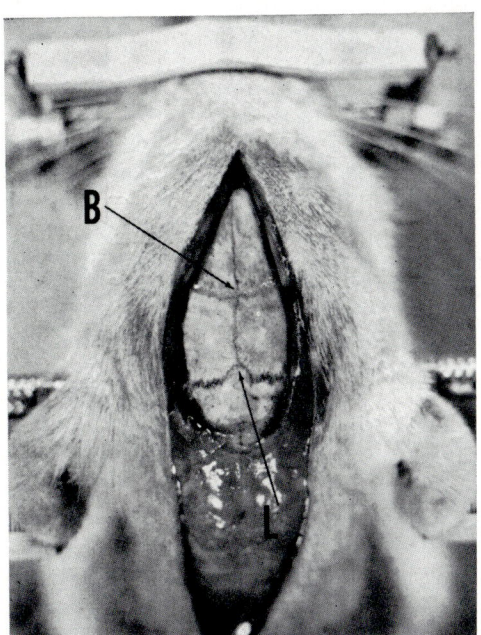

FIG. 5. Dorsal view of albino rat's skull showing location of Bregma (B) and Lambda (L)

lambda is about 0·5 mm anterior to stereotaxic zero in rats weighing 200–300 g, but becomes zero in the anterior-posterior plane in rats weighing more than 400 g. In fact, the relationship between lambda and stereotaxic zero is so consistent that this landmark can be used exclusively, in conjunction with the Massopust (1961) atlas, in the calculation of the frontal level at which the lesion is to be made.

It is not uncommon that in the monkey stereotaxically-placed lesions may err considerably in the anterior-posterior plane. I have found that bregma is approximately 6·0 mm anterior to stereotaxic zero for monkeys weighing between 2·0 and 5·0 kg. On the basis of this information, it is possible to "correct" the stereotaxically defined coordinate for the frontal plane and avoid the error that would otherwise be inevitable.

E. Know the Depth of the Structure to be Lesioned

Increased precision in the horizontal plane can be obtained by knowing the distance that the lesion electrode must travel through the brain in order to reach the target structure. With respect to the placement of subcortical lesions in the rat, the vertical accuracy can be increased by calculating how deep to insert the electrode beyond the surface of the dura.

VIII. Verification of Lesion Placements—Some Rapid Techniques

It is clear that the researcher who decides to study the brain by means of stereotaxic lesion procedures must consider the use of adequate histological controls. It must be emphasized here that it is inexcusable to rely even to the smallest degree upon the stereotaxic coordinates for the position and size of a lesion. Only by applying appropriate histological controls can the researcher obtain information about the placement and extent of a lesion.

Numerous techniques are available which serve to identify lesions of the brain (see Chapter 9). For those who will require immediate records about the location and extent of a lesion, the method described below yields permanent histological records of brain sections within a day or two after the animal has been sacrificed. These procedures are based upon the work of Guzman-Flores *et al.* (1958), who showed that the unstained brain section, when used as a negative film in a photographic enlarger, will provide an image simulating a fiber stain. The enlarged image also clearly differentiates the three zones of the lesion (see Fig. 1). A permanent record of the enlargement can be obtained either by exposing photographic paper to the image and developing a positive print, or by sketching the image with pencil and paper. Since the brain sections shown in most atlases are stained for fibers, the photographed or sketched enlargement of the unstained section affords accurate localization of the brain lesion.

The specific procedures involved in sacrificing the animal, removing and fixing the brain, and sectioning the brain block are described in Chapter 9.

A. Equipment and Supplies

In addition to a freezing microtome, the most important single item of equipment needed will be a 35 mm photographic enlarger. The one that is used in many laboratories for histological purposes is the Leitz Focomat 1c (E. Leitz, Inc.), costing approximately $250. However, Kodak and other companies offer enlargers which can be purchased for as little as $50, and a local camera shop can provide catalogues with this information. Other items needed are a black-and-white print dryer, pans for the prints, a timer for checking exposures, a darkroom light (see Fig. 6), an assortment of small camel-hair brushes, glass slides, small wide-mouth jars, photographic paper and processing liquids.

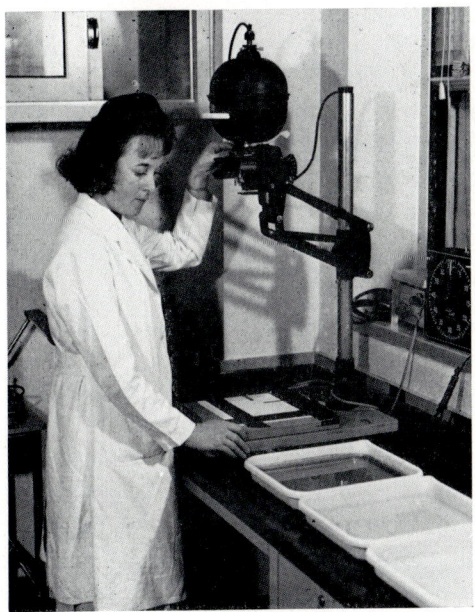

FIG. 6. Some items of equipment necessary to make photographs of unstained brain sections.

B. Obtaining the Brain Sections

Because a freezing microtome will be used, the brain must be sufficiently hardened in formalin prior to sectioning. The rat brain ordinarily is kept in 10% formalin for at least two days, but the brain of a larger animal may require as long as five days. This period of fixation can be reduced if the brain is blocked prior to immersion into the formalin. Blocking the brain involves trimming tissue which is distant from the expected locus of the lesion. For the rat, it is only necessary to block in the frontal plane, allowing at least 3·0 mm on either side of the expected locus of the lesion. For a larger brain, blocking requires the removal of tissue lateral, dorsal, and ventral to the lesion.

At this point in the procedure, it is important to emphasize that comparisons of the brain sections with those of the brain atlas can best be achieved by cutting the brain at an angle which corresponds to that illustrated in the atlas. The appropriate angle can be attained by blocking the caudal part of the brain at an orientation paralleling that illustrated in the atlas and by adjusting the angle of the microtome stage during the initial stage of the sectioning process.

In order to differentiate the left side of the brain section from the right side, a notch is made on the brain block on the right side prior to sectioning.

After the block is frozen, cut it coronally at a *uniform thickness*. Excellent prints can be obtained from sections having a thickness between 30–90 μ. Place every third section showing the lesion in a dish or jar of water, with a camel-hair brush. The remaining sections showing the lesion may be discarded or retained in a separate dish in case of damage to the original set.

C. Photographing Brain Sections

While it is not necessary to photograph the brain tissue immediately after sectioning with the microtone, it should be done within a matter of a week. Under no circumstances should the sections be transferred from water to formalin during the interval between sectioning and photography. This transfer may cause the sections to shrink and wrinkle and thus prevent clear prints from being obtained.

(a) The developing liquids should be mixed according to their instructions. Three pans will be needed, each measuring at least 6 in wide, 12 in long and 2 in deep. In addition, a water bath or sink must be available. The first pan should contain a solution of Kodak Dektol Developer; the second, Kodak acetic acid and the third Kodak fixer. Use single weight, F-3, F-4, or F-5 Kodak Kodabromide paper, cut into 5 in by 8 in sections.

(b) Pour the sections into a dark bowl filled with water. Gently place one section onto a glass slide with the use of a small camel-hair brush. Wipe off excess water. It is now ready to be used as a negative film (see Fig. 7).

(c) Set the enlarger so that the projected, focused section will be enlarged at least 10 times if brain tissue from the rat is involved and proportionately less for brain tissue of a larger animal. As in all phases of photography, two variables determine the degree of contrast of the positive print: (1) the amount of light going through the diaphragm of the enlarger; and (2) the exposure time of the projected section onto the photographic paper. It may be

necessary to attempt several different time exposures and light settings before a sharp photograph of a section is obtained.
(d) Place the exposed paper into the first pan (Dektol) until the picture becomes clear. Then dip the paper into the second pan (acetic acid) for approximately 10 sec and finally place it into the third pan (fixer) for at least 30 min. During this time interval, the lights may be turned on for the purpose of inspecting the quality of the print and placing a second section on a slide to be photographed.

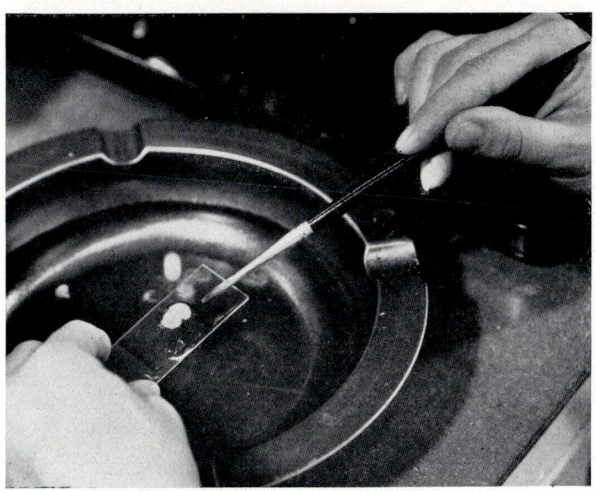

FIG. 7. Placing an unstained section of rat brain on glass slide preparatory to sketching or photographing the tissue.

(e) Put the print into the water bath for at least 30 minutes.
(f) If a print dryer is to be used, be sure to transfer the prints from the water bath to a pan containing a solution of Kodak Photo-Flo. After about five minutes, the prints are ready to be placed on the dryer.

D. Sketching Brain Sections

Although less desirable, a permanent record of the locus and extent of a lesion can be obtained by sketching the enlargement of each informative unstained section. The adequacy of this method depends heavily upon the number of anatomical details included in each sketch. If certain distinguishing features are omitted from the drawings, then reference to these records at some future date might lead to doubt concerning the exact frontal (A-P) level at which the lesion was made or the amount of damage to certain nuclei and fiber systems.

E. Use of Work Sheets in Mapping Lesions

In lesion research, it is often obligatory to make rather precise comparisons of lesions in different animals. Such comparisons are important for determining a "focal" area for a particular behavioral deficit and for assessing the relationship between the extent of damage to a given structure and the magnitude of the behavioral deficit. These can be achieved by making use of "work sheets" in conjunction with a photographic enlarger.

(a) A stencil must be made of a series of line drawings of certain sections in the brain atlas, including the boundaries of those structures relevant to the lesion analysis. Run off as many copies of these work sheets as needed.
(b) For each animal, select those unstained brain sections showing the lesions which correspond to the sections included on the work sheet.
(c) With the use of a photographic enlarger, superimpose each section upon the appropriate section of the work sheet and draw in the lesion. In this manner, lesions of different animals will be reconstructed on the same work sheet and will greatly facilitate comparisons of lesion locus and size.
(d) It is particularly important to draw only the central necrotic zone of the lesion. Since the area of central necrosis is smaller than the entire fulgurated zone, and since a significant proportion of normal functioning cells and fiber systems may exist within the surrounding gliotic field, the probability of discovering a critical focus is considerably enhanced (see Thompson *et al.*, 1967).

IX. An Evaluation of the Lesion Method

Like all neuropsychological methods used in the experimental laboratory, the lesion method has its weaknesses as well as its strengths. First of all, let us examine some of the advantages.

Undoubtedly, the greatest strength of the lesion method lies in its simplicity and straightforwardness in investigating the functional significance of specific parts of the central nervous system. Assuming that no data exist on the possible function of a given structure within the midbrain, no approach is simpler or more to the point than to destroy the structure and observe the subsequent behavior of the animal in various situations. In some instances, the changes may be so subtle that no conclusions can be drawn about the functions. However, striking modifications in behavior may also occur to the extent that several hypotheses about the functional significance of the structure can be developed.

Another advantage of the method revolves about the historical fact that it has been used with remarkable success in localizing functions within the brain. Few would argue that much of what is known about the structures involved in sensory, motor, motivational, emotional, attentional, perceptual, learning and memory functions has been acquired through the study of animals and humans with localized brain lesions. Thus, the lesion method is of inestimable value whenever the primary goal of a neuropsychological experiment involves the identification of those pathways or groups of nuclei which underlie the performance of learned or unlearned responses.

Finally, the lesion method is ideally suited to test certain neuropsychological theories. Lashley (1950), for example, employed the lesion method to test the Pavlovian theory that there are stimulus-response connections at the neocortical level concerned with learning and memory. There is little doubt that this method will continue to be used in a variety of ways to obtain data which provide the basis for the construction of new theories.

Probably the most serious weakness of the lesion method centers on the difficulty of interpreting behavioral or physiological changes following local brain damage. For example, a particular thalamic lesion may lead to a severe impairment in retention of a learned habit. At first glance, it might be assumed that the deficit is due to defective memory of the habit. But alternative interpretations must be considered, such as disturbances in emotionality, motivation, attention or sensory-motor capacities. Although it may seem to be a relatively easy task to decide which one of these is involved in the impairment in retention, it may, in fact, be quite difficult to analyse, at least in relation to delayed-response deficits following prefrontal lesions or visual discrimination deficits following inferotemporal lesions (Morgan, 1965).

A second weakness of the method is that most lesions destroy fiber bundles as well as cell bodies. If a conspicuous deficit in behavior develops postoperatively, an explanation of the results in terms of the elimination of nerve cells within the central necrotic zone may be in error. Conceivably, the deficit could arise either from the severance of a critical conduction pathway coursing through the central necrotic area or from an abnormal activity of a remote brain structure which was de-afferented by the lesion. One case in point deals with the motivational disturbances following local lesions of the hypothalamus. There is some reason to believe that certain disturbances in motivated behavior may more appropriately be attributed to the disjoining of specific pathways traversing the hypothalamic area rather than destruction of neurons located in the hypothalamus (Morgane, 1961; Stokes and Thompson, 1970).

A third weakness of the method stems from the secondary chemical effects arising from lesions of the brain. For example, there is increasing evidence that local lesions of the hypothalamus or midbrain will significantly alter the concentrations of serotonin and norepinephrine within parts of the brain far removed from the central necrotic zone (Heller et al., 1962; Lints and Harvey, 1969). These findings, of course, put further restraints on the traditional conclusion that a behavioral deficit is caused by the destruction of nerve cells.

Fourth, the lesion method suffers from the fact that the appearance of a behavioral deficit often depends upon such factors as the size of the lesion, the sensitivity of the behavioral test, the length of the recovery period, the age and prior experience of the animal, and the number of stages involved in the production of the lesion. For example, the effects of a lesion can be attenuated or even totally abolished by the production of a second lesion (King and Meyer, 1958; Lubar, 1964; Stokes and Thompson, 1970; Vanderwolf, 1964) or by the administration of drugs (Braun et al., 1966; Meyer et al., 1963).

Nevertheless, the advantages of the lesion method, in the opinion of some investigators, can outweigh the weaknesses. The usefulness of the method cannot be denied, and its value is clearly seen in the classic studies of Lashley (1950) and Sperry (1967). New developments in the appropriate use of the lesion method, such as the "double-dissociation" design suggested by Teuber (1955), are inevitable and will certainly add power to the method.

REFERENCES

Aronow, S. (1960). *J. Neurosurg.* **17**, 431–438.
Braun, J. J., Meyer, P. M. and Meyer, D. R. (1966). *J. comp. physiol. Psychol.* **61**, 79–82.
Breen, T. E. (1965). Unpublished doctoral dissertation, Louisiana State University, Baton Rouge, Louisiana, U.S.A.
Carpenter, M. B. and Whittier, J. R. (1952). *J. comp. Neurol.* **97**, 73–131.
Ferrier, D. (1886). "Functions of the Brain," Smith and Elder, London.
Fulton, J. F. and Jacobsen, C. P. (1935). *Sec. Internat. Neurol. Congr.*, London, 70–71.
Guzman-Flores, C., Alcaraz, M. and Fernandez-Guardiola, A. (1958). *Bol. Inst. Estud. med. biol., Univ. nac. Mex.* **16**, 29–31.
Heller, A., Harvey, J. A. and Moore, R. Y. (1962). *Biochem. Pharmacol.* **11**, 859–866.
Herrero, S. (1969). *Am. J. Physiol.* **217**, 403–410.
Hetherington, A. W. and Ranson, S. W. (1942). *Anat. Rec.* **78**, 149–172.

Hoebel, B. G. (1965). *Science, N.Y.* **149**, 452–453.
Horsley, V. and Clarke, R. H. (1908). *Brain* **31**, 45–124.
King, F. A. and Meyer, P. M. (1958). *Science, N.Y.* **128**, 655–656.
Lashley, K. S. (1950). *Symp. Soc. exp. Biol.* **IV**, 454–482.
Lints, C. E. and Harvey, J. A. (1969). *J. comp. physiol. Psychol.* **67**, 23–31.
Lubar, J. F. (1964). *J. comp. physiol. Psychol.* **58**, 38–46.
Massopust, L. C. (1961). *In* "Electrical Stimulation of the Brain" (D. E. Sheer, ed.), pp. 182–202. University of Texas Press, Austin, Texas, U.S.A.
McNew, B. R. and Thompson, R. (1966). *J. comp. physiol. Psychol.* **62**, 125–128.
Meyer, P. M., Horel, J. A. and Meyer, D. R. (1963). *J. comp. physiol. Psychol.* **56**, 402–405.
Morgan, C. T. (1965). "Physiological Psychology," McGraw-Hill, New York.
Morgane, P. J. (1961). *Am. J. Physiol.* **201**, 420–428.
Peters, M. and Cooper, R. M. (1969). *Psychon. Sc.* **14**, 97.
Pool, R. (1964). *Dissert. Abstr.* **24**, 4819–4820.
Pool, R. (1967). *Am. J. Physiol.* **213**, 31–35.
Reynolds, R. W. (1965). *Psychol. Rev.* **72**, 105–116.
Roussy, G. (1907). "La Couche Optique." Thesis No. 165, G. Steinheil, Paris.
Snider, R. S. and Lee, J. C. (1961). "A Stereotaxic Atlas of the Monkey Brain." University of Chicago Press, Chicago, Illinois, U.S.A.
Sperry, R. W. (1967). *In* "The Neurosciences" (G. C. Quarton, T. Melnechuk and F. O. Schmitt, eds), pp. 714–722. Rockefeller University Press, New York.
Stokes, L. D. and Thompson, R. (1970). *J. comp. physiol. Psychol.* **71**, 303–310.
Sweet, W. H., Mark, V. H. and Hamlin, H. (1960). *J. Neurosurg.* **17**, 213–225.
Teuber, H. L. (1955). *Ann. Rev, Psychol,* **6**, 267–296.
Thompson, R. (1969). *J. comp. physiol. Psychol. Monogr.* **69**, Part 2, 1–29.
Thompson, R., Lukaszewska, I., Schweigerdt, A. and McNew, J. J. (1967). *J. comp. physiol. Psychol.* **63**, 458–468.
Thompson, R. and Rich, I. (1961). *Exp. Neurol.* **4**, 436–443.
Vanderwolf, C. H. (1964). *J. comp. physiol. Psychol.* **58**, 31–37.

Appendix

Electrode Supplies

Becton, Dickinson and Company, Rutherford, New Jersey, U.S.A.
Clay-Adams Inc., 141 E. 25th Street, New York 10, N.Y., U.S.A.
Epoxylite Corporation, South El Monte, California, U.S.A.
Insl-x Products Corporation, 115 Woodworth Avenue, Yonkers, N.Y., U.S.A.
Turtox Biological Supplies, 8200 S. Hoyne Avenue, Chicago, Illinois 60620, U.S.A.

Lesion-makers

C. H. Stoelting Company, 424 N. Homan Avenue, Chicago, Illinois 60624.
Grass Instrument Company, Quincy. Massachusetts 02169.
Lehigh Valley Electronics, Fogelsville, Pennsylvania.

Surgical Instruments and Supplies

American Hospital Supplies, 2020 Ridge Avenue, Evanston, Illinois 60201, U.S.A.
Clay-Adams Inc., 141 E. 25th Street, New York 10, N.Y., U.S.A.
Turtox Biological Supplies, 8200 S. Hoyne Avenue. Chicago, Illinois 60620, U.S.A.

Photographic Equipment

E. Leitz Inc., 468 Park Avenue South, New York 16, N.Y., U.S.A.

Chapter 6

Recording Changes in Electrical Properties in the Brain: the EEG

RAY COOPER

Burden Neurological Institute, Bristol, England

I. Historical Introduction 156
II. Origins of Brain Activity 157
III. Applications of Implanted Electrodes for Encephalography . . 158
    A. Clinical 158
    B. Research 159
IV. The Electrodes 161
    A. Construction 162
    B. Operational Characteristics 171
V. The Recording 181
    A. Connection to Amplifiers 181
    B. Amplifiers and Display 181
    C. Montage 182
    D. Electrode Distribution Board 183
VI. Interpretation of the Records 185
    A. The Data 185
    B. Artefacts 191
    C. Relationship between Scalp and Depth EEG . . . 194
    D. Analysis of the EEG 194
References 201
Appendix A. Manufacturers of Electroencephalographs . . . 204
Appendix B. Wire tables 205

THERE are many methods of studying the brain. Some investigators seek detailed anatomical information about structures and structures of structures; other workers investigate biochemical systems with the underlying faith that all the events in the brain are based on these processes; still others treat the brain as a black box considering only behaviour, and the brain as a controller of this behavior. All of these methods are necessary in our search for understanding of brain function.

One method of studying brain function is by recording and analysing its electrical activity. There is little doubt at the present time that the flow of impulses and waves is the primary method of transfer of information between the brain and the peripheral sense organs, and from one part of the brain to another. A limited amount of this information is available from scalp EEG recordings, which as we shall see later, reflect the cortical activity beneath the electrodes. This two dimensional approach has made a valuable contribution to our knowledge of the brain, but the third dimension provided by the use of depth electrodes has increased the basic knowledge enormously.

If at times we seem to be swamped by information it is because, at present, we are lacking the basic natural laws of the brain equivalent to the gas laws or the periodic tables in physics and chemistry which condense information into an orderly pattern. If there are doubts that these laws exist, take heart from Francis Bacon (1561–1626): "They are ill discoverers that think there is no land when they can see nothing but sea."

I. Historical Introduction

"Feeble currents of varying direction pass through the multiplier when the electrodes are placed on two points of the external surface, or one electrode on the grey matter, and one on the surface of the skull." Thus, Caton in a report published in the *British Medical Journal* about 100 years ago described the discovery of the electroencephalogram.

Before 1875 most of electrophysiology was concerned with the study of peripheral nerves and muscle, and it was through such work that Caton and other workers were investigating the function of exposed cortical areas in animals. The experiments carried out by these early workers was of an exceptionally high standard and many frustrating months must have been spent repairing the galvanometers used for recording the cerebral activity. It is of interest that these scientists were mainly concerned with slow changes of the cerebral activity as few of them had any means of recording the higher frequency components. Caton's description of his work indicated that he had difficulties due to movement artefact and made considerable effort to fix the electrodes so that "no movement of the animal's body could affect the position of the electrodes of the brain". The electrodes used had been developed by Du Bois-Reymond and were non-polarizable. Although electrodes were not "implanted", in the modern sense, great efforts were made for the animal to be unrestrained, and light wires, suspended from a support over the animal, connected the electrodes to the galvanometer. The animal was "allowed to move about, eat and drink at its pleasure".

In the years between 1890 and 1930 there was much animal experimentation on exposed cortex of animals. In 1932 Hans Berger, the discoverer of the scalp electroencephalogram in man, recorded from the exposed human cortex, and in the following years the recordings from exposed cortex were used mainly to validate the cortical origin of scalp activity, localize epileptogenic foci near scar tissue, and study temporal lobe foci prior to temporal lobectomy for psychomotor epilepsy.

From about 1940 electrodes were implanted in animals, culminating in the early 1950s with implants in man (Delgado 1952; Delgado et al. 1952; Bickford et al., 1953). Since then implantation in animals and man has become routine procedure in many laboratories. The animal work has concentrated on the study of the function of the normal and abnormal brain, whereas the work in man has necessarily concentrated on the clinical and therapeutic uses.

For the early investigations of cerebral activity the reader is referred to Brazier (1961) and Gloor (1969).

II. Origins of Brain Activity

One of the obvious signs of electrical activity in the nervous system is the nerve action potential that transfers information from the periphery to the brain. The need for these narrow pulses (1 msec) for transmission of sensory experiences arises because of the extremely high resistance of the very thin nerve fibres along which information must flow. This high resistance attenuates the electrical signals and they have to be amplified or renewed in some way from mm to mm. Multiple amplification of graded information (amplitude of signal proportional to stimulus strength) on its passage from the periphery to the brain would distort the signal so much that all messages would be totally incoherent. Pulse rate modulation systems in which the information is carried by the *rate* of amplitude saturated pulses do not suffer distortion by multiple amplification and is the method used in the nervous system.

On entering the cortex, the axons along which the pulses are travelling terminate in neurones that are triggered by the action potential. This neuronal action potential is accomplished by a relatively slow change of membrane potential. These changes are small (0·5 mV) compared with a spike discharge or the resting membrane potential (40–80 mV), and can be both positive and negative. If the intracellular potential change is positive the cell is more likely to discharge although it may not do so. These charges are called excitatory post-synaptic potentials (EPSP). Conversely a negative potential will inhibit the cell and reduce the likelihood of discharge, inhibitory post-synaptic potentials (IPSP). Although much analysis has been performed, there has been no consistent relationship between the EEG activity as recorded by macroelectrodes and the unit spike activity recorded by intra- or extra-cellular microelectrodes.

A relationship was found between the EEG and the EPSPs by Creutzfeldt et al., 1966, who showed that in the motor cortex of anaesthetized cats there was a strong positive correlation between the surface negativity of the regular, surface negative, spindle waves and cellular depolarization composed of EPSPs. As the discharge of the cell is dependent largely on the EPSPs, a loose relationship is established between the cellular-spike activity and the EEG. It is clear from these and other studies, that the EEG is only partially related to the neuronal spike activity (Buchwald et al., 1966), and the earlier hypothesis that the EEG is the summation or envelope of populations of spike discharges is not tenable. A more consistent, but not yet fully established, relationship exists between the post-synaptic potentials, which themselves are partially related to the spike discharge, and the EEG.

The chemical events causing the changes of the membrane potentials and their transmission to neighbouring neurones are not yet known, but acetylcholine which is considered a transmitter substance could be involved (see review by Jasper, 1966).

III. Applications of Implanted Electrodes for Encephalography

A. Clinical

The clinical use of implanted electrodes can be separated into two categories; those implanted for treatment of psychiatric and other illnesses by coagulation of selected tissue, and those implanted for localization of EEG abnormality to be followed by surgery.

From the standpoint of the electrical activity, the first group is very important as it provides EEG information from patients who do not have organic lesions. Of course, the electrodes are implanted in specific regions, for example, in the frontal lobes for treatment of anxiety or the thalamus for dyskinesia, and the activity recorded cannot be compared directly with the recordings in the temporal lobe in other types of patients. However, this group has contributed a great deal to the knowledge of the general properties of human brain tissue such as the extent of volume conduction (Cooper *et al.*, 1965), the type of EEG activity in "normal" brain tissue (Sem Jacobsen, 1956, and others), the relationships between depth and scalp recordings (Abraham and Ajmone-Marsan, 1958; Cooper *et al.*, 1965; DeLucchi *et al.*, 1962), and the distribution of evoked responses (Walter, 1964; Cooper, 1968; Weinberg *et al.*, 1970). Further studies with this group include the effect of repetitive electrical stimulation (Crow *et al.*, 1961; Walter, 1962), activity evoked at distant sites from single-pulse electrical stimulation (Crow *et al.*, 1965), changes in brain volume and other variables (Moskalenko *et al.*, 1964) and local changes in oxygen availability and blood flow (Cooper *et al.*, 1966).

The similarity between the brain properties in this group and the animal studies provide a bridge between the species so that discoveries in animals can be applied to man.

In the second group of patients, the EEG is used to identify malfunctioning tissue. The need for implanted electrodes arises in some cases of temporal-lobe epilepsy, because the scalp and sphenoidal EEG do not provide the necessary information to state with certainty the position of the lesion. There are many advantages to this type of investigation: (1) the investigative procedures can be done under better conditions than in the operating room when vital decisions have to be taken under the pressure of time; (2) the recordings can be repeated many times; (3) the patient is usually fully conscious and can describe his sensations; (4) on-line or off-line computer analysis of the data can be performed in a specialized laboratory; (5) drugs can be withdrawn slowly over a period of days to reveal any abnormalities being suppressed by medication; (6) physiological stresses can be imposed on the patient such as hypoglycaemia and hyperpnoea without endangering the patient, and (7) the records are not contaminated by the effects of an anaesthetic.

Against this, must be balanced the risks of brain haemorrhage and infection during implantation and the inevitable trauma of insertion. It cannot be emphasized too strongly that the patient who is considered for this type of investigation is seriously ill and the operative procedures likely to be performed after investigation, for example lobectomy, are traumatic and irreversible. The risks of implantation are small, however, when compared with the suffering that could be caused by a misdiagnosis and maloperation.

B. Research

All of the work in which electrodes have been implanted for research investigations in humans has also been done in animals. This research falls into two main categories: (1) the study of the normal brain and (2) the study of a malfunctioning brain usually induced by chemical or electrical methods.

(1). *Normal brain function*

Some of the electrical concomitants of brain function have been studied using the EEG. They can be classified in five ways:

First are the electrical activities of specific structures identified by the anatomists (reticular formation, amygdala and hippocampus, for example) with the object of determining the function of these structures. In this work, accurate placement of electrodes is essential and the positions have to be verified histologically at the end of the experiment. The behaviour of the animal is correlated with the change of EEG activity in the structures being studied, and film or videotape records can be taken at the same time as the EEG to provide detailed descriptions of the behaviour.

Second, there are the investigations of the cerebral-data processing systems such as the visual cortex and association areas. In some ways, this work is simpler than the one just described as the amount of data collected can be much less, since most of the relevant EEG activity is contained within a few seconds following the presentation of the stimulus. The repetitive nature of some of the stimuli, flicker for example, facilitates the necessary enhancement of the signal over the background activity by computer techniques such as averaging or correlation analysis (Section VI *D*).

Third, there are the studies on the EEG correlates of learning. Much of the work in this group is a combination of the two previous groups. The presentation of a novel stimulus to an animal is accompanied by a change of behaviour (orienting reflex) and EEG in various parts of the brain. On further presentation of the same stimulus the behaviour response gradually disappears (habituation) as does the electrical-evoked response in the non-specific areas of cortex, leaving only a "localized" response in the specific areas.

Fourth, changes of level of consciousness, as seen in sleep, hibernation and hypnosis, are accompanied by marked changes of cerebral electrical activity. For example, during the rapid-eye-movement stage of sleep, when dreaming usually occurs, there is a clear desynchrony of the EEG record.

Finally, there are the EEG correlates of stresses on the cerebrovascular system. Hypoglycaemia, hypoxia, ischemia often cause generalized increases of low frequency abnormal activity in the EEG and exposure to high pressure oxygen can cause epileptic seizures. In these fourth and fifth groups the EEG changes are more generalized, and there is not such a severe limitation on the experiments by the need for accurate placement of the electrodes. It must always be remembered that, however many electrodes are implanted, much brain tissue is not being monitored.

(2). *Abnormal brain activity*

In animals, focal epileptogenic lesions can be produced by chemical means, and the establishment of these epileptic zones and the effect on the brain as a whole are matters of vital clinical concern, and intracerebral recordings are providing valuable information. Epileptiform activity can also be produced by direct electrical stimulation of cortical or midbrain electrodes. Other studies of brain activity include abnormalities induced by surgery, toxins, nutritional deficiencies and irradiation as well as the naturally occurring vascular disorders, brain infection and hydrocephalus.

One of the more recent and sophisticated animal experiments was described by Delgado *et al.* (1969) in which the EEG activity from implanted electrodes in the amygdala of an unrestrained chimpanzee was transmitted to recording equipment and subjected to computer analysis. When rhythmic (28 Hz) activity was present at certain electrodes, other electrodes in the mesencephalic reticular formation were electrically stimulated by telemetered signals from the computer. This stimulation modified the electrical activity and over a period of days changed the animal's behaviour, which persisted for weeks after the stimulation was discontinued. This experiment is described, not for its scientific value but to illustrate the type of experiment that can be done with the advanced technology already available. The social implications of such changes of animal behaviour should be made clear to all, for we are not just trying to understand and control the brain of a monkey but through these experiments we are trying to understand and therefore be in a position to control the mind of man. The ethical difficulties facing life scientists and clinicians in this field will be great—how we handle them will be a test of our civilization.

IV. THE ELECTRODES

The design of electrodes for recording the EEG depends upon the problem being investigated. The factors that will be considered are:

(A) Construction, including consideration of type of metal, insulation and size.
(B) Operational characteristics.

A. Construction

(1). Metal

Any foreign body implanted in tissue is likely to evoke a reaction. Fischer *et al.* (1957), Collias and Manuelidis (1957), Chusid *et al.* (1957), and Robinson and Johnson (1961) investigated the reaction of brain tissue to various metals. Electrodes were implanted in a group of animals that were sacrificed at various times following the implantation. Histological examination of the brain tissue in the region of the metallic electrodes showed that silver/silver chloride, copper, tungsten, tantulum and platinum evoke reactions when left in the brain for a week or more. The lesions caused by tantulum and platinum were smaller than those from tungsten and all three were relatively innocuous compared with the violent reactions to silver, chlorided silver and copper. Gold and stainless steel (18/8, 18% Chromium, 8% Nickel) were inert.

For silver and copper electrodes a lesion was clearly seen after one week of implantation. This consisted of a central region of necrotic tissue surrounded by a broader zone of swollen microglia. After two weeks, the central area was surrounded by a fibroblastic wall with leukocytic infiltration. After four weeks, the acute reaction was no longer present and the lesion was walled off by fibroblasts. The size of the lesions were 1 to 1·5 mm diameter for silver and from 1·5 to 7 mm for copper.

The conclusion from this work is that silver and copper are unsuitable materials for depth electroencephalography and that stainless steel and gold are the preferred metals from the standpoint of tissue reaction. It is unfortunate that the recording characteristics of stainless steel and gold are much inferior to silver/silver chloride (Section IV *B*). One useful characteristic of gold as compared to stainless steel is that the density of the wires on the X-ray photographs is very much greater, which facilitates localization.

The toxicity of various metals when implanted is clearly undesirable both for the destruction of brain tissue and contamination of EEG records by the abnormal electrical activity due to the inflammatory reaction. Cooper and Crow (1966) showed that silver electrodes when implanted in the brain caused high-amplitude, low-frequency activity developing over a period of days and persisting many months. Figure 1(A) shows the EEG recorded on the fourth post-operative day. This record was considered satisfactory as the slight amount of abnormal activity could have been due to the insertion trauma. However, by the 11th post-operative day, the EEG record was dominated by

6 Recording Changes in Electrical Properties

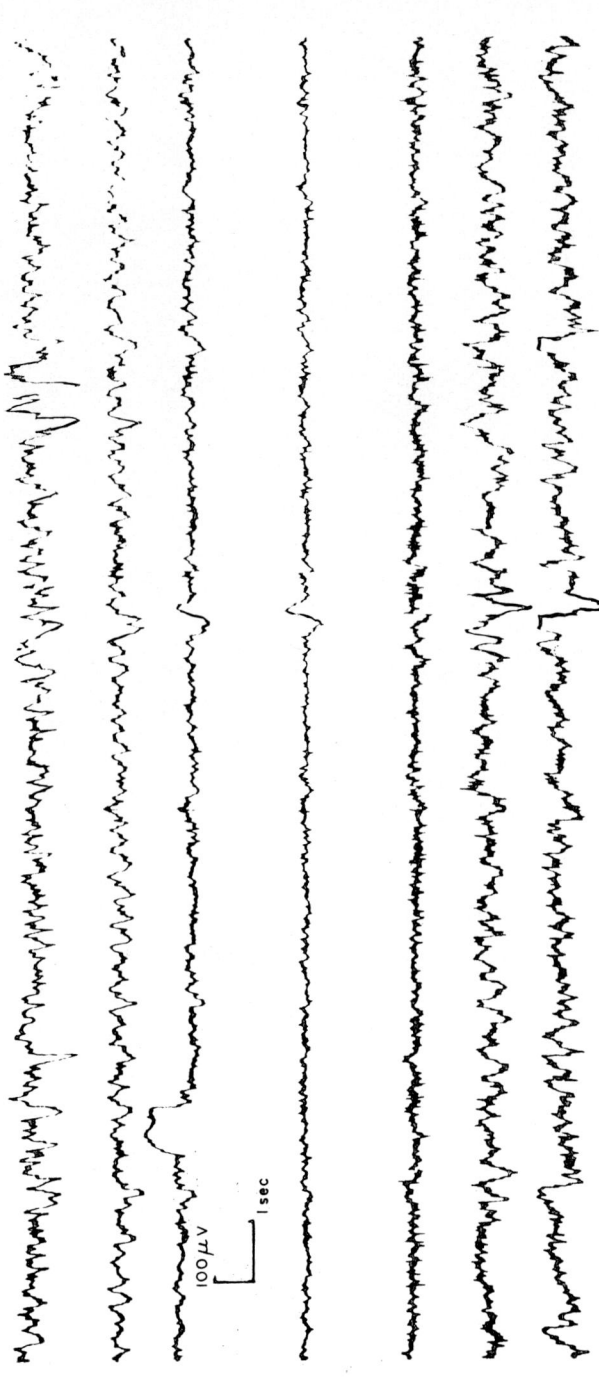

Fig. 1 (A)

Fig. 1 (A). Intracerebral EEG record on fourth day after insertion of electrodes. Channels 1–7 are recordings from 7 electrodes in left frontal lobe each referred to average of 60 other electrodes. Time constant 1·0 sec. (B) On eleventh post-operative day, high-amplitude low-frequency activity is seen at all electrodes. Note loss of low-amplitude fast activity on Channels 5, 6 and 7. Time constant 1·0 sec. (C) Three months after insertion the EEG still shows an excess of low-frequency activity but the low-amplitude fast activity has returned on Channels 5, 6 and 7. Time constant 1·0 sec. Figures 1 (A), (B) and (C) reproduced with permission from Cooper and Crow (1966).

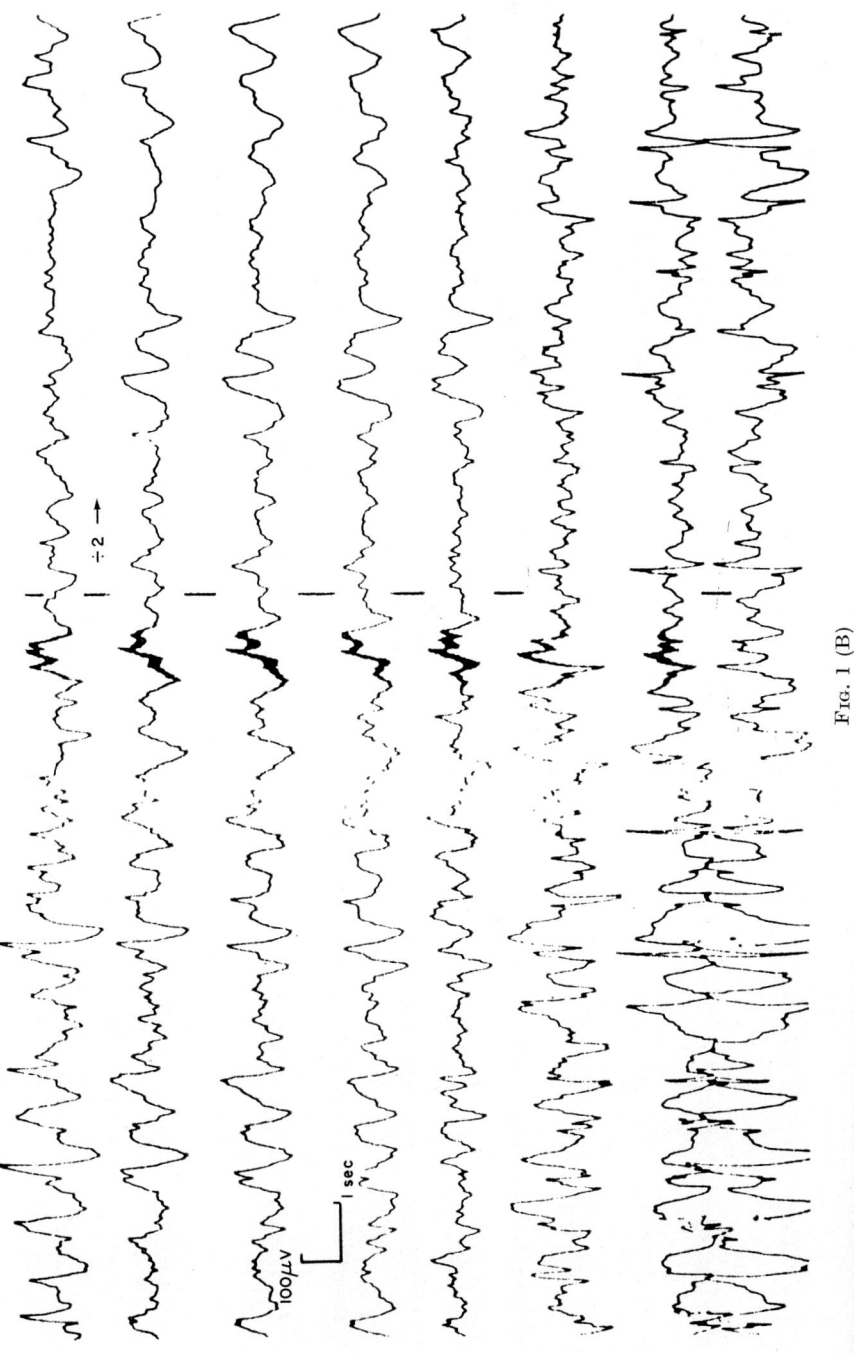

Fig. 1 (B)

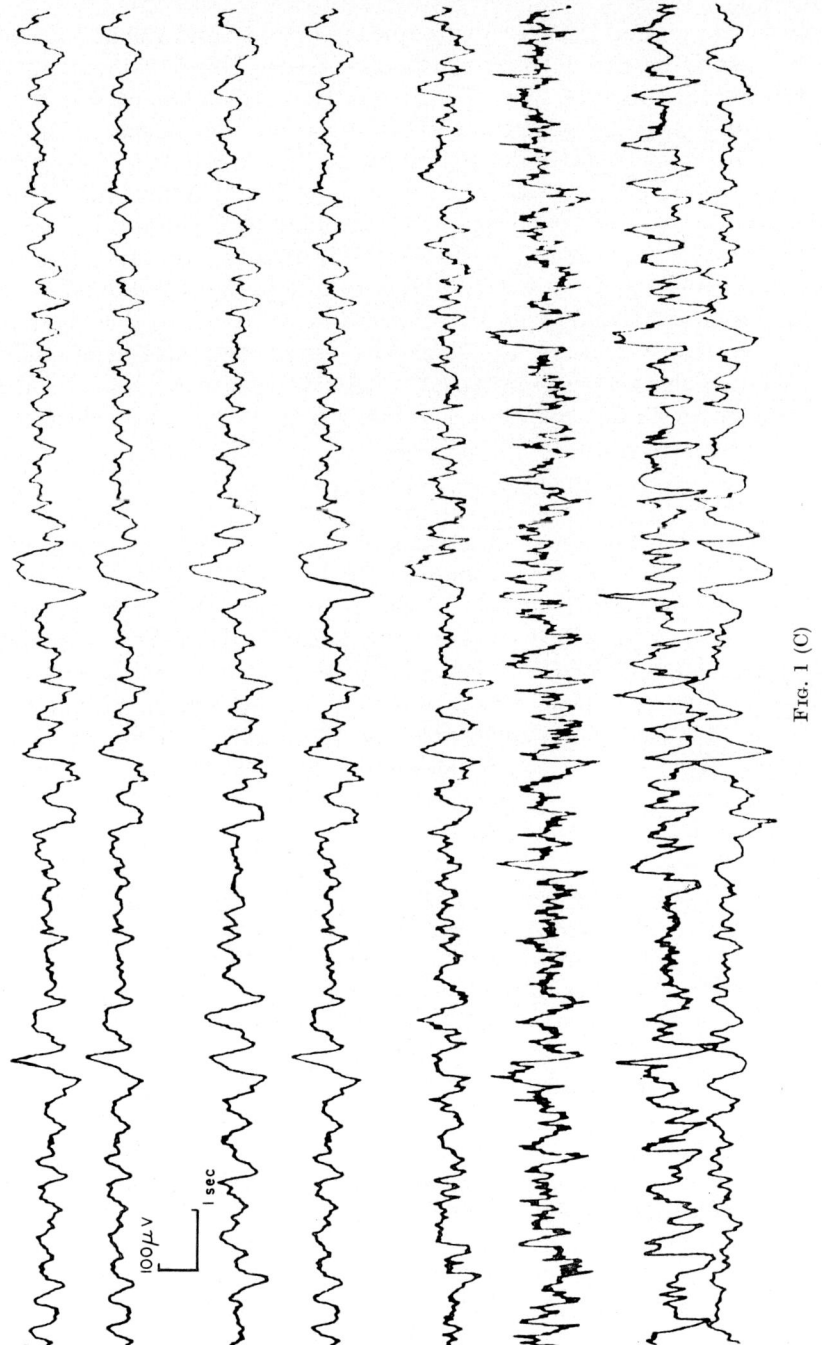

Fig. 1 (C)

widespread high-amplitude low-frequency activity and the absence of normal activity, Fig. 1(B). This activity persisted for several weeks and even after three months some abnormal activity still remained, Fig. 1(C). It is highly probable that the EEG from chronically indwelling silver (or copper) electrodes will be heavily contaminated for weeks and months following implantation. It is doubtful whether the intracerebral EEG activity recorded by these metals can ever be considered normal. Whether *cortical* electrodes made from silver, separated as they are from the brain tissue by the meninges, also cause inflammatory reaction does not appear to have been adequately investigated, although many workers use silver as cortical electrodes in animals. In view of the very abnormal EEG activity caused by silver in the depths of the brain, cortical recordings using this metal as electrode must be viewed with honest suspicion.

(2). *Insulation*

Wire used for implanted electrodes is insulated except for a short length at the tip. The insulation must be both thin and inert. Fischer et al. (1957) showed that tygon, formvar and polyethylene were inert and some forms of silicon rubber, such as the medical grade supplied by Dow Corning, are also inert. Plastic or silicone rubber insulation is rarely used for intracerebral implantation as there is a minimum thickness of insulation of about 0·005 in, 125 μ, necessary for adequate covering. This enlarges the overall diameter of the implant considerably and increases the risk of insertion trauma. Enamel when used for insulating electrode wire can be much thinner than plastic and is more commonly used. Formvar has been widely used in America and Diamel (Johnson, Matthey Metals Ltd., 81 Hatton Garden, London E.C.1) is available in Europe.

It should not be assumed that all epoxy resins are inert, as fillers might have been included for convenience of use. For example, Araldite, an epoxy resin available for household use in Great Britain, is not completely inert and should not be used for insulation of electrodes or transducers if implantation of more than a few days is required.

The enamel covering of electrode wire used for recording the EEG need not be very thick as the voltages are usually less than 1 mV. However, during winding, implantation and use, the wire is subject to considerable handling and mechanical stress that can cause cracks in the insulation. For this reason it is desirable that the insulation should be at least 0·0008 in (20 μ) thick and the baking temperature, during the coating of the wire by the manufacturer, set to give flexible frequencies. Figure 8 shows the attenuation caused by the electrode characteristics of stainless-steel or gold electrodes for two different DC amplifier input impedances 2 and 10 megohms. It will be seen that for the lower amplifier input impedance, serious attenuation of the signal can take place at frequencies less than 1 Hz. A phase shift

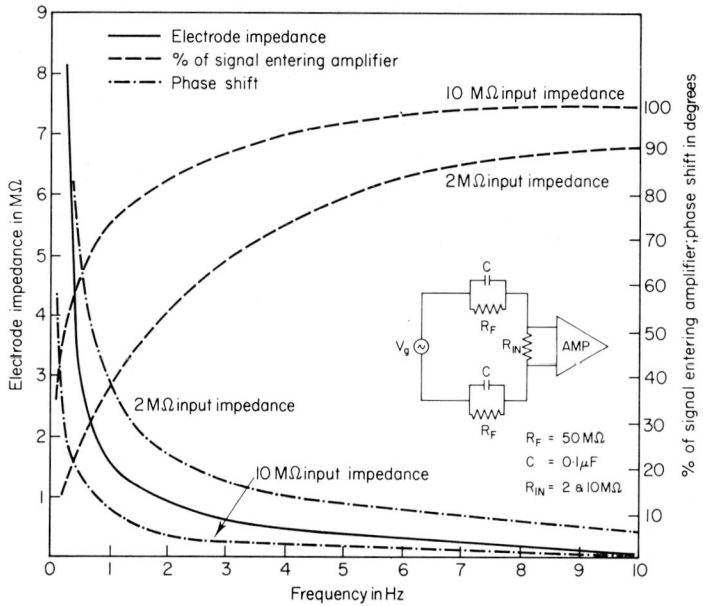

FIG. 8. Reduction of signal entering amplifiers (dashed line) by frequency response of electrodes (thick line). The phase shift due to the electrodes is shown by the dotted lines. Two amplifier input impedances 2 and 10 MΩ are considered.

also occurs at the electrode (dotted line) and could cause errors in timing very low frequency events if the records from different electrode metals are compared, or if the intracerebral recordings from polarized electrodes are compared with the scalp EEG recorded from silver/silver chloride electrodes. The combined low-frequency response of the polarized electrodes and amplifier is improved if the input impedance is high.

(6). *Measurement of "electrode resistance"*

On many EEG machines the electrode resistance is measured with a DC milliammeter in series with a 1·5 volt battery and the electrodes. Although this method is tolerable for scalp records using AC recorders, previous eye movement and saline tank were measured with an ordinary 1000 Hz, AC bridge with 150 mV peak-to-peak amplitude. The values measured were: stainless steel, capacitance 0·06 uF, resistance to 20 k Ω; gold, capacitance 0·08 uF, resistance 15 k Ω; silver/silver chloride, capacitance 0·4 uF, resistance 5 k Ω. Even though the capacitance values are not too far away from those measured in the bath and eye movement experiments, the resistance values for the polarized electrodes differ by many orders of magnitude. These gross differences are due to the different method of measurement, in particular the use of 1000 Hz as a generator. This AC bridge method does not give an indication of the effectiveness of the electrode for DC measurements and is not recommended for investigation of electrode characteristics. It is of interest to note that the measurements by Porter et al. (1964) showed progressive changes of impedance (measured at 1000 Hz) for some days after implantation, but it is not known whether these are due to changes of the electrode surface or tissue reaction to the electrode.

(5). Effect of electrode characteristics on the EEG

Like any capacitor, the impedance of a polarized electrode rises as the frequency falls. For AC recordings this rising value is of little importance as the amplifiers themselves have high pass characteristics, suppressing signals of less than about 1 Hz. However, with DC amplifiers there is no such suppression; but the very low frequency components, less than 1 Hz, and the steady levels are difficult to record because of the polarized electrodes. The problem arises because the input impedance of most EEG amplifiers is small compared with the high value of the low-frequency impedance of the electrodes. We have seen in Fig. 7(B) that at frequencies between 1 Hz and DC the electrode impedance rises to many megohms, and if this is equal or greater than the input impedance of the amplifier the signal is seriously attenuated.

A simplified diagram of the electrodes and input circuit is shown in the inset of Fig. 8. As the two electrodes, each of combined impedance R_E, are in series with the input impedance R_{IN}, the voltage entering the amplifier is given by

$$\frac{R_{IN}}{2R_E + R_{IN}} \cdot V_G$$

If $R_E = R_{IN}$ the voltage entering the amplifier is only one-third of the true voltage V_G. As many EEG machines have input impedances of a few megohms, there can be considerable attenuation of the low

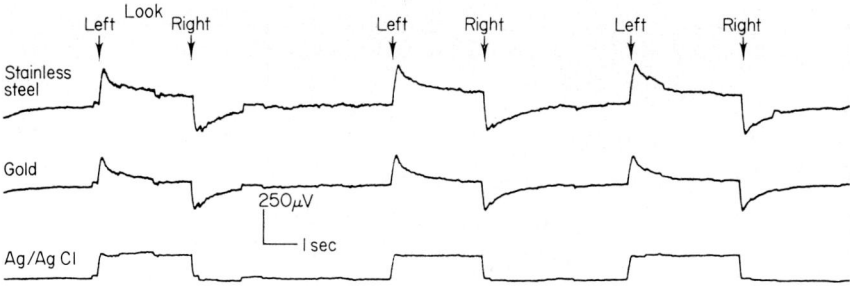

Fig. 6. Measurement of electrode characteristics using eyes as generator.

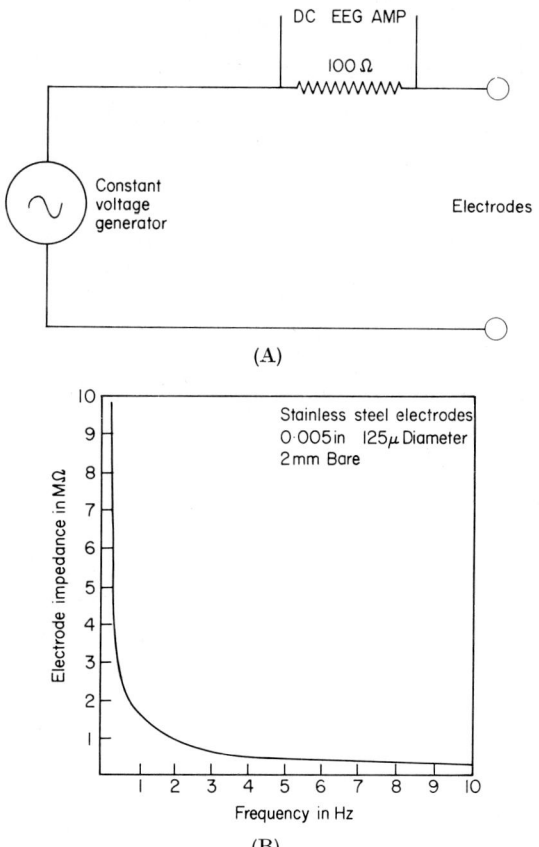

Fig. 7 (A). Circuit for measurement of frequency response curve of electrodes. (B) Frequency response curve of a pair of stainless-steel electrodes.

6 Recording Changes in Electrical Properties

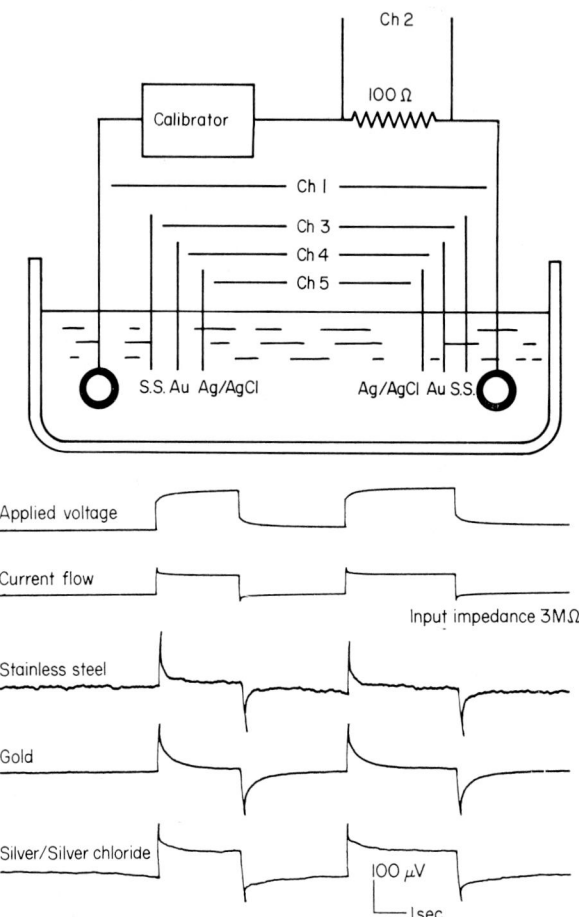

Fig. 5. Measurement of electrode characteristics showing accurate reproduction of silver/silver chloride and differentiation by stainless-steel and gold electrodes.

It was found impossible to draw the response curve of silver/silver chloride electrodes on the same scale as the impedance went from 6 k Ω at 10 Hz to 12 k Ω at 0·2 Hz.

An AC bridge can be used for measuring the electrical properties of electrodes in a bath of saline or in the brain. Porter et al. (1964) measured the impedance of specially prepared stainless-steel implanted electrodes using a 1000 Hz Wheatstone bridge with an amplitude of about 50 μ V. They found the resistive value of electrodes was about 15 k Ω and the capacitance 0·01 uF. The electrodes used for the

The low DC resistance of non-polarized electrodes would be of great value in depth electroencephalography, but as yet there are no suitable non-toxic metals. The potentials between electrodes are added or subtracted to the measurements obtained from the circuit in Fig. 4 and can cause confusing results. The battery voltage should be reversed and the mean value across R taken. If necessary the voltage applied to the electrodes can be increased by increasing the value of the battery or the 100 Ω attenuator resistance.

(ii) *Measurement of combined impedance* As just shown, the DC resistance of polarized electrodes is so large that in many situations the effective circuit becomes a series capacitor C. With the input impedance of the EEG amplifier, this capacitor acts as a time constant or high pass filter differentiating the input signals. This time constant can be demonstrated using the circuit shown in upper part of Fig. 5. A square wave calibrator similar to those in the EEG recorder is used to pass current through two large silver/silver chloride electrodes in a bath of saline. The voltage applied is recorded in channel 1 and the current in channel 2, Fig. 5. The other channels in this figure record the field potentials in the saline using different pairs of electrodes. It will be seen that the stainless-steel and gold electrodes differentiate the square pulse, whereas the silver/silver chloride electrodes record the true potential.

The effective time constant of the pair of stainless-steel electrodes shown in Fig. 5 was 0·2 sec and that of the gold 0·5 sec. As the input impedance of the amplifiers used was 3 M Ω, the capacitance of each stainless-steel electrode was 0·13 uF and each gold electrode 0·3 uF.

Another method of displaying the time-constant effect uses the eyes as a DC generator. The electrodes under investigation are placed on the skin near the outer canthus of each eye and used for recording lateral eye movements. The recordings using similar electrodes to those in the saline-tank experiment are shown in Fig. 6. Again the stainless-steel and gold electrodes differentiate the eye potentials which were recorded accurately by the silver/silver chloride electrodes.

The low-frequency characteristics of an electrode can also be expressed as a response curve in which the impedance is plotted against frequency. This can be done using the circuit shown in Fig. 7(A). The method is the same as measurement of the DC resistance except that in place of a source of steady potential a low-frequency constant-voltage oscillator is used. For these measurements a DC EEG machine can be used to measure the current through the series resistor R. Fig. 7 (B) shows how the electrode impedance of a pair of stainless-steel electrodes rises at low frequencies to values greater than 10 M Ω.

most convenient instrument to use although a DC EEG machine can also be used, with some loss of accuracy. Whether the measurements taken before sterilization and implantation indicate how the electrodes will behave after implantation is open to question. The value of the measurements before use is that they indicate the range of voltages to be expected from the electrode metals themselves. If the measurements taken *in vivo* are very much greater than those taken *in vitro* it is likely, but not certain, that the potentials are arising from the tissue.

(b) *Equivalent circuit* The values of R_F and C should be determined in similar conditions to those experienced in use, that is, when recording small voltages, mV or less. If the test voltages are too high, greater than about 1·3 volts, the electrical double layer is seriously disrupted with misleading results.

(i) *Measurement of DC resistance* (R_F) This value determines the ability of the electrode to record steady potentials in tissue. The most satisfactory method of measurement uses the circuit shown in Fig. 4.

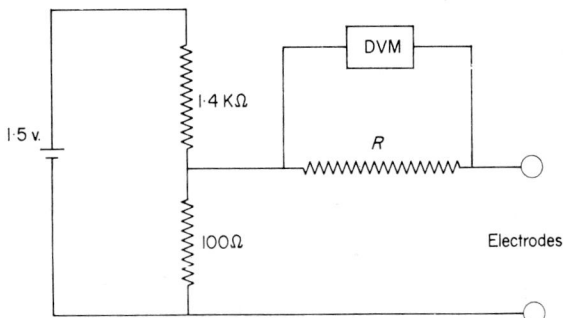

FIG. 4. Circuit for measuring DC resistance of electrodes.

A low impedence, low voltage generator is constructed from a 1·5 volt battery. This voltage (100 mV) is applied to the electrodes through a resistance R and the current flowing is calculated (by Ohms law) from the voltage across R measured with a high impedance ($>$100 M Ω) voltmeter. The current flowing through polarized electrodes is so small (nA) that the resistance R might have to be as high as 10 M Ω before an appreciable voltage is recorded. For example, using a pair of gold electrodes (2mm bared, 0·006 in, 150μ diam) it was found that the voltage across a 10 M Ω resistance (R) was about 10 mV. The electrode resistance was therefore about 100 M Ω. The resistance of a pair of stainless-steel electrodes was about 50 M Ω, whereas the resistance of a similar pair of non-polarizable silver/silver chloride electrodes was 30 k Ω.

Grahame (1952). Rs is the resistance of fluid in contact with the electrode. Its value is of the order of hundreds of ohms. C is the capacitance of the electrical double layer and is usually of the order of microfarads/sq mm of electrode surface. R_F is the equivalent resistance of the chemical change taking place when current flows. –W– is called the Warburg impedance and is equivalent to a resistance and capacitor, the values of which are proportional to frequency. At the frequency of EEG activity –W– can be ignored as can C_0, a small capacitor made up from strays.

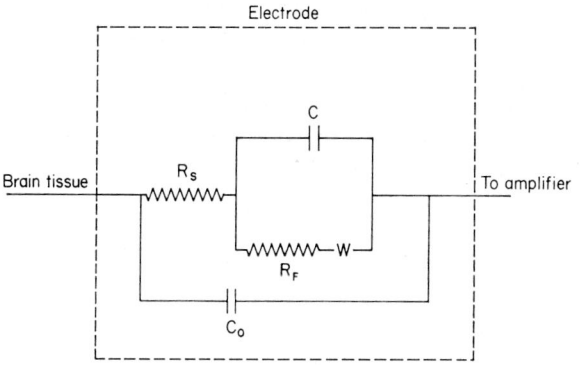

FIG. 3. Equivalent circuit diagram of an electrode in solution.

The most important elements are C shunted by R_F. In a reversible, non-polarized, electrode R_F is small and bypasses the capacitor C, thus providing a DC path for measurement of steady levels. The value of R_F of polarized electrodes is large, many megohms, and the effective equivalent circuit is the capacitor C in series with the electrode. The electrical double layer is similar to a parallel plate capacitor and the capacitance is proportional to the area of electrode surface; large electrodes have a high value of capacitance, small electrodes have a low value.

(4). *Measurement of electrode characteristics*

(a) *Electrode potential* The measurement of electrode potential of a metal is difficult, since a standard hydrogen electrode or a secondary standard silver/silver chloride electrode is required. In EEG work the electrode potential *per se* is not required but rather the differences between the various electrodes in use. These can be measured with the electrodes in a bath of saline prior to implantation. A high-impedance digital milli- or micro-voltmeter (input impedance >100 M Ω) is the respect to a hydrogen electrode (hydrogen absorbed on platinum black). The electrode potential of silver/silver chloride, for example, is -222 mV.

The potential exists whenever a metal is placed in solution and cannot be eradicated. However, it two *similar* metals are placed in the same solution, the voltage between them is the difference of the two electrode potentials and should be zero. Unfortunately, it is almost impossible to find two electrodes exactly alike because of metallic differences and surface contamination, and it is unusual to find zero voltage between a pair of electrodes. With careful preparation the differences might be less than a millivolt when tested *in vitro*.

If AC amplifiers are used for the EEG recording, this steady level does not appear in the recording but can cause an artefact such as blocking when changing montages. If one wishes to measure the steady potentials of the cerebrum, using implanted electrodes, the electrode potentials are a major difficulty.

(2). *Polarization*

Since EEG recordings are possible only if current flows from the cerebral "generators" through the electrodes to the input circuit of the amplifiers, the behaviour of electrode metals in passing small currents is of great importance.

Application of a voltage to two electrodes either from an external battery or from the internal cerebral generators disturbs the equilibrium of the electrical double layer. Whether appreciable current flows through the electrode depends upon the type of metal and those metals that pass only small currents; that is, those that have a high resistance, are said to be *polarized*. Stainless steel, gold and platinum are all polarized electrodes. Silver/silver chloride in saline, and copper in copper sulphate solution have a low resistance and considerable current can flow; this type of electrode is called *non-polarizable* or *reversible*.

A polarized electrode has a very high resistance to slowly-changing and steady voltages and has characteristics similar to a capacitor. That is, the resistance or more correctly impedance, decreases as the frequency of the exciting voltage increases.

(3). *Equivalent circuit of an electrode in a solution*

It is useful to consider the equivalent circuit of an electrode although it must be noted that there is no *a priori* reason why such an equivalent circuit can be drawn using resistors, capacitors and inductances. Figure 3, from Cooper (1962), is an equivalent circuit suggested by is dissolved in water, and application of an external electrical field will cause the charges to separate and current to flow.

Solutions, like metals, obey Ohms law and although the specific resistance is many orders higher than the metallic conductors, it is still only hundreds of ohms. Any deviation from Ohms law is usually due to the method of measurement which has to include electrodes. For reasons that will become apparent, the resistance of a solution on tissue is usually measured using alternating current which avoids some of the difficulties experienced with electrodes.

(1). *Electrode potential*

When a metal is placed in a solution a potential difference, known as the electrode potential, is established between the electrode metal and the bulk of the solution. This electrode potential is believed to be due to the separation of electrical charge into an electrical double layer at the metal/liquid interface, thus giving rise to a potential difference between metal and liquid.

The establishment of the electrical double layer is illustrated in Fig. 2. Immediately after the metal is placed in a solution, ions leave

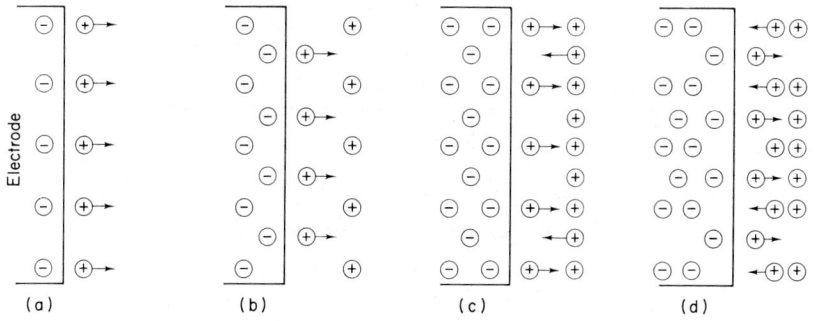

FIG. 2. Formation of electrical double layer: (a) Ionic flow into solution immediately after immersion; (b) accumulation of ions in solution; (c) ionic flow into and out of solution at different rates; (d) equilibrium when rates are equal. Note excess of positive ions in solution giving electrical double layer. Reproduced with permission from Cooper (1962).

the metal (a), but as the charge builds up in the solution (b) the ions begin to return (c). An equilibrium becomes established when the excess of charge in the solution forces more ions back to the metal and the rates of leaving and returning are equal (d). When this has occurred the electrode exhibits its electrode potential.

The value of the potential is usually quoted as measured with a considerable distance between the brain and the skull either on top of or below the dura. Electrode sheaves made from very thin stainless-steel or soft gold wire bend when pushed and have to be stiffened with additional stainless-steel wire.

Since accurate placement of an array of electrodes is often required for certain animals the wires are usually held in a thin plastic plate that is placed on a selected part of cortex. Hughes (1959) describes a method in which small stainless-steel discs are embedded in a thin polyethylene sheet (0·5 mm thickness). The discs are exposed to the cortex on one side of the sheet and are spot welded to stainless-steel lead wires on the other. To avoid the spot-welding, the enamelled lead wire can be bared at the end and wound into a flat spiral which is placed in contact with the cortex. Petsche and Rappelsberger (1970) describe arrays of 4×8 electrodes embedded in a thin plate made from dental cement which is screwed to the under-surface of the skull. If only a few cortical electrodes are needed, metallic studs can be placed in holes bored in the skull.

For recording steady or slowly-changing cortical potentials, non-polarizable electrodes are necessary and much care is required. Rowland (1961) describes a method using a silver/silver chloride electrode with a saline bridge for making contact with the cortex. These electrodes are less liable to damage than the calomel electrodes used by Gumnit and Grossman (1961) and Wurtz (1965). Details of construction of silver/silver chloride and calomel electrodes suitable for implantation are given by Wurtz (1965) and Bond and Ho (1970).

B. Operational Characteristics

The most important characteristic of an electrode is its ability to transform the electric field and current circulating in the tissue into voltages available for amplification. The atomic processes involved in the transfer of energy from ionic conduction in solution to electron conduction in the wires to the amplifier are beyond the scope of this chapter. The following description is presented so that the reader can obtain some idea of the basic mechanisms and the problems when electrodes are used in biological measurements.

Electrical current in solutions is carried by electrically charged particles called ions. A cation is a positively charged particle that is attracted to a cathode; the negative ion, attracted to an anode is called an anion. When sodium chloride becomes ionized, an atom of sodium loses an electron (negative charge) and becomes a cation (Na^+); the chlorine atom acquires an electron and becomes an anion (Cl^-). Both are free to move independently when the sodium chloride example). Some household paint-removers can be used. The stripper should be viscous so that it can be painted only on to the end of the electrode, and care must be taken to prevent the stripper from getting onto other portions of the wire. After the intracerebral end of the sheaf has been prepared, the outer ends of the wires are coded for postoperative identification. The easiest method is to cut them to different lengths, the longest wire on the outside corresponding to the tip electrode inside and so on. These outer ends are then stripped so that they can be soldered to the socket assembly after implantation.

The electrode wires are usually brought through the scalp and soldered to thicker flexible wires connected to a multiway socket. The soldering of many fine wires is a tedious job especially with stainless steel which does not solder easily. Gold wire presents a different problem in that, at normal soldering temperatures, the gold alloys with the solder and disappears. Low-melting-point solder (150°C) and a cool soldering iron should be used for gold wire. The soldering can be done immediately after implantation or even some days later.

After each solder joint is made, it should be tested for continuity by checking its impedance, against several others in common with an AC impedance meter as described in Section IV B6. After each sheaf is connected, the joints can be insulated from each other by sandwiching them between two pieces of sticky polythene tape; and then the sheaves are bundled together by more tape.

An alternative method of construction and insertion, in which the electrodes are connected to the sockets before implantation and recording can be started immediately after implantation, has been described by Chatrian et al. (1959b).

For investigations specifically with animals, many methods of electrode implantation have been described (see Klemm, 1969). Most use sockets fitted to the skull of the animal so that there are no loose wires, and during the recordings, the socket is mated with a plug leading to the EEG amplifiers. Although most electrodes are not moveable in the brain after implantation, Long and Tapp (1965) describe a method in which implanted electrodes can be moved over a 5 mm range. The electrode wires are usually soldered to the sockets and particular care must be taken to preserve correct identification of electrodes.

(6). *Construction of cortical electrodes*

Sheaves of electrodes such as those just described for intracerebral studies can also be used for cortical recordings. If the electrodes have to be inserted through a small burr hole, the sheaves have to be pushed being 1 mm bared, and the separation between electrodes about 1 or 2 mm.

Consideration of separation of electrodes raises fundamental problems concerning the minimum size of a cerebral region which generates its own characteristic activity. As will be seen in more detail in Section VI *A* different EEG activities can be observed from electrodes only 1 or 2 mm apart. This means that to provide complete information about the electrical activity of a particular region many electrodes, each about 1 mm long and separated by 2 mm, would have to be implanted. Under these conditions a number of electrode sheaves would have to be implanted close together. The number of electrodes soon becomes impossibly large and the recording apparatus becomes the limiting factor in the collection and analysis of the information. In practice, electrodes are usually bared for 1 or 2 mm at the tip and wound into sheaves with 5 to 10 mm between adjacent electrodes.

It should be noted that even if 100 electrodes are implanted, the EEG recorded represents but a small sample of the total electrical activity of the brain. For example, in man the recordings from 100 electrodes each 2 mm long represents only about 0·01 % of the total electrical activity of the brain. Of course, if a specific structure, such as the hippocampus, was being investigated, a relatively small number of strategically placed electrodes gives adequate coverage.

(5). *Construction of intracerebral sheaves*

For intracerebral use, the electrodes are inserted into the brain either through an introducer or pushed into place if they are stiff enough. For these leads, several wires are twisted together into a sheaf and the wires cut off at various distances from the end of the sheaf giving a number of electrodes along the length of the sheaf. On the cortex, especially in animal work, a matrix of electrodes is often required, and the electrodes are held in position on a plastic plate.

For intracerebral use, several lengths of wire are wound together on a winding machine (see, for example, Chatrian *et al.*, 1959a). Seven wires wound together (six wires round a central core) lie tightly together and can be made into a very smooth sheaf which eases the implantation through a cannula. The overall thickness is three times the diameter of an individual wire.

The enamel on the ends of the wires, after being cut to the appropriate length, is removed either by scraping with a knife or by using a chemical solvent, such as that available for stripping enamel (Strip-X by GC Electronics Co., Los Angeles 18, California, for especially when three or more strands are wound together, but there are practical difficulties in bending this diameter wire to conform with the shape of the skull. This difficulty is not experienced with gold wire and a sheaf of seven strands of 0·006 in, 150 μ, diameter wire is easily bent to fit the contours of the skull. In practice, therefore, the diameter of gold wire used for intracerebral electrodes is about 0·006 in, 150 μ and stainless-steel wire 0·004 in, 100 μ.

For cortical electrodes the diameter of the wire is not limited by the trauma of insertion, as the electrodes do not penetrate brain tissue and larger diameters are possible. However, as mentioned above, thick electrodes can be very stiff and often the same wire is used for cortical as well as for depth electrodes.

An alternative method for depth recordings in man using a rigid probe has been described by Ray (1966). Eighteen electrodes of platinized platinum wire (0·003 in, 75 μ, diam.) are supported on a stainless-steel tube fixed into the skull. The overall diameter is 0·030 in, 0·75 mm. It is claimed that this technique has advantages over the flexible wire method although it is considerably more expensive. As there can be considerable natural movement of the brain within the skull, a rigid intracerebral probe fixed to the bone might cause some trauma or movement artefact in the EEG.

During anodic, direct current coagulation stainless-steel electrodes erode and the metal goes into the tissue (Loucks et al., 1959). Thin electrodes erode more quickly and the electrolytic lesion might not be large enough before the electrode has dissolved. Electrodes of 0·004 in, 100 μ will pass only about 10 mA for 30 sec before dissolving, whereas similar wire of diameter 0·008 in, 200 μ, will pass this current for more than three minutes. This erosion does not occur with 0·007 in, 150 μ gold electrodes which pass 20 mA with ease.

(4). *Length of electrode tip and separation*

The length of metal exposed is determined by the clinical and experimental requirement. An electrode in tissue will pick up the electrical activity at all points along the exposed surface. Thus an electrode with 4 mm of tip bared will show the average of the EEG activity from a column of tissue slightly longer than the 4 mm and cannot discriminate where the activity arises in that column. If such an electrode was lying through cortex and the electrical activity of this cortex was such that the deep layers became positive as the surface was negative, it is possible that no EEG would be recorded. Greater accuracy can only be achieved by using several electrodes each tip insulation (if the temperature is high a very hard coating is obtained but will crack easily on bending). This thickness of enamel, if properly applied, is adequate for all voltages used in intracerebral work including stimulation, DC and AC coagulation.

One minor but annoying feature of some types of enamel insulation on *gold* wire is that the colour of the enamel is almost identical to that of the metal and it is very difficult to see how much of the insulation has been stripped from the tip during preparation of the electrode. As the colour of the enamel is a function of the baking temperature, the manufacturer can arrange to make the colour darker than the metal, but enamel tints should not be used because of possible toxic reactions.

One of the problems of coating thin wire is that the enamel does not wet the metal easily and small areas of wire can be left uncoated. Repeated applications of enamel reduce the number of pinholes but even after 6 or 8 coats they can still occur. When the wire is to be immersed in electrolyte, as in the brain, a pinhole in the insulation will act as a conductor and EEG activity from the site of the pinhole will contaminate the EEG from the electrode tip.

The electrode wire is tested before being formed into electrodes by measuring the insulation resistance of the wire as it is drawn through a conducting liquid. One lead of an insulation test-meter is connected to the end of the electrode wire and the other lead to a metal plate (a scalp electrode is satisfactory) in a bath of saline. The insulation resistance is monitored continuously as the wire is drawn through the saline. The resistance of intact enamel when measured using a few volts will be very high (greater than 500 M Ω) but will fall to less than a megohm if there is a pinhole in the length of wire currently immersed in the liquid.

(3). *Diameter of wire*

To reduce the trauma of implantation the diameter of the wire should be as small as possible. The minimum diameter is set by mechanical strength, ease of handling and operational characteristics. The tensile strength of stainless steel is very much greater than that of gold and thinner electrodes can be made with this metal. Gold wire less than 0·004 in, 100 μ, diameter breaks easily and is not rigid even when several strands are wound together. Stainless steel less than 0·002 in, 50 μ, diameter is difficult to handle and this wire too is not rigid when wound together. The relationship between size of electrode and recording characteristics will be discussed in Section IV B. Stainless-steel wire diameter greater than 0·007 in, 175 μ, is very stiff it is unsuitable for implanted electrodes for two reasons. First, 1·5 volts is sufficient to disrupt the electrical double layer and a false reading of electrode impedance can be obtained. Second, the tissue can be affected by small currents even though they may be flowing only for a short time while the measurement is taken. In our laboratory, the mental state of a psychiatric patient has been changed temporarily by direct current of less than 500 μA passed through electrodes in the frontal lobes.

Intracerebral electrode resistance should be measured using a low-amplitude (less than 200 mV peak to peak) sin wave generator, with a frequency within the EEG band (preferable at the upper end at about 40 Hz).

V. THE RECORDING

A. Connection to Amplifiers

In an experiment with an unrestrained animal the lead from the plug and socket on the head to the amplifier is liable to considerable movement. This movement causes static charges to build up on the insulation and artefact is seen in the EEG recording. The basic remedy is to coat the leads so that a charge does not build up. One method is to use "Mini-Noise" cable (Microdot, Inc., South Pasadena, California) but a multilead cable can be stiff and bulky.

An alternative method described by Kamp *et al.* (1965) is used for connecting the head socket to multichannel telemetry equipment on the dog's back. This is so effective that the animal can jump about without any movement artefact. Clinical investigations in man are usually performed with the patient relatively immobile in a chair or bed and movement artefact is not much of a problem.

B. Amplifiers and Display

Any high-grade differential amplifier can be used for intracerebral EEG investigations. A multichannel recorder is essential for the number of electrodes implanted. The frequency and amplitude of the intracerebral activity is similar to the scalp EEG and commercially available electroencephalographs are suitable for these recordings. Pen recorders are the most convenient method of display although for evoked responses, an oscilloscope is better since the sweep can be synchronized to the stimulus.

Most intracerebral recording is done using polarized electrodes, but it is useful to have high-gain DC amplifiers available for recording. The input impedance of the amplifier should be as high as possible to lessen the droop of the response at very low frequencies described in

Section IV B. Five megohms should be considered the minimum and 50 megohms is desirable.

(C). *Montage*

All methods of recording use the same basic information from the electrodes; however, some are less confusing than others. There are three types of recordings: (1) common reference, (2) bipolar, and (3) average reference.

(1). *Common reference*

In this method, sometimes called unipolar or monopolar, the activity at each electrode is referred to another, usually distant, inactive electrode. If the inactive electrode is reliable, the common reference recording is perfectly satisfactory, and each channel will show the activity at each electrode. A difficulty may arise if the common reference electrode is active. In this situation, the activity at the reference electrode appears in all channels and can cause misinterpretation.

(2). *Bipolar*

In this method, two electrodes assumed to be active are connected to each amplifier. On the scalp, potentials change only slowly from electrode to adjacent electrode and the phase reversals observed with a bipolar chain can provide accurate location of a focus of activity [see, for example, Hill and Parr (1963), Cooper et al. (1969)]. However, in the depths of the brain and often on the cortex the EEG activity from adjacent electrodes is very different even when the electrodes are only a few mm apart. This means that a channel connected to two electrodes showing independent activity will show the algebraic difference of these two activities, and it is impossible to state which activity is occurring at which electrode. A bipolar chain, within a sheaf of electrodes, for example, can help to remove some of this ambiguity, but there is little advantage in using bipolar recording for depth electroencephalography. A further disadvantage is that timing errors can occur if the bipolar method is used for similar but time-displaced signals (Cooper 1959).

(3). *Average reference*

This method is based on the premise that the summation of a large number of independent generators is about zero for most of the time. On the scalp there is rarely a sufficient number of independent sources for the method to be of much value, but deep in the brain, the generators are often independent and many electrodes are usually available. Provided that many electrodes are not concentrated in a small area, the average reference method of recording is probably the most useful.

The average reference point is generated by connecting a high resistance from each electrode to a common point, Fig. 9. The value of the resistor has to be high and is determined by the number of electrodes available. If the impedance of each electrode is about 30 k Ω (at say 40 Hz) then the combined impedance of all the electrodes connected through the resistors to the average reference point should

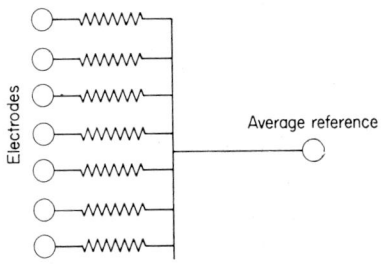

FIG. 9. Generation of average reference.

be approximately equal to this value. This preserves an adequate amplifier discrimination against inphase artefact. Thus, if 60 electrodes are available, then they should be connected through 200 k Ω resistors (the combined parallel value of 60 resistors, each of 200 k Ω, is about 30 k Ω). If a smaller number of electrodes is used, smaller values could be employed. It must be remembered that whatever the value of the average reference resistors, they are across the amplifier inputs and reduce the effective input impedance of each amplifier; thus, the attenuation of the low frequencies by the characteristics of polarized electrodes is increased.

This problem can be solved by making it possible to switch out the average reference resistors of a particular electrode when recording from that electrode. This makes little difference to the average reference point and preserves the high input impedance of that amplifier. A selector board with this facility will be described in the next section.

If there is coherent activity at many electrodes, the average reference system can be misleading, as the average of the activities will contain the coherent activity and will be subtracted from all channels. It might be added that if this were the case, the two other methods, common reference and bipolar, would probably be equally unsuitable.

D. *Electrode Distribution Board*

A distribution system to connect any of the input terminals of 16 channels (32 inputs) to any of 60 electrodes can be quite complex. A simple method which avoids the use of switches has been described by Cooper and Warren (1959). In this system each electrode is terminated on a board by a 4 mm socket. The input terminals of the amplifiers are also terminated by 4 mm sockets, and there are two sockets in parallel for each input terminal, Fig. 10.

The electrode montage is set up by using leads with 4 mm plugs on each end. One end is placed in the socket of the desired electrode and the other in one side (black or white) of the amplifier. The opposite side of the amplifier is connected with another lead to a second electrode if common reference or bipolar recording is required, or to the average reference point if this method is being used.

Whatever montage is being used, there will always be a spare socket available for leads on the amplifier input terminals. Each average reference resistor is fitted with a switch so that any particular electrode can be disconnected from the average reference point. The connecting leads are of many colours to facilitate checking of the electrode pattern. A board similar to the one shown in Fig. 10 has been used with complete success for many years in our laboratory.

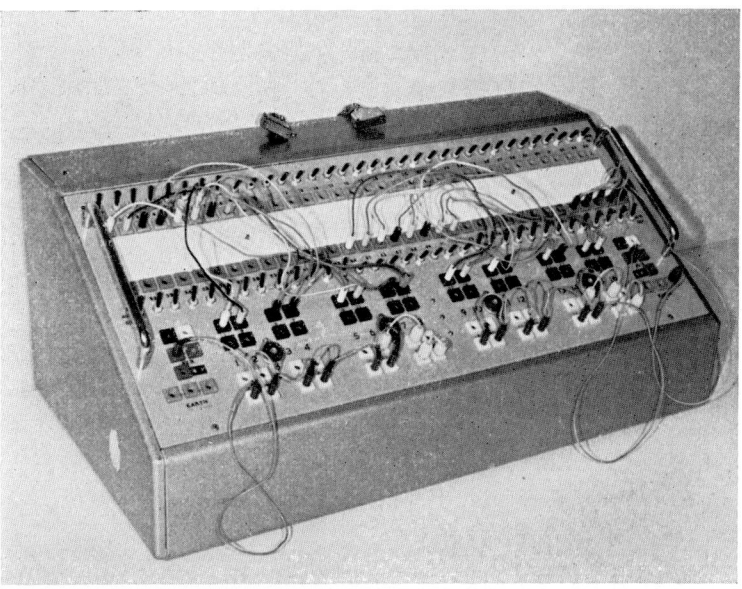

FIG. 10. Photograph of electrode selector board for selecting 16 channels (lower half) from 68 electrodes (upper). An average reference is generated from all electrodes, but those being used for recording can be switched out of system. The two 34-way plugs and leads to the head are shown on top.

VI. Interpretation of the Records

A. The Data

Recordings from intracerebral electrodes are very similar in amplitude and bandwidth to the scalp EEG. That is, peak-to-peak amplitude of the activity is about 50–100 μV, although voltages up to 1 mV can be recorded in certain conditions; the bandwidth is DC to 100 Hz, although higher frequencies and spike activity have been reported. Figure 11 shows an EEG record obtained from a psychiatric patient. The electrodes, which were in the frontal lobes, were referred to the average of 68 electrodes in the frontal and cingulate gyri regions. Each gold electrode was 4 mm long, 0·006 in, 150 μ diameter and the tips of electrodes in a sheaf were separated by 8 mm. The activities from adjacent electrodes, for example, on channels 7 and 8, are considerably different. This rapid changeover a distance of a few mms, is a characteristic of the recordings from intracerebral electrodes. In contrast, the recordings from scalp electrodes separated by about 20 mm are always very similar. The cause of this and the relationship between the scalp and intracerebral EEG will be discussed later.

The differences in activity from closely spaced intracerebral electrodes presents at once the difficulties and fascination of these recordings (the difficulties of handling such a large quantity of data and the fascination of such a variety of signals from a living brain). The differences arise because the spread of electrical activity by volume conduction, that is by the establishment of electrical lines of force, in the intact brain is extremely small, probably less than 1 mm in living tissue. Thus, electrodes separated by more than 1 or 2 mm will be displaying their own local activity and will not pick up the field from the tissue more than 1 mm away. This means that when similar activity occurs at electrodes over 1–4 mm apart, the spread is due to physiological conduction along fibres.

The extent of the interacting intracerebral regions can be determined by measuring the similarities of the EEG, as for example using cross correlation techniques, described later, at electrodes separated by varying distances. Fig. 12 shows a plot of cross-correlation coefficient against distance for electrodes in the frontal lobe in man. It will be seen that the cross correlation coefficient (a value of 1 indicates identical waveforms, 0 means complete dissimilarity) tends to fall with distance, i.e. the EEG becomes less coherent at longer distances. The more surprising feature of Fig. 12 is the enormous scatter of the coefficient even when the electrodes are close together. This means that the activities at such electrodes can be similar or dissimilar. If

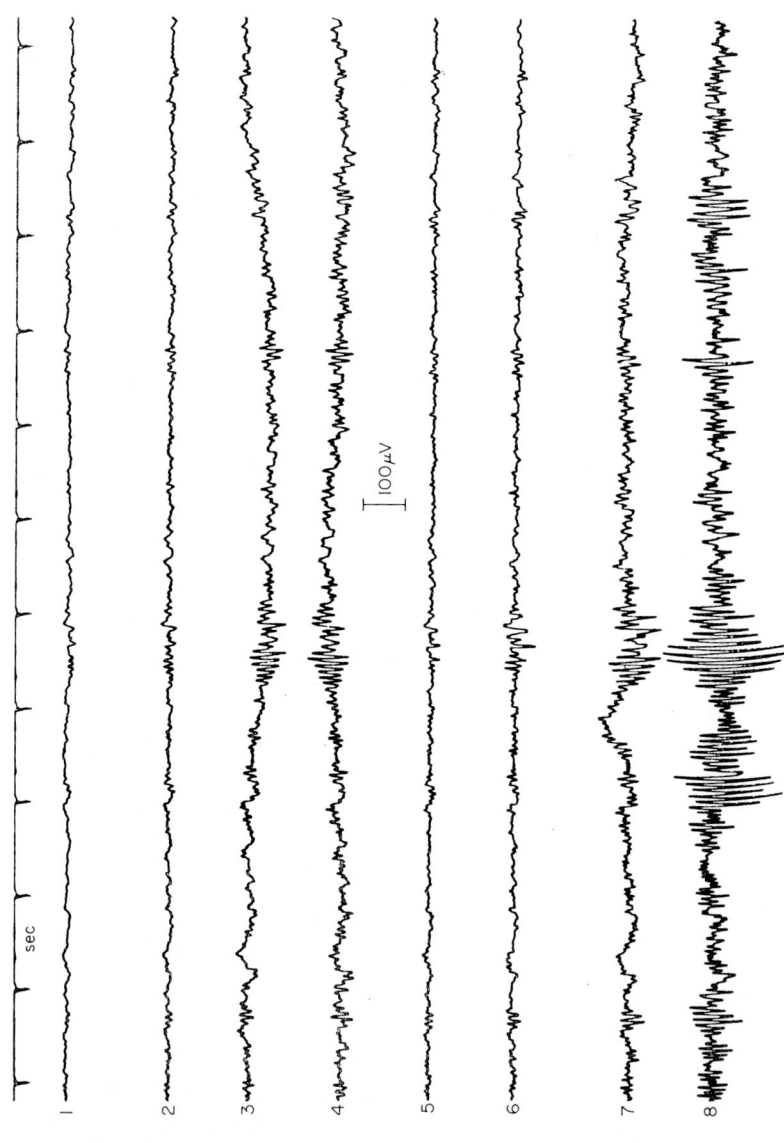

FIG. 11. EEG from psychiatric patient. Channels 1 through 4 are from sheaf of gold electrodes terminating in orbital cortex. Channels 5 through 8 are from electrode sheaf 8 mm lateral from first. Electrodes in each sheaf are 4 mm long, separated by 8 mm.

the spread of activity was due to the decline of an electrical field, the scatter would be much less and follow a regular curve.

In depth encephalography, the significance of the electrical activity is assessed in the same way as similar activity when observed on the scalp. As already described in Section II, the origins of the EEG have not yet been completely determined. More important, there is at

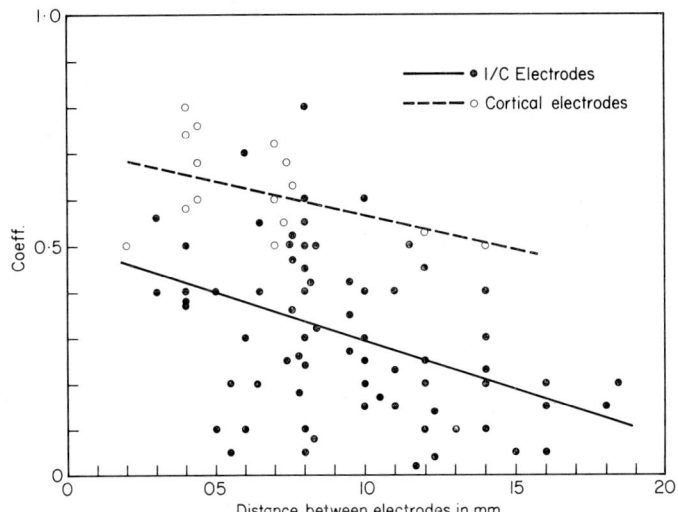

FIG. 12. Cross correlation of EEG activities from electrodes in 12 psychiatric patients. The thick line is the least squares fit of intra-cerebral electrodes. Dashed line best fit of subdural activities.

present no adequate theory about the *function* of the various types of EEG activity. All that has been established is that certain types of EEG activity are usually associated with certain patterns of pathology or behaviour, for example, low frequency activity with a cerebral tumour or spike and wave with *petit mal* epilepsy.

Broadly speaking, the interpretation of the depth recordings are similar to those on the scalp. For example, if in the investigation of temporal-lobe epilepsy an electrode or group of electrodes showed high amplitude low frequency activity or wave and spike associated with psychomotor fits in one temporal lobe and not the other, then this would be considered good evidence of malfunction in one lobe, as shown in Fig. 13. However if, as is sometimes the case, there are EEG abnormalities in both temporal lobes, then there is no clear indication which lobe is the cause of the psychomotor epilepsy.

The same type of activity as shown in Fig. 13 would be considered

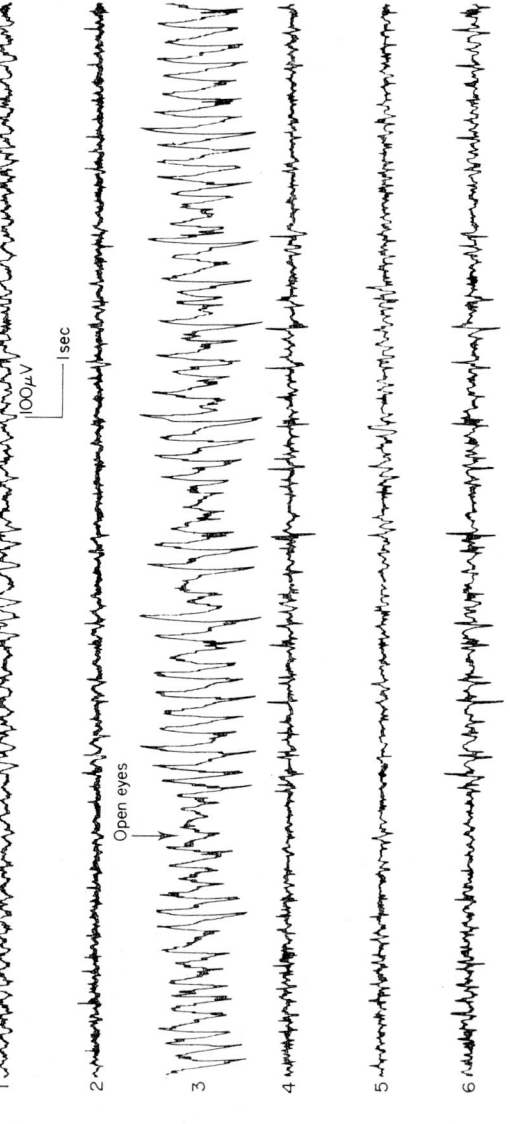

Fig. 13. Delta activity (channel 3) associated with organic lesion in patient with temporal lobe epilepsy. Channels 2 and 4 from electrodes 10 mm above and below that in channel 3.

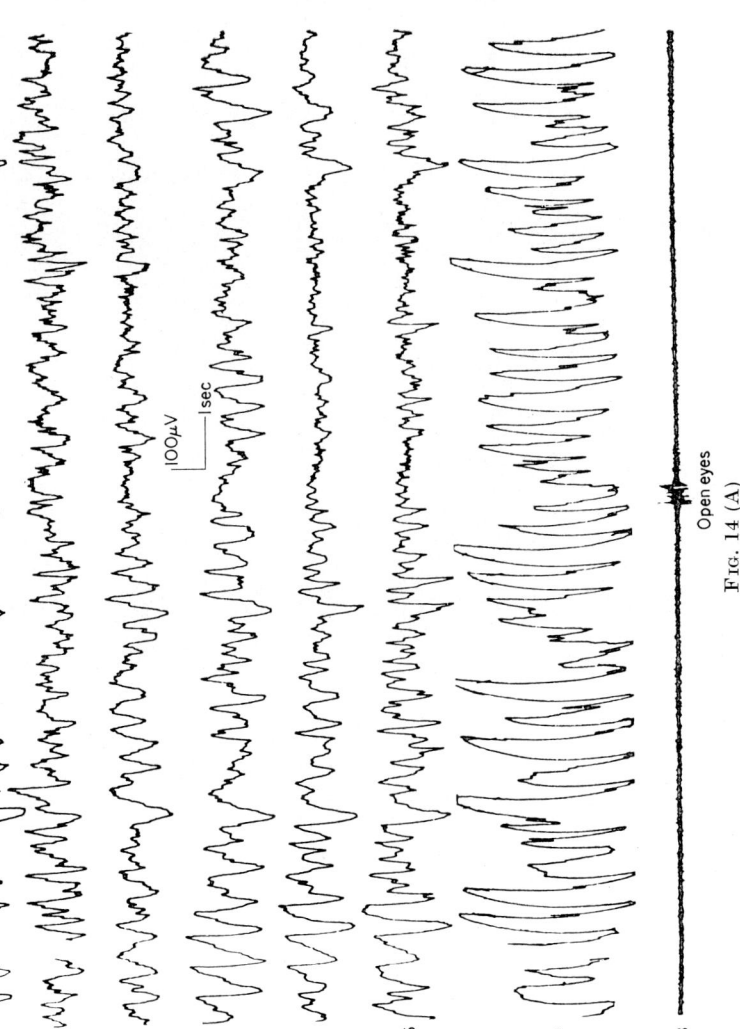

Fig. 14 (A). Widespread delta activity on channels 1 through 6 partly blocked by opening eyes. Channel 7 not affected. (B) Delta activity on channels 1 through 6 blocked by mental arithmetic and that on channel 7 reduced.

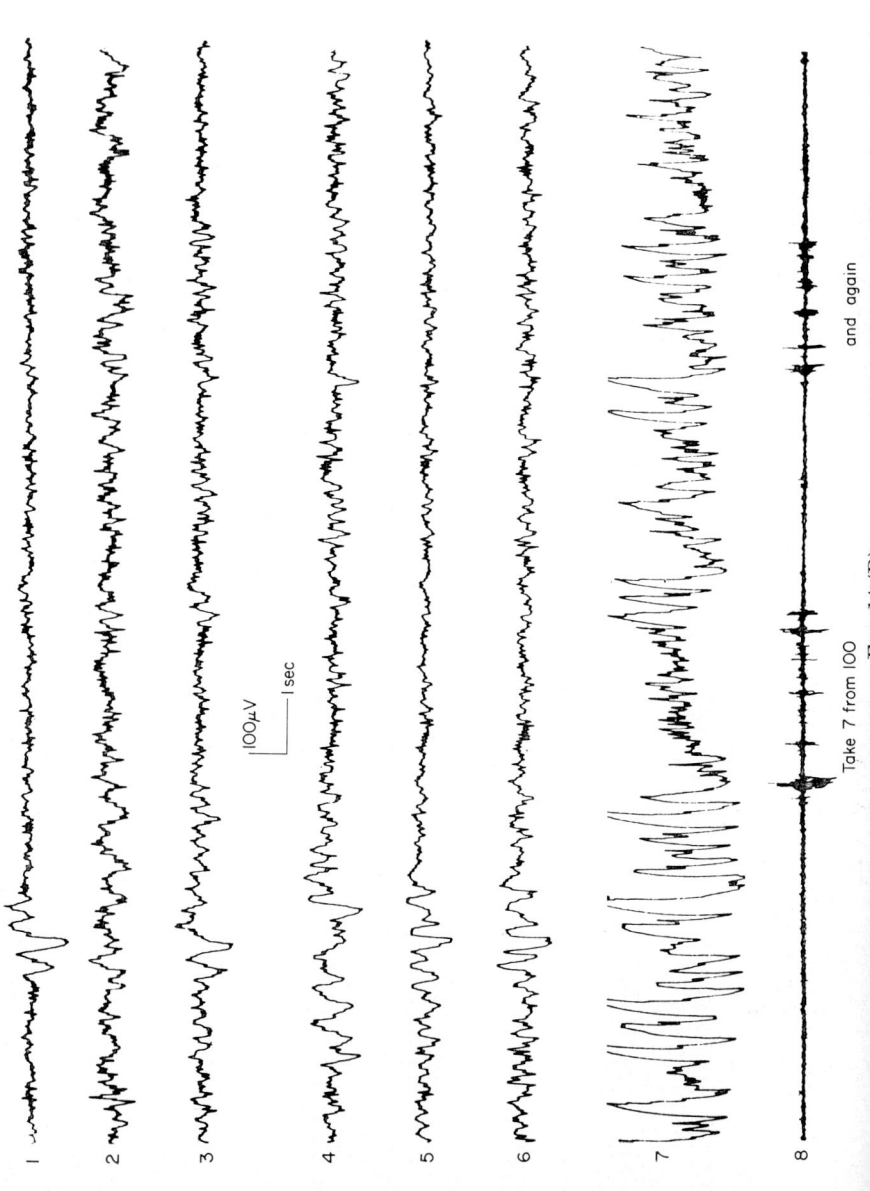

differently if observed in a psychiatric patient. In this case, the delta activity could be due to insertion trauma, the medication that some patients often receive, or possibly the residual effects of other treatments such as electro-convulsive therapy. The important point is that the interpretation of the EEG has to be made within a total experimental or clinical framework.

Delta, or low frequency activity, is not uncommon in patients, especially at recording sessions within a few days after implantation. There appear to be two types of this activity. First, widespread rhythmic delta activity occurs which is blocked by changes of the patient's state, eye opening, counting or casual conversation (Fig. 14(A) and (B), Channels 1 through 6). This is considered to be generalized abnormal activity of normal tissue caused by lesions elsewhere. Second, there is the type of localized delta activity which is not blocked entirely by such changes of state. This is probably caused by damaged cortical cells, and such regions can be the cause of widespread activity already described, Channel 7, Fig. 14(A) and (B). As time progresses, the generalized activity disappears, leaving the localized lesions which sometimes persist for weeks after implantation.

In animal research, the emphasis has been on the EEG correlates of behaviour, and the interpretation of the record is a search for a consistent relationship between the EEG pattern and a change of state of the animal. The changes may be related to different stages of sleep, epileptic fits caused by drugs or hyperbaric oxygen, surgical lesions of the brain stem, acquisition of conditioned reflexes, orienting reflex, and so forth. The changes of the EEG vary considerably from variations of steady potentials to wave and spikes. Most of the interpretation is done by scanning the original records, but more sophisticated methods of analysis, some of which are described in Section VI *D*, are now being reported.

B. *Artefacts*

The artefacts experienced in depth electroencephalography are fewer than those seen on the scalp. The most serious artefacts are caused by movements of the leads. Eye movements (Fig. 15(A)) which are very troublesome in the scalp EEG are negligible in implanted electrodes in man, but are more annoying when recording in animals (Klemm, 1969). There is no muscle artefact in the recordings from the depth electrodes.

A troublesome artefact from gold electrodes when using amplifier time constants greater than 0·3 sec is very slow baseline shifts with

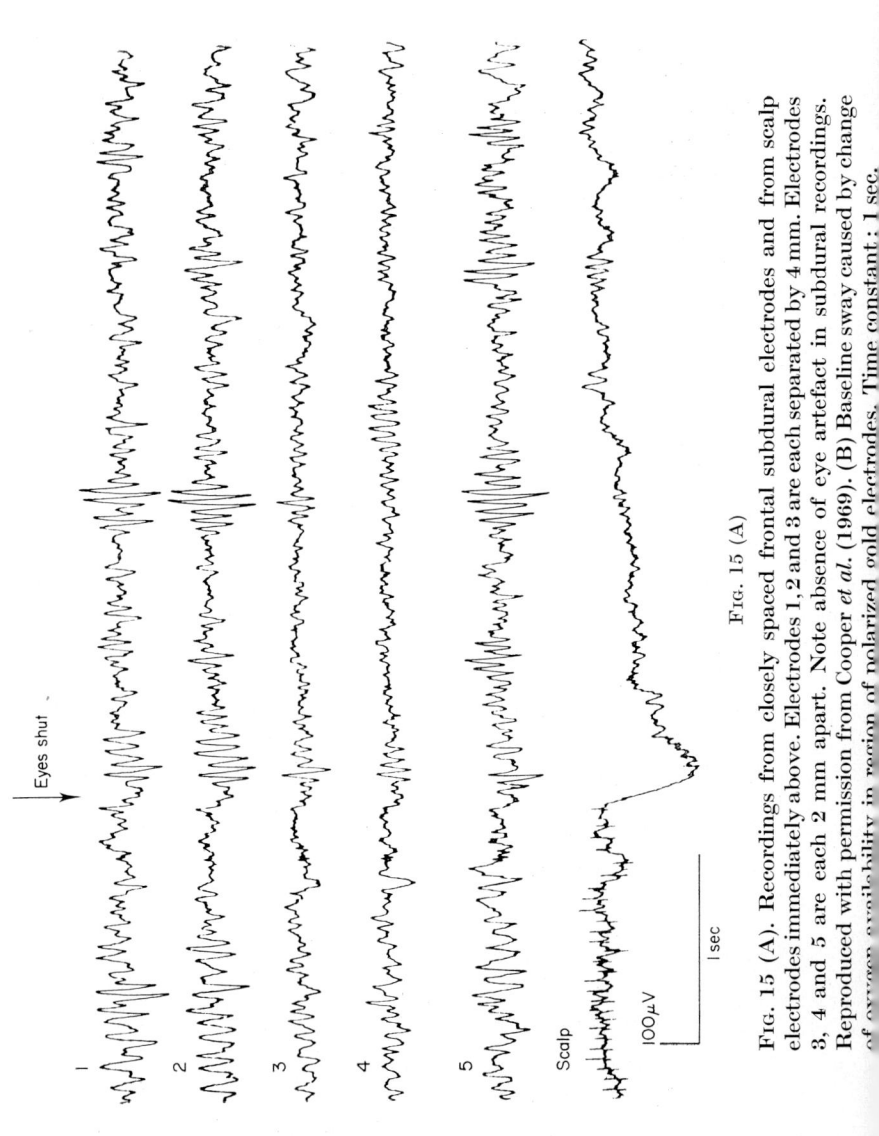

Fig. 15 (A). Recordings from closely spaced frontal subdural electrodes and from scalp electrodes immediately above. Electrodes 1, 2 and 3 are each separated by 4 mm. Electrodes 3, 4 and 5 are each 2 mm apart. Note absence of eye artefact in subdural recordings. Reproduced with permission from Cooper et al. (1969). (B) Baseline sway caused by change of oxygen availability in region of polarized cold electrodes. Time constant: 1 sec.

6 Recording Changes in Electrical Properties

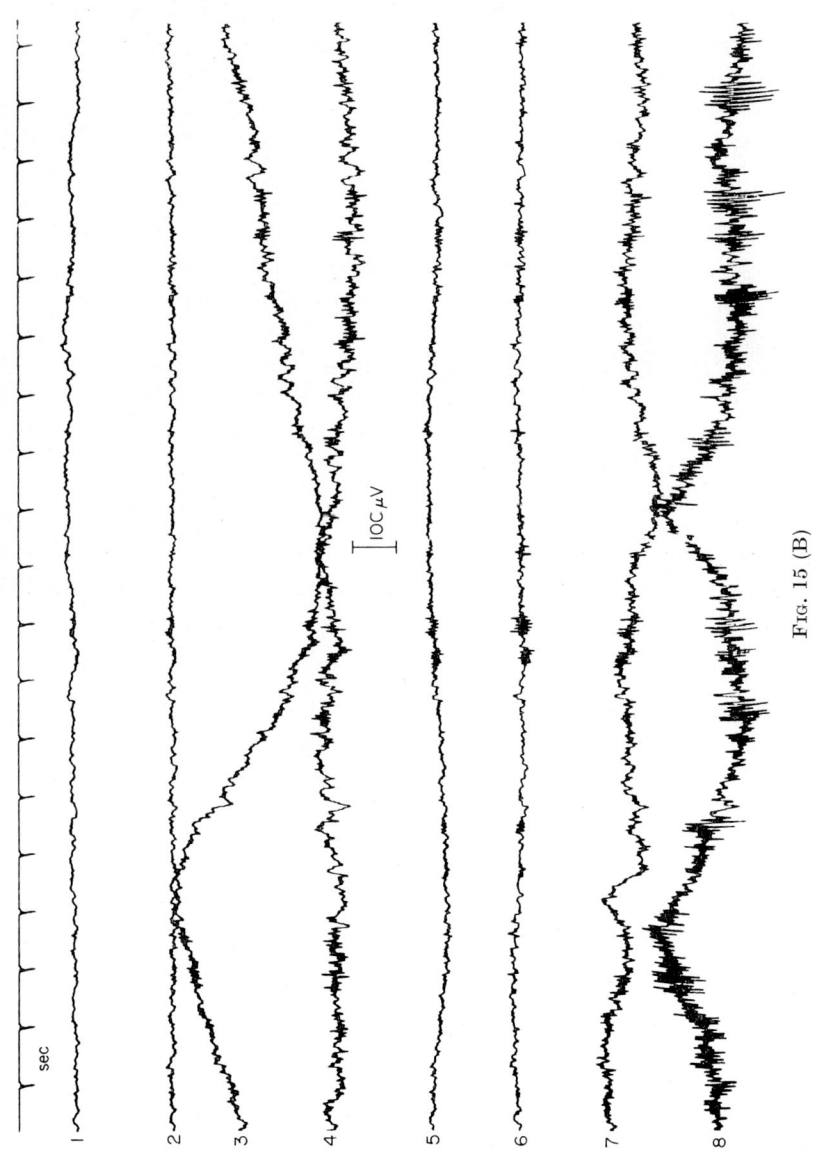

Fig. 15 (B)

periods of about 10 sec, Fig. 15(B). These are due to oxygen fluctuation in the regions of polarized electrodes.

In animals, chewing or lip smacking can be associated with large amplitude activity in the EEG, but it is difficult to determine whether this activity reflects a genuine neuronal change or is an artefact. Generally speaking, it is most unusual to find changes at electrodes in the depths of the brain caused by extracranial electrical disturbance because of the small volume conduction of brain tissue.

This applies to all external fields, including the 50 or 60 Hz line voltages. As the implanted electrodes are enclosed in a saline-saturated skull and scalp, they are screened from external fields and any artefact at line frequency is due to pickup in the leads to the input selector board and amplifiers or inadequate grounding of the patient or animal. When recording, the intracerebral electrodes not being used should be connected together to the common ground terminal of the input amplifiers. There should be only one ground connector to the animal or human. All other metallic objects, such as chains, in the vicinity should be grounded to the same point. If ancillary pieces of equipment such as stimulators or oscilloscopes are line operated, they should be connected to the same power outlet as the EEG recorder to avoid ground loops. In most cases it is unnecessary to work in a screened room.

C. Relationship between Scalp and Depth EEG

Although there is often little sign on the scalp of the activity recorded subcortically (Abraham and Ajmone-Marsan, 1958; DeLucchi et al., 1962; Cooper et al., 1965), there is little doubt that the activity recorded by scalp electrodes arises from the upper layers of the cortex beneath the electrode (see Brumlik et al., 1966, 1967 for reference). Furthermore, the intervening passive tissues (skull and scalp) act like an averager, and only activity that is synchronous over a considerable area of cortex (Cooper et al. 1965 quote 6 sq cm), will be recorded by the scalp electrodes. Activity of areas less than this are grossly attenuated by the skull and scalp. Figure 16 is a diagrammatic representation of signal transmission from cortex to scalp.

D. Analysis of the EEG

The most common kinds of analysis performed on EEG data fall into four groups:

(1) Frequency analysis, designed to provide quantitative measures of particular frequency components, which are then associated with changes of behaviour.

(2) Correlation analysis, which will extract rhythmic components in a signal (auto-correlation) or test for similarity (cross-correlation). Pattern recognition can be included in this group.
(3) Signal/noise enhancement for study of evoked responses. In this method a time-locked signal (evoked response) can be extracted from background activity by summation or averaging techniques.
(4) Spatial and temporal analysis. In this group the distribution of the electrical activity in time and space is determined.

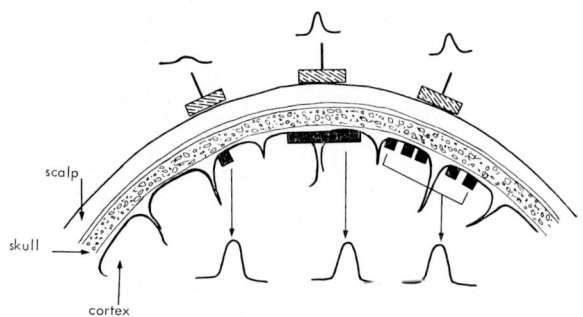

FIG. 16. Diagrammatic representation of signal transmission from cortex to scalp. (From Cooper *et al.*, 1969.)

(1). *Frequency analysis*

The most common form of frequency analysis is that originally proposed by Fourier. In this method a complex waveform is split up into a series of harmonically related components. This is illustrated in Fig. 17 in which each of the complex waveforms (upper traces) is made from the eight components shown superimposed just below. The differences between the two waveforms is due to an alteration of the relative phases of the components and an adequate description by Fourier analysis is only given by both the sin and cosine components of the harmonics. This figure also shows that the power spectrum in which the sin and cosine components are combined (losing the information about phase) is the same for both waveforms and cannot be considered an adequate or unique description. In Fig. 18 the sin and cosine components are combined together to resynthesize the waveform, thus giving an indication of the accuracy of the analysis. The sin and cosine components can also be displayed as vectors and the phase angles compared in different situations.

There is no doubt that Fourier analysis is a powerful method for isolating particular components and can be very useful for detectingrhythms related to flicker for example. However, there are

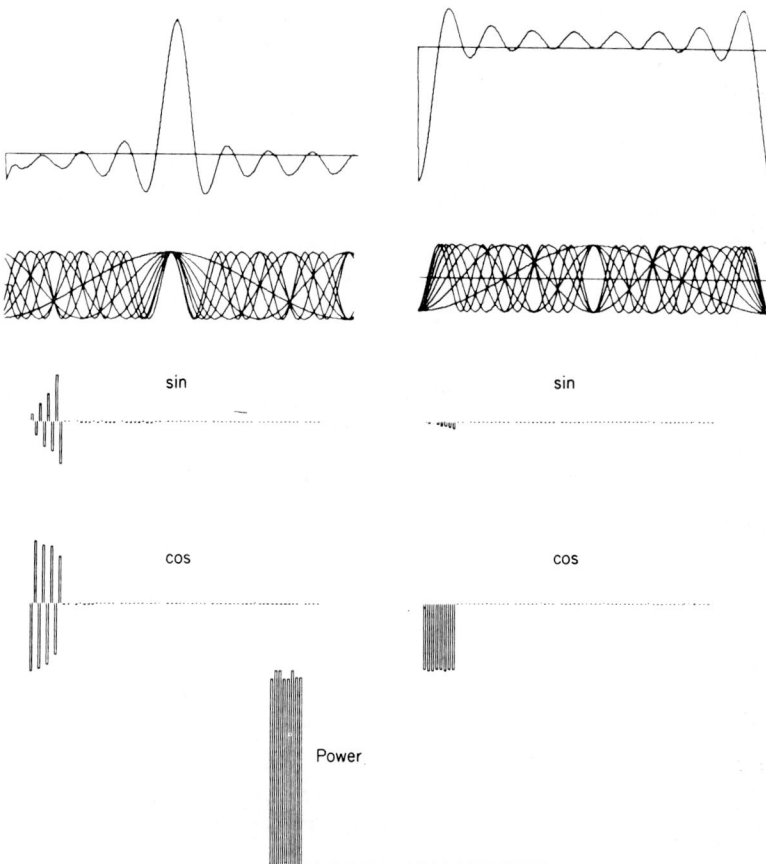

Fig. 17. Addition of 8 equal amplitude components, shown superimposed in second trace, to give two different complex waveforms by changes of phase. Power spectrum are the same for both waveforms.

limitations, and the reader is referred to other literature, Blackman and Tukey (1958), Jenkins and Watts (1969), Manley (1950), Brazier (1961).

(2). *Correlation analysis*

In this form of analysis, tests are made of the similarity of two waveforms. If they are similar, then the integrated cross product (corrected for mean level and amplitude) of the two waveforms will be equal to unity. If the waveforms are different, then the cross-correlation coefficient can have any value between 1 and −1. If zero, the waves are completely dissimilar and if −1, one wave is the inversion of the other.

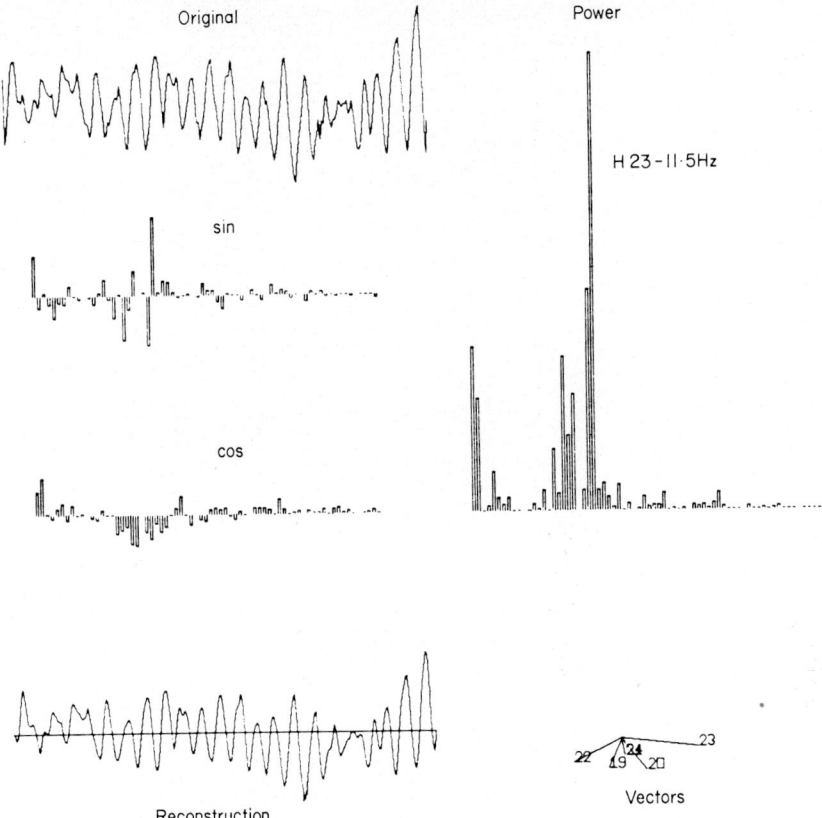

FIG. 18. Fourier analysis of 2 sec sample of alpha rhythm showing sin and cosine components and power spectrum. Spectra is $\frac{1}{2}$ Hz steps. Sin and cosine components combined to give resynthesis and vectors.

If two similar signals occur at different times, then the cross-correlation coefficient will be maximum when one signal is displaced in time with respect to the other. If the time difference is not known, it can be found by calculating the correlation coefficient for a number of values of time displacement between the two signals. The resulting relationship between the correlation coefficient and the time-delay is called the correlation function. Figures 19(A) and (B) show the correlation function of similar (a) and dissimilar (b) waveforms. If one of the waveforms is a particular pattern, the EEG can be "scanned" for this waveform which is indicated by a high value of the correlation coefficient.

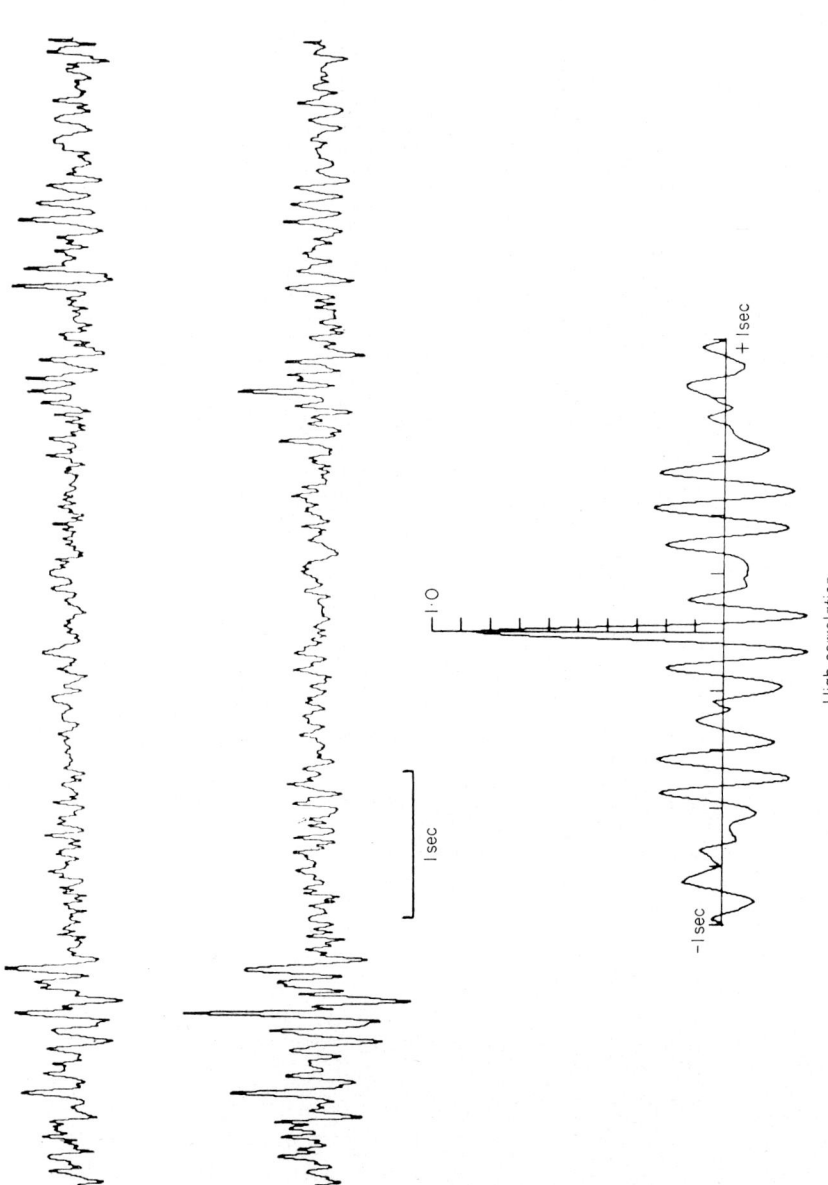

FIG. 19. Cross correlation functions of two samples of EEG from intracerebral electrodes (A) showing high correlation of similar record, (B) showing low correlation of dissimilar records.

6 Recording Changes in Electrical Properties

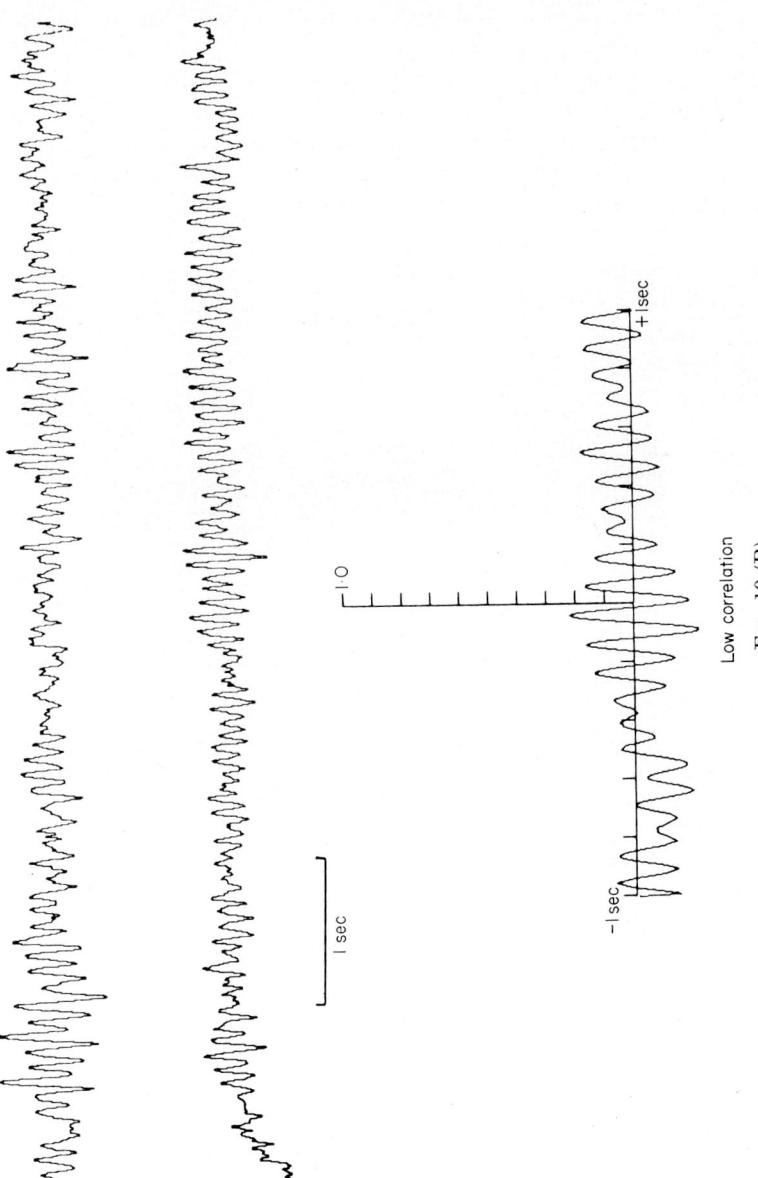

Low correlation
Fig. 19 (B)

(3). *Signal/noise enhancement*

The evoked response in the brain to a stimulus is usually equal to or less than the spontaneous activity at that particular site, and the shape of the evoked response is difficult to determine without some form of noise reduction. This can be achieved by repeated presentation of the stimulus and a superimposition of the responses on a cathode ray oscilloscope or YT plotter, or by averaging the evoked responses with a computer, Fig. 20. The advantage of the superimposition method is that it gives some idea of the variability of the signal which is not seen in the average unless the variance is also calculated and displayed. However, the average often gives a clearer response and is more often used.

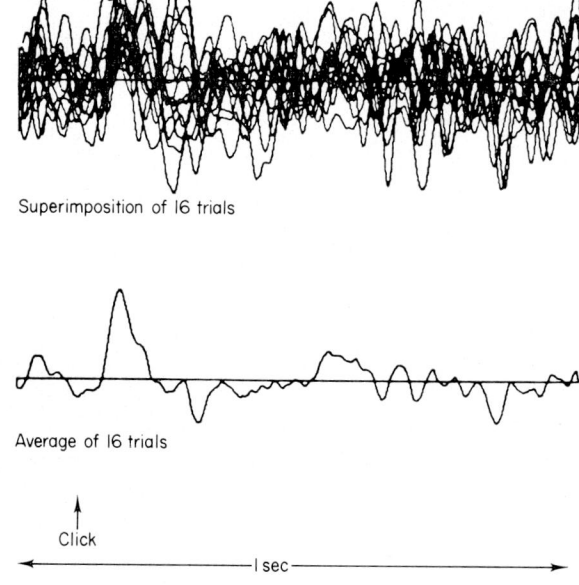

Fig. 20. Comparison of superimposition and average of intracerebral evoked responses.

The availability of computers has given momentum to averaging methods (see, for example, Katzmann 1964; Cobb and Morocutti, 1966), and much work is being done in this field. One serious disadvantage of this type of signal to noise enhancement is that it is dependent upon the response to the stimulus being the same, irrespective of the number of times the stimulus has been previously given to the subject. In certain parts of the brain this is not true, as the amplitude of the evoked response decreases with repetition (habituation).

(4). *Spatial and temporal analysis*

The mechanisms involved in the spread of electrical activity through tissue is of fundamental importance in the understanding of the brain. This problem can be studied using an array of cortical electrodes but presents great problems in the analysis of the data. These arise because the activities at different cortical sites have to be tested for similarities and the time differences between the similar components measured. Since the time differences are small (msec) any technique has to have high resolution and be capable of dealing with a large amount of data. Although some analogue devices have been used successfully (Storm van Leeuwen and Bekkering (1958), Livanov (1958), Petsche and Sterc (1968), Petsche and Rappelsberger (1970)), it seems likely that large capacity digital computers will be necessary for these investigations.

REFERENCES

Abraham, K. and Ajmone-Marson, C. (1958). *Electroenceph. clin. Neurophysiol.* 10, 447–461.
Bickford, R. G., Petersen, M. C., Dodge, H. W. and Sem-Jacobsen, C. W. (1953). *Proc. Staff Meet. Mayo Clin.* 28, 181–193.
Blackman, R. B. and Tukey, J. W. (1958). "The Measurement of Power Spectra." Dover, New York.
Bond, H. W. and Ho, P. (1970). *Electroenceph. clin. Neurophysiol.* 28, 206–208.
Brazier, M. A. B. (1961). "Computer Techniques in EEG Analysis." *Electroenceph. clin. Neurophysiol.* Suppl. 20.
Brazier, M. A. B. (1961). "A History of the Electrical Activity of the Brain. The First Half-century." Pitman Medical Publishing Co., London.
Brumlik, J., Richeson, W. B. and Arbit, J. (1966–1967). *Brain Res.* 3, 227–247.
Buchwald, J. S., Halas, E. S. and Schramm, S. (1966). *Electroenceph. clin. Neurophysiol.* 21, 227–238.
Chatrian, G. E., Dodge, H. W., Petersen, M. C. and Bickford, R. G. (1959a). *Electroenceph. clin. Neurophysiol.* 11, 165–169.
Chatrian, G. E., Pollack, C. S. and Petersen, M. C. (1959b). *Electroenceph. clin. Neurophysiol.* 11, 358–361.
Chusid, J. G., Kapeloff, L. M. and Kapeloff, N. (1957). *Electroenceph. clin. Neurophysiol.* 9, 178.
Cobb, W. and Morocutti, C. (eds) (1966). "The Evoked Potentials." *Electroenceph. clin. Neurophysiol.* Suppl. 26.
Collias, J. C. and Manuelidis, E. E. (1957). *J. Neurosurg.* 14, 302–328.
Cooper, R. (1959). *Electroenceph. clin. Neurophysiol.* 11, 819–820.
Cooper, R. (1962). *Proc. electrophysiol. Technol. Ass.* 9, 22–33.
Cooper, R. (1968). *In* "Computers and Electronic Devices in Psychiatry" (Kline, N. S. and Laska, E. eds), pp. 169–177. Grune and Stratton, New York.
Cooper, R. and Crow, H. J. (1966). *Med. biol. Engng.* 4, 575–581.

Cooper, R., Crow, H. J., Walter, W. G. and Winter, A. L. (1966). *Brain Res.* **3**, 174–191.
Cooper, R., Osselton, J. W. and Shaw, J. (1969). "EEG Technology." Butterworth and Co., London.
Cooper, R. and Warren W. J. (1959). *Electroenceph. clin. Neurophysiol.* **11**, 810–811.
Cooper, R., Winter, A. L., Crow, H. J. and Walter, W. G. (1965). *Electroenceph. clin. Neurophysiol.* **18**, 217–228.
Creutzfeldt, O. D., Watanabe, S. and Lux, H. D. (1966). *Electroenceph. clin. Neurophysiol.* **20**, 1–18 and 19–37.
Crow, H. J., Cooper, R. and Phillips, D. G. (1961). *J. Neurol. Neurosurg. Psychiat.* **24**, 353–360.
Crow, H. J., Tomka, I. and Walter, W. G. (1965). *J. Physiol.* **178**, 50–51P.
Delgado, J. M. R., Hamlin, H. and Chapman, W. P. (1952). *Confin. Neurol.* **12**, 315–319.
Delgado, J. M. R. (1952). *Yale, J. Biol. Med.* **24**, 351–362.
Delgado, J. M. R., Johnston, V. S., Wallace, J. D. and Bradley, R. J. (1969). *Electroenceph. clin. Neurophysiol.* **27**, 701–702.
DeLucchi, M. R., Garoutte, B. and Aird, R. B. (1962). *Electroenceph. clin. Neurophysiol.* **14**, 191–196.
Fischer, G., Sayre, G. P. and Bickford, R. G. (1957). *Proc. Staff Meet. Mayo Clin.* **32**, 14–22. Also appears in "Electrical Stimulation of the Brain" (1961), (Sheer, D. E., ed.), University of Texas Press, Austin, Texas, U.S.A.
Gloor, P. (1969). "Hans Berger on the Electroencephalogram of Man." *Electroenceph. clin. Neurophysiol.* Suppl. 28. Elsevier, Amsterdam.
Grahame, D. C. (1952). *J. Electrochem. Soc.* **99**, 370C.
Gumnit, R. J. and Grossman, R. G. (1961). *Am. J. Physiol.* **200**, 1219–1225.
Hill, D. and Parr, G. (1963). "Electroencephalography", 2nd Ed. Macdonald, London.
Hughes, J. R. (1959). *Electroenceph. clin. Neurophysiol.* **11**, 447–458.
Jasper, H. H. (1966). *In* "Brain and Conscious Experience" (J. C. Eccles ed.), pp. 256–282. Springer, Berlin.
Jenkins, G. M. and Watts, D. G. (1968). "Spectral Analysis and Its Applications." Holden-Day, San Francisco.
Kamp, A., Kok, M. L. and DeQuartel, F. W. (1965). *Electroenceph. clin. Neurophysiol.* **18**, 422–423.
Katzmann, R. (ed.) (1964). "Sensory evoked response in man." *Ann. N.Y. Acad. Sci.* **112**, 1, 1–546.
Klemm, W. R. (1969). "Animal Electroencephalography." Academic Press, New York and London.
Livanov, M. (1958). *In* "Int. Coll. EEG Higher Nerv. Activity", pp. 185–198. *Electroenceph. clin. Neurophysiol.* Suppl. 13.
Long, C. J. and Tapp, J. T. (1965). *Electroenceph. clin. Neurophysiol.* **19**, 412–413.
Loucks, R. B., Weinberg, H. and Smith, M. (1959). *Electroenceph. clin. Neurophysiol.* **11**, 823–826.
Manley, R. G. (1950). "Waveform Analysis." Chapman & Hall, London.
Moskalenko, Yu. E., Cooper, R., Crow, H. J. and Walter, W. G. (1964). *Nature, Lond.*, **202**, 159–161.
Petsche, H. and Rappelsberger, P. (1970). *Electroenceph. clin. Neurophysiol.* **28**, 592–600.
Petsche, H. and Sterc, J. (1968). *Electroenceph. clin. Neurophysiol.* **25**, 11–22.

Porter, R., Adey, W. R. and Kado, R. T. (1964). *Neurology (Minneap.)*. **14**, 1002–1012.
Ray, C. D. (1966). *J. Neurosurg.* **24**, 911–921.
Robinson, F. R. and Johnson, M. T. (1961). ASD Technical Report 61–397, Wright-Patterson A.F.B. Ohio.
Rowland, V. (1961). *Electroenceph. clin. Neurophysiol.* **13**, 290–291.
Sem-Jacobsen, C. W., Petersen, M. C., Dodge, H. W. Jr., Lazarte, J. A. and Holman, C. B. (1956). *Electroenceph. clin. Neurophysiol.* **8**, 263–278.
Storm van Leeuwen, W. and Bekkering, D. H. (1958). *Electroenceph. clin. Neurophysiol.* **10**, 563–570.
Walter, W. G. (1962). *In* "Progress in Neurobiology." *Neural Physiopathology* (Grenell, R. G. ed.) Vol. V. Hoeber, New York.
Walter, W. G. (1964). *Ann. N.Y. Acad. Sci.* **112**, 1, 320–361.
Weinberg, H., Walter, W. G. and Crow, H. J. (1970). *Electroenceph. clin. Neurophysiol.* **29**, 1–9.
Wurtz, R. H. (1965). *Electroenceph. clin. Neurophysiol.* **18**, 649–662.

Appendix A

Manufacturers of Electroencephalographs

These are the addresses of the Head Offices from whom the name of the local agent can be obtained:

Ahrend-van Gogh,
P.O. Box 70, Singel 130,
Amsterdam, The Netherlands.

Alvar-Electronic,
6 bis, Rue de Progrès 93-Montreuil,
Paris, France.

Beckman Instruments,
3900 North River Road,
Schiller Park, Illinois 60176

Brush Division,
Clevite Corporation,
Cleveland, Ohio.

Devices,
Welwyn Garden City,
Herts., England.

E.C.E.M.,
95 rue de Flandre,
Paris 19, France.

Electro-Medical Engineering,
Burbank, California.

Elema-Schonander,
S 17120 Solna 1, Sweden.

Galileo, P.O. Box 402,
50100 Firenze, Italy
and
S.L.E.,
Campbell Road,
Croydon CR0 2SQ, England.

Grass Instrument Co.,
Quincy, Massachusetts 02169.

E. Kaisers Laboratorium A/S,
36 Linde Alle, Van Løse,
Copenhagen, Denmark.

Minneapolis-Honeywell,
Denver, Colorado, U.S.A.

Niohn Kohden Kogyo Co.,
Shinjuku-Ku, Tokyo, Japan.

San-Ei Instrument G.,
Shinjuku-Ku, Tokyo, Japan.

Sanborn Div.,
Hewlett Packard,
Waltham, Massachusetts.

Schwarzer,
Barmaunstra. 38,
Munich 60, W. Germany.

Appendix B

American and British Wire Gauges

Gauge number	American Brown and Sharpe		British Standard Wire Gauge	
	Inch	mm	Inch	mm
24	0·0201	0·511	0·022	0·559
25	0·0179	0·455	0·020	0·508
26	0·0159	0·404	0·018	0·457
27	0·0142	0·361	0·0164	0·417
28	0·0126	0·320	0·0148	0·376
29	0·0113	0·287	0·0136	0·345
30	0·0100	0·254	0·0124	0·315
31	0·0089	0·226	0·0116	0·295
32	0·0080	0·203	0·0108	0·274
33	0·0071	0·180	0·0100	0·254
34	0·0063	0·160	0·0092	0·234
35	0·0056	0·142	0·0084	0·213
36	0·0050	0·127	0·0076	0·193
37	0·0045	0·114	0·0068	0·173
38	0·0040	0·102	0·0060	0·152
39	0·0035	0·090	0·0052	0·132
40	0·0031	0·079	0·0048	0·122
41	0·0028	0·071	0·0044	0·112
42	0·0025	0·063	0·0040	0·102
43	0·0022	0·056	0·0036	0·091
44	0·0020	0·051	0·0032	0·081
45	0·00176	0·045	0·0028	0·071
46	0·00157	0·040	0·0024	0·061
47	0·00140	0·036	0·0020	0·051
48	0·00124	0·031	0·0016	0·041
49	0·00111	0·028	0·0012	0·030
50	0·00099	0·025	0·0010	0·025

1 mm = 0·040 in = 40 thousandths
1 mm = 1000 μ
1 thou = 0·001 in = 25 μ

Chapter 7

Electrical Stimulation of the Brain

F. R. ERVIN and G. J. KENNEY

Harvard Medical School, Stanley Cobb Laboratory;
Massachusetts General Hospital, Boston, Massachusetts, U.S.A.

I.	Introduction	207
	A. Why Stimulate the Brain?	209
	B. Effect of Electrical Stimulation	210
	C. Usefulness of this Method	211
II.	Types of Electrodes	212
	A. Monopolar Electrode	213
	B. Bipolar Electrode	214
	C. Multipolar Electrode	214
	D. Concentric Electrode	214
III.	Electrode Construction	215
	A. Insulation	218
	B. Bipolar and Multi-lead Electrode	218
	C. Concentric Electrode	219
	D. Cortical Stimulating Electrode	220
IV.	Implantation Procedures	220
	A. Pedestals, Sockets and Connectors	221
	B. Potential Problems	225
V.	The Electrochemical Interface and Problems of Polarization	230
	A. The Stimulator	232
	B. Frequency, Amplitude and Duration of Pulse	233
	C. Wave Forms	236
	D. The Conscious Animal	237
	E. Telestimulation	238
VI.	Interpretation	238
VII.	Conclusion	242
References		243
Appendix		245

I. INTRODUCTION

FOCAL stimulation of the brain was the earliest to be utilized of the three classic techniques of ablation, stimulation and recording. For the observations of Hippocrates and his followers this focal stimulation arose from pathologic processes in the brain itself, but the symptomatology of spontaneously arising epileptic seizures was then, and remains, a rich source of information about functional brain organization. It was, however, after the introduction of experimental stimulation of the brain with electricity by Fritsch and Hitzig that clinicians were able to exploit seizure symptomatology in a systematic way to examine brain structure.

Jackson provided a model for such studies and much of the fundamental information until it became supplemented in the middle of this century by observation at surgery of direct electrical stimulation of the brain under reasonably controlled conditions. Fritsch and Hitzig carried out their experiments making use of the advances in bioengineering and bioelectronics introduced by Helmholtz and du Bois-Reymond, as well as an adaptation of the induction coil devised by Farraday in 1834 for physiological work. They addressed their studies to the philosophical problem of intent in physiology, i.e. whether the mind was a reflection of physical processes in the brain or whether, as the vitalists argued, they arose in relationship but transcendental to the material processes of the brain.

Specifically, as with many physiologists of the day, they were concerned about the problem of cerebral localization, about which there were two strong points of view. The dominant theory of the day was that of Flourens, who maintained that unity was the great reigning principle of the nervous system and that the brain tended to act as a unit. His own position in regard to this "action commune" was in direct rebuttal to the then phrenological teaching of Gall. His holistic ideas, however, were less convincing after the careful demonstration in a series of experiments, that specific movements could be elicited in the neck, face and limbs of a dog by stimulating separate and precise points in the anterior portion of the brain. These experiments were the more exciting at the time because earlier attempts, by Bernard, for example, had been interpreted to suggest that nervous tissue could not be electrically stimulated to perform a natural function. When Müller, the most influential physiologist of his day, formulated his doctrine of specific nerve energies in 1838, he considered all of the methods then employed to stimulate nervous tissue artificially and the principle of nervous propagation to be immeasurable. When Fritsch and Hitzig further demonstrated that movements in man could be elicited electrically by taking advantage of an individual's open head wounds, during the Franco-Prussian War, the doctrine of cerebral localization was widely accepted and gained rapid support from the beginning expansion of neuroanatomical studies. These young investigators summed up their work in 1870 by saying: "The mind is not all, as Flourens and most others following him thought, a kind of holistic function of the total cerebrum . . . but more likely there are separate psychical functions, which are probably dependent on circumscribed centers of the cerebrum for their entry into or origin from material form."[1] It is clear, however, that they did not resolve the controversy once and for all, for it continues today, and, with advances in techniques of electrical stimulation, has moved from the cortex through the subcortex and indeed, to the single cell. It is probably true that the experimenter's implicit bias as to a holistic or particulate organization of the brain determines his interpretation of stimulation-evoked responses.

A. Why Stimulate the Brain?

In general, the goal of experimental stimulation of the brain is obviously to reproduce the function of the region stimulated, so that the complicated circuitry of the central nervous system can be functionally dissected. It is tempting, therefore, when one finds that stimulation has elicited some observable function to conclude that function is controlled by, represented in, or caused by the region of stimulation. This tempting logic is of course by no means true. Even if one considers only the complexity of tissues stimulated by any given electrical current, there are fibers, inhibitory and excitatory cells, dendrites, cell bodies and so on, all synchronously influenced in a way which must never occur in response to a naturally-occurring incoming volley of nerve impulses with their precise temporal-spatial patterning. Sober reflection on the difficulties of interpreting stimulation data can lead one to philosophic despair, and particularly to wonder why electrical stimulation should be used.

The classic work of Sechenov in demonstrating the role of the midbrain recticular formation utilized crystals of salt as the stimulating element, and in that tradition, investigators since have turned increasingly to the use of ions such as potassium or sodium, or presumed transmitters such as acetylcholine or norepinephrine to try more precisely to replicate the natural processes of the brain.

These techniques are discussed in Chapter 8, and with a rapidly advancing technology may well at some point replace electrical stimulation. In the meantime, however, electricity provides certain advantages. It can be delivered to a precise point within the brain by a relatively small mechanical unit, a wire. The dimensions of the stimulus delivered, that is, its amplitude, duration, shape and frequency of

[1] As quoted by D. E. Sheer in "Electrical Stimulation of the Brain", p. 12.

repetition, can be precisely controlled and measured. The stimulus may be applied conveniently by remote control, and the onset and termination of its effect may be quite prompt as compared to similar changes following chemical stimulation. For all these reasons, it remains a powerful and useful experimental tool.

B. Effect of Electrical Stimulation

Since electrical change is a basic aspect of the changing patterns of neuronal organization in the living brain, brain function is responsive to imposed electrical fluctuations which produce ion flow through neuronal membranes or in extraneuronal space. It is perhaps worth a reminder that electric flow in biological systems is not in general accompanied by electron flow, but rather by the movement of ions and perhaps by small movements of macromolecules. The use, therefore, of an electrode for stimulation or recording requires that electron flux be converted into ion flux, or conversely. This conversion gives rise to many of the small technical problems associated with electrophysiology and is sometimes misunderstood by students or non-biologically trained engineers. The immediate effect of electrical stimulation of the brain, therefore, is to alter the state of organization of those neural elements in the field of the electrode. Those elements may be cell bodies, dendrites, axons, glia, or even subcellular structures. The change of organization induced in these elements may in turn either activate or inactivate their "usual" function. Since this modified function may in turn be either inhibitory or excitatory in terms of further neuronal organization, and may have its maximum effect either locally or remotely as in the case of fibers of passage, the behavioral result may be exceedingly difficult to interpret. This also implies that since the effect of stimulation viewed from the perspective of the whole organism is to modify only one small aspect of the total cerebral organization, the result may be quite dependent on the initial state of the organism, environmental stimuli, or fortuitous metabolic factors.

In view of the complexity of these interactions, it is impressive that so much of the literature on stimulation can describe orderly and predictable consequences, even in complex systems such as those dealing with motivation. In each instance, however, one must be careful in interpreting the relevance of the site of stimulation to the observed effect. If one is stimulating close to the origin of the final common effector pathway, then one may obtain highly stereotyped, completely reproducible phenomena and be tempted to think of "centers" of action. It was this, of course, which marked the pioneering work of Hess in the late 1920's, which has served as a model, both technically and conceptually, for much subsequent work, particularly on subcortical brain stimulation. It is worthwhile to re-read the early studies of Hess for the careful attention he paid to parameter control, techniques of placement, and so on. Conceptually, however, the facile identification of sites from which fixed motor patterns could be elicited with the notion of precise cerebral localization of complex function can no longer be supported. In behavioral research particularly, it is important to think carefully through the implicit assumptions in the interpretation of stimulation data. The failure to do this in a rigorous way has given rise to much empty polemic in the field. A particularly thoughtful discussion of this problem can be found in the review of electrical stimulation of the brain by Doty (1969), whose own work on conditioning of the brain by electrical stimulation is an exceedingly important contribution to our understanding of this tool. It is clear from this work that although the stimulus is "artificial" and complex as described above, it can be discriminated by the brain and responded to as biologically "meaningful". He has also defined the limits within which this discrimination can occur.

C. *Usefulness of This Method*

In this chapter, we have emphasized the use of stimulation as a behavioral tool. The most traditional use in nerve physiology, is of course the investigation of the organization of neural pathways, by electrically recording the activity of single fibers and cells following stimulation. This same technique is extremely useful in following pathways of intercerebral communication, and is important in "the electroanatomy" of the brain. It is a particularly useful supplement to histological methods because it can elucidate differing states of organization over time or in various experimental conditions in ways in which stained material cannot quite yet achieve. Thus, in our technical descriptions to follow we shall pay attention to the requirements of experiments in which electrical recording in response to stimulation is necessary as well as those behavioral experiments in which it is not.

In using brain stimulation as an experimental tool two approaches are possible. One is to consider all of the complexities of the tool and to dissect it at length, the other is to use that which works empirically most of the time and not worry about the fine details. We have worked with brain stimulation techniques in animals and in man for the past twenty years and have concluded that all of the most interesting questions about the technique are still not answered, and many of them have not even been asked. On the other hand, many people do not use the technique because of ostensible methodological complexities which, in fact, for many purposes, can be considered almost trivial. We shall try in the following discussion to emphasize the simple pragmatics of the matter, noting from time to time, references to extended articles which explore at greater length the details of those elegant or more demanding procedures. Basically it is our position that a piece of insulated wire *can* be placed into the brain and stimulated with a doorbell buzzer and a six-volt battery to produce interesting and analysable phenomena. Indeed, most of the classic studies in the field have been done in essentially this fashion.

II. Types of Electrodes

Although a number of commercially produced electrodes are available (see appendix) they are generally expensive for the academic laboratory and are not necessarily superior to the home-produced electrodes.

There are a variety of materials and methods employed to manufacture electrodes for extracellular stimulation (and recording) and a number of equally suitable techniques described in the literature (see Delgado, 1961, 1964; Bureš *et al.*, 1960).

The physical configuration of any electrode, its size and length, the amount of exposed tip and so on, will depend upon its intended use. The techniques discussed below describe the manufacture of a number of electrode types which can be used to stimulate or record population responses (gross evoked potentials, slow wave potentials, or massed unit discharges) in either acute or chronic preparations. Except for the dimensions, the basic decision to be made in constructing electrodes has to do with their spatial configuration: monopolar, bipolar (or multipolar) or concentric. The electrode array is after all an antenna which is broadcasting a field of excitation, the shape of which is dependent on the spatial configuration of the electrode points, other stimulus parameters being constant. That is to say, in principle, one could shape a highly directional or precisely shaped field of excitation by choosing the right antenna array.

The three basic types of configurations have very characteristic and useful fields. It is of value to the beginner to utilize various kinds of electrodes with a standard stimulus pulse either in a beaker of saline while mapping the potential field in three dimensions with an exploring electrode, or to use a current-sensitive paper, such as Teledeltos paper on which one can actually see a two-dimensional section of the field generated by the electrode.

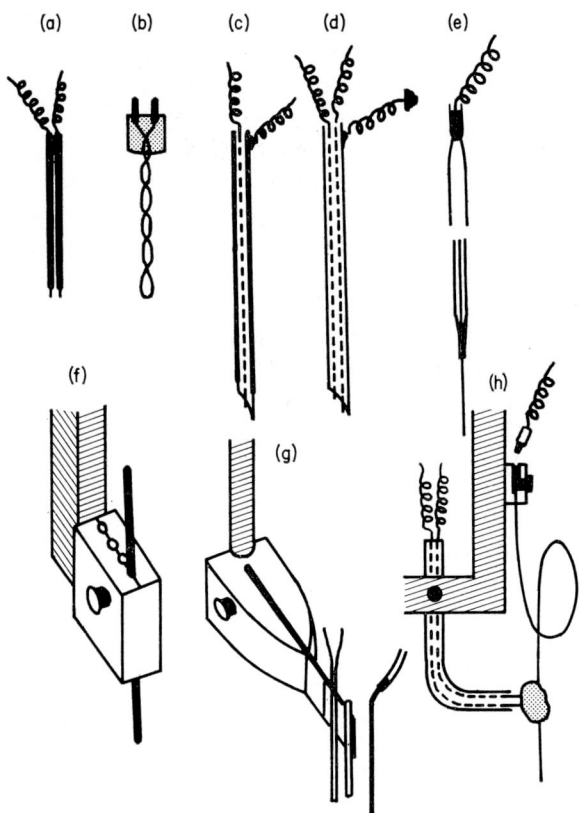

FIG. 1. Different types of electrodes and electrode carriers used with stereotaxic apparatus: (a) bipolar needle electrodes; (b) bipolar electrodes made from insulated twisted silver wire; (c) concentric electrodes; (d) bipolar electrodes with needle sheath; (e) electrodes for implantation with the connecting plug and socket arrangement; (f, g and h) different types of electrode carriers. (From Bureš et al., 1960.)

A. Monopolar Electrode

The monopolar electrode with a reference lead elsewhere on the animal stimulates the largest area. For practical purposes, in a small brain, the electrode can be assumed to stimulate the brain as a whole with the point of most intense stimulation, of course, being the tip of the electrode. The intensity falls off as the square of the distance away from the electrode. The intervening tissue between the brain and the reference point which may include muscle, heart, retina, or other tissues is also stimulated. For this reason, the monopolar electrode is in general unsatisfactory for precise work. The large stimulus field, however, does increase the chance of finding an excitable area and may sometimes be useful in a preliminary exploration of the cortex or some subcortical point.

B. Bipolar Electrode

The bipolar electrode is composed of two monopolar electrodes placed close together but with tip separations of one-half to one millimeter. The most intensely stimulated region is that lying between the two electrode tips where the lines of force are concentrated, and a symmetrical field surrounding them. In the recording situation, the reverse is true; there exists an isopotential plane between the two electrode tips from which no potentials are recorded. The bipolar electrode provides a much more discrete localization of the stimulus than does the monopolar and is generally preferred, particularly when stimulating with a movable, exploratory electrode.

C. Multipolar Electrode

The multipolar electrode is ordinarily used only in bipolar configuration, the larger array serving as a convenience to the experimenter to permit exploration of a series of brain sites without the trauma of moving the electrode. This has been particularly valuable in human studies with chronically implanted electrodes. Our group ordinarily uses a twelve-to-fourteen lead electrode with tip separations of about one to two millimeters permitting laboratory testing of responses to stimulation between adjacent pairs of electrodes and ultimately exploring a sizeable structure. These electrodes have also been useful in animal work and can be designed with the aid of a stereotaxic atlas to permit a single penetration of the brain with an array which, for example, will concentrate a bipolar pair of electrodes with the tips in one nucleus and another pair five millimetres away in another subcortical structure. An evenly spaced array of such points at, for example, half-millimeter intervals, allows for rapid surgical implantation in a region where the desired result is the optimization of some behavioral response. After recovery from surgery, the electrode pairs can be explored sequentially and the optimal site chosen for further work.

D. Concentric Electrode

The so-called concentric electrode, usually made with the exposed tip of a cannula or hyperdermic needle within which is an insulated wire bare only at the tip, has an even "tighter" field pattern than does the bipolar. Its field can be thought of as sharply focused between the protruding central tip and the surrounding circle so that it stimulates predominantly in the direction in which it is aimed and thus allows for some accurate positioning for exciting structures which are not mechanically penetrated by the electrode. The recording field for this electrode is rather tear-drop shaped, focused again at the tip of the electrode but allowing for some directionality for recording not obtained with the other configurations. To our knowledge, none of the other possible antenna arrays have been systematically exploited, although some interesting use has been made of three-electrode recording to obtain vector fields, both by Adey and his group in California and in our own laboratory.

III. Electrode Construction

The basic monopolar electrode is easily constructed of tungsten, stainless steel or platinum irridium. Tungsten and stainless steel are both accessible to most laboratories and are biologically well-tolerated by the brain. It should be pointed out, however, that both may be unsuitable for certain applications as stimulating electrodes. Loucks *et al.* (1959) have demonstrated that both metals erode with the passage of AC and DC currents as small as 0·1 mA at 60 Hz, and the passage of two mA for two minutes causes a mushrooming of the tips. (See Fig. 2.)

Delgado (1964) has found the erosion of stainless steel to be slight when short-pulsed durations of the order of 0·2 msec are used. These short durations are common in most animal work and stainless steel is very useful indeed for such application particularly if there are no concerns about the possible deposition of iron. Tungsten, on the other hand, reacts in a peculiar way with current densities greater than 100 mA cm^{-2}. Weinman and Mahler (1964) found that with one pulse per M/sec stimulation, the voltage across the electrode began to rise, becoming greater with each additional pulse, even though current-density and pulse duration remained constant (Fig. 3). Neither of the above effects was found for platinum irridium electrodes used in both of these studies. Platinum is the most generally suitable material for stimulating electrodes when high current-densities and long stimulus durations are applied, and in its non-brittle alloy with irridium is a generally useful electrode material.

Tungsten is particularly suitable for monopolar electrode construction because of its extreme rigidity. It is commercially available in a variety of lengths and diameters and can be obtained pre-straightened (see Appendix for a partial list of suppliers of materials mentioned in this section). The pre-straightened tungsten is more attractive than

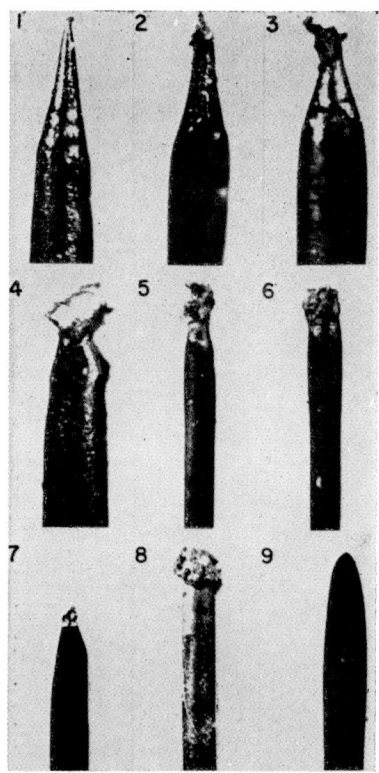

FIG. 2. Erosion of electrode tips in electrolytic solutions with passage of currents within normal stimulus range for neurophysiological experiments. Nos. 5 and 6 were implanted in the brain of an experimental animal and show mushroom-like accretions typical of AC stimulus. No. 8 is sterling silver; No. 9, platinum irridium. (From Loucks et al., 1959.)

stainless steel since the latter is more flexible at small diameters, 0·010–0·012 inches, and usually comes in spools of wire which require straightening before it can be accurately implanted. Because tungsten is brittle, care must be taken to avoid splitting the metal when cutting it into exact lengths. This can be accomplished with sharp wire-cutters or may be done with a small grinding wheel. The cut end should be examined under a magnifying glass to be sure it is evenly cut. Tungsten can be electrolytically etched and polished to a few microns in diameter without pitting. This makes it ideal for microelectric studies as well. To electro-etch tungsten an AC current of about 10 volts is passed between the electrode wire and a carbon rod immersed in an

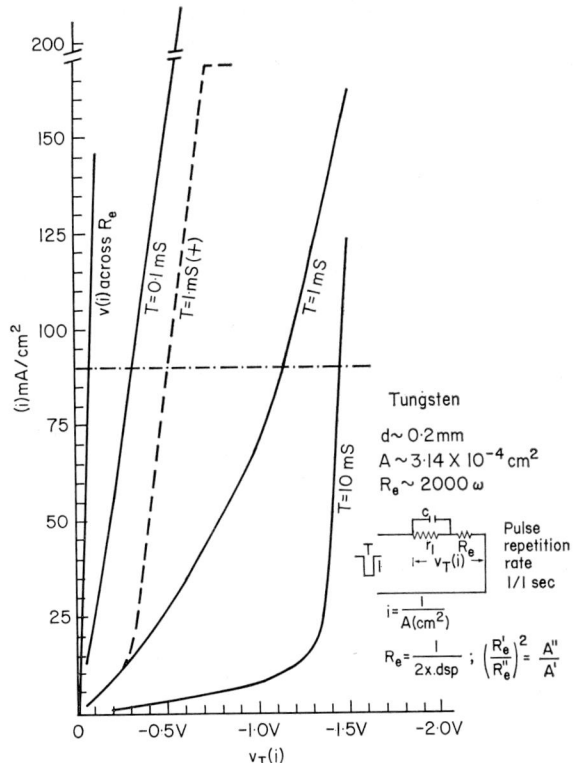

FIG. 3. Peculiar behavior of tungsten electrode with positive current. Graph shows increase in electrode impedance indicated by growing $vT(i)$ as a function of increasing number of pulses, although current-density and duration (indicated by horizontal interrupted line) remained constant. (From Weinman and Mahler, 1964.)

aqueous saturated solution of potassium nitrite. To polish it, the same procedure is followed, with a reduced voltage of 2–5 volts. A variable transformer is used as the current force, and a smooth taper can be produced at the tip by dipping the electrode wire up and down in the solution at a constant rate. Because the commercial production procedures usually leave the wire somewhat oily at the surface, the authors usually electro-polish the whole shaft before cleaning and insulating.

All electrode materials should be thoroughly cleaned and dried before the insulating material is applied. This can be done by pulling the electrode wire through a surgical sponge saturated with absolute alcohol and held tightly between the thumb and index finger. This should be done several times, and the process repeated with anhydrous ether and finally, with a dry surgical sponge. If stainless steel is used, it can be straightened either by hand drawing, or by hanging heavy weights on the cut pieces of wire for several days. Stainless steel can be electro-etched and polished by the above procedure using 6 volts AC and the following solution: 34 ml sulphuric acid, 42 ml phosphoric acid, 24 ml distilled water.

To electro-polish platinum irridium electrodes, one should use a current of 5–6 volts AC and a solution of 50% sodium cyanide and 30% sodium hydroxide (Kinnard and McLean, 1967).

A. Insulation

A great number of insulating varnishes are commercially available which provide well-tolerated insulation for all types of electrodes.

Insl-X can be applied easily full strength with a minimum of beading if the electrode is drawn out of the varnish at a slow, steady rate and at an angle of about 45 degrees. This can be done by hand, but is nicely accomplished by a clock motor. The major advantages of this insulation are that it is thick and a single coat is usually sufficient, and it will dry fully in the air in only a few hours. Because it is a vinyl-based plastic, however, it is better suited for recording electrodes than for stimulating ones.

Epoxylite is a resin-based varnish which is extremely versatile as an insulating material. It provides a tough, thin coating when cured, and, unlike many other materials, will allow the insulated electrode to be cleaned with alcohol and hydrocarbon solvents without causing a break in the insulation. Epoxylite, however, is thin even at full strength, so that it tends to bead easily when an electrode is drawn out of the varnish. This problem really requires a mechanical dip-coater, which draws the electrode out of the varnish at a controlled rate. Since the varnish is thin, several coatings will be necessary in order to fully insulate the electrode. The insulation is then oven-cured at 50 to 60°C overnight and the desired amount of surface area can be exposed by scraping off the insulation under a magnifying glass or loupe.

B. Bipolar and Multi-lead Electrode

The electro-etching and insulating procedures described above are applied also to the construction of bipolar and multi-lead electrodes. Stainless steel is a more useful material than tungsten for this purpose because it is flexible and is readily available in a pre-insulated form.

We prefer to use it insulated with Formvar, which can be purchased locally.

The simplest technique for constructing bipolar electrodes is to cement two straightened lengths of pre-insulated stainless-steel wire together. The distance between the tips is determined by the nature of the experiment but is usually 0·5–2 mm. One should test both wires for breaks in the insulation before cementing, as straightening sometimes stretches the insulation and creates a crack. Testing can be done by connecting an ohmeter to a bare end of the wire and the other to a piece of absorbent cotton soaked in normal saline. By running the cotton up and down the electrode wire, any discontinuity in insulation will be detected by short circuit on the meter.

If both electrodes are well insulated, they can be cemented together with Epoxylite. They should then be re-insulated and cured, and the tips bared by scraping or by simply cutting across the wire, being sure that the two tips are not put in contact. After this process, the ohmmeter again allows for testing to see if there are any short circuits between the two wires. Before baring the tips of either monopolar or bipolar electrodes to be used for stimulation, they also should be tested by being placed in a beaker of saline with a bare electrode and a high DC voltage (400 volts) placed across them. Observation for a few minutes will show bubbles being formed by electrolysis at any points of break in the insulation.

For extracellular recording and stimulation, the wires are usually about 0·010–0·014 inches in diameter. To make multi-lead electrodes one uses a finer-diameter wire of about 0·004 inches. One simply twists together the desired number of wires of differing lengths. If one desires to use extremely fine wires for the bipolar pair, it is frequently useful to twist them about a heavier "strut". This is particularly useful in chronic implantation, for the "strut" can be used in the electrode carrier of the stereotaxic instrument; to assure rigidity after fixation of the electrode at the skull, the "strut" can be cut off at the surface and the electrode wires which are small and flexible can be easily positioned to connect to an electrode socket.

C. Concentric Electrode

The concentric or coaxial electrode is made easily by using a stainless-steel cannula readily obtained as hypodermic needle stock of 24 or 28 gauge. This stock is cut to the desired length with a high-speed drill and an abrasive wheel as described in Chapter 8. An insulated, tested stainless-steel wire is then inserted through the cannula so as to protrude a millimeter or so from the end of the tube. For chronic implantation, one should predetermine the depth of the target site from the surface of the skull. Slightly above this level, a small cut is made into the side of the cannula and just below it a flexible pigtail lead is affixed to the cannula. This preparation allows the inner wire to be inserted through the side of the tubing, where it is then fixed in place with a tiny drop of dental cement; then the cannula is insulated and cured. After exposing the tip and scraping a small spot of insulation from the cannula at the desired distance, the shaft should be tested for a break in the insulation or a short between the two components. Prior to the insertion of the center wire, a pigtail lead is soldered to the cannula shaft for easy connection to the plug or stimulator apparatus. The electrode is lowered into position with the electrode carrier of the stereotaxic instrument fixed to the tubing above the cut. Once the electrode is fixed to the skull, the excess protruding cannula can be easily broken off by hand.

D. *Cortical Stimulating Electrode*

Several electrode arrangements have been used to stimulate the cortex and are described by Delgado (1964). "Blind" techniques in which insulated steel phonograph needles are hammered into the skull may be unrealiable since the exact tip locations cannot be certain. Because of the configuration of volume-conducted electrical spread over the cortex, ideal cortical electrodes should be small and located on the surface of the brain itself, with little exposure to the spinal fluid which easily shorts out large electrodes. Such electrodes can be simply constructed out of insulated stainless-steel wires with only the cardion spared and inserted through small trephine holes in the skull after the dura has been spread with a needle probe. A better technique is to lace such wires through a flexible material such as the rubber dams commonly used in surgery and then to bear only the flat surface which will lie next to the cortex. With more elegant technology available, one could of course print such connectors onto flexible mylar.

IV. IMPLANTATION PROCEDURES

The use of a stereotaxic instrument is essential for accurate depth stimulation and indispensable for a chronic implantation in which the electrodes must be placed as closely as possible to the structures under study. The electrode carriers are calibrated so that any position in a set of three rectangular coordinates can be obtained. With the animal fixed in this instrument, an electrode can be accurately placed anywhere on or within the brain, as described by Pellegrino and Cushman in Chapter 3.

A. Pedestals, Sockets and Connectors

Once the electrodes have been implanted and tested *in situ* a number of techniques can be employed for chronic fixation to the skull. In general, the first step, while the electrode is held rigidly in the carrier, is to fill the drill hole in the skull with dental cement or an acrylic resin. One should be sure that the hole and area of skull surrounding it are not wet with spinal fluid. By carefully flowing dental cement of proper consistency into the hole, it tends to spread out on the undersurface of the skull like a rivet and secure the electrode rigidly. Once all necessary holes are thus filled and the electrodes firmly fixed, the stereotaxic machine can be removed and the leads fixed to some kind of convenient connectors. The classic description of the ideal way to do this for large animals such as the cat and monkey is that of Sheatz (1961). (See Fig. 4.) A triangular-shaped platform is mounted on

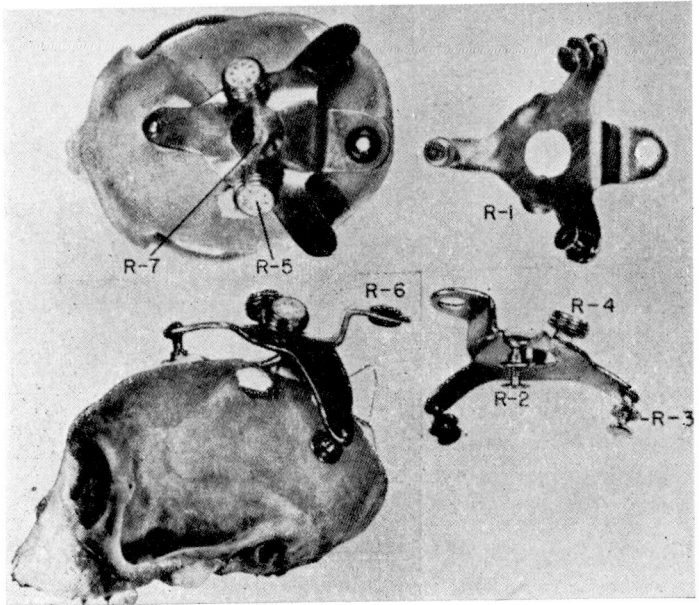

Fig. 4. Skull-mounted Sheatz Pedestal and tripod array. (From Sheatz, 1961.)

adjustable anchor screws, forming a tripod which can be adjusted to fit the curvature of the skull. The anchor screws are inserted into burr-holes drilled in the skull and secured with hex-nuts. Dental cement is applied over the nuts to assure rigidity. The electrodes are drawn through a hole in the center of the pedestal and fixed to the connector. Sheatz' connector is interesting because it eliminates the need to solder wires during surgery. The connector-pins are spring-mounted in a plexiglass cup and the free ends of the electrodes are inserted in the holes of the female element of the lucite connector. The holes are then packed with silver dental amalgam, an excellent conductor, and a solder-free connection is the result.

Miller et al. (1961) describe a simple electrode holder for use with chronic implantations in the rat. (Fig. 5.) After stereotaxic implantation the electrode should be allowed to protrude about 2 mm from the skull. Four jewelers screws (stainless steel, SAL #46) are positioned in front of and behind the electrode sites. After the leads have been soldered to the electrodes, dental cement is applied to the total area, adhering first to the screws. When a small pool of cement has hardened, the wire leads are drawn back toward the animal's back and the male element of a dress snap is soldered to the lead. The structure is built up again with dental cement. The female element of the dress snap provides the connector during the experiment.

Roth (1966) has recently described a method for attaching electrical connectors to the skull which involves the use of "pop" rivets, which have had a wide industrial use. Stainless-steel rivets one-eighth and one-quarter inch are used and are applied through the phalanges of the connector with a special plier-like tool and to a #30 burr-hole in the skull. This technique has been successfully used in Rhesus monkeys. These rivets are used to hold a Sheatz-type connector or other device, and simplify the problem of rigid permanent mounting under the head.

The connector itself is chosen for the size of the animal and to contain enough connectors for the number of electrodes involved. A wide assortment of miniature and microminiature connectors are available from industrial firms, some of which are listed in the Appendix. Small connectors, including those made by Winchester, can be bolted together and are particularly attractive for insuring tight connections. In certain stimulation experiments it is desirable to have electrodes which will pull apart at the connector, should the animal have a convulsion or move with unexpected vigor; however, a satisfactory disconnect device is not readily available commercially.

The fixed electrode has of course the disadvantage of assuming that one has predetermined desirable target area, or at best, one has been able to "straddle" it with a multi-lead electrode. If it is desirable to carry out exploratory stimulation on an awake animal, the ingenious approach best described by MacLean (1967) can be used. This technique replaces fixed electrodes with a platform permanently mounted

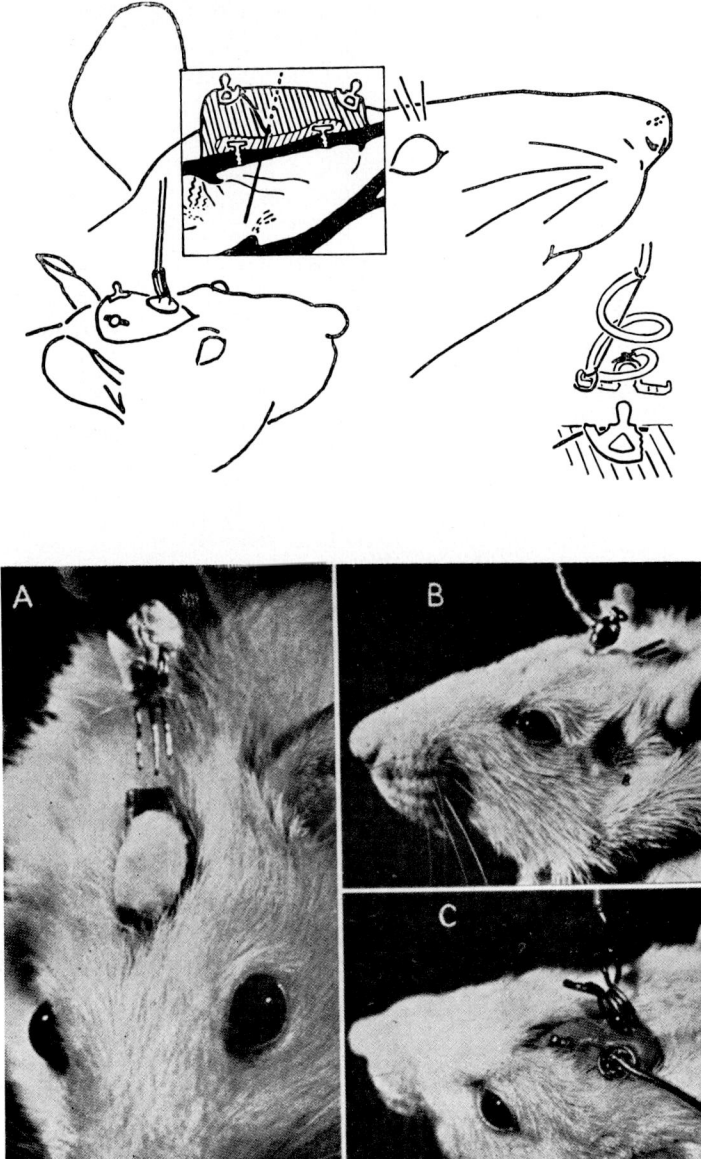

Fig. 5. *Top:* Main features of the Chronic implantation technique. *Bottom:* Various connector arrays for the technique described by Miller *et al.*, showing two methods (in photo C) for connecting male elements of dress snaps, with a spring or female dress snap. (From Miller *et al.*, 1961.)

on the skull parallel to the plane of the stereotaxic atlas. The platform, usually of lucite, consists of 20–30 perpendicular holes, one millimeter apart, and stereotaxically aligned before fixation on the skull. (Fig. 6.) Through these already aligned holes, the experimenter may enter the skull by making a small twist-drill opening, then by treating the dura and lowering an electrode, either with a micrometer drive or to some prefixed depth by hand. Thus the experimenter may gain access to practically all points of the brain with the movable electrode and the awake animal. This has been particularly useful in the study of chaired squirrel-monkeys who do not tolerate large numbers of intracerebral electrodes well. In addition to the convenience of this method for large electrodes, the platform has been successfully used for microelectrode recording.

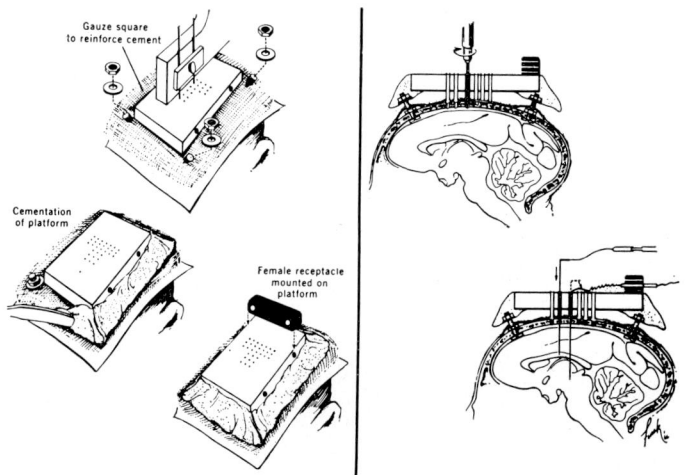

Fig. 6. MacLean chronically fixed stereotaxic platform, showing final mounting and electrode implantation procedures. (From MacLean, 1967.)

All of the above techniques assume a rigid electrode fixed at the skull for stability. This method seems to be entirely satisfactory for practical purposes in most animal studies. In the human, however, a problem is created by the fact that the brain is free to move a considerable distance in the cranial cavity, particularly if there is any cerebral atrophy. In this situation, rigid electrodes are a potential hazard to the brain, and in our own laboratory, we have avoided them by using a flexible electrode which is placed into position with a rigid guide which is subsequently withdrawn; the flexible wire is thus free to move with the brain. Serial X-rays show that they remain in position for many months (Fig. 7) and post-mortem histological studies show a minimum of traumatic changes in the surrounding tissue. This technique may be indicated in dealing with animals with unusually large brains, or in unusual situations where problems of acceleration and deceleration are prominent.

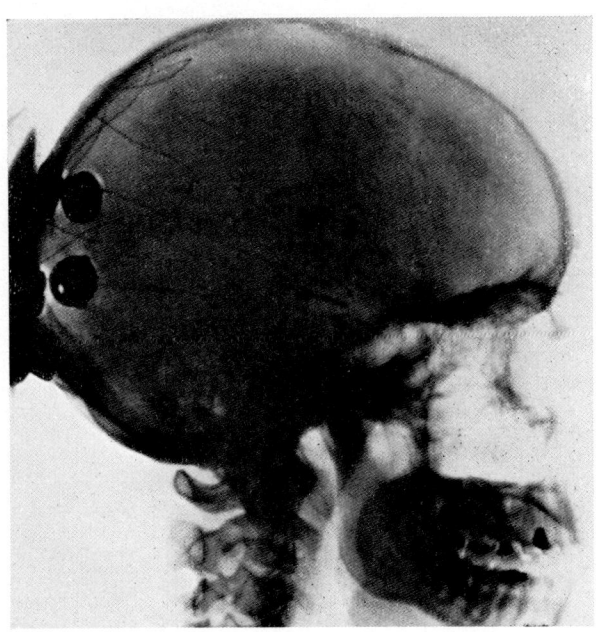

FIG. 7. X-Ray photograph of electrodes implanted in the amygdala of a human patient.

B. Potential Problems

When implanting either surface or depth electrodes, the investigator will produce some mechanical trauma, which is inevitable and must be taken into account when interpreting the results of an experiment. If this seems to be a critical issue, it is advisable to use the neuroanatomist's strategy of placing the electrode in sequential experiments from different entry points so as to distribute randomly the cell damage.

The most critical aspect of the technique is simply that of any good surgical technique. As described in Chapter 4, one should minimize trauma and avoid extraneous foreign bodies such as cotton sponges. Sterilization of the electrodes is quite important, since a microabscess at the tip of an electrode can substantially alter stimulation results. The electrode can be sterilized by vigorous cleaning with soap and water, careful rinsing, soaking for two hours in 1:1000 Zephiran solution, and careful rinsing with sterile distilled water. Attention to the physical construction of the electrode to avoid beading of insulation, bending of small wires, and the presence of other protuberances also minimizes trauma. With good technique, one should have difficulty in finding the track of an electrode which has been in place for a few months. (See Fig. 8.) Some testimony to the brain's resistance

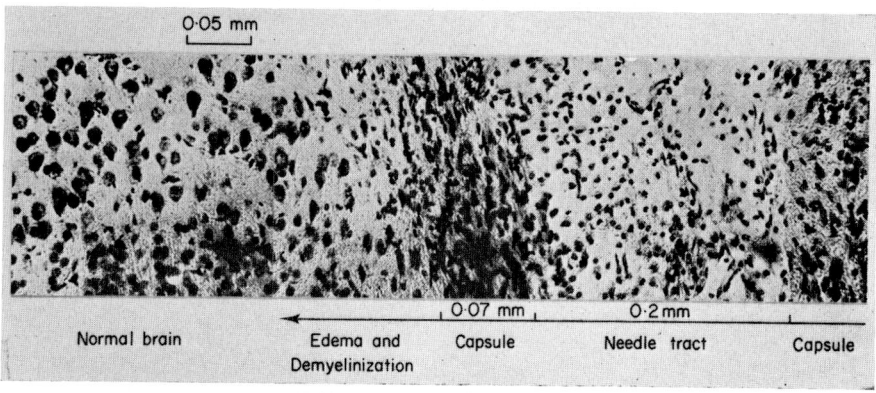

Fig. 8. 325 Magnification of monkey brain section (frontal plane) 3 months after implantation of S.S. electrode, showing extent of neural damage surrounding needle tract. (From Delgado, 1961.)

to trauma is given by Delgado (1961) who reported that as many as fifty electrodes could be left for long periods of time without significantly altering the normal functioning of the monkey brain.

A second source of tissue trauma may result from chemical irritation due to the composition of the metal electrode or of the insulating material. A great variety of metals have been used for chronic implantation. These include copper, silver, stainless steel, platinum, gold, tungsten, molybdenum and platinum chloride and silver chloride. Fischer et al. (1961) implanted insulated and uninsulated copper, silver chloride, and stainless-steel wires in the cat's brain for periods of 2–4 months to test for toxicity. Silver chloride and the copper electrode were poorly tolerated even when insulated and caused extensive tissue degeneration in the area surrounding the uninsulated wire (Figs 9 (A) and (B)). There was no noticeable tissue reaction to stainless steel, even around the bare wire. Subsequent work has confirmed the general conclusion that highly reactive metals such as copper and silver should not be used for chronic implantation and perhaps should be viewed with suspicion, even in prolonged acute experiments.

A third, troublesome problem is created by the finding that with prolonged implantation and particularly repeated stimulation, microscopic quantities of iron diffuse from the tip of steel electrodes into the surrounding tissue. In certain regions, such as the hypothalamus, the iron can be a source of excitation to the cells, independent of the electric current.

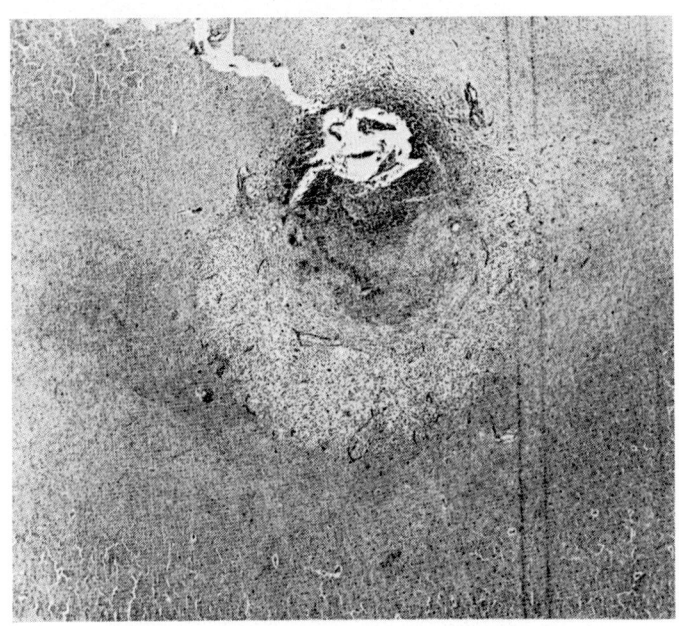

Fig. 9 (A)

Fig. 9. (A) Brain tissue reaction to bare silver wire, one week after implantation.

In the experiments cited by Fischer *et al.* a number of insulating materials were similarly tested: Tygon, Formvar, Thermobond, M472 and Polyethylene, were all found to be well-tolerated as are many newer plastics, including Teflon and Epoxylite, which are in common commercial use. Most insulating materials referred to in the literature are biologically well-tolerated, although vinyl-based insulating materials are generally unsatisfactory for stimulating electrodes because they tend to adhere poorly to metal and pull away from the electrode tip. Teflon, unless specially bonded, is particularly poor and may sometimes develop microcracks which reduce the impedance to leakage current.

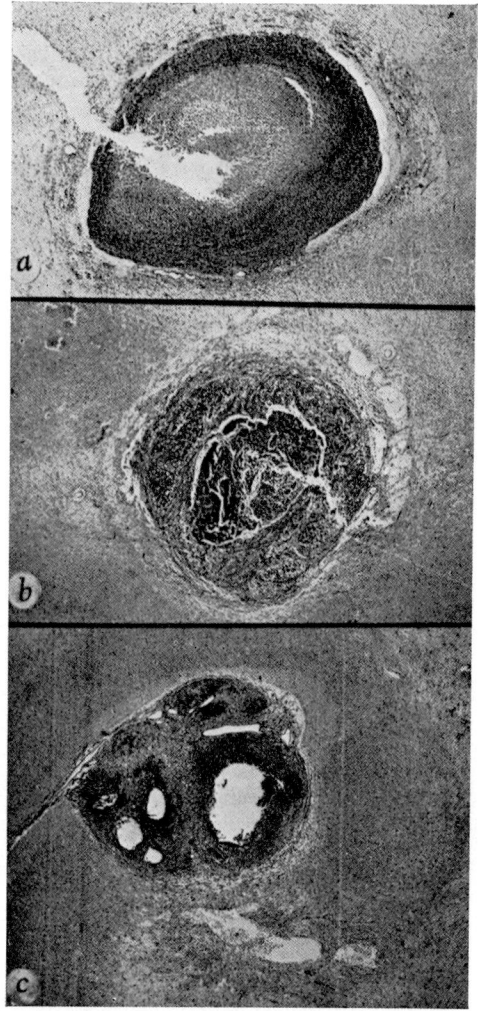

Fig. 9 (B)

(B) Effects of bare copper wires on brain tissue, after: (a) one, (b) three, and (c) four weeks' implantation. (From Fischer et al., 1961.)

A potential source of tissue damage is the stimulating current itself. (See Fig. 10 for different stimulus pulse types.) There are basically two types of such damage, thermal and electrolytic. Electrolytic damage is easily caused by unidirectional DC even at relatively low current densities. This is particularly to be guarded against because a few tens of microamperes can pass undetected in the usual monitoring situation and may be an artifact of malfunctioning or poorly designed equipment. Unidirectional pulsating DC (as is produced by most commercially available stimulators with "square wave" output) can also cause electrolytic damage according to Mickle (1961). He recommends the use of pulses of alternating polarity to avoid this problem.

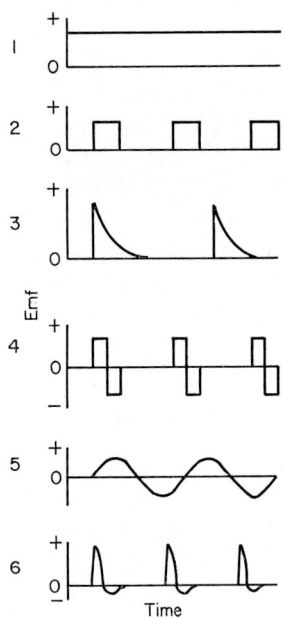

FIG. 10. Schematic representation of different monophasic waveforms commonly employed as stimuli: 1—continuous monophasic (pos) DC; 2—rectangular DC pulse (pos); 3—capacitor discharge; 4—AC, rectangular pulses; 5—AC sine wave; 6—mixture of AC and DC. (From Delgado, 1964.)

Lilly (1961) has suggested that using a differentiated sinusoid which creates brief pulses of alternating polarity is an even better stimulus. Some measure of the magnitude of this problem comes from a consideration of the average current versus time which flows in a pulsed stimulation. If one stimulates with one millisecond "square wave" pulses at 100/sec with a peak voltage of 10 V (not uncommon parameters in the laboratory) the unidirectional current flow is a minimum of 100 μA for train durations longer than ten seconds and as high as 500 μA for shorter periods. This current flow, sustained for any length of time, is sufficient to damage tissues.

For practical purposes, one may use the figures given by Lilly (1961) for 5 sec long pulse trains at 60 pulse periods per second repeated at 30 sec intervals. He found that pulse durations above 5 msec caused rapid electrolytic injury. Durations below 0·2 msec, on the other hand, caused thermal injury if given at threshold turn. Within these limits of practical applications for repetitive stimuli of 0·1–1·0 msec, one should create little or no electrolytic damage if peak currents are kept below about 10 mA for electrodes of usual size. (A critical variable is of course the current density, i.e. mA/cm^2, which can become extremely high if the electrode tip is quite small.)

Sinusoidal alternating current with symmetrical positive and negative cycles minimizes all of these problems and is used by some investigators. Oddly enough, it is not incorporated into most commercially available machines, probably because the history of electrical stimulation has focused on the use of single or paired shock stimuli for neurocircuit analysis, where the abrupt rise time and limited duration of the square wave has been of considerable value.

V. THE ELECTRICAL INTERFACE AND PROBLEMS OF POLARIZATION

The wave form delivered to tissue by the stimulator may be quite different than that produced on the oscilloscope by the stimulating device. An electrode of whatever kind and the surrounding tissue have a complex physicochemical relationship, even under the best of conditions. Problems created by this interaction are compounded in chronic preparations in which electrodes remain in contact with the tissue for some time. The processes that occur alter the electrical characteristics of both the conducting medium and of the electrode. In general, these phenomena include an exchange of ions between the electrode and the surrounding tissue which polarizes either the electrode, the tissue, or both (see Fig. 11). This polarization process can be so severe as to block or sizably alter the measurement of cell-generated currents and may seriously distort stimulating processes. The ideal electrode would be one which maintains a constant electrode potential when immersed in a physiological solution and should remain independent of the flow of stimulating current supplied by the external device. These two criteria are rarely achieved, but much of the choice of metals and wave-forms mentioned above is determined by attempts to approach this condition in situations where polarization may be intense. The constant current stimulator bucks the polarization by achieving high voltage outputs. Since the degree of polarization can change rapidly, a continuous monitoring of the stimulating current is essential to avoid an unstable preparation.

In addition to the polarization problem and the related problems which may arise from electrolytic actions of the electrode tip which by displacing small impurities, particularly in steel electrodes, can

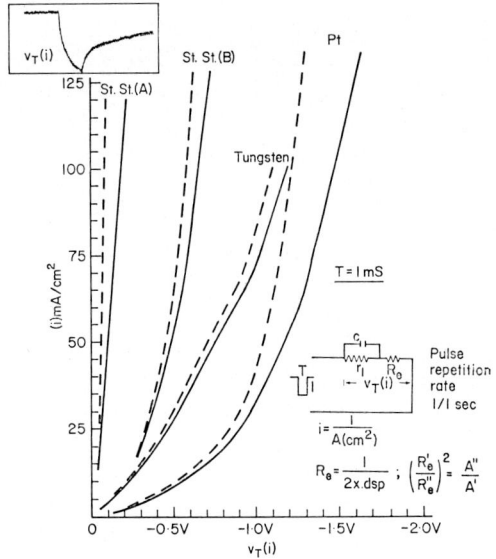

FIG. 11. Difference in impedance properties of four metal electrodes, after 1 msec pulse, as a function of current density. Broken line shows same for positive pulses. (From Weinman and Mahler, 1964.)

create sudden fluctuations in potential, one must pay attention to the electrode capacitance. Every metal in equilibrium with a surrounding tissue fluid has a characteristic capacitance which acts as a filter during the recording of signals and which distorts wave-forms applied by the stimulator. This problem is most easily detected when one is using "square wave" stimulation. This phenomenon emphasizes the importance of monitoring simultaneously the voltage and current, not only as to amplitude, but as to wave-form to maintain careful control over experimental conditions. Because the electrochemistry of interface phenomena is both complex and rather poorly understood, the interested reader is referred to a lucid summary of the problem by Weinman and Mahler in their article on the electrical properties of metal electrodes (1964).

A. The Stimulator

The stimulator consists of two parts. One supplies the control of time parameters including the stimulus duration, the repetition rate, the delay between a synchronizing pulse and the effective stimulus, the delay between two or more stimuli or the duration of a train of repetitive stimuli. For the experimental laboratory, this section of the stimulator should in fact be made up of modular timing pulse and logic units to allow for maximal flexibility.

The other part of the stimulator is a source of power to be delivered to the electrode and a unit which couples that power source to the electrode and hence to the organism. Some debate has come into the question as to whether that power source should supply a constant voltage or a constant current. The ideal stimulator should probably supply either on demand, but if limited should supply constant current. At least for equal potentials the critical parameter may in fact be power, that is volts × current × time, producing equivalent responses. There are two things the stimulator should not supply: one is undetected DC, the other is an unexpected ground return circuit from the organism which at its best produces large stimulus artifacts or, at its worst, may shock or even electrocute the organism. To protect from all of these hazards, it is customary to isolate the "stimulator" from the organism. The simplest method of doing this is with a transformer, allowing the stimulator to drive the primary of the transformer with the secondary tied to the pair of stimulating electrodes. This method poses a difficulty for pulse stimulation since few transformers can pass a "square wave" without appreciable distortion. Since the shape of the wave is not particularly critical for some purposes, a high quality audiotransformer will serve this purpose nicely. More commonly, one uses a radio frequency isolation unit designed by O. H. Schmitt, which includes a small radio frequency oscillator intercharged from the output of the stimulator. The pulse from the stimulator modulates the radio frequency carrier which is coupled to a secondary of a radio frequency isolation transformer, subsequently rectified so that the original wave shape is restored. A radio frequency isolation transformer is much easier to design and build than one designed to handle a "square wave" with high fidelity; it also has extremely low capacitance to ground which is of protective value.

More recently, isolation units have been designed which take advantage of the high frequency response of light-emitting semi-conductors and light-sensitive photodiodes to couple the timing information to a self-contained and isolated power source. The concern for isolation, for fail-safe protection against DC on the stimulating leads and fail-safe correction against spurious grounds as well as high voltage on the stimulating leads are all absolute essentials for human stimulation, and are not adequately met by any existing commercial stimulator. These requirements need not be quite so rigorous for the experimental animal but are nevertheless important. In addition to the above essentials a well-designed stimulus set-up will allow for easy monitoring of voltage and/or current, will provide timing pulses at the leading and trailing edges of the stimulus wave-form, will allow for easy inversion of the wave-form, and will make it easy to add second and third stimulus sources for studies of interaction. The power, as we have indicated, need only reach 5–10 mA and never for prolonged periods of time.

B. Frequency, Amplitude and Duration of Pulse

One way to consider the parametric issues is to say that those parameters are ideal which repeatedly elicit the biologic phenomena which one wishes to study. Probably in most experiments, this rule applies. However, there have been some systematic studies of these parameters since the time of Hess. Such studies have fundamentally asked two questions: what parameters may be troublesome? These we have discussed above in the section on tissue damage. Second, are there optimal parameters for evoking certain kinds of response? If one is recording evoked potentials, one is ordinarily using single shock stimuli and is usually concerned that these be of short duration to minimize stimulus artifact in the recording. In this situation, pulse durations of 0·01–0·1 msec are customary, although longer durations may be required to activate very fine fibers which characterize much of the structure of the brain.

This issue has never been explored thoroughly, but in peripheral nerves it is also necessary to utilize 3–5 msec duration impulses of high amplitude in order to activate the C-fiber components. Single shock stimuli on the other hand rarely elicit behavioral responses and, when these responses are seen, they consist of single muscle twitch, a whispered twitch, and so on (Buchwald and Ervin, 1957). If one wishes to elicit organized behavior, one is required to use trains of repetitive stimuli. These trains need not be very long, often a few pulses at high frequency, or at most, a few seconds will suffice to evoke a meaningful response. The optimal frequency for these repetitive bursts, the duration of the burst, and the recovery time before a second stimulus is identical with the first, are all extremely dependent upon location within the brain. For example, the reticular formation is most effectively excited by high-frequency stimulus of 100–200 cycles per second, and the hippocampus is most powerfully activated by frequencies of 4–6 cycles per second close to its spontaneous activity. In general frequencies of 60–100 cycles are most likely to be effective. Figure 12(A) and (B), taken from Mihailovic and Delgado (1956) show the relationship between threshold and frequency for somatic and autonomic responses in the unanesthetized monkey. These findings are consistent with those of Hess (1954), who further suggested that in the hypothalamus low frequencies, i.e. below 50/sec, were more likely to produce parasympathetic effects, whereas higher frequencies, sympathetic effects. For the amygdala, Buchwald and Ervin (1957) described a wide range of elicited behaviors dependent on the frequency used as well as on other factors. All of this suggests that for a given locus or for a given behavior, one must find the optimal frequency; that is, if one is exploring for an excitable area it probably makes sense to explore with a 60–1–0 cycle stimulus.

In our own work with man, we start with slow frequencies and test for threshold effects at 1, 6, 20, and 60 Hz. Pulse duration has been discussed briefly, and train duration for repetitive stimulation has been much less systematically explored. In general, once a behavior is clearly evoked, termination of the train seems to be desirable, because if it is continued, there is some hazard of its recruiting increasing numbers of neurons and producing an epileptic seizure. To sustain an activity for a prolonged period of time, it is generally better to give regular intermittent kinds of stimulation adjusted to the particular experimental conditions. We have, for example, used half-second on, half-second off cycles at a 30/sec repetition rate for sustaining certain motivational states. Perhaps of more importance in train duration, if one is making repeated observations in a preparation, is the duration of the intertrial interval. For example, Delgado has pointed out that in studies of the motor cortex one should wait approximately one minute between successive stimulations to maintain stable thresholds. There should be a period of 5–10 sec of rest, and in general the obvious rule should be that the interval between two stimulations should be longer than the duration of the local excitatory state following the first stimulation. This factor again varies widely by locus and perhaps other metabolic variables. Of particular importance may be the sequential and potentially irreversible changes in response to stimulation from some parts of the brain. Delgado, for example, reported nearly ten years ago that repetitive stimulation of the amygdala produced sequential behavioral changes in monkeys. Shagass (personal communication) reported similar changes in cats

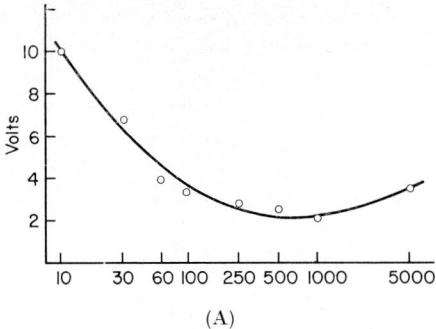

(A)

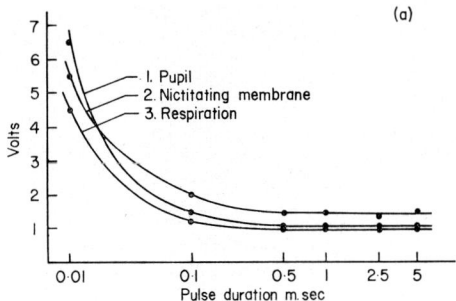

(B)

FIG. 12. (A) Effect of varying frequency of pulses upon threshold of motor response. (Pulse duration constant); localization brachium conjunctiuum. (B) Effect of varying duration (a) and frequency (b) of pulses upon thresholds of automatic responses. Localization No. 1, lateral hypothalamus; No. 2, superior border of the red nucleus; No. 3, Medulla oblongata. Note similar curve pattern in different species. (From Mihailovic and Delgado, 1956.)

stimulated in the septal region. An elegant and detailed analysis of this phenomenon has been made by Goddard et. al. (1969). (Fig.13.) He reports that in a rat given single bursts of stimulation, particularly in the amygdala, as well as in other anterior limbic structures, the threshold for seizure discharge sequentially drops, and after several such stimuli the animal shows spontaneous convulsions. This phenomenon seems to be dependent on the interstimulus interval and to

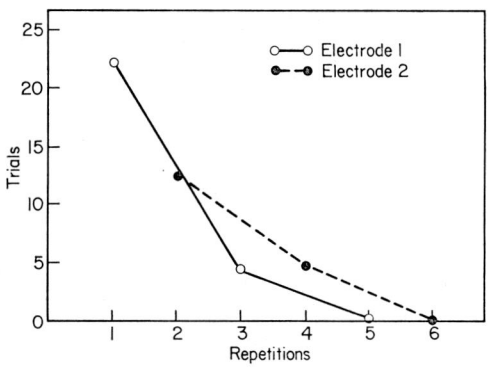

FIG. 13. Changes in brain function. Permanent effect of non-polarizing electrical stimulation on brain function. Graph shows a decrement in the number of daily trials before convulsions were elicited from electrodes implanted in the amygdala of the rat. (From Goddard et al., 1969.)

be modified by stimulation at other points within the brain. His careful work supports the impression of many clinical epileptologists that spontaneous seizures, particularly in the amygdala, tend to lower the threshold for other seizures, and to sequentially impair function in the region. Thus, in certain species and in certain regions, there may exist an infinite hysteresis to electrical stimulation.

C. Wave Forms

In describing the stimulator earlier, we avoided making any requirements as to the characteristics of the output. We did imply earlier that most available stimulators simply supply pulses of DC, that is, "square waves". By the time these have passed through the usual electrode array, they may be slightly differentiated, which accentuates the rising and falling phase. These sharp changes of voltage against time are quite effective in exciting certain neural elements, particularly relatively large fibers. This stimulus pulse is used widely for stimulating the brain in spite of the fact that "square" is the most unlikely shape of any biological event. Although there has been much discussion about optimal wave-forms for stimulation or stimulation of certain kinds, there is little systematic information published. One would think that stimulation would have been carried out from tape recordings of spontaneous EEG rhythms, by evoked potentials, by pathological events, such as epileptic spike, and so on. But either this has not been done, or has not produced any interesting information.

In addition to the pulsed DC already mentioned, three basic kinds of stimulus pulses have been used. Sine waves (see Fig. 10, No. 5) for trains of repetitive stimulation seem to be not only perfectly adequate biologically, but considerably safer in regard to electrolytic damage of tissue. They should probably be used more often than they presently are. Lilly (1961) has argued that, by differentiating a sine wave, one has both a more effective stimulus of a pulsed pair of opposite polarity and a stimulus which can be utilized for single or double shock stimulation, and so on. He has described the circuit necessary to produce this wave-form, and it has been utilized by a number of people around the world. In ordinary laboratory usage, there seems to be no great advantage and it has slowly been neglected. Hunsperger in Germany uses an extremely high frequency sine wave of several kilocycles presented as a shaped burst, and has explored the effect of changing the envelope of that burst. With a gradual increase in amplitude at the onset of the burst, one may produce an extremely smooth and "natural looking" onset of animal behavior (NRP Symposium, Boston 1967). John has used a similar approach, but has used the high-frequency sine wave essentially as a carrier and modulated it with other information, such as a low-frequency sine wave. Using this mode of stimulation, he was able to teach animals to differentiate between two different low-frequency modulations on such carriers, suggesting again that it was the envelope information which effectively excited the nervous tissue. These techniques should be explored in much greater depth as they promise the possibility of a different approach to modifying central nervous organization. The danger of producing thermal effects from the high-frequency stimulation can probably be controlled if it is carefully monitored.

Excluded from this discussion is the usefulness of the technique of stimulation with DC fields, which are of particular value in electrophysiological studies as well as to the analysis of conditioned reflexes, as explored by Rusinov and other Soviet investigators.

D. *The Conscious Animal*

For behavioral analyses, stimulation of the conscious animal is desirable. The advantages are that one can see rather rapidly if the animal seems to be in pain, if a seizure state seems to be developing or if gross uncoordinated involvement of the motor system is occurring to preclude other analyses. The techniques are essentially two-fold. The most straightforward is to connect the stimulating electrode via a long wire protected in a leash to the stimulus isolation unit on the top of the cage or some distance away from the animal by having a long light leash conveniently fixed to the ceiling in the cage by a spring or elastic which permits unstressed movement of the wire. Or a swivel-connector is used which allows for free rotation on a mercury joint without loosing electrical contact. Animals such as rats and cats, are observed through a window from a darkened room into a lighted cage; movies or video tapes can be taken of the elicited activity. With monkeys, it is more convenient to use a restraining chair and to position the electrodes above the head so that they move within the limits imposed by the chair. If one wishes simultaneously to record and stimulate these behaving animals, a similar connection is made utilizing Microdot or similar low-noise cable for the recording leads. In this situation, the stimulating electrode leads should be carried as a twisted pair and shielded, and the shield carefully grounded.

E. Telestimulation

Since even a single light pair of wires on the head of an animal may restrict movement, several devices have been described in the literature for remote or telestimulation. Even with the work of Delgado who has recognized the tremendous importance for free field or social studies, it is remarkable that there is not an adequate telestimulator on the market as of this writing. One of the problems of telestimulation is the dependence of the stimulus pulse on such variables as position and distance from the stimulator, which may be overcome by mounting the stimulus power supply on the animal with the triggering pulse and timing controlled by radio. Delgado has used a self-contained recycling stimulator built into a watch case which is worn around the neck by his monkeys. These stimulators deliver a preset stimulus at regular intervals and the animal can then be observed in his colony or other free-living situation while he is being subjected to regular intermittent stimulation of some brain structure. This technique loses a certain flexibility of control by the experimenter, but is relatively straightforward and economical.

VI. Interpretation

Finally, we may consider what measures of the stimulus effect are available, which may very often be combined, as one tries simultaneously to follow electrophysiological and behavioral changes in response to a given stimulus. An example of such a study is given in Buchwald and Ervin (1957) where an attempt was made to correlate behavior, evoked potentials and stimulation of subcortical sites in various modes.

Perhaps the very simplest measure of stimulus effect is the electrical recording in the field of the stimulation. The most striking phenomena here is that of the after discharge, that is to say, a self-sustained electrical hypersynchrony which continues after the cessation of the stimulus, but by definition does not build up into an epileptic seizure. Localized after-discharge phenomena have been used as test systems for drug effects, and have been used to locally interfere with neural function, producing a kind of temporary electrical ablation in behavioral studies.

Further, one may examine remote electrical effects of focal stimulation by usual electrophysiological recording techniques, most commonly either EEG recording, or the observation of more rapid time-locked potentials evoked by the electrical stimulus. The shift from cortical synchrony in the EEG to low-voltage fast activity, induced by burst stimulation of the midbrain reticular formation, is the classic example of the former. Such an effect is shown in Fig. 14, taken from a study in which the sensitivity of the reticular formation to that stimulus was systematically varied by local cooling.

By triggering the recorded electrical event from the same clock which starts the stimulus, one may look at time-locked events, or evoked potentials, which are in general too fast to be observed in the slow recording of the EEG machine, but which reveal a great deal of information, both about conduction pathways, and/or about the organization of the neural aggregate where the information is received. Figure 15 shows the response elicited "antidromically" by stimulating the optic tectum of the pigeon and recording the contralateral optic nerve. These data show clearly the absence of projecting fibers from the one side and the complexity of the reponse evoked from the other.

This supplemental information from stimulation was not only consistent with, but clarified pre-existing anatomical information about these projections. There are time-locked evoked responses to stimulation which are relatively slow and related to the intrinsic rhythms of the brain, and so stand somewhere between the diffusely altered states of the first kind mentioned above and the quite precise projections of the second kind. The recruiting response is such a phenomenon and is characteristically elicited from certain specific nuclei of the thalamus. Figure 16 illustrates the usefulness of depth stimulation for the localization of an anatomical structure. In this experiment an electrode was

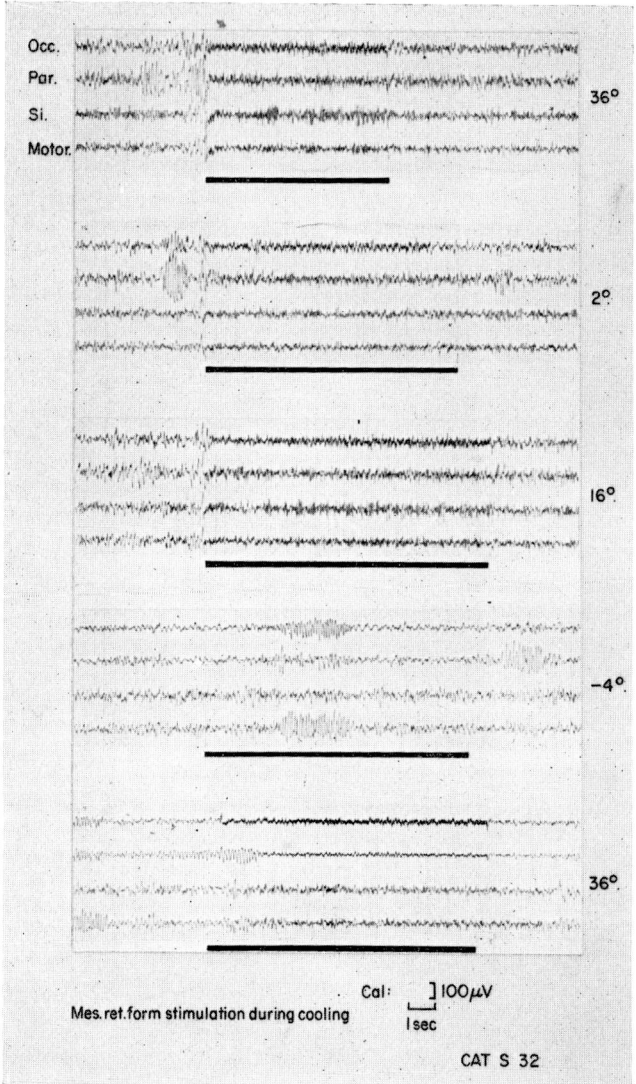

Fig. 14. Reticular formation. Stimulation during cooling using a cold probe.

sequentially lowered into the brain, aimed hopefully at the anterior nucleus of the thalamus which was finally identified by the characteristic response evoked in the overlying frontal cortex. It is interesting to note in this situation that even the artifact is useful, for its magnitude clearly outlines the lateral ventricle through which the electrode

7 Electrical Stimulation of the Brain

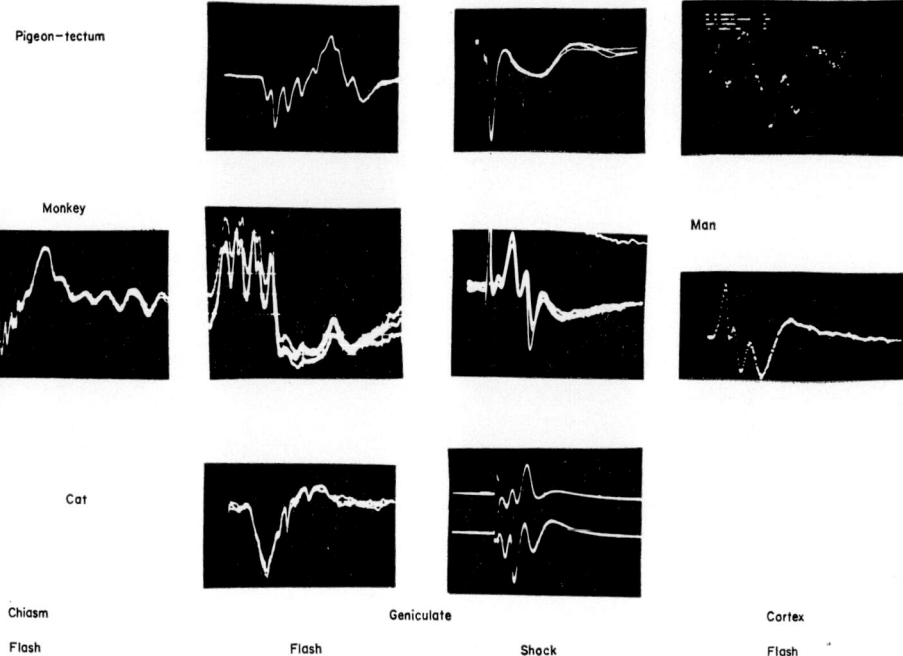

Fig. 15. Comparative visual responses of pigeon, monkey and cat.

passes on the way. This technique of identifying subcortical structures by their response to stimulation is particularly useful in human stereotactic surgery where the surgeon is faced with necessity for precise localization in often distorted brains hidden within the extremely variable human cranial vault. Under these conditions, strict anatomic or radiologic landmarks are only suggestive, not definitive of nuclear location.

Moving away from electrophysiologic recording techniques, one may look for some readily identifiable effector event, the twitch of a muscle, the dilation of a pupil, the change in heart rate, etc. as either the threshold phenomena to stimulation of the site or the identification of the site in response to a moving electrode being stimulated suprathreshold. Perhaps the most classic example of this kind is self-stimulation in which the availability of a threshold stimulus or its disappearance is very promptly reflected in the behavior of the animal under observation.

Most complex probably are the phenomena of self-report available only to man who can give verbal descriptions of his own awareness of change in response to brain stimulation. Although such material is

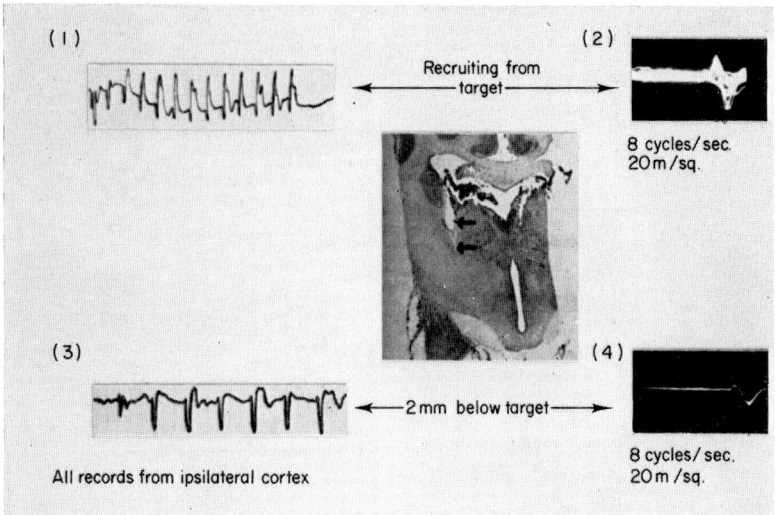

Fig. 16. Recruiting response; definition of ventricular floor by electrical stimulation.

collected under clinical conditions which make much of it not as rigorous as the experimenter could desire, it is extremely illuminating for the brain stimulator to re-read the reports over the years of Forster, Penfield, White and other neurosurgeons who have stimulated man at the operating table in the course of clinical surgery. While these reports are somewhat less anecdotally fascinating, they are probably more useful in the present state of our knowledge than the more elaborate statements that come from schizophrenic subjects who have also had an opportunity to respond to brain stimulation.

VII. Conclusion

Brain stimulation is only one of many tools which contribute to the understanding of man's mind and behavior, and it is unlikely that it will ever fulfill the fantasy of some, of reproducing exactly a predictable and desired state of the whole organism. Still, it is a tool which widely used provides another bridge between those events observed as behavior by the experimenter, and those more private events which reflect the ongoing spatiotemporal patterning of the most complex mechanism known in the universe, the brain. It would be desirable if this potentially powerful technique were thought about conceptually, developed with the same parametric rigour as recording techniques have been and supported with the superb technology that is in principle now available.

REFERENCES

Bak, A. F. (1967). *Electroenceph. Clin. Neurophysiol.* 22, 186–187.
Brazier, M. A. B. (1968). "The Electrical Activity of the Nervous System." Williams and Wilkins, Baltimore.
Brazier, M. A. B. (1959). In "Handbook of Physiology" (J. Field, H. W. Magoun, and V. E. Hall, eds), Vol. 1, Sec. 1, pp. 1–58. Am. Physiol. Soc., Washington, D.C.
Broca, P. (1861). In "A Source Book in the History of Psychology" (Herrnstein and Boring, eds), pp. 223–229. Harvard University Press, Cambridge.
Buchwald, N. A. and Ervin, F. R. (1957). *Electroenceph. Clin. Neurophys. J.* 9, No. 3, 477–496.
Bureš, J., Petráů, M. and Zachar, J. (eds), "Electrophysiological Methods in Biological Research." Academic Press, New York and London.
Chatrian, G. E., Dodge, H. W., Jr., Petersen, M. C. and Bickford, R. G. (1959a). *Electroenceph. Clin. Neurophysiol.* 11, 165–169.
Chatrian, G. E., Pollack, C. S., and Petersen, M. C. (1959b). *Electroenceph. Clin. Neurophysiol.* 11, 358–361.
Delgado, J. M. R. (1959). *Elenceph. Clin. Neurophysiol.* 11, 591–593.
Delgado, J. M. R. (1961). In "Electrical Stimulation of the Brain" (D. E. Sheer, ed.), pp. 25–37. University of Texas Press, Austin, Texas, U.S.A.
Delgado, J. M. R. (1964). In "Physical Techniques in Biological Research" (W. L. Nastuk, ed.), Vol. 5, pp. 89–138. Academic Press, New York and London.
Doty, R. W. (1969). *Ann. R. Psychol.* 20, 289–320.
Ebbinghaus, H. (1885). In "A Source Book in the History of Psychology" (Herrnstein and Boring, eds), pp. 517–530. Harvard University Press, Cambridge.
Fechner, T. (1860). In "A Source Book in the History of Psychology" (Herrnstein and Boring, eds), pp. 66–74. Harvard University Press, Cambridge.
Fischer, G., Sayre, G. P. and Bickford, G. (1961). In "Electrical Stimulation of the Brain". (D. E. Sheer, ed.), pp. 55–60. University of Texas Press, Austin, Texas, U.S.A.
Flourens, J. M. (1824). In "A Source Book in the History of Psychology" (Herrnstein and Boring, eds), pp. 220–223. Harvard University Press, Cambridge.
Franz, S. I. (1915). In "A Source Book in the History of Psychology" (Herrnstein and Boring, eds), pp. 237–244, Harvard University Press, Cambridge.
Fritsch, G. and Hitzig, E. (1870). In "A Source Book in the History of Psychology" (Herrnstein and Boring, eds), pp. 229–233. Harvard University Press, Cambridge.
Gavalas, R. J., Walter, D. O., Horner, and Adey, W. R. (1970). *Brain Res.* 18, 491–501.
Gengerelli, J. A. (1961). In "Electrical Stimulation of the Brain". (D. E. Sheer, ed.), pp. 155–164. University of Texas Press, Austin, Texas, U.S.A.
Goddard, G. V., McIntyre, D. C. and Leech, C. K. (1969). *Exp. Neurol.* 25, 295–330.
Hess, W. R. (1954). "Diencephalon, Autonomic and Extrapyramidal Functions." Grune and Stratton, New York.
Kinnard, M. A. and MacLean, P. D. (1967). *Electroenceph. Clin. Neurophysiol.* 22, 183–186.

Lashley, K. A. (1929). In "A Source Book in the History of Psychology" (Herrnstein and Boring, eds), pp. 244–248. Harvard University Press, Cambridge.
Lilly, J. C. (1961). In "Electrical Stimulation of the Brain" (D. E. Sheer, ed.), pp. 60–64. University of Texas Press, Austin, Texas, U.S.A.
Loucks, R. B., Weinberg, H., Smith, M. (1959). *Electroenceph. Clin. Neurophysiol.* **11**, 823.
MacLean, P. D. (1967). *Electroenceph. Clin. Neurophysiol.* **22**, 180–182.
Mickle, W. A. (1961). In "Electrical Stimulation of the Brain" (D. E. Sheer, ed.), pp. 67–74. University of Texas Press, Austin, Texas, U.S.A.
Mihailovic, L. and Delgado, J. M. R. (1956). *J. Neurophys.* **19**, 1.
Miller, N. E., Coons, E. E., Lewis, M. and Jensen, D. H. (1961a). In "Electrical Stimulation of the Brain" (D. E. Sheer, ed.), pp. 51–55. University of Texas Press, Austin, Texas, U.S.A.
Miller, N. E., Jensen, D. O. and Myers, A. K. (1961b). In "Electrical Stimulation of the Brain" (D. E. Sheer, ed.), pp. 64–67. University of Texas Press, Austin, Texas, U.S.A.
Müller, J. (1838). In "A Source Book in the History of Psychology" (Herrnstein and Boring, eds.), pp. 26–33. Harvard University Press, Cambridge.
Nastuk, W. L. (ed.) (1964). "Physical Techniques in Biological Research", Vol. 5, Academic Press, New York and London.
Plonsy, R. (1969). "Bioelectric Phenomena." McGraw-Hill Series in Bioengineering, New York.
Robinson, D. A. (1968). *Proc. IEEE* **56**, 6. June, 1968.
Roth, J. G. (1966). *Electroenceph. Clin. Neurophysiol.* **20**, 618–619.
Sechenov, I. M. (1965). "Reflexes of the Brain." The M.I.T. Press, Cambridge.
Sem-Jacobsen, C. W. (1968). "Depth-Electrographic Stimulation of the Human Brain and Behavior." Charles C. Thomas, Springfield, Illinois.
Sheatz, G. C. (1961). In "Electrical Stimulation of the Brain" (D. E. Sheer, ed.), pp. 45–51. University of Texas Press, Austin, Texas, U.S.A
Sheer, D. E. (ed.) (1961). "Electrical Stimulation of the Brain." University of Texas Press, Austin, Texas, U.S.A.
Sherrington, C. S. (1947). The Integrative Action of the Nervous System." Yale University Press, New Haven, Connecticut, U.S.A.
Stevens, C. F. (1966). "Neurophysiology: A Primer." John Wiley & Sons, New York.
Suckling, E. E. (1964). In "Physical Techniques in Biological Research" (W. L. Nastuk, ed.), Vol. 5, pp. 1–20. Academic Press, New York and London.
Suckling, E. E. (1961). "Bioelectricity." McGraw-Hill, New York.
Thompson, R. F., Lindsley, D. B., and Eason, R. G. (1966). In "Experimental Methods and Instrumentation in Psychology" (J. B. Sidowski, ed.), pp. 117–176. McGraw-Hill, New York.
Thompson, R. F. (1967). "Foundations of Physiological Psychology." Harper and Row, New York.
Thorndike, E. L. (1898). In "A Source Book in the History of Psychology" (Herrnstein and Boring, eds), pp. 534–544. Harvard University Press, Cambridge.
Weinman, J. and Mahler, J. (1964). *Med. Electron. Biol. Engng.* **2**, 299–310.
Wundt, W. (1896). In "A Source Book in the History of Psychology" (Herrnstein and Boring, eds), pp. 399–406. Harvard University Press, Cambridge.

Appendix

List of Equipment Suppliers

CHEMICAL REAGENTS
Fisher Scientific Co.
1458 N. Lamon Ave.
Chicago, Illinois, U.S.A.

COMMERCIAL ELECTRODES
Biocom Co.
9522 W. Jefferson Blvd.
Culver City, Colorado 90230, U.S.A.

Bioelectric Instruments
Box 24, Hastings on Hudson,
New York, New York 10706, U.S.A.

E. & M Instruments
Box 12511
Houston, Texas 77017, U.S.A.

Grass Instrument
101 Old Colony Ave.
Quincy, Massachusetts 02169, U.S.A.

David Kopf Institutes
7324 Elmo Street
Tujunga, California 91042, U.S.A.

COMMERCIAL STIMULATORS
Bioelectric Instruments
Box 204, Hastings on Hudson,
New York, New York 10706, U.S.A.

E & M. Instruments
Box 12511
Houston, Texas 77017, U.S.A.

Grass Instrument
101 Old Colony Ave.
Quincy, Massachusetts 02169, U.S.A.

David Kopf Institutes
7324 Elmo Street
Tujunga, California 91042, U.S.A.

Harvard Apparatus Co.
150 Dover Rd.
Millis, Massachusetts 02054, U.S.A.

Phipps & Bird
303 56th St.
Richmond, Virginia 23205, U.S.A.

Ortec Institutes
267 Midland Rd.
Oak Ridge, Tennessee 37836, U.S.A.

CONNECTORS
Amphenol Connector Division
Amphenol-Borg Electronics
1830 South 54th Ave.
Chicago, Illinois, U.S.A.
(Available also at most Radio and Electronics Supply Houses.)

ELECTRODE MATERIALS
Tungsten Wire
General Electric Co.

Lamp Metals and Component Division
21800 Tungsten Rd.
Cleveland, Ohio, U.S.A.

Cleveland Tungsten Inc.
10200 Meech Ave.
Cleveland 5, Ohio, U.S.A.

Stainless Steel Wire
Driver Harris Co.
202 Middlesex St.
Harrison, New Jersey, U.S.A.

Stainless Steel Hypodermic Tubing
Available at most Hospital Supply Houses

Platinum Wire
Available at Dental and Jewlers supply houses.

Electrode Varnishes
The Epoxylite Corporation of New York
42 Brekenridge St.
Buffalo, New York, U.S.A.

Insl-X E-33
Insl-X Products Co.
115 Woodworth Ave.
Yonkers, New York, U.S.A.

Fisher-Payne dip coater
Fisher Scientific Co.
1458 N. Lamon Ave.
Chicago, Illinois, U.S.A.

STEREOTAXIC APPARATUS AND ACCESSORIES

David Kopf Instruments
7324 Elmo Street
Tujunga, California 91042, U.S.A.

MISCELLANEOUS MATERIALS
Dental Cement
S. S. White, Co.
1480 Soldiers Field Road
Brighton, Massachusetts, U.S.A.
(Also avallable at Local Dental Supply Houses)

Dremel drill kit
Dremel Manufacturing Co.
Industrial Division
Racine, Wisconsin, U.S.A.
(Drill-bit takes dental drills of all sizes, available at dental supply houses)

Pop Rivets and Tool
United Shoe Machinery Corporation
Shelton, Connecticut, U.S.A.

Chapter 8

Methods for Chemical Stimulation of the Brain

R. D. MYERS

*Laboratory of Neuropsychology, Purdue University,
Lafayette, Indiana, U.S.A.*

I. Introduction	247
A. Rationale for Chemical Stimulation	248
B. Differences between Injections into the Ventricles and Tissue	249
II. Construction of an Intracerebral Cannula	250
A. Cannula for Injection into Brain Substance	250
B. Cannula for Intraventricular Injections	255
C. Multiple Cannula Array	257
D. Chemitrodes	258
III. Implanting the Cannula into Brain Tissue	259
IV. Methods of Applying a Chemical	260
A. Micro-injection of a Solution	261
B. Micro-injection of a Solution by Pump and by Hand	262
C. The Problem of Volume and Diffusion	265
D. Application of Crystals	268
V. Interpretation of Data	270
A. Pharmacological Aspects of Chemical Stimulation	272
B. Anatomical Aspects of Chemical Stimulation	274
C. Physiological Aspects of Chemical Stimulation	275
Acknowledgements	278
References	278
Appendix	280

I. INTRODUCTION

EVER since the beginning of this century, scientists have been interested in what happens when a chemical substance is injected directly into the brain. As early as 1916, Schütz infused magnesium and calcium chloride solutions in 3 to 10 ml volumes in the tuberal region of the rabbit. Somewhat later, Demole (1927) and Clöetta and Fischer (1930) showed that calcium and magnesium injected in similar volumes into the infundibular region of the cat caused a depression in activity, whereas potassium produced excitation, and sodium had no significant effect. In the same era, Hasama (1930) examined the effects of injecting a number of salt solutions into brain tissue of the cat and found that magnesium, calcium and other ions affected the body temperature of this animal.

In the late 1930's, Masserman (1938, 1940) injected strychnine and other drugs, in large doses and volumes, directly into the hypothalamus of the unanesthetized cat, and demonstrated that a drug applied to brain tissue may exert a different action from that observed when the drug is given systemically. During the same period, Comroe (1943) also showed that differences between electrical and chemical stimulation exist. He found that potassium ions applied to the brainstem could either depress or excite the depth and rate of respiration; this finding suggested that ionic stimulation does not necessarily mimic the effect of electrical stimulation.

Other significant milestones in the field of chemical stimulation, other than ones involving hormone implants, were the experiments of: Kennard (1953) who provided some of the first direct evidence of cholinergic systems in the spinal cord; MacLean (1957) who first used crystals of cholinomimetic compounds to investigate the origin of hippocampal seizures; Olds and Olds (1958) who found that a rat would press a lever to self-inject iproniazid directly into the hypothalamus; and Rech and Domino (1959) who explored the effects of pH, tonicity, volume and temperature of a solution injected into the brain stem. Following these papers, the decade of the 1960's has witnessed a dramatic increase in the use of the methods of chemical stimulation, and in a sense, the technique itself has only come into its own during the last ten years. For this reason, certain difficult questions such as those pertaining to reliability and diffusion continue to persist, and a large number of other technical problems associated with the method have not as yet been resolved.

A. Rationale for Chemical Stimulation

Why should anyone want to inject a chemical substance into brain tissue? Isn't stimulation with an electrical current a more valid approach to the experimental investigation of the brain and its function? These two questions, put to the author more than 10 years ago by a well-known neurologist, are not as easy to answer as one might expect.

In one sense, chemical stimulation can be viewed perhaps as an extension or refinement of the method of electrical stimulation. We know, for instance, that an electrical current, in an artificial way, depolarizes (or hyperpolarizes) a large population of neurones indiscriminately, and the firing or discharge rate of all the neurones in the area of stimulation is altered. In order to "dissect out" the function of a given region of the brain, the local application of a chemical transmitter, for example, probably parallels more closely what is actually occurring biologically at that local site. What is the evidence for this?

In examining the mechanisms of brain function, it is essential to know which humoral factors are involved in the mediation of the activity of a given structure, and hence a given behavioral response. Since the non-specificity of the blood stream precludes this route of study, and because the whole-brain assay is of limited value (Myers, 1969a), the direct injection of a chemical substance has arisen as the most feasible approach to this problem at the present time. One reason revolves about the principal criterion required for establishing a specific chemical as a putative neurotransmitter: that the substance excites nervous tissue. A most powerful argument for the use of chemical stimulation, then, is that different transmitter substances may exert different kinds of physiological responses when micro-injected at the *same* site. In the case of several specific candidate transmitters, acetylcholine, norepinephrine and serotonin, different kinds of physiological responses may be elicited when they are selectively micro-injected at one site (Myers and Yaksh, 1969), whereas electrical stimulation produces only one of these responses.

Another strong justification for its usage is the fact that different neurotransmitters may be released in functional opposition to one another within the very same site in the brain (Myers and Sharpe, 1968a). Therefore, by the local application of a candidate transmitter, one may be able to simulate or mimic the differential release of a humoral factor and thereby determine which substance is involved in the activation of a specific physiological or behavioral response (Myers, 1964b).

B. Differences between Injections into the Ventricles and Tissue

When a chemical substance is injected into the cerebral ventricles, it is difficult to localize anatomically its pharmacological action. The reason for this is that cerebrospinal fluid carries the substance throughout the ventricular system either by way of diffusion, active transport, or circulation. Nevertheless, if one wishes to obtain a first approximation of a specific central effect of a given compound, leaving for the moment the question of localization out of the picture, the intraventricular route has great utility. For example, chemical substances may exert vastly different actions when given by the intraventricular as opposed to the common intravenous or intraperitoneal routes. When the catecholamine, norepinephrine, is given systemically, the effect is excitatory; but the amine has a depressant action when administered by the intraventricular route (Feldberg, 1963). In this case, not only was a physiological demonstration of the blood brain barrier to this amine illustrated, but also this procedure provided an entirely new approach to the concept of the central function of this neurohumoral substance.

II. Construction of an Intracerebral Cannula

The fabrication of a cannula for injecting a solution or depositing crystals into the brain of an experimental animal will vary depending upon the species used. Generally, because of the problem of tissue damage, a cannula of a small diameter should be used for an animal with a relatively small brain (Fisher and Coury, 1964). However, there are certain basic principles which apply for the construction of the cannula and a subsequent micro-injection, regardless of the species.

A. Cannula for Injection into Brain Substance

The micro-injection cannula assembly consists of two parts: (1) an outer guide cannula and (2) an inner injector cannula. The gauge of each of these will depend upon the preparation, a 28 gauge injector cannula being suitable for cats and monkeys and a 30 gauge for rats and other small animals. The gauge of the guide will, of course, depend on the outside diameter of the injector cannula, but ordinarily a thin-walled 22 gauge guide cannula can be used for a 28 gauge injector cannula. At the other extreme, a 26 gauge guide tube will accommodate a 32 gauge inner cannula. These sizes have been used successfully for the infusion of solutions into the brain of an unanesthetized rat (Myers, 1963; Ankier and Tyers, 1969).

Figure I illustrates a lightweight, inexpensive cannula which may be constructed easily. The plastic base is cut from the end of a 1 ml disposable tuberculin syringe. Both the external top of the cannula base and the internal part of the cap, which covers the end of the syringe barrel, are threaded with a $\frac{3}{16}$ in die and tap. The guide cannula is cemented in place with epoxy resin cemnet packed into the core of the base. Similarly, after the 28 gauge injector cannula is inserted through the cap, it is cemented to the top with epoxy-resin cement. This particular cannula assembly has been used in a number of different laboratories for stimulating hundreds of animals.

When a needle tubing of 28 to 32 gauge is cut with wire-cutters, a small grinding wheel, obtainable from any hardware store, is used to

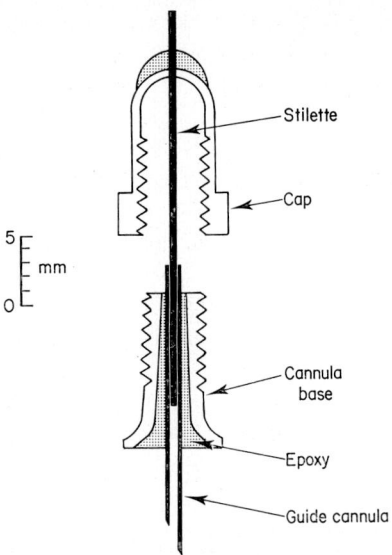

FIG. 1. A guide cannula cut from 22 ga needle tubing, beveled at an angle of 60°. The needle is cemented with epoxy resin glue into the plastic cannula case which is the needle end of a 1 ml disposable syringe that is threaded. The cap, threaded internally, is the dust cap which covers the end of the disposable syringe. The 28 ga stylet (shown) or injector cannula is cemented to the cap with epoxy resin cement. (From Myers et al., 1967.)

bevel the end of the tube. In our laboratory, the grinding wheel is mounted on a utility motor having a variable speed so that the grinding rate can be more easily controlled. To open the lumen at the cut end, the uncut or open end is affixed to a 2 to 3 foot length of PE tubing, filled with distilled water; the tubing is fitted to a tuberculin syringe via a 27 gauge needle. As the cannula is ground away at a 45° to 60° angle, the plunger of the syringe is squeezed so that a stream of water keeps flowing. This internal pressure within the cannula tubing tends to "blow-open" the cannula, and it can then be ground to any length.

When a finer-gauge cannula is made, the PE-10 tubing to which it is attached must be drawn to a finer taper. This is accomplished simply by grasping the tubing between both thumbs and forefingers, and holding the 2 cm space of tubing between the thumb and forefinger, over an extremely cold flame (yellow) of a bunsen burner or butane lighter. The PE tubing is drawn apart slowly, and cut with a scalpel at the point in the taper at which the 28 gauge tubing will fit tightly.

The ends of both the guide and injector cannulae to be placed in brain tissue are always beveled at a 45 to 60° angle. The reasons for this are as follows: (1) during implantation, the pointed guide penetrates the pia-arachnoid layer more easily after the dura is cut; (2) the guide cannula will incise rather than tear the neural tissue as it is lowered through the brain tissue; and (3) for the subsequent verification of the position of the cannula, the angulated lesion made by the tip often provides additional visible cues for histological localization of the injection site. It is also important to remember to cut the stylet, which will be positioned inside the guide tube during implantation, to the same length and tip bevel as the guide tube. Most investigators always keep the stylet, which extends to the tip of the guide, in place at all times except for the period of the actual stimulation.

Figure 2 shows a 32 gauge cannula with its outer wall notched for better adhesion to cranial cement (Epstein, 1960). When the microinfusion is made in the rat, for example, an injector needle is inserted

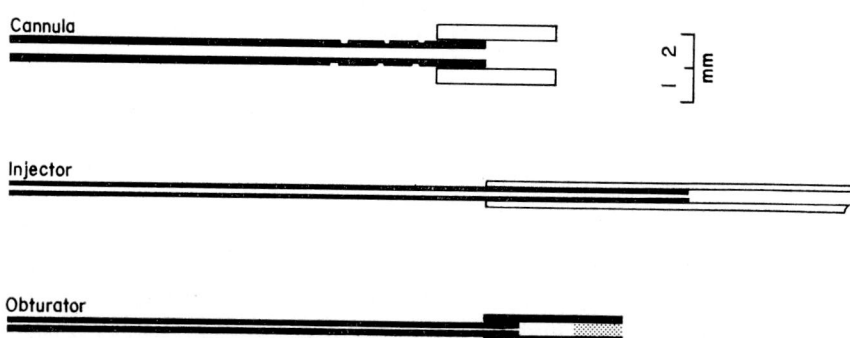

FIG. 2. Guide cannula (top), notched for better adhesion to cranial cement, is fitted with a plastic tube. Injector cannula (middle) is lowered into the guide to a depth limited by the PE tubing containing the solution for injection. The obturator or stylet (bottom) is kept in the guide cannula at all times, except when an injection is made. (From Epstein, 1960.)

inside this guide cannula to a depth which is limited by the polyethylene collar positioned by friction-fit over the injector needle. Again, a 29 gauge stylet or "obturator" is kept inside the cannula throughout the experiment. If the animal is to be retained for any length of time, it is best to have a somewhat more rugged pedestal or base into which the guide cannula is cemented. This tends to reduce the possibility that the guide, the stylet, or injector tubes will be displaced or dislodged during the period of chronicity. It has been our experience that in animals larger than rats, a pedestal base as illustrated in Fig. 1 is usually required.

Another type of cannula which possesses the special properties of fluid seal and accuracy of depth (Marley and Stephenson, 1968) is illustrated in Fig. 3. A steel collar that is cemented to the inner (injector) cannula with epoxy-resin cement (Araldite), butts up against the top or external edge of the guide cannula. The polyethylene sleeve which fits snugly on the outer surface of the steel collar prevents

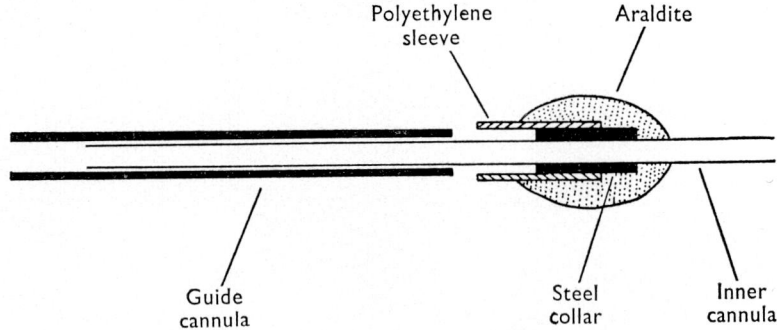

FIG. 3. Inner injector cannula with steel collar cemented by epoxy resin glue (Araldite). Steel collar limits the depth of the micro-injection beyond the tip of the guide cannula. The polyethylene sleeve provides a fluid seal and prevents the injected solution from leaking into the shaft of the guide cannula. (From Marley and Stephenson, 1968.)

leakage and backflow of the injected solution into the guide cannula. The depth of the site at which the micro-injection is made for this as for the other two cannulae illustrated in Figs 1 and 2 can be varied simply by altering the length of the inner injector cannula. The diversity of application of this cannula, shown in Fig. 3, is illustrated by the fact that it was used in experiments in which drugs were micro-injected into young chickens (Marley and Stephenson, 1968).

Another cannula assembly which utilizes a base for more permanent fixation was devised by Decima and George (1964) and is illustrated in Fig. 4. In this case, the removable threaded connector (B) of a banana plug becomes the base into which the guide cannula is cemented. When the leaves are cut away from the banana plug, a protective screw cap (A) can be fashioned. The stylet and injector tubes (C) are soldered into a hexagonal nut which in turn has been soldered to a "holder" (D). For a micro-injection, the injector tube (C, right) is attached to a microliter syringe via a polyethylene tube.

To explore different sites in the vertical dimension for their sensitive ity to a specific substance below the tip of the guide tube is a very simple matter. Two procedures are used. First and the most direct

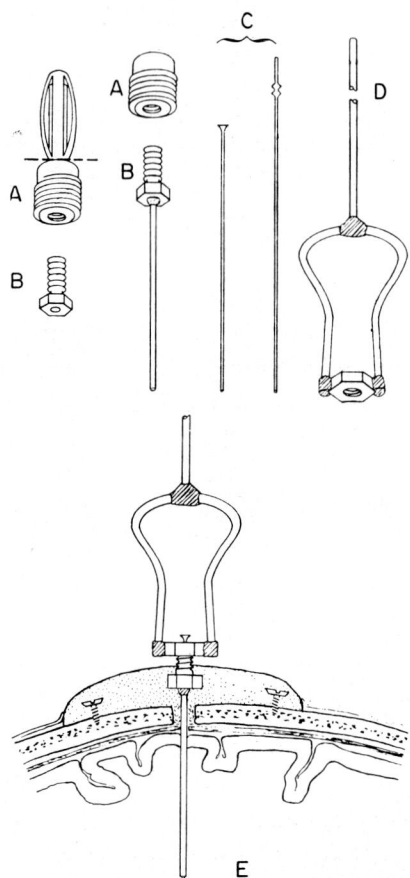

Fig. 4. The cannula assembly is constructed as follows: First, the four-leaved springs of the banana plug are cut away (broken line), leaving parts which become a screw cap (A) for the implanted cannula unit and an inner threaded brass guide holder (B). Second, the larger tubing, cut to the desired length, is passed through the guide holder (B) and soldered in place. Third, two lengths of small diameter tubing are cut (C), with one serving as the injector cannula and the other as a stylet. Fourth, a cannula holder (D) is made by soldering a $\frac{1}{8}$ in hexagonal nut to a "Y-shaped" piece of wire. The position of each part is represented in E after implantation. (From Decima and George, 1964.)

way, is to have on hand a series of injector needles or cannulae cut to different lengths in millimeter steps. Thus, the deeper the site, the longer the needle which is used to extend beyond the guide. Second, spacers or shims of different lengths can be placed over an injector needle which is of uniform length. We have used shims cut from polyethylene tubing which fit snugly over the injector needle. The disadvantage in the use of a metal spacer is the fact that it may fall off accidentally prior to the micro-injection; however, a metal shim cannot be compressed.

B. Cannula for Intraventricular Injections

For injecting solutions of drugs into the cerebral ventricles of cats and larger animals, a unique cannula was devised by L. Collison, of the National Institute for Medical Research, Mill Hill, London, which has been used successfully for many years (see Feldberg, 1963). It is commercially available from Palmer, Ltd., or other biological supply houses. A special feature of this cannula is a polyethylene or polyvinyl chloride extension tube with an opening cut in the side, which is

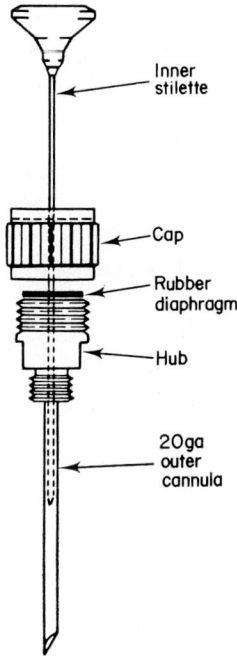

FIG. 5. A modified Collison cannula, by which the threaded segment at the base of the hub permits the cannula to be screwed into the skull. Through the holes in the top surface of the cap, the inner stylet (shown) or injector cannula is lowered. A rubber diaphragm, cut from the septum of a gas chromatograph, is inserted between the cap and the Collison hub to maintain a fluid- and air-tight seal.

fitted over the metal cannula. The tip rests permanently in the ventricular lumen so that injections can be made repeatedly. Among other cannulae for intraventricular infusions are those described by Clark et al. (1968), Goodrich et al. (1969) and Grunden and Linburn (1969).

Because of the possible effects caused by a fluid remaining in the hub of the cannula, we devised a procedure (Myers, 1964b; Villablanca and Myers, 1965) whereby a 20 gauge guide cannula is implanted into the cerebral hemisphere so that the tip rests just above the ventricular lumen. A modified Collison cannula, illustrated in Fig. 5, can also be used for this purpose. When an injection is made, the stylet (Fig. 5) is removed and an injector cannula is pushed through the rubber diaphragm of the cap and into the guide until contact with the ventricle is made. After the injection is made, the injector needle is removed and the stylet is replaced through the rubber diaphragm so that a leak-proof seal is retained.

For smaller animals a cannula was devised which can be used either

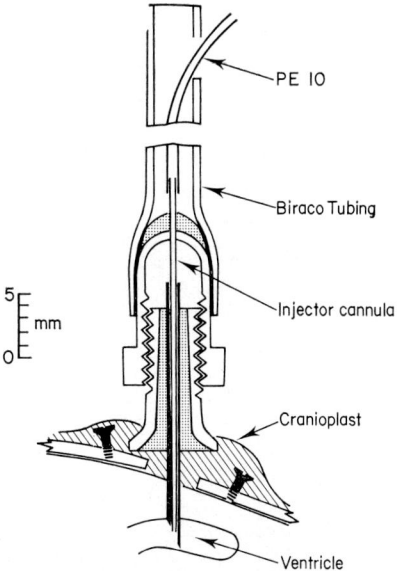

FIG. 6. An injector cannula, for making injections into the ventricle (or brain tissue) is kept in place as a result of screwing the cap assembly onto the guide cannula base. The guide cannula is fashioned in the same way as that described in Fig. 1 and is held in place by cranioplast cement packed in and around the anchor screws. Biraco or other plastic tubing is cemented over the cap, and PE-10 tubing containing the solution for the micro-injection is run through a hole in this tubing, which protects the PE tubing and injector cannula. (From Myers et al., 1967.)

for single intraventricular injections or for infusions given intermittently over a long period of time (Myers, 1963). The cannula shown in Fig. 1 is modified slightly so that the injector needle and polyethylene tubing containing the solution is well protected. A 4 cm length of polyvinyl chloride (PVC) tubing is attached to the top of the cap by epoxy or other cement. As shown in Fig. 6, the PE-10 tubing is then threaded through a 3 mm hole cut in the upper and posterior portion of this tubing. Then, surgical adhesive tape is wrapped tightly around both the PE-10 and vinyl tubing so that both are held together. This outward extension of PVC tubing protects the polyethylene tubing when the rat tucks its head under its body against the cage floor, a typical position during sleep. Also, it is sufficiently strong to prevent the animal from grasping the PE tubing, containing the chemical, with its paws as it washes and grooms itself. Figure 6 also illustrates how the base of the cannula is cemented to the skull with cranioplast cement which is packed in and around the two retaining or anchor screws inserted in the calvarium.

C. Multiple Cannula Array

In many experiments, it is expedient to implant more than one cannula into the brain of the animal. Among the reasons for this is the desirability of simultaneous bilateral stimulation at two homologous sites. Also, one site can often be used as an anatomical control for another, particularly for "mapping" studies, and for the accurate localization of a given behavioral response to a specific chemical. In 1960, the author devised a method for implanting an array of two or more cannulae in cats. The guide tubes were lowered through the core of a modified Sheatz-type pedestal (Sheatz, 1961), bolted to the cranium and held in place by dental cement packed within the pedestal and over the screws. The external end of each guide tube extended beyond the dental cement. A plastic cap was screwed onto the pedestal to protect the ends of the cannulae and to retain a sterile preparation for the duration of the experiments (Myers, 1964b).

Recently, a much simpler method has been devised in our laboratory for implanting a multiple cannula array (Myers and Sharpe, 1968b; Sharpe and Myers, 1969). The pedestal itself is fashioned from any small-mouthed plastic bottle; this eliminates the problems associated with the machining of stainless steel. As shown in Fig. 7, the top of a 2 oz polyethylene bottle is cut away so that only a small portion of the plastic remains below the threaded mouth of the bottle. After the cannula array, in this case four 22 gauge guide-cannulae, is lowered simultaneously to the appropriate position in the brain, cranioplast cement is packed inside the mouth of the bottle top and around the screws which are used for anchoring the bottle top onto the skull. Such an array implanted in a cat is shown in Fig. 9. The external ends of the cannulae are protected and kept aseptically by simply screwing the sterilized bottle cap (not shown) onto the threads of the pedestal.

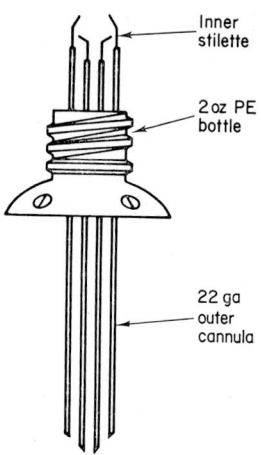

Fig. 7. A four-cannula "array" held in place by cranioplast cement packed in the mouth of a 2 oz plastic bottle. The top has been cut away from the bottle and serves as a pedestal onto which the bottle cap can be screwed to protect the cannula array. The 28 ga inner stylets are replaced by injector cannulae which extend beyond the tips of the 22 ga outer guide cannulae. With this array, it is possible to stimulate, independently, different anatomical sites.

D. Chemitrodes

Cannula assemblies which can also be used for electrical stimulation of brain tissues are sometimes referred to as "chemitrodes." Delgado (1966), Morgane (1969) and others have used these devices for alternate stimulation with either electrical current or a chemical substance. Ordinarily, an insulated wire is lowered in place of the stylet for monopolar stimulation, the guide serving as the indifferent electrode. For bipolar stimulation, both the stylet and the guide cannula are insulated except for a 1 mm area at the tip of each one. For the details of electrical stimulation, coating of the electrodes, and fabrication of the connectors, the reader is referred to Chapter 7 by Ervin and Kenney.

III. Implanting the Cannula into Brain Tissue

Stereotaxic procedures described by Pellegrino and Cushman (Chapter 3) are required for implanting an intracranial cannula. The anatomical site for each implantation must be selected according to a co-ordinate system which on histological verification provides reasonable accuracy and reliability.

Perhaps the most important point to remember is that the guide tube does not necessarily have to rest in the intended structure of stimulation. In our experience, we have found that it is always better to lower the tip of the injector cannula to a site for stimulation which is 1 mm or more beyond the tip of the guide tube. The reason for this is that the area surrounding the shaft of the guide tube often becomes impacted with glial tissue and fibrous formations which are many cell layers in thickness. In order to stimulate an area which is not composed of nervous tissue or not free from necrosis, it is therefore necessary to penetrate beyond the encapsulation of tissue. Moreover, if the depth of the injector cannula is increased in 1 mm steps beyond the end of the guide tube, it is possible to explore to a considerable extent the tissue below the end of the guide for its sensitivity to the presence of a chemical or drug. In our laboratory, the guide tube is usually implanted 2 to 4 mm above the intended site of stimulation. Then, as an anatomical control, injections can be made at 1 mm depths above and even below the so-called "prime" site of stimulation. The details of the surgical methods and precautions to be taken are described in Chapter 4 by Meyer and Meyer. Generally, the basic principles inherent in these procedures should be followed closely. In addition, several other important factors must be taken into account.

First, it is necessary that a small wedge or strip of gelfoam is placed into the craniotomy hole before the cannula is lowered. The gelfoam insulates and protects the surface of the dura which should be completely covered. Without this protection, the cranioplast or other cement may damage seriously the superficial portion of the cortex because of the intense heat of fusion common to these acrylic cements. Second, the stylet or obturator must always be inserted into the guide cannula before it is lowered through the tissue. This will prevent the brain tissue from entering the shaft of the guide tube, which will clog the cannula even before the experiment begins. Third, the stylet and cannula tip should be beveled at the same 45 to 60° angle. Both tips should coincide spatially and be positioned so as to face the same direction. If the stylet is turned slightly, a larger lesion will be caused at the tip. Fourth, the concentric assembly should be lowered very slowly through the tissue, with care taken that the dura mater is not compressed. As the outer wall of the guide passes through the dura mater, it is sometimes necessary to grasp each of the two edges of the incised dura with fine iris forceps held in each hand and used for retraction. In instances where a compression occurs on one side of the brain, a clear-cut distortion of the hemisphere can be visualized easily on post-mortem examination.

As shown in Figs 4 and 6, anchor or retaining screws are usually inserted into the calvarium at positions rostral and caudal to the craniotomy hole. Only a minimum amount of dental acrylic or cranioplast cement should be flowed in and around the cannula and the retaining screws, and then packed down with a spatula. If a cannula pedestal or base is not used, it is essential that several notches are filed on the outer guide cannula so that the cement adheres more strongly and the cannula does not loosen or rotate post-operatively.

After the cement has dried, the skin is usually brought up over the hillock of cement, and with a purse-string suture (Markowitz, et al. 1959), the skin is drawn up around the cannula. We have also used the standard procedure adopted by Hubel (1959), which is used by surgeons for the infection-free closure around gastric or other fistulae. The original longitudinal incision must be made off the mid-line several mm lateral to the intended position of the cannula. After the cannula has been cemented in place, a small incision of a length which will accommodate the width of the cannula base is made in the skin. Then, by grasping both edges of the incision with iris forceps, the skin is pulled over the cannula base. The main incision is then closed with continuous subcutaneous sutures according to procedures described in Chapter 4.

IV. Methods of Applying a Chemical

Generally speaking, the particular problem under investigation will dictate the procedure used to introduce a chemical into the brain. When one wishes to activate or inhibit a distinct neural pathway with, let us say, two individual candidate transmitters, then the chemical would be applied either in solution or in crystalline form directly to that structure. If, on the other hand, the problem centers on a more permanent alteration of the so-called biochemical "environment" of the brain, then repeated infusions are made chronically for pays or even weeks (Myers, 1963). In this section, we will be concerned with the technique of relatively short-term or acute stimulation with a chemical substance.

A. Micro-injection of a Solution

Although the term micro-injection should more properly be applied to the iontophoretic application of a solution, many scientists have accepted the convention that when one infuses a solution in a microliter volume or a fraction thereof with a microliter syringe, the term "micro-injection" has utility and a legitimate meaning.

Since one of the critical factors pertaining to the application of drugs to selected areas of brain tissue is the extent of diffusion, it is essential that extremely small quantities are used for stimulation (Olds et al., 1964). For this reason, a Hamilton or other microliter syringe of 10 or 50 μl capacity is required. The usage, care and maintenance of such a syringe is described fully on a brochure included in the package. It is our practice always to keep the microliter syringe in a covered vessel or beaker filled with 70% alcohol. Never, under any circumstances, is the barrel of the syringe itself filled with a drug, dye, ink, or chemical solution of any kind.

To fill the microliter syringe, only the dust-free alcohol solution or distilled water is used. After a 27-gauge syringe needle is attached to the tip of the barrel and lowered into the alcohol solution, the syringe is held in an upright position, and the plunger is pumped vertically until all air bubbles are removed. Then, as the plunger is drawn out of the barrel slowly, the syringe is filled to a point beyond the scale. When the syringe is set aside, care must be taken that air does not enter the syringe needle or the barrel.

Next, the PE-10 tubing connected to the 28 or other gauge injector cannula is filled with the chemical to be used for stimulation. The solution to be injected is thus "back-loaded." Care, again, is taken to ensure that minute particles are absent from the solution and the tubing. A disposable syringe or a sterilized glass tuberculin syringe is usually used for filling the PE tubing with the chemical solution to be micro-injected. Once the tubing is filled and the flow at the end of the injector cannula is not only unimpeded but streams like a "geyser," the PE tubing is cut with scissors at a point close to the disposable syringe needle. This end of the PE-10 tubing is attached immediately to the needle of the micro-syringe.

At first, the syringe plunger is moved inwards very slowly until 2 μl, as denoted on the barrel scale, is delivered at the tip of the injector cannula. A droplet which should measure exactly 1·5 mm in diameter should appear and its size determined by a mm ruler. This droplet is blotted then with a sterile gauze. Next, the plunger is moved in by 1 μl on the barrel scale. A droplet at the end of the injector cannula about 1·1 mm in diameter will appear, which again should be measured. As this procedure is repeated several times, the patency and accuracy of delivery can be assured.

Should an occlusion occur just prior to the micro-injection, or between a series of micro-injections, the injector cannula is removed from the PE tubing and the inner bore is reamed either with a stylet wire, which is usually included in the box of syringe needles, or with a strand of hi-fi or other fine hook-up wire obtainable commercially. An alternative and often easier procedure is to remove the injector cannula, reverse its position and attach it to another length of PE-10 tubing filled with distilled water. By exerting a rapid thrust of the plunger of a 1 ml syringe attached to the other end of this second PE tubing, the occlusion can usually be washed out.

To monitor the flow of the solution as well as its actual injection into the brain tissue, it is common practice to introduce a tiny bubble of about 1 mm dia into the PE-10 tubing. The best location for the bubble in the length of tubing is about 10–15 cm from the injector needle. When the micro-injection is actually made, the bubble should move at a steady speed. If the tip of the micro-injector cannula is blocked, the bubble will not move at all, and instant verification of occlusion is obtained. A reference tab can be made from a 1×2 cm rectangle of paper which is punctured at either end and slipped over the PE tubing. In our laboratory, the paper is calibrated in terms of the distance (mm) that the bubble travels down the tube per microliter, or fraction thereof, injected.

B. *Micro-injection of a Solution by Pump and by Hand*

The point can be argued indefinitely as to whether it is more desirable to use a pump for driving the plunger of the micro-injection syringe or to make the micro-injection by hand. Thousands of micro-injection experiments have been done in our laboratory using both techniques. In general, the pump procedure is somewhat more satisfactory, since the rate and volume of the delivery of a microliter droplet can be controlled so precisely. In terms of the repeatability of an effect, dose response and other types of experiments, infusing the chemical into the brain by a pump cannot be surpassed. This is not to say, however, that similar physiological and behavioral responses are not evoked by the same chemical applied at the same site by driving the plunger with one's finger.

The procedure used for making a micro-injection by hand in a conscious animal is illustrated in Fig. 8(A) and (B). Note how the barrel is held by one hand and plunger tip of the micro-syringe is grasped between the thumb and forefinger of the other. With practice, accurate and reliable injections of a specified volume can be made by moving the plunger exceedingly slowly, a fraction of a millimeter at a time. The cannula shown implanted in this rat is the same as that portrayed in Fig. 1, and in the monkey, the same as in Fig. 7.

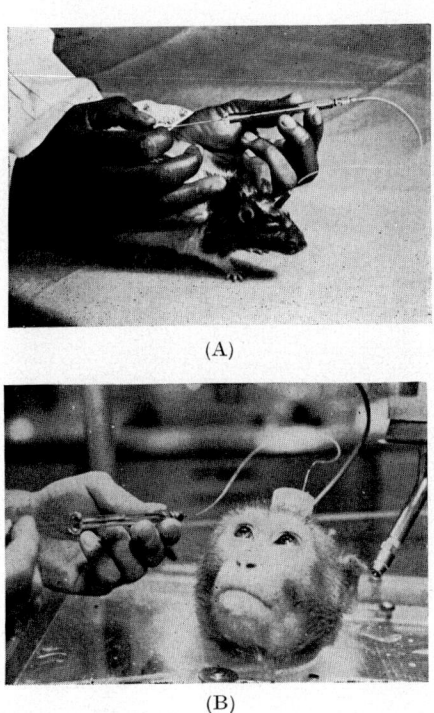

(A)

(B)

FIG. 8 (A) and (B). (A) Micro-injection of a solution of a putative transmitter into the hypothalamus of an unrestrained rat, and (B) restrained rhesus monkey. The plunger of the 50 μl syringe is gently pushed inward until 0·5 μl is delivered. The injector cannula is kept in place for 30 to 60 sec after the injection has been made. The cannula assembly in the rat is that portrayed in Fig. 1, whereas in the monkey, a multi-cannula array, illustrated in Fig. 7, was used.

Before a solution is micro-injected by means of a pump, it is essensial that the syringe is mounted *first* on the pump holder or the syringe rack *before* the injector cannula is lowered into the tissue to the intended site of stimulation. A Hunter or other interval timer is used for switching the pump motor on and off. The rate of delivery of the micro-injection is varied quite easily simply by altering the gear ratio of the pump; however, after this is done, the volume per unit time must always be calibrated. Then the pump-syringe system is tested several times before the injector needle is lowered into the brain. Figure 9 illustrates an actual micro-injection of a possible transmitter substance, serotonin, into the brain of an unrestrained cat. In this case, 0·8 µl was delivered into the animal's hypothalamus over a 36 sec interval.

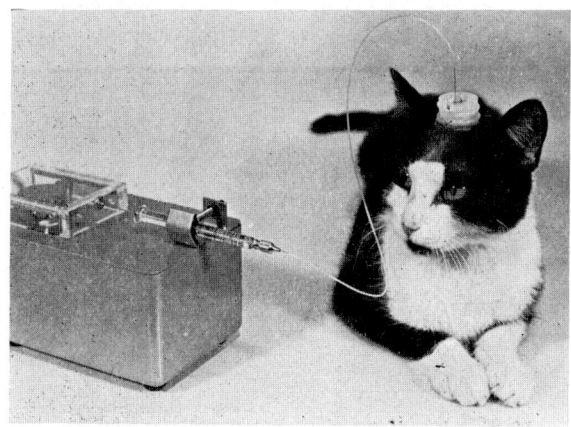

FIG. 9. Micro-injection of a putative transmitter into the hypothalamus of an unrestrained cat. A four-cannula array (see Fig. 7), held in place by a plastic-bottle-top pedestal, had been implanted one week earlier. The sage pump is timed to deliver 0·8 µl over an interval of 36 sec.

At the end of the injection, the injector cannula is left in place in the brain for an interval of: (a) 30 to 40 sec when 0·8 µl or less is microinjected; or (b) 45 to 50 sec if a slightly larger volume such as 1·2 µl is infused. Dye diffusion studies done in our laboratory have revealed that this extra, post-injection interval provides sufficient time for the chemical substance to infiltrate into the tissue immediately surrounding the site of injection. If the injector is taken out as soon as the pump stops, or removed too quickly, there is the danger that a large part of the microliter droplet will be drawn up into the tissue beyond the end of the guide tube or into the shaft of the guide tube itself.

As mentioned earlier, it must be remembered that the injector needle is replaced with the stylet which was cut to fit that specific guide tube. In experiments in which a multiple cannula array is used, for making bilateral injections, both the injector and stylet tubes should be distinctly separated. To label clearly a stylet or injector cannula, we use a numbered "flag" which can be cut from adhesive tape or from the plastic tape used in a Dymo pressure label-maker machine. Either of these is affixed to the external tip of the injectors and stylets.

When exploring sites at different depths below the tip of the guide tube, it is also necessary to "tag" or label each injector needle having a different length. For example, an injector needle which extends 1 mm beyond the tip of the guide when lowered to the maximal depth can be designated as a *number 1* cannula; a *number 3* injector cannula is cut 2 mm longer and extends 3 mm beyond the guide.

C. *The Problem of Volume and Diffusion*

Although it was made quite clear from the strong condemnation of MacLean (1957), who described the extraordinary diffusion following the injection of a large volume of a solution into the brain substance, and by the additional evidence provided by Rech and Domino (1959) on the lesions caused by such injections, the literature continues to grow with papers in which a very large volume of a fluid is injected with reckless abandon into cerebral tissue. In spite of the fact that one is a student or beginner, there is no defensible reason to make this same mistake, particularly with our present state of knowledge.

As a direct example of how critical the volume of injection is, in terms of interpreting whatever experimental findings are obtained, one can simply measure the diameter of the droplet at the end of the injector cannula. Then, the overall dimension of the structure into which this droplet is to be infused can be calculated. The main point to be recognized here is that the droplet will displace, in large part, that amount of tissue which corresponds to the diameter or dimension of a given droplet (Myers, 1964a).

A coronal section from the de Groot (1959) atlas at the level of the rat's hypothalamus can be used to illustrate the danger of an excessive volume, since this species is commonly used for chemical stimulation experiments. If, as shown in Fig. 10, the micro-injection is made into the lateral hypothalamus, at a point adjacent to the fornix, a 1 μl droplet which measures 1·1 mm in diameter would displace the entire lateral hypothalamic region from the median forebrain bundle to the dorsomedial nucleus. A 2·0 μl droplet which measures 1·5 mm in diameter injected at the same site would reach the zona incerta. A 5·0 μl droplet measuring 2·0 mm in diameter touches all of these structures in this part of the hypothalamus, and would also reach the optic tract and internal capsule. It is apparent, therefore, that the cerebral tissue simply cannot accommodate a 5·0 or 10·0 μl droplet, illustrated in Fig. 11. Even if there would be an uncommon amount of extracellular fluid, it is essential that for smaller species such as the rat a microliter droplet of 0·5 μl or less be used as the stimulation volume (Myers and Sharpe, 1968b). In a monkey or cat in which individual structures in the brain are significantly larger than those of the rat, the volumes used in our laboratory for a micro-injection experiment are ordinarily 0·8 to 1·0 μl. Up to 1·2 or 1·8 μl has been

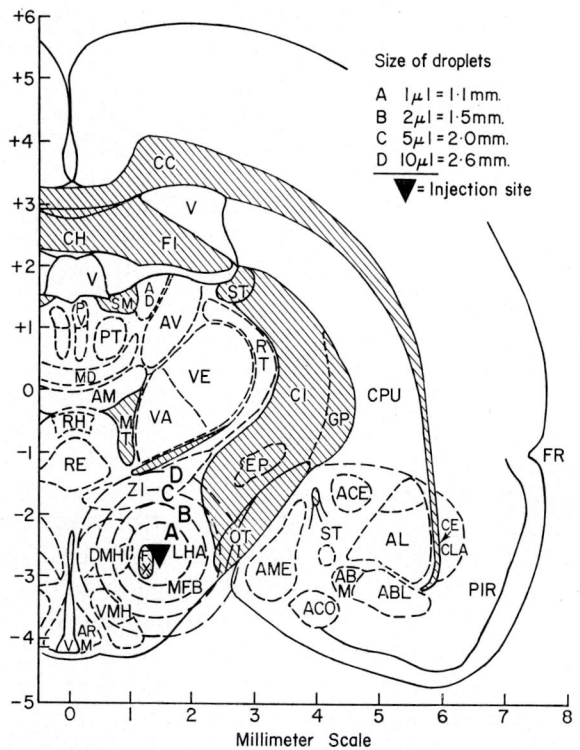

FIG. 10. Diagrammatic reconstruction from the de Groot atlas of the rat brain at the coronal level of AP 5·4. The volume of brain tissue which would be displaced by each microliter droplet is depicted by the dashed lines, if the micro-injection were made in each case in the lateral hypothalamus. The actual size of each microliter droplet is given in millimeters in the legend. (From Myers, 1964.)

used in these larger animals if the intent of the infusion is to "inundate" an entire nucleus or mass of tissue within a given area.

In test animals, it is possible to determine empirically how large an area is reached by a droplet of the injected solution. A dye or stain, such as bromophenol blue or Evans blue, which has been employed in the past, is extremely useful for investigating the extent of diffusion, following a micro-injection (Myers, 1966). Figures 11 (A), (B), (C) and (D) illustrate the amount of diffusion following a micro-injection in an anesthetized rat of 0·5 µl, 1·0 µl, 2·0 µl and 3·0 µl, respectively. Once again, it is clear from these illustrations that for any sort of "mapping" investigation in which the micro-injection must be localized exactly,

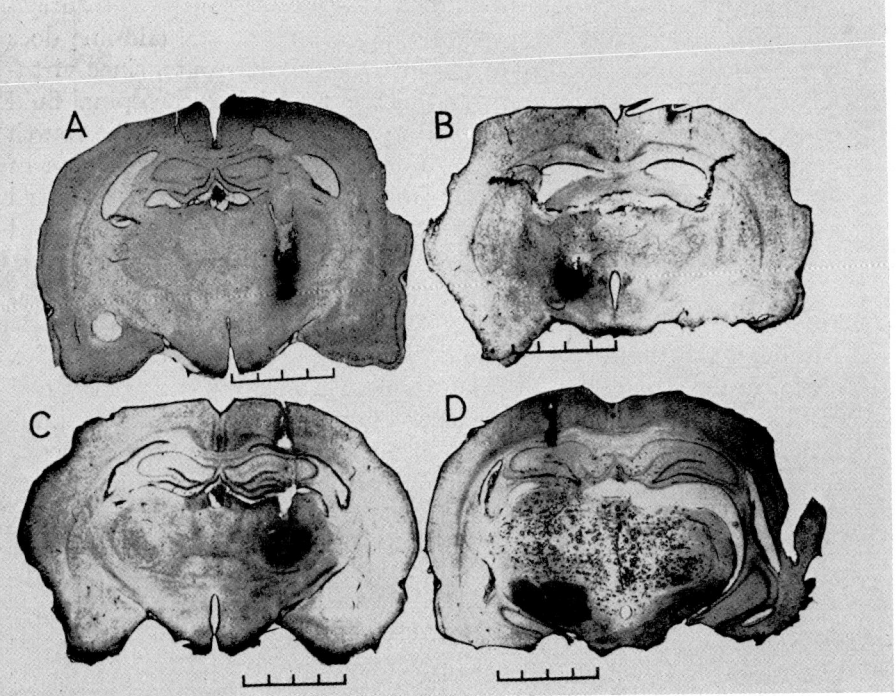

FIG. 11. Photomicrographs of the diffusion of dye in partially fixed and unstained 50 µ coronal sections. (A) 0·5 µl Evans blue at the border of the ventral thalamic nucleus and medial lemniscus. (B) 1·0 µl picric acid into the dorsolateral area of the hypothalamus. (C) 2·0 µl bromophenol blue into the lateral nuclear mass of the thalamus. (D) 3·0 µl Evans blue into the ventral thalamic nucleus just dorsal to the zona incerta. Magnification ×5. Scale is in millimeters. (From Myers, 1966.)

the maximum volume that can be used for a small animal, such as the rat, is 0·5 µl.

Recently, a study has been completed in our Laboratory in which tritiated or ^{14}C labelled serotonin, norepinephrine or acetylcholine have been injected at similar sites in the lateral hypothalamus in a volume of 1·0 µl in each instance. In general, the results correspond nearly identically to the dye diffusion studies reported earlier (Myers, 1966). Nevertheless, structures at points located at some distance from the site of the micro-injection were found to contain radio-active material, although in a concentration which would have no apparent pharmacological action (Myers, *et al.*, 1971). This confirms the findings of Grossman and Stumpf (1969).

Perhaps the most interesting fact is that a substance such as acetylcholine micro-injected at a site 1·5 mm lateral to the mid-line does not exert its action by way of the intraventricular route, since virtually no radioactivity was detected in the artificial cerebrospinal fluid collected following its perfusion from the lateral through the fourth ventricle. This result, of course, fails to support the suggestion of Baxter and others (Baxter, 1967; Routtenberg, 1967) that a chemical injected into the brain may act at a distant site after it has passed into the cerebral ventricles.

D. *Application of Crystals*

Although the disadvantages and advantages of using crystals of a chemical for stimulation of brain tissue will be dealt with at the end of this section, it should be mentioned here that the crystalline stimulation technique is relatively straightforward. There are several ways for applying crystals, at a specific site, although the general technique described originally by MacLean (1957) is still a satisfactory one.

After the stylet is removed from the guide tube, the injector tube, into which crystals have been tamped, is lowered to the appropriate depth. Then, the needle is fixed to the guide and the substances are allowed to dissolve and diffuse away from the site. The crystals may also be ejected by a wire stylet placed within the shaft of the injector needle (MacLean, 1957). Nashold and Gills (1960) have found that the stimulation is more reliable if the tip of the injector needle is sealed with a relatively inactive substance such as carbon, or in the case of acetylcholine, with physostigmine. This not only helps to prevent the escape of the drug but also helps to mark the site of the application.

Another procedure is to melt the chemical by gentle heating. By rotating the end of the injector needle in the warmed, liquified drug, a film of the substance is deposited on the tip. Since the dose of the drug is difficult, if not impossible, to determine by MacLean's procedure of tamping crystals into the tip of an injector tube, this latter method provides a way of gross estimation of the weight of drug to be deposited (Nashold and Gills, 1960). Grossman and others have developed further the method of crystalline application so that it is now a routine procedure (for example, see Grossman, 1964; Fisher and Coury, 1964).

In addition, radioactive tracer methods are now used for assessing the spread of the crystalline substance (Grossman and Stumpf, 1969).

One attempt to quantify the dose of a crystal given was based on an empirical finding of Stein and Seifter (1962), who discovered that when the injector cannula was "tapped" three times immediately after it was inserted into a guide, a behavioral response occurred in a rat which could be elicited reliably at a later date by the same number of "taps." If the injector was "tapped" more than three times, the likelihood of convulsions increased. For the beginner, this procedure would appear to be a rather difficult one to use because of: (a) the variation in the strength of one's tapping finger; (b) the movement of the animal's head during tapping; and (c) the variability in the number of crystals of a given drug that are tamped into the tip of the injector (tapper) cannula.

A rather unique cannula was developed by Hernández-Peón, Morgane and their colleagues (Hernández-Peón et al., 1963) for crystalline stimulation of brain tissue. This cannula, illustrated in Fig. 12, consists of an exploring guide cannula which can be locked into place at

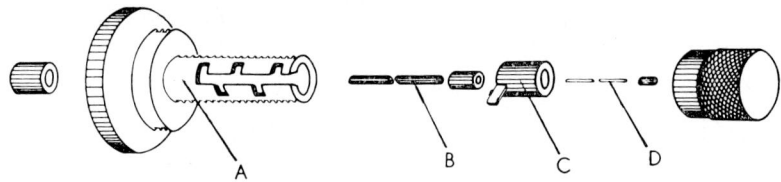

Fig. 12. A cannula system for the application of crystals at specific loci. The actual size of each part is indicated in brackets. (A) The notched base for moving and locking in the cannula system at one mm depths (10 mm); (B) The outer barrel of the guide cannula (22–25 mm); (C) Exploring guide holder (about 5 mm); (D) Tamping needle cannula which holds the crystals (22–25 mm). (From Hernández-Peón et al., 1963.)

depths separated by 1 mm. The crystals are deposited into the tip of the tamping needle, and the needle is then lowered into the brain to a depth limited by the locked guide. Through the use of this cannula, the action of a chemical substance at different levels of the brain can be explored in a precise way.

Whether or not one should design one's experiments around the method of either injecting a solution of a drug or by applying crystals of the compound cannot be specified without serious thought and several considerations. For instance, in a symposium sponsored by the New York Academy of Sciences, Grossman (1969) has stated that

". . . If the main purpose of the experiment is to describe the probable site of drug action in terms of specific anatomically defined structures, or to test routinely a large number of drugs in a large number of animals in behavioral situations which require unrestrained subjects, the procedure of choice is, quite clearly, the crystalline technique." Myers (1969b) has written, however, that ". . . From a pharmacological standpoint, a dose-response relationship is a fundamental and most critical need in any experiment in which the local endogenous concentration of a given substrate such as a biogenic amine is elevated. Put simply, the exact dose must be specified. The only reasonable experimental recourse, therefore, is to inject a drug in a known concentration." Fisher (1969) has concluded that "I will hold to my position that the best procedure is to use as many delivery methods as appear necessary to afford adequate control and answer relevant questions."

For the newcomer to this field, it would appear logical if not essential to examine carefully the details and variables of the two procedures for chemical stimulation of different structures in the brain. Table I presents a comparison of the two procedures, each contrasted in terms of a specific variable. One clear revelation of Table I is the number and variety of different problems associated with chemical stimulation experiments which are not inherent in a method by which electrical current is used to stimulate a given structure.

V. Interpretation of Data

The results of experiments in which a local region of the brain has been stimulated by a chemical may require a somewhat different kind of interpretation than that based on a more traditional method such as the production of a lesion or electrical stimulation. One reason for this is that more parameters must be considered. In relation to this is the observation that different endogenous neurohumoral substances applied to one site may produce entirely different responses, whereas electrical stimulation would produce one response at that site and a lesion of the area could obliterate that response. Since there may well be a number of different transmitter systems in the brain, including noradrenergic, dopaminergic, serotonergic or cholinergic, it is possible that by the use of the technique of chemical stimulation, one of these systems may be activated independently at a discrete locus, and the functions can be experimentally delineated even in the face of intricate anatomical overlapping. This then would seem to be the chief contribution of the chemical stimulation method. Before one can evaluate and subsequently interpret the data obtained from an experiment using the method, however, three important aspects of chemical

TABLE I

Summary comparison of the variables and questions pertaining to the use of solutions *vs* crystals for the local stimulation of brain tissue with a chemical substance

Variable	Micro-injection of solution	Application of crystals
1. Anatomical localization of action	Precise	Precise
2. Dose at site	Accurate estimation	Approximation only
3. pH	Precise control	No control
4. Temperature	Irrelevant (attains ambient level)	Irrelevant
5. Osmolarity (tonicity)	Precise control possible	No control
6. Lesion produced	Dependent on volume of injection	Dependent on size of injection needle or amount of ejected crystals
7. Necrotic tissue at site	Present	Present
8. Mechanical pressure or deformation	Dependent on rate of injection	Minimal
9. Diffusion	More immediate but volume dependent	More gradual
10. Convenience factor	Less	More
11. Use of compounds of low solubility	Difficult	Possible
12. Action of blocking agents at site	Effective	Effective
13. Control anatomical placements	Required	Required
14. Action via ventricular route	Ruled out	Ruled out
15. Dissolution of substance as injector is lowered through tissue	None	Possible

stimulation should be considered: those which are (1) pharmacological, (2) anatomical, and (3) physiological in nature.

A. Pharmacological Aspects of Chemical Stimulation

If it is assumed that a transmitter stimulates the receptors on the post-synaptic or sub-synaptic membrane, then a chemical applied locally is not acting on the axonal fibers in a discrete area. A strong possibility does exist, however, that the chemical in a high enough dose will produce toxicological or other effects. For this reason, it is essential that the effects of different doses must be clearly established in experiments in which a given volume of the micro-injected substance is held constant. The importance of this can be illustrated by an actual experiment.

If one wants to test the hypothesis that the level of the endogenous monoamine, serotonin (5-HT), within the anterior part of the hypothalamus is responsible for hyperthermia, this amine could be micro-injected at that site and the temperature monitored closely. When 5-HT is micro-injected in a dose of 10 μg into the anterior hypothalamus of a monkey, the animal's temperature falls (Myers, 1969a,b). One would suspect immediately that within the classic thermoregulatory area, 5-HT is involved in the mediation of the *heat loss* mechanism for body temperature. If this experiment were repeated time and again with the same result, the suspicion about 5-HT would become even more firm. But, it would turn out to be incorrect.

Actually, a high dose of a number of chemical substances produces what is thought to be a depolarizing blockade of neuronal activity, after which the firing rate of the nerve cells in a given area declines drastically. Further, with a large dose of a compound, receptor sites may also be occupied, and a local "inactivity" of the area of stimulation occurs which would account for the suppression of the physiological or behavioral response under investigation. Regardless of the mechanism, the interpretation of one's experimental data would be incorrect. In actuality, serotonin micro-injected in a low dose into the anterior hypothalamic area of several species evokes a sharp rise in body temperature to fever level (Myers, 1969c). This phenomenon is, in fact, dose-dependent, but only at the lower doses. This is illustrated in Fig. 13 which shows the hyperthermic effect of 5 μg of 5-HT as well as the pronounced fall in temperature caused by 10 μg of 5-HT. Once the effect of the large dose is dissipated, the hyperthermic response to 5-HT then ensues after all.

Another important consideration related to the pharmacological aspect of chemical stimulation is the need to block the action of the

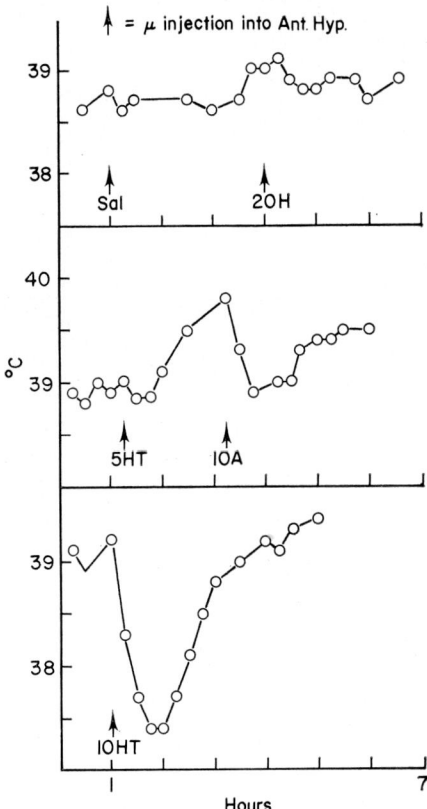

FIG. 13. Amines microinjected in 0·5 to 1·0 µl volumes into the anterior hypothalamus of an unanesthetized rhesus monkey. Upper: 1 µl normal saline at first arrow and 20 µg histamine at second arrow. Middle: At first arrow 5 µg 5-HT and at second arrow 10 µg A. Lower: At arrow 10 µg 5-HT. Temperature in degrees centigrade was monitored colonically in the monkey. (From Myers, 1968.)

chemical at the site of stimulation. At the present time, this appears to be a valid way to demonstrate a certain pharmacological specificity of a compound. A sufficient amount of research has not been done, however, to delineate both the excitatory property of a candidate transmitter, as well as the blockade of this property by a specific antagonist of the transmitter substance. Nevertheless, atropine and succinylcholine may be used to inhibit the excitatory effects of acetylcholine, whereas Brom-LSD or methysergide may block the actions of 5-HT. α- or β-adrenergic antagonists have also been used to distinguish between the stimulating or inhibitory properties of adrenergic compounds.

Recently, attempts have been made to use agents which inhibit the synthesis of a compound which occurs endogenously in brain tissue. These agents include p-chlorophenylalanine which lowers serotonin content, and α-methyl-tyrosine which reduces norepinephrine levels in the brain. Again, it remains to be seen whether some sort of valid interpretation can be made when these compounds are applied onto collections of nerve cells (Myers, 1970a). For a more complete discussion of central pharmacological antagonists and agonists, the reader should consult a standard, comprehensive textbook of pharmacology. It is particularly important, for example, to be aware of the limitations of those agents which mimic the actions of a candidate transmitter. The use of synthetic compounds, including carbachol, often presents certain difficulties associated with the interpretation of one's results, but these problems are beyond the scope of the present discussion.

B. Anatomical Aspects of Chemical Stimulation

The verification of the site of chemical stimulation is perhaps the most important part of the experiment. Since certain chemical substances may act to produce extraordinarily different responses at different sites, it is essential for the investigator to know exactly which part of a structure within the brain mediates the physiological or behavioral response to the chemical stimulus. The putative transmitter, norepinephrine, excites a behavioral response when applied to one region of the brainstem and inhibits a physiological system when applied to another (Myers and Sharpe, 1968b).

1. *Verification of the micro-injection site.* Before the animal is sacrificed, the site of the micro-injection must be marked. To do this, the same microliter syringe, tubing, injector needle and pump are required as those used for the actual experiments. Although the decision as to where to inject the dye is simply based on the results obtained following stimulation of a particular site, the microliter droplet of ink or dye is usually deposited at the deepest injection site.

India ink is probably the best substance to be used for marking a micro-injection, since the particles of carbon do not interfere with the histological staining procedure. However, Evans blue, bromophenol blue, or pyronin Y are dyes which have also been employed for visualizing the locus of stimulation as the brain is being sectioned. In some instances, these dyes may stain the tissue so that the histological photomicrograph will appear darker at the injection site. Commercial

India ink available for drafting purposes is prepared in distilled water in a concentration of 25 or 50%. Solutions of Evans and bromophenol blue are made up in concentrations of 1·0 or 2·0% in the same way. It is best to determine by trial and error the concentration of ink or dye which portrays the site most satisfactorily. Generally, a 25% solution of India ink and 1·0% of the blue dyes is adequate. One important caution to be taken is *never to fill* the microliter syringe with an ink or dye, but rather fill or "backload" the PE tubing and injector cannula with the marking solution, by the procedure described under Section IV, *A*.

When the brain is sectioned on a microtome, as described in Chapter 9 by Wolf, the site of the micro-injection is clearly delineated by the ink. If only a small sample of sections will be taken for subsequent staining, the presence of the ink at the micro-injection site will facilitate the selection of the histological material to be mounted on the microscope slide. In fact, the number of histological sections to be cut can be reduced considerably as a result of the marking ink.

After the histological sections have been stained and covered with glass slips, a thorough microscopic examination of the injection site or sites along the vertical axis below the guide cannula is carried out. Procedures to be followed are outlined in Chapters 9 by Wolf and 5 by Thompson. In view of the question of diffusion, it is always necessary to examine closely the area surrounding the site of micro-injection. Evidence of the degree of penetration or infiltration of the substance, absence of cells, signs of tearing, or lesions in the medial direction toward the lumen of the ventricle are all important parts of the histological study required for the interpretation of one's data. Information about these signs is often very helpful, particularly when non-specific responses occur, or if a site which was an "active" one suddenly does not mediate a response after a micro-injection of a specific chemical.

C. Physiological Aspects of Chemical Stimulation

A specific response to the local injection of a putative neurotransmitter or other substance can be of great functional importance. If other neurotransmitters evoke other responses when applied at the same site, or fail to exert any action, then this first observation takes on additional significance. Why?

Each year, more and more evidence accumulates which supports the concept of a chemical "coding" of brain function; this evidence has been reviewed by several authors, including Miller (1965) and Myers and Sharpe (1968b). What this concept implies is that the behavioral or physiological mechanism subserved at one anatomical site may be mediated by two or even more neurotransmitter substances. One may activate and another inhibit a given function, or two substances can independently activate separate parts of the same mechanism. For example, 5-HT injected in the anterior hypothalamus will elevate temperature, whereas norepinephrine, similarly applied, will have the opposite effect and lower temperature (see review of Myers, 1970a).

As a corollary to a neurotransmitter "code" of a function at one site, it is also apparent that one neurotransmitter substance may anatomically "code" different functions at separate sites. That is, one neurohumoral agent, acting in several different ways, may serve in a modulating, excitatory, inhibitory, or neutral capacity, depending upon the anatomical locus. For example, norepinephrine, which, as mentioned earlier, inhibits heat production when applied in the anterior hypothalamus, will stimulate a feeding response when microinjected into the lateral hypothalamus (Myers, 1969b) or may cause sedation when injected at more medial loci of this diencephalic structure. Because of these findings, the method of chemical stimulation becomes a valid one, in a physiological sense, only when an area of the brain is "mapped" chemically. What does this entail for the student or the established investigator?

First, a single, intermediate dose of a compound can be used to "test" all sites in one animal to obtain information on the site-specificity of each response that is observed. Then, two or preferably three doses of each chemical substance under study would be microinjected at the same sites in order to determine whether the response is enhanced or attenuated by the alternate elevation or lowering of that dose of the chemical.

Second, a functional "map" of the animal's responses is constructed for each compound used for stimulating the brain. The sites of stimulation, together with the physiological responses, are localized by means of the histological sections. As an example of this procedure, one such "map" is illustrated in Fig. 14 in which those sites at which 5-HT evoked hyperthermia in the monkey are designated by the triangles (▲) and those at which 5-HT had no effect are signified by the open circles (○). From an analysis of these data, it is possible to ascribe a function to this neurohumoral substance and to localize the function to specific anatomical regions within the brain.

Finally, it is important to consider the two most important physiological limitations of the method of chemical stimulation. First, the stimulus cannot be turned on and off repeatedly at various intervals as can be done with an electric current. Second, the duration of the

5-HT MICRO-INJECTION SITES

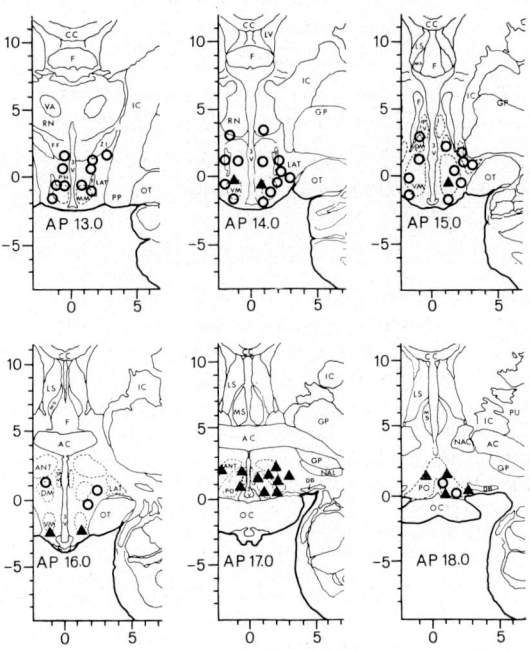

▲ = HYPERTHERMIA
○ = NO RESPONSE

FIG. 14. Anatomical "mapping" at six coronal (AP) levels of sites in the hypothalamus at which micro-injections of 5-HT in doses of 2–5 μg produce hyperthermia (▲). Sites at which 5-HT injections cause no change in temperature are also indicated (○). AC, anterior commissure; ANT, anterior hypothalamic area; CC, corpus callosum; DB, diagonal band of Broca; DM, dorsomedial nucleus; F, fornix; FF, fields of Forel; GP, globus pallidus; IC, internal capsule; LAT, lateral hypothalamus; LV, lateral ventricle; LS, lateral septal nucleus; MM, mammillary body; MS, medial septal nucleus; NAC, nucleus accumbens; OC, optic chiasm; OT, optic tract; PH, posterior hypothalamic area; PO, preoptic area; PP, cerebral peduncle; PU, putamen; PV, paraventricular nucleus; RN, reticular nucleus of the thalamus; VA, anteroventral nucleus of the thalamus; ZI, zona incerta; 3V, third ventricle. Horizontal and lateral scales are in mm. Vertical zero represents the stereotaxic zero plane 10 mm above the interaural line. (From Myers and Yaksh, 1969.)

stimulus again cannot be controlled, since this parameter is determined by the dissolution characteristics of the chemical and/or its rate of metabolic degradation. In the future, these limitations may be at least partially overcome by technological advances. For example, a method for accurate and repeated perfusions of an isolated region of brain tissue of the conscious animal has already been developed (Myers, 1970b). This procedure may enable one to simulate the activity of a chemical transmitter in terms of its release and turnover. Thus, our goal of understanding precisely what happens within a circumscribed area of the brain may ultimately be achieved.

ACKNOWLEDGEMENTS

Many of the developments contained in this Chapter have been made possible by the support given to the author over the years by the National Science Foundation, Office of Naval Research, National Institutes of Health, Wallace Laboratories and the Purdue Research Foundation. I am deeply grateful to my technicians, students, and colleagues who contributed in so many ways to the ideas presented here, and in particular to: Dr L. G. Sharpe, for his part in devising the cannulae shown in Figs 5 and 7, and to Peter Curzon and Raymond Baxter, staff members of the Laboratory of Neuropsychology.

REFERENCES

Ankier, S. I. and Tyers, M. B. (1969). *Br. J. Pharmacol.* **37**, 548P.
Baxter, B. L. (1967). *Fedn. Proc.* **26**, 289.
Clark, W. G., Vivonia, C. A. and Baxter, C. F. (1968). *J. appl. Physiol.* **25**, 319–321.
Clöetta, M. and Fischer, H. (1930). *Archs Exp. Path. Pharmakol.* **158**, 254–281.
Comroe, J. H., Jr. (1943). *Am. J. Physiol.* **139**, 490–498.
deGroot, J. (1959). *Verh. K. Ned. Akad. Wet.* **42**, 3–40.
Decima, E. and George, R. (1964). *Electroenceph. Clin. Neurophysiol.* **17**, 438–439.
Delgado, J. M. R. (1966). *Arch. Int. Pharmacodyn.* **161**, 442–462.
Demole, V. (1927). *Archs Exp. Path. Pharmakol.* **120**, 229–258.
Epstein, A. N. (1960). *Am. J. Physiol.* **199**, 969–974.
Feldberg, W. (1963). "A Pharmacological Approach to the Brain from its Inner and Outer Surface." Edward Arnold, London.
Fisher, A. E. (1969). *Ann. N.Y. Acad. Sci.* **157**, 984.
Fisher, A. E. and Coury, J. N. (1962). *Science, N.Y.* **138**, 691–693.
Fisher, A. E. and Coury, J. N. (1964). *In* "Thirst in the Regulation of Body Water" (M. Wayner, ed.), pp. 515–526. Pergamon Press, New York.
Goodman, L. S. and Gilman, A. (1965). "The Pharmacological Basis of Therapeutics." MacMillan Co., New York.
Goodrich, C. A., Greehey, B., Miller, T. B. and Pappenheimer, J. R. (1969). *J. appl. Physiol.* **26**, 137–140.
Grossman, S. P. (1964). *In* "Thirst in the Regulation of Body Water" (M. Wayner, ed.), pp. 902–912. Pergamon Press, New York.
Grossman, S. P. (1969). *Ann. N.Y. Acad. Sci.* **157**, 902–918.

Grossman, S. P. and Stumpf, W. E. (1969). *Science, N.Y.* **166**, 1410–1412.
Grunden, L. R. and Linburn, G. E. (1969). *J. Pharm. Sci.* **58**, 1147–1148.
Hasama, B. (1930). *Archs Exp. Path. Pharmakol.* **153**, 291–308.
Hernández-Peón, R., Chávez-Ibarra, G., Morgane, P. J. and Timo-Iaria, C. (1963). *Exp. Neurol.* **8**, 93–111.
Hubel, D. H. (1959). *J. Physiol.* **147**, 226–238.
Kennard, D. W. (1953). *In* "CIBA Foundation Symposium on the Spinal Cord", pp. 214–221. Little, Brown & Co., Boston.
Kottler, P. D. and Bowman, R. E. (1968). *J. Exp. Anal. Behav.* **11**, 536.
MacLean, P. D. (1957). *A.M.A. Arch. Neurol. Psychiat.* **78**, 113–127.
Markowitz, M. B. E., Archibald, J. and Downie, H. G. (1959). "Experimental Surgery." The Williams and Wilkins Co., Baltimore.
Marley, E. and Stephenson, J. D. (1968). *J. Physiol.* **196**, 97–99P.
Masserman, J. H. (1938). *J. Pharmacol. exp. Ther.* **64**, 335.
Masserman, J. H. (1940). *J. Pharmacol. exp. Ther.* **70**, 450.
Morgane, P. (1969). *Ann. N.Y. Acad. Sci.* **157**, 806–849.
Miller, N. E. (1965). *Science, N.Y.* **148**, 328–338.
Myers, R. D. (1963). *J. appl. Physiol.* **18**, 221–233.
Myers, R. D. (1964a). *In* "Thirst in the Regulation of Body Water" (M. Wayner, ed.), pp. 533–549. Pergamon Press, New York.
Myers, R. D. (1964b). *Can. J. Psychol.* **18**, 6–14.
Myers, R. D. (1966). *Physiol. Behav.* **1**, 171–174.
Myers, R. D. (1969a). *Science, N.Y.* **165**, 1030–1031.
Myers, R. D. (1969b). *Ann. N.Y. Acad. Sci.* **157**, 918–934.
Myers, R. D. (1969c). *In* "The Hypothalamus—Anatomical, Functional and Clinical Aspects" (W. Nauta, W. Haymaker, E. Anderson, eds), pp. 506–523. Charles Thomas, Springfield, Illinois, U.S.A.
Myers, R. D. (1970a). *In* "Physiological and Behavioral Temperature Regulation" (J. D. Hardy, ed.), pp. 648–666. Charles Thomas, Springfield, Illinois, U.S.A.
Myers, R. D. (1970b). *Physiol. Behav.* **5**, 243–246.
Myers, R. D. and Sharpe, L. G. (1968a). *Science, N.Y.* **161**, 572–573.
Myers, R. D. and Sharpe, L. G. (1968b). *Physiol. Behav.* **3**, 987–995.
Myers, R. D. and Yaksh, T. L. (1969). *J. Physiol.* **202**, 483–500.
Myers, R. D., Casaday, G. and Holman, R. (1967). *Physiol. Behav.* **2**, 87–88.
Myers, R. D., Tytell, M., Rudy, T.A. and Kawa, A. (1971). *Physiol, Behav.* **7**, in press.
Nashold, B. S. and Gills, J. P. (1960). *J. Neuropathol. Expl Neurol.* **19**, 580–590.
Olds, J. and Olds, M. E. (1958). *Science, N.Y.* **127**, 1175–1176.
Olds, J., Yuwiler, A., Olds, M. E. and Yun, C. (1964). *Am. J. Physiol.* **207**, 242–253.
Rech, R. H. and Domino, E. F. (1959). *Arch. int. Pharmacodyn.* **131**, 429–442.
Routtenberg, A. (1967). *Science, N.Y.* **157**, 838–839.
Schütz, J. (1916). *Archs Exp. Path. Pharmakol.* **79**, 285–290.
Sharpe, L. G. and Myers, R. D. (1969). *Exp. Brain Res.* **8**, 295–310.
Sheatz, G. C. (1961). *In* "Electrical Stimulation of the Brain" (D. E. Sheer, ed.), pp. 45–51. University of Texas Press, Austin, Texas, U.S.A.
Stein, L. and Seifter, J. (1962). *Am. J. Physiol.* **202**, 751–756.
Villablanca, J. and Myers, R. D. (1965). *Am. J. Physiol.* **208**, 703–707.
Wagner, J. W. and de Groot, J. (1963). *Electroenceph. Clin. Neurophysiol.* **15**, 125

Appendix

Chemicals and Dyes
Sigma Chemical Co.
3500 DeKalb Street
St. Louis, Missouri 63118, U.S.A.

Cal Biochem
Box 54282
Los Angeles, California 90054, U.S.A.

Du Pont
El DuPont Nemours & Co., Inc.
Organic Chemicals Department
Wilmington, Delaware 19898, U.S.A.

Eastman Organic Chemicals
Division of Distillation Products Inc.
Rochester 3, New York, U.S.A.

The Matheson Co., Inc.
P.O. Box 966
Joliet, Illinois 60434, U.S.A.

Mann Research Labs, Inc.
Subsidiary B-D-Labs, Inc.
136 Liberty Street
New York, New York 10006, U.S.A.

Electrical
Allied Electronics
2400 W. Washington Boulevard
Chicago, Illinois 60680, U.S.A.

Newark Electronics
2114 S. Division Street
Grand Rapids, Michigan, U.S.A.

Milli-Pore Filters
The Millipore Corporation
Bedford, Massachusetts 01730, U.S.A.

Pedestal Bases (Polyethylene bottle)
Dynalab Corporation
Box 112
Rochester, New York 14601, U.S.A.

C. F. Palmer, Ltd.
Myographic Works
Effra Road
Brixton, London S.W. 2
England

Plastpak Disposable Plastic Syringe
Becton, Dickinson & Co.
Rutherford, New Jersey, U.S.A.

Pumps
Sage
230 Ferris Avenue
White Plains, New York 10693, U.S.A.

Harvard Apparatus Co.
150 Dover Road
Millis, Maryland 02054, U.S.A.

Watson-Marlow, Ltd.
Marlow, Bucks.
England

Screws
Albany Products Co., Inc.
3046 W. 77th Street
Chicago, Illinois 60652, U.S.A.

Syringes
Hamilton Co., Inc.
Whittier, California, U.S.A.

PE-Tubing
Clay-Adams, Inc.
141 East 25th Street
New York 10, New York, U.S.A.

Portex Plastics, Ltd.
Hythe, Kent
England

Syringe Needle Tubing for Cannulae
Superior Tube
Norristown, Pennsylvania, U.S.A.

Cooper's Needle Works (Redditch) Ltd.
Birmingham 20, England

C. A. Roberts
2300 S. Tibs Avenue
Indianapolis, Indiana, U.S.A.

Becton, Dickson & Co.
Rutherford, New Jersey, U.S.A.

Chapter 9

Elementary Histology for Neuropsychologists

GEORGE WOLF[1]

Division of Natural Sciences, State University of New York, Purchase, New York, U.S.A.

I.	Introduction and Historical Background	281
II.	Preparation of Sections	283
	A. Perfusion	283
	B. Removal of Brain	284
	C. Sectioning	286
III.	Preparation of Slides	287
	A. Mounting	287
	B. Cover Slips	289
IV.	Introduction to Staining	290
V.	Staining Recipes	292
	A. Cells: Cresyl Violet Method	292
	B. Fibers: Modified Weil-Weigert Method	293
	C. Cells and Fibers: Modified Klüver-Barrera Method	295
	D. Cells and Fibers: Auletta Method	296
VI.	Analysis of Brain Sections	297
	A. Drawings of Histological Sections	297
	B. Localizing Electrode and Cannula Tips	297
	C. Determining Tissue Damage	298
	References	299
	Appendix	300

I. Introduction and Historical Background

STAINS are used to color specific components of tissue. Neuropsychologists stain slices of brain tissue so that they can identify fiber tracts and cell groups for the purpose of determining the locations of lesions or of probes. To the extent that we are interested in identifying

[1] Work on this chapter was done during the tenure of an Established Investigatorship of the American Heart Association and was supported by Grant #70-684 from the American Heart Association. The author is grateful to J. W. Kelly for frequent advice, to J. P. Auletta for collaboration in developing the staining procedures, and to S. Rustin for photographic work.

nuclei and tracts rather than individual units, we need utilize only the simplest of the many specialized staining methods available. We rarely require magnification of more than 100 times to obtain the necessary histological information. Depending on the particular brain structures under investigation, a cell stain, a fiber stain, or a combined cell and fiber stain may be most useful. Refined methods for applying each of these types of stains are available.

The problem of cell staining was essentially solved about 100 years ago (Conn, 1933) by the use of the basic aniline stains which combine with acidic molecules such as proteins and nucleic acids (Nissl substance) in the cell bodies. These stains are relatively easy to apply and control.

Fiber (myelin) staining is somewhat more complex, both in chemistry and in practical application. The oldest and most widely used fiber stain is the iron-hematoxylin method which gives black fibers on a diffuse light-brown background. The iron atoms link the hematoxylin to the fibers by forming a bridge between the dye molecules and phosphate molecules in the myelin (chelation). The iron-hematoxylin method dates back to the latter part of the nineteenth century when Weigert and other histologists described a number of procedures using different metallic salts (Conn, 1933).

A relatively facile and reliable method for staining both cells and fibers was described by Klüver and Barrera (1953). With this method the myelinated fibers are first stained blue with a phthalocyanine pigment and the cells are then "counterstained" with a red or reddish-blue basic aniline stain. A new method for cell and fiber staining has recently been developed by J. P. Auletta in this laboratory and will be described for the first time in this chapter. This method makes use of the phenomenon of metachromasy (two colors from one stain) to produce differential pigmentation of cells (blue) and fibers (burgundy red) with a single stain.

This chapter will present simplified methods for preparing and analysing histological material. The procedures to be described have been developed for use with rats; however, they are applicable to other species of experimental animals with generally minor and obvious modifications. Each of the steps involved in the preparation of histological material will be described in detail. However, one should keep in mind that a written description cannot entirely replace direct observation; and if one is entirely naïve one can save oneself a great deal of trial and error simply by watching an experienced worker, even though his techniques differ in detail from those presented here.

II. Preparation of Sections

A. Perfusion

(1) *Equipment*

Large surgical scissor

2 small curved hemostats

Blunted 17 ga hypodermic needle connected by tubing to a 50 ml syringe containing 10% phosphate buffered formalin

(2) *Procedure*

Anesthetize the animal deeply. An overdose of nembutal (60 mg/kg) is good for this purpose. Figure 1 shows a rat prepared for perfusion.

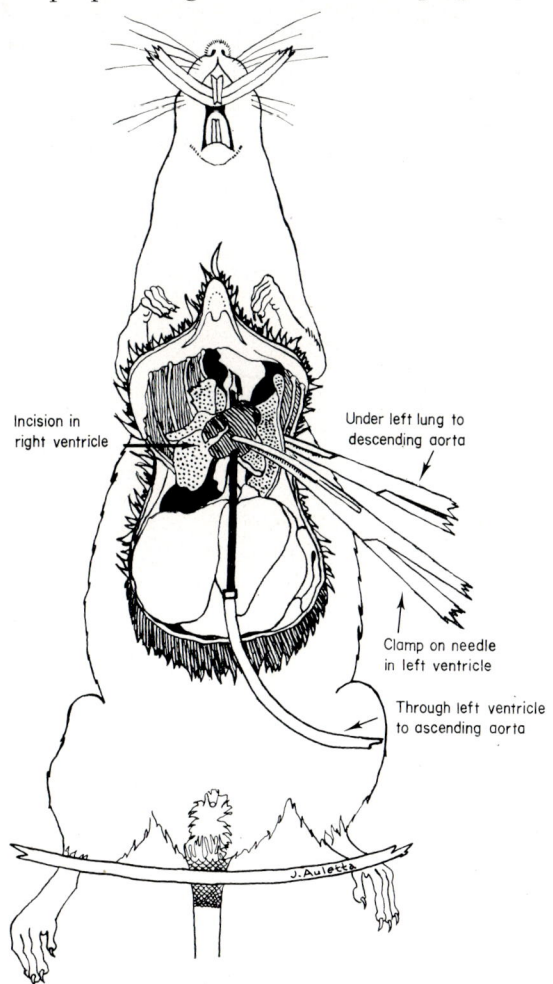

FIG. 1. Rat prepared for perfusion.

The rat is placed in a supine position on a grill over a sink or pan and held in place by rubber bands over the snout and hind legs. Cut a large crescent-shaped opening which severs the abdominal wall below the sternum and enters the rib cage laterally. Sever the diaphragm, and reflect the rib cage. It may be helpful to clamp the xiphisternum to the lower incisors to better expose the thoracic cavity while inserting the hemostats and perfusion needle. Lift the left lung and clamp-off the descending aorta. Clear the pericardial membranes from the heart. Pinch the right ventricle between the thumb and forefinger of the left hand and pull downward gently so that the ascending aorta can be seen. With the right hand insert the perfusion needle through the bottom of the left ventricle in line with the lumen of the aorta and guide it gently upward until it is about $\frac{1}{2}$ cm into the lumen. The needle can be easily seen through the wall of the aorta. Clamp the needle in place with a small hemostat on the left ventricle. Sever the wall of the right ventricle. Perfuse rapidly with the 10% buffered formalin; 50 ml perfused over a 30 sec period is sufficient for a rat. It is customary to perfuse physiological saline prior to the formalin, but this is not necessary for the present histological methods.

B. Removal of Brain

(1) *Equipment*

Large surgical scissors
Small surgical scissors
Narrow rongeurs

(2) *Procedure*

The procedure for removing the brain is shown in Fig. 2. It is most conveniently done immediately after perfusion before the brain hardens too much. Decapitate at the neck and cut off the mandible. Cut the scalp along the midline and reflect it forcefully to the side to reveal the temporal muscles. Implanted electrodes should be removed carefully at this time. Cut forward along each side through the attachments of the muscles and zygomatic arch to bare the sides of the skull. The skull can now be broken off in large pieces by grasping the edge lightly with the rongeurs and pulling outward rather than biting through the bone. Begin at the foramen magnum, work forward over the dorsal surface to the bregma, and finally remove the sides of the skull to the floor of the cranial cavity. The bone and dura between the cerebrum and the cerebellum should be removed carefully using the scissors rather than the rongeurs. The brain stem can now be lifted slightly from the floor of the cranial cavity to reveal several attachments of cranial nerves and dura which can be cut with the small scissors. Now grasp the nasal bone at the orbits with the rongeurs and squeeze. The frontal bone will split down the midline and the brain will fall out intact.

The brain should be allowed to harden in 10% phosphate-buffered formalin for at least a day before blocking and sectioning. Generally, sectioning is done in a frontal plane corresponding to the plane of a particular stereotaxic atlas. Many workers use the stereotaxic instrument and block the brain *in situ* after perfusion to ensure accuracy and consistency in the plane of the sections. Standardized blocks can be obtained more easily by means of a blocking guide such as the one shown in Fig. 2 (e), which can be made by embedding the top half of a rat's skull in a slicing block to form a mold for the brain and a guide for a razor blade.

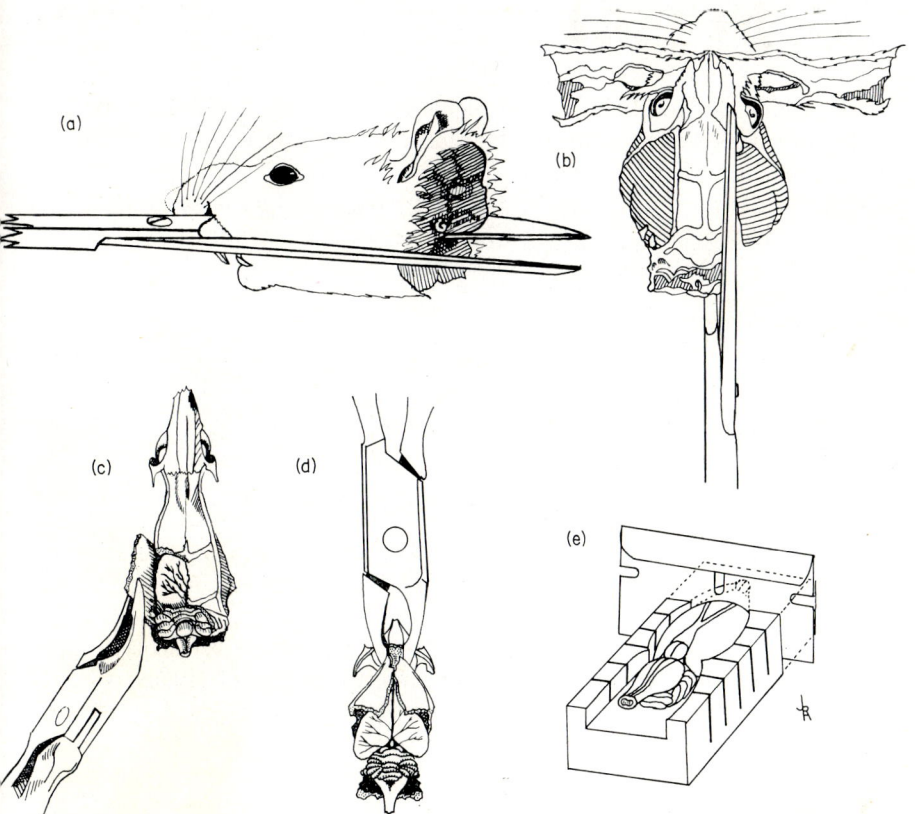

FIG. 2. Removal of brain from cranium ((a) through (d)) and blocking guide (e).

C. Sectioning

There are a number of methods for preparing sections. The "frozen" method described below is perhaps the most popular because it is the most simple and rapid. The main alternatives are the paraffin and the celloidin methods in which the tissue is embedded in material which hardens to allow thin sections to be cut from the block. While there are some advantages to these embedding methods, they do not generally outweigh the extra work involved. Frozen sectioning can be done on tissue embedded in gelatin and this is sometimes useful when sections contain separate pieces of tissue because they will be held together by the hardened gelatin. We have used the following procedure slightly modified from Luna (1960, p. 31) with satisfactory results.

Wash the tissue block in running water for a few hours to clear out the formalin. Impregnate successively in 5%, 10% and 20% aqueous gelatin solutions at 40°C for 24 hr at each concentration. Allow the 20% gelatin to cool slightly so that a thick film remains over the block when it is removed. Place the block in 10% formalin for one or two days to harden the gelatin. The block is now ready for sectioning on the freezing microtome.

The cutting and the cytology of frozen sections is somewhat improved if the block is soaked in "sweetened" formalin (10 g sucrose per 100 ml 10% buffered formalin) for a day before sectioning.

(1) Equipment

Sliding microtome with freezing stage
Camel-hair brush
Absorbant tissue paper
Multicompartment tray containing buffered formalin

(2) Procedure

Place the block of brain containing the target area on the stage of the microtome over a piece of wet paper toweling and freeze. Place a few drops of water around the edges of the block to fix it firmly to the paper. The paper can be peeled off the stage after sectioning is completed without waiting for the remaining piece of tissue to thaw. Mark one side of the brain by puncturing with a fine hypodermic needle. One can trim away the cortex when it is not of interest, to reduce the size of the sections. When the top of the block appears dry and feels hard it is sufficiently frozen to begin sectioning. Slide the knife smoothly through the tissue and adjust the rate of each excursion so that the section begins to curl just slightly as the knife passes through, the colder the block the slower the excursions. Pick the sections off the knife with the brush and place them in order in the cubicles of the tray. Wipe the knife dry with tissue paper after each cut. The sections may be stored indefinitely if the tray is sealed and refrigerated.

The proper care and use of the microtome knife is important. The cutting edge must be sharp and smooth in order to obtain good sections. To utilize the entire length of the knife evenly, we begin at the left end, and after sectioning each brain, we move the knife 1 mm to the right. The edge of the knife can probably stand a lot more cutting but it pays to play it safe here and thus ensure the best possible sections. Also, it is a good practice to clean the blade with absolute alcohol after sectioning is completed.

Most microtomes allow variable angles of the knife. The horizontal angle is not too critical; we usually set it about 20° off the line of excursion, to slice through the block rather than strike it head on. The vertical angle (clearance angle) is more important and should be set so that the bottom surface of the bevel is about 5° off the horizontal, thus allowing only the cutting edge to contact the block.

The uniformity of the stain depends to a large extent upon the uniformity of the thickness of the sections. Often when one finds different sections or different parts of the same section stained at differential intensity it will be due to some flaw in the sectioning procedure. Be certain that the knife is firmly held in the carrier, that it is wiped dry before each cut, and that excursion through the block is at a smooth, even rate.

III. Preparation of Slides

A. Mounting

Sections can be mounted on slides either before or after staining While slides are easier to handle than loose sections, there are a number of advantages to staining unmounted sections which, in my opinion, make this method preferable. Total staining time is reduced because there are two free surfaces for impregnation of the solutions and the overall quality of the stained sections appears substantially enhanced. Even more important, the unmounted staining method allows staining of thick sections which do not adhere well to slides when subjected to chemical treatments during staining.

At 100 μ thickness, the sections provide excellent definition for localization work. Indistinct nuclear groups and diffuse fiber tracts are more apparent in thick sections because of (a) the greater number of intact cells (cell fragments at the surfaces of "frozen" sections often loose their cytoplasm) and (b) the greater length of fibers in the section. Moreover, thick sections are easier to mount on slides. They resist fragmentation, distortion, and wrinkling so that mounting proceeds rapidly, even for the less-skilled worker. Thick sections are especially advantageous when electrode tracts or lesions leave large cavities in the tissue, because the sections remain intact even though only small shreds of tissue connect the portions. However, thick as well as thin sections tend to fold and one has to get accustomed to unfolding them on the slide. This takes practice.

Certain potential disadvantages of thick sections should be noted at this point. While various cell types can be identified, the sections are not suitable for detailed cytologic analysis requiring high magnification, and photography requires focal depth so that a dissecting scope or macro-lens camera must be used to obtain a sharp picture. Also, certain treatments (e.g. acid) cause some shrinkage of unmounted sections. Shrinkage also occurs in paraffin and celloidin embedded tissue and can be avoided only by staining mounted unembedded sections. However, since the shrinkage is uniform it does not interfere with the usual identification and analysis of lesions, or electrode or cannula tracks. If necessary, shrunken sections can be re-expanded by placing them in a weak phosphate-buffered solution at pH 7·0 (such solutions are used for setting pH meters), but this is somewhat detrimental to the quality of the basic aniline cell stains.

(1) *Equipment*

Glass microscope slides and cover slips
2 fine camel-hair brushes
1·0% aqueous pigskin gelatin solution (store in refrigerator)
Eye dropper.
Hard filter paper (S&S #597)

(2) *Procedure*

Analysis of the sections is facilitated if many sections are placed on the same slide because they can be scanned rapidly under the microscope without continually removing and replacing slides. Thus, when there is a large series of sections to be studied, the use of large slides which can accommodate 10–20 sections of rat brain is suggested. However, this should not be attempted until one has mastered the mounting procedure. Stained sections should be soaked in warm (about 40°C) gelatin solution for a few minutes prior to mounting. Place a slide on a transparent or black surface which allows the sections to be seen clearly when they are floated on the slide. The slide should be at room temperature during and after mounting of the sections. Put a few drops of gelatin solution on the slide. Pick up a section on a brush and lay it on the gelatin solution. Use two brushes, one in each hand, to unfold and orient the section. After all the sections are mounted, remove the excess gelatin with the eye dropper or by tipping the slide. Now one can easily move the sections into their final positions and they will not float out of alignment. Lay the filter paper over the slide to absorb additional fluid and remove slowly. The procedure may require some practice. If one finds that the sections stick to the filter paper, one can try using a piece of cigarette-paper first, but this should not be necessary once one gets the knack of it. Finally, place a dry portion of the filter paper on the slide and press firmly over the sections to flatten them against the slide and to absorb the final bit of fluid. Let the sections dry at room temperature for a few minutes to an hour before final dehydration in alcohol and clearing in xylene. If the sections loosen in the alcohol, let them dry longer. If the sections are decolorized in an acidic solution and are not rinsed well before soaking in gelatin, they will tend to crack while drying. This will also happen if the gelatin is too acidic (pH < 5.0).

The mounting procedure for sections to be stained on the slides is similar to the above except that pre-soaking in gelatin solution is not necessary. The slides should be kept on a warming plate at about 60°C overnight to increase adherence before staining. An alternative method is to smear a drop of albumin fixative on the slide, place it on the warming plate, and then place a few drops of water on it. Float the sections in place and allow the water to evaporate. Leave the slides on the warming plate overnight before staining.

B Cover Slips

(1) *Equipment*

Slide carrier
4 slide trays with 50% alcohol, 75% alcohol, absolute alcohol, and xylene
Permount

(2) *Procedure*

To prepare the slides for cover slips, pass them successively through 50%, 75% and absolute alcohol for about 1 min in each solution, agitating them to wash off the excess gelatin. We usually add a *few drops* of dilute acetic acid to the 75% alcohol to finish the last bit of decolorization of cell stains and sharpen the differentiation. Then place the slides in xylene to clear the sections. They are now ready to be covered. Place a few drops of Permount along the left perimeter of the sections. Thicker sections require somewhat more Permount than thinner sections. Hold the corners of the right edge of the cover slip in the right hand and lay the left edge of the cover slip along the left edge of the Permount. Now, with a dissecting pin or with a mounting brush held upside down, press down lightly on the cover slip and "roll" the cover slip across the sections from left to right. In this way, any air bubbles will be pushed to the right edge of the cover slip.

IV. Introduction to Staining

Staining procedures can be approached more like cooking recipes than like chemical-treatment methods. Unlike many laboratory procedures in which success depends upon rigid adherence to instructions, certain steps of the staining procedures must be modified occasionally for optimum results and instructions can serve only as rough guidelines. However, one doesn't have to know much chemistry to get good histology. Given that the sections have been prepared properly, most problems that occur in staining can be solved by simply changing the concentration of one or another solution or changing the duration of one or another treatment.

I suggest one begins by following our recipes rather closely, but if things do not work out do not be afraid to *"patchka"*. It will be very fortunate if good results occur on the first attempt. Try the simple cell stain first. If fixation and sectioning procedures have been performed properly, good results should be obtained within a few trials. Figures 4 and 5 show color photographs of frontal sections at a different rostro-caudal level for each of the four stains. Use corresponding sections for comparison, and do the staining prior to mounting.

Containers for staining unmounted sections are commercially available. Figure 3A shows a covered multicompartment tray which contains the sections. Perforations in the bottom and top allow the various staining solutions to flow into the compartments when the tray is submerged in the staining pans (Fig. 3B).

A convenient way to stain unmounted sections when serial order is not important (e.g. when trying a new stain) or when the order can be determined after staining, is to use (a) a small porcelain (Gooch) crucible with a perforated bottom to carry the sections, and (b) small jars or a cup-cake pan for the solutions (Fig. 3(c)). A few dozen sections can be stained at one time in this way.

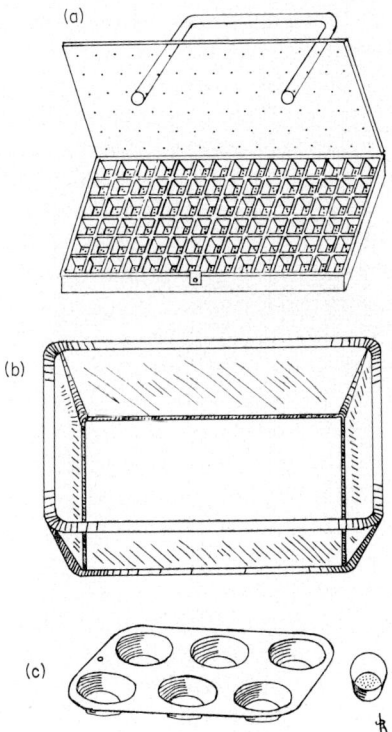

Fig. 3. Multicompartment perforated tray (a) and staining-pan (b), for staining unmounted sections, and Gooch crucible and cup-cake pan for staining when maintenance of serial order is not necessary (c).

Since we do not know all of the variables which affect the quality of the stain, it is a good rule to be a bit compulsive. When rinsing is called for, do it thoroughly with a few changes of distilled water. Rinse especially well before beginning any staining procedure to wash out all the buffered formalin, and again after completing the staining so as to wash out all of the decolorizing solution. Decolorizing solutions should be discarded after one use. Use the inexpensive fiber-staining solutions only once also.

The general principle underlying the staining methods described here is that the sections are first overstained and then the excess stain is removed (decolorization). The rate of decolorization depends on the pH of the decolorizing solution: acid for the cell stains, basic solution for the fiber stains. (Also note that acids harden and contract the sections, whereas bases soften and expand them.)

The sections should be deeply and uniformly colored when they are removed from the staining solutions. If one can distinguish between white and grey matter, place the sections back in the stain for a longer impregnation. If one finds that the fiber stains have not completely penetrated dense, heavily myelinated fiber tracts, increase the duration of pretreatment in acetone which dissolves some of the fat. Acetone pretreatment can also be used for the luxol blue stain but is not necessary here since the alcohol solvent has a similar effect.

The stains from different producers and even different batches from the same producer may vary somewhat in composition. We use Matheson, Coleman and Bell stains, except for Pyronin GS which is made by Chroma-Gesselschaft, and have found them relatively consistent in composition. Stock solutions of the stains can be made up and stored indefinitely. The solutions should be stirred well to dissolve all the stain, and then filtered through glass wool. For simplicity we use only absolute alcohol in the staining recipes when staining unmounted sections. When staining mounted sections, 70% and 95% alcohol are used to gradually dehydrate or rehydrate the sections. Otherwise, the recipes are directly applicable to mounted as well as unmounted sections. Optimal results can generally be obtained with the cell stains and with Auletta's cresyl violet fiber stain without individual treatment of the sections during decolorization. To obtain perfect results with the iron-hematoxylin and luxol blue fiber stains, it is sometimes necessary to decolorize some sections for a longer period of time than others. This is especially true when sections from different parts of the brain are being stained.

Finally, I think it's important to consider that in some ways staining is an art. It is an art because mysterious things happen, but it is an art also in an aesthetic sense. The structures of the brain are beautiful and their beauty is enhanced by the brilliant colors we apply to them. Considerable personal gratification can be gained by creating beautiful brain sections—indeed the experiences you have looking through your microscope can be ecstatic.

V. STAINING RECIPES

A. Cells: Cresyl Violet Method

Each type of stain has specific advantages and disadvantages. A simple cell stain is unexcelled for identification of nuclei and glial borders of lesions and electrode tracks. Fiber counterstaining causes an inevitable loss of definition of some nuclear groups when diffuse fiber systems obscure their boundaries or cytoarchitectonic characteristics. Therefore, certain structures are best seen in simple cell-stained material.

Cresyl violet acetate is an excellent cell stain. It provides a very strong contrast between stained elements (cytoplasm of neurons and nuclei of glial cells) which are blue and unstained elements which remain white. The staining process is simple and results are consistently good without individual treatment of sections. Unlike some other basic aniline stains such a thionin, cresyl violet does not fade with time.

(1) *Solutions*

    0·1% aqueous cresyl violet acetate solution
    Acid alcohol decolorizing solution
        1 part 10% acetic-acid solution
        9 parts absolute alcohol
    Absolute alcohol
    Xylene

(2) *Procedure (Steps)*

1. Water rinse
2. Alcohol: 2–5 min
3. Xylene: about 10–20 min
4. Alcohol: 2–5 min (agitate well)
5. Water rinse
6. Cresyl violet solution: 2–10 min
7. Water rinse
8. Acid alcohol to decolorize
9. Water rinse

(3) *Comments*

The purpose of the xylene step is to remove some of the lipid substances in the cells and fibers which impair the specificity of the stain. The rate at which the section decolorizes depends upon the amount of acid in the decolorizing solution. If the section is not decolorizing rapidly enough, add some 10% acetic acid. The decolorizing step need not be longer than five minutes but requires some attention. When the fiber areas and the molecular layer of cortex are pure white (except for scattered glial cell nuclei) by gross appearance the decolorizing is complete. Generally, one has plenty of leeway after the optimum point so that considerable over-decolorization is possible without great loss of utility.

B. *Fibers: Modified Weil-Weigert Method*

In the same way that the presence of stained fibers obscures certain nuclei, the presence of stained cells can impede the delineation of diffuse fiber systems. A simple fiber stain is of value in cases where special attention to individual fiber detail or to the exact borders of fiber tracts is called for as well as when diffuse fiber systems are to be identified. Iron-hematoxylin is undoubtedly the best myelin stain giving intensely impregnated black fibers on a uniform light brown background.

(1) *Solutions*

Acetone
Iron-hematoxylin solution
  1 part 10% alcoholic hematoxylin solution (1 g hematoxylin per 10 ml absolute alcohol)
  9 parts distilled water
  10 parts 4% aqueous solution of ferric ammonium sulfate
Decolorizing solution
  25 g potassium ferricyanide
  plus 25 g sodium borate per liter water

(2) *Procedure*

1. Water rinse
2. Acetone: 10–20 min
3. Water rinse
4. Iron hematoxylin solution: about 60 min at 50–60°C
5. Water rinse
6. Decolorizing solution till fibers are differentiated
7. Water rinse
8. Alcohol: about 5 min
9. Water rinse

(3) *Comments*

Hematoxylin is said to improve its staining characteristics if the 10% alcoholic solution is allowed to "ripen" (oxidize) for a few weeks, but I have found little evidence for this when using the above recipe and the suggested stain. Also, the iron hematoxylin staining solution appears stable for at least a few weeks so that it is not necessary to make it up immediately before staining. Those familiar with the Weil-Weigert Method (Drury and Wallington, 1967; Lillie, 1965) will see that the present procedure omits decolorization with iron alum prior to borate-ferricyanide treatment. We have omitted this step for although it may result in a lighter background, it appears to diminish the intensity of the fiber stain. Step #8 shrinks and hardens the sections to facilitate mounting.

FIG. 4. Frontal sections of rat brain cut on freezing microtome and stained according to recipes in text: 100 μ thick section through caudal diencephalon—cresyl violet method (A); 50 μ thick section through rostral diencephalon—Modified Weil-Weigert Method (B).

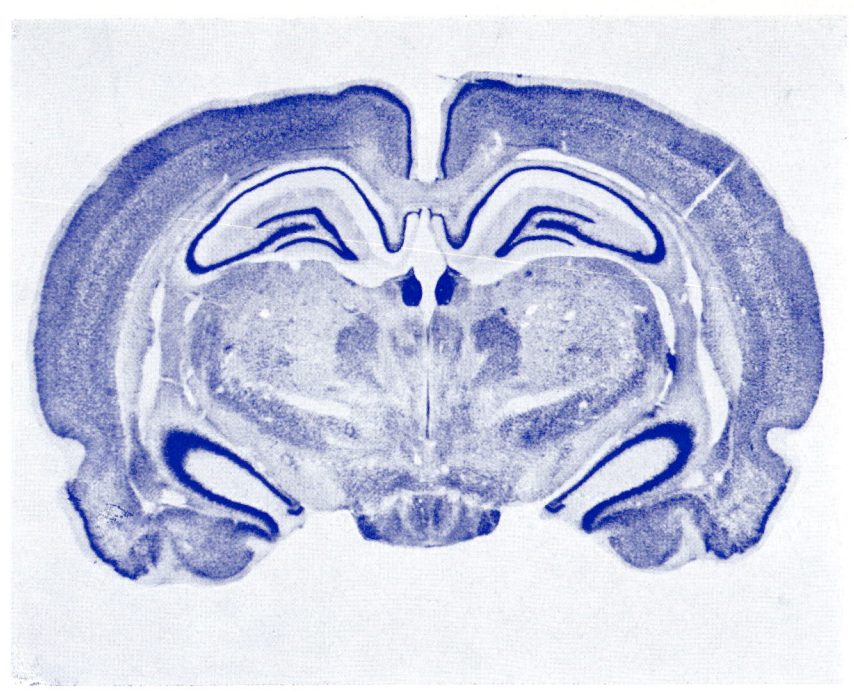

A

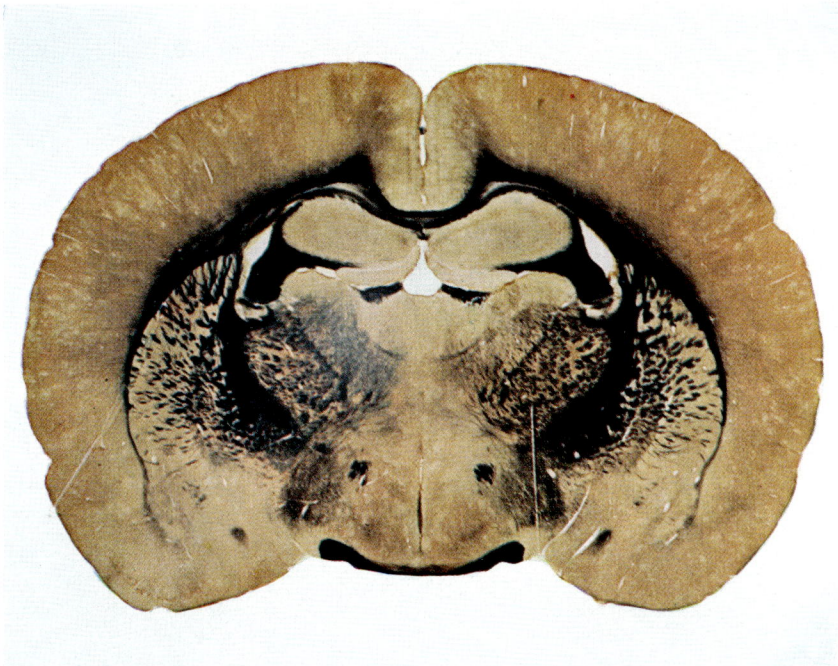

B

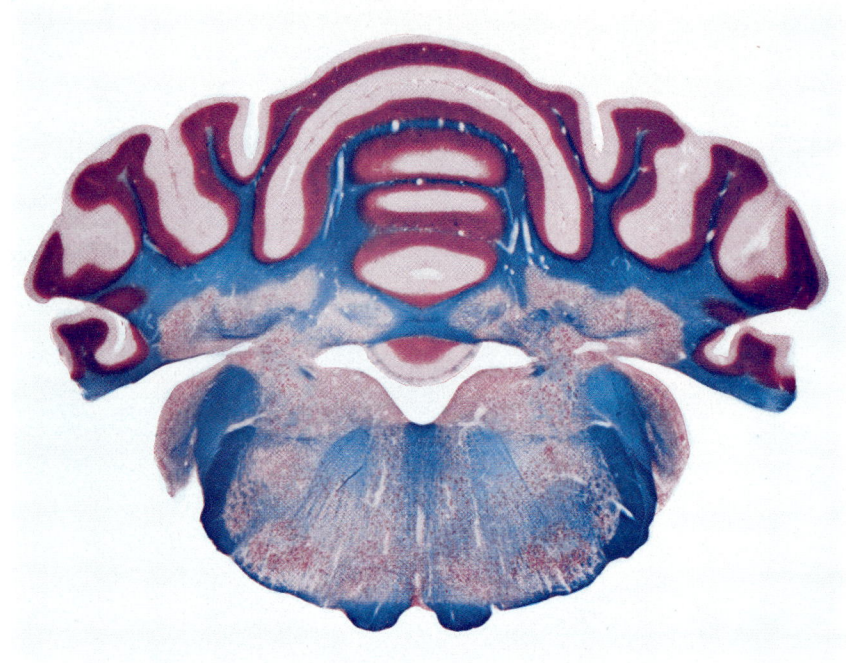

A

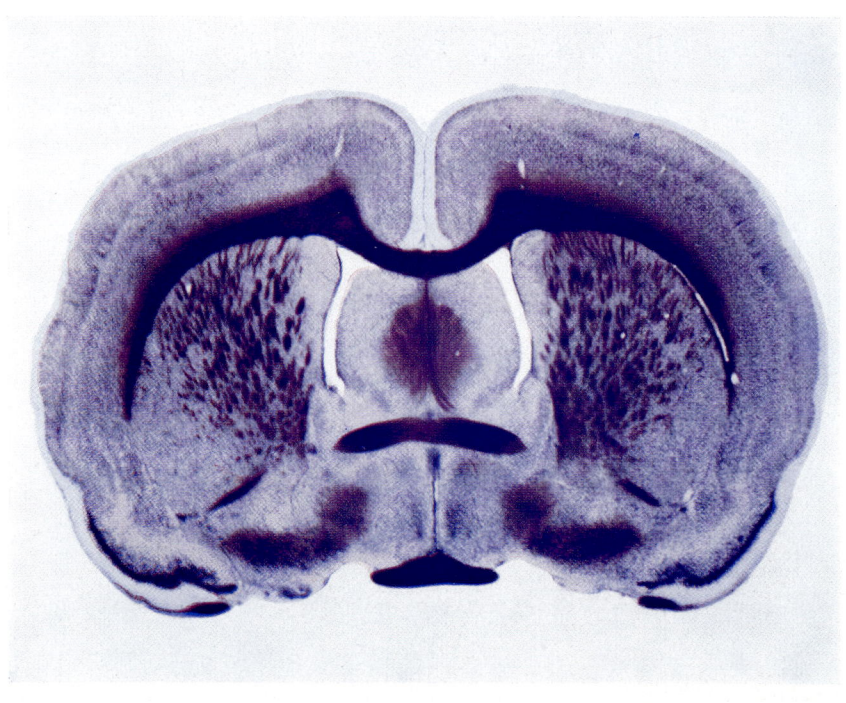

B

The decolorization step is tricky because visually the rate of decolorization is positively accelerated, so that the sections which are uniformly black may sit in the solution for a few minutes without apparent change and all of a sudden begin to differentiate rather rapidly, the background turning from black thru deep brown to a lighter brownish color. Unlike the cell stains, this stain cannot be over-decolorized without considerable loss. The appearance of a properly decolorized Weigert section depends on its thickness; the thicker the section the deeper the background will be at optimum differentiation. For this reason I prefer 50 μ sections to more thick ones on aesthetic grounds, although thicker sections are effective for most practical purposes.

C. Cells and Fibers: Modified Klüver-Barrera Method

When general orientation and identification of fairly distinct nuclei and fiber tracts is called for, methods which stain both in contrasting colors are very useful. The Klüver-Barrera Method has been the most popular counterstaining method. The fibers are stained with luxol blue which, although not as intense as iron-hematoxylin, can show individual fiber detail quite clearly. The cells are generally stained with a red or reddish-blue basic aniline stain. Red basic aniline stains are somewhat inferior to the blue ones but provide a much better contrast with the blue fibers. A number of red stains are available and will be listed in the recipe according to our preference.

(1) *Solutions*

Luxol blue solution
   10 g luxol blue and 1 ml glacial acetic acid in 1 l absolute alcohol
Ammoniacal alcohol solution
   1 part 5% ammonium hydroxide
   9 parts absolute alcohol
1% aqueous solution of cell stain
   (pyronin GS, pyronin Y, safranin O, neutral red, or Darrow red)
Acid alcohol solution
   1 part 10% acetic acid
   9 parts absolute alcohol

FIG. 5. Frontal sections of rat brain cut on freezing microtome and stained according to recipes in text: 100 μ thick section through cerebellum and lower brain stem—Modified Klüver-Barrera Method (A); 100 μ thick section through septal area—Auletta Method (B).

(2) *Procedure*
  1. Water rinse
  2. Luxol blue solution: 2 hr to overnight at 50–60°C
  3. Water rinse
  4. Ammoniacal alcohol solution (to loosen stain from cellular areas): about 15 sec
  5. Water rinse to wash out stain
  6. Cell-staining solution: 2–10 min
  7. Water rinse
  8. Acid alcohol to decolorize cell stain
  9. Water rinse

(3) *Comments*
In my experience it seems that long impregnation in luxol blue reduces the amount of variability during decolorization but has little advantage otherwise. Steps 4 and 5 should be repeated until the background is white; 2 or 3 times back and forth between the two solutions should be enough. The relative intensity of the fibers and cells can easily be controlled via the decolorization steps to meet specific needs.

D. *Cells and Fibers: Auletta Method*
This method provides a very rapid and reliable cell and fiber counterstain by utilizing a metachromatic reaction (Kelley, 1956) of cresyl violet acetate. The main advantages of the method are its simplicity and fine cell-staining qualities. The stain is very useful for localization work, although it has some drawbacks. The apparent redness of the fibers depends on the light source, standard microscope illumination from below being the best. Further, individual fibers are not well defined and the fibers cannot readily be decolorized to control their intensity.

(1) *Solutions*
  Acid-acetone solution
    1 part glacial acetic acid
    4 parts acetone
  1% aqueous cresyl violet acetate solution (the Matheson, Coleman, and Bell Product gives the best metachromatic reaction)
  Acid alcohol solution
    1 part 10% acetic acid
    2 parts absolute alcohol

(2) *Procedure*
  1. Water rinse
  2. Acid-acetone solution: 10–20 min
  3. Water rinse
  4. Cresyl violet solution; 2–10 min
  5. Water rinse
  6. Acid alcohol to decolorize
  7. Water rinse

(3) Comments

The acid alcohol decolorizes the cells only—the intensity of the fiber stain is not affected. Since the reddish metachromatic effect is specific to myelin no differentiation of fibers is necessary. However, in areas such as the reticular formation which are permeated with diffuse fiber systems, it may be desirable to diminish the intensity of the fiber stain so that the nuclear groups will become more apparent. One way to do this is to use a weaker cresyl-violet acetate solution which will tend to diminish the fiber stain but not the cell stain; but this stain is most suitable for areas with distinct fiber bundles. Thus, I would suggest the use of the Klüver-Barrera stain which allows more control of fiber intensity for counterstaining in areas such as the lower brain stem.

VI. Analysis of Brain Sections

(1) Equipment
Microprojector
Microscope

(2) Procedure

A. Drawing of Histological Sections

Much of this work can be done with a microprojector. Project each relevant section on paper and trace the outlines of the nuclei and fiber tracts. Trace the cavity made by the electrode or lesion and the surrounding area of necrosis and gliosis. Sections at the beginning, middle, and end of the lesion or electrode tip should receive the closest study. After making projection drawings of these 3 levels, the sections should be inspected under the microscope to confirm the gross observations made with the projector. Additional details which were not apparent with the projector can now be filled in if necessary.

B. Localizing Electrode and Cannula Tips

There are some points to keep in mind when attempting to localize an electrode or cannula tip. When the sections are cut in the plane of the track the analysis is straightforward, because the center of the stimulated area lies midway between the anterior and posterior edges of the track. However, if the sections are cut at a tangent to the track they will contain an ovoid cavity rather than a fissure, and if the track is several hundred microns in diameter it may be somewhat difficult to determine which of several sequential sections contain the midpoint of the stimulated area. In such cases it is helpful to reconstruct the track in the sagittal plane with the aid of an appropriate parasagittal diagram from a stereotaxic atlas (see Chapter 3).

C. Determining Tissue Damage

Determination of lesion damage in the histological sections can be simple and straightforward if the animal is sacrificed at a time when the apparent lesion size represents the actual extent of tissue damage. Lesions change in apparent extent as a function of post-operative recovery, the most significant change being a progressive contraction beginning within a week or two after lesioning. Accurate estimation of tissue damage with contracted lesions depends on reconstruction of an area whose size and structural relations are distorted. While in some cases this may be accomplished by detailed comparisons with a normal brain, I would suggest that, when exact anatomical delineation is required and when the experimental design allows, this problem be circumvented entirely by sacrificing the animals before contraction begins (see Wolf and DiCara, 1969, for details).

It is also important to be aware of the fact that the abnormal tissue surrounding an electrolytic lesion cavity changes in appearance as a function of postoperative survival time (Wolf and DiCara, 1969). One hour after operation necrotic tissue surrounding the cavity may be largely indistinguishable from normal tissue. About one day after the surgery the outer portion appears pale in comparison to the surrounding tissue, because the dead nerve cells are disappearing. At some time beginning one day to one week after the operation, the abnormal area becomes filled with small cells such as lymphocytes and glia, which give it a dense, intensely stained appearance. After this time there is a progressive disappearance of the glial cells till only a narrow border surrounds the cavity.

In some cases volumetric analyses of lesions may be useful and can easily and accurately be carried out by the following procedure. Determine the weight per area of a good-quality paper. Determine the magnification of your projected image. Trace on the paper the outer borders of the lesion from beginning to end through sequential sections which are a fixed distance apart. Cut out the traced outlines of the lesion and weigh them all together. Apply the following formula:

$$V = \frac{(WO)}{(WA)} \frac{(D)}{(M)^2}$$

Where V = volume of the lesion in mm³
WO = total weight of the outlines in mg
D = distance between successive sections (including the thickness of each section) in mm
WA = weight per area of the paper in mg/mm²
M = magnification of projected image

This procedure can also be used to assess the percentage of a given structure which was destroyed by the lesion by determining the volume of the structure from a normal brain prepared in the same way as the lesioned brain and determining the volume of the intact remnants of the structure in the lesioned brain.

REFERENCES

Conn, H. J. (1933). "The History of Staining." The W. J. Humphrey Press, Geneva, New York.

Drury, R. A. B. and Wallington, E.A. (1967). "Carleton's Histological Technique." Oxford University Press, New York, New York.

Kelley, J. W. (1956). In "Protoplasmatologia" (L. V. Heilbrun and F. Weber, eds), IID2, pp. 1–98, Springer-Verlag, Vienna.

Klüver, H. and Barrera, E. (1953). J. Neuropath. Expl. Neurol. 12, 400–403.

Lillie, R. D. (1965). "Histopathologic Technic and Practical Histochemistry", 3rd Ed., McGraw-Hill Book Company, New York, New York.

Luna, L. G. (1960). "Manual of Histologic Staining Methods of the Armed Forces Institute of Pathology", 3rd Ed., McGraw-Hill Book Company, New York, New York.

Wolf, G. and DiCara, L. (1969). Exp. Neurol., 23, 529–536.

Appendix

Manufacturers

Most of the general laboratory and histological supplies are readily available. The products of different manufacturers which are found in many Biological Supply catalogues are about equally good. Therefore, I have listed below only those products of which a particular brand is preferred.

Phosphate Buffered 10% Formalin Gelatin (purified pigskin) Permount	Fisher Scientific Co. 53 Fadem Road Springfield, New Jersey, U.S.A.
Staining Tray	Klett Instrument Co. 177 E. 87th Street New York, New York, U.S.A.
Stains	Matheson, Coleman & Bell 2909 Highland Avenue Norwood, Ohio, U.S.A.
Pyronin GS	Chroma-Gesellschaft Stuttgart, West Germany

Chapter 10

Determining Changes in Vital Functions: Ingestion

J. L. FALK[1]

Rutgers University, New Brunswick, New Jersey, U.S.A.

I.	Introduction	301
	A. Rationale	303
II.	Mechanical Arrangements for Presenting Foods and Fluids	305
	A. Basic Considerations	305
	B. Food Intake	305
	C. Water Intake	309
III.	Special Diets	313
	A. Solid Diets	314
	B. Liquid Diets	315
IV.	Spatio-Temporal Arrangements: Their Influence on Intake and Choice	316
	A. Position	317
	B. Sequence	317
V.	Extraneous Environmental Variables	319
VI.	Acceptance, Rejection and Preference	320
	A. Concentration and Intake	320
	B. Terms and Methods	321
VII.	Analysis and Interpretation of Food and Fluid Intake Patterns	323
	A. Theoretical Considerations	325
References		327
Appendix		330

INTRODUCTION

It would seem that the ingestive functions, with their obvious relevance to the sustenance of life, have always held a high fascination for man. Along with the activities identified with the other deadly sins, gluttony has generated its share of dramatic passion and humor. In the early French Renaissance, Rabelais (1532) chronicled the exploits of his

[1] This project was supported by Grant MH 18409 from the National Institute of Mental Health, National Center for Prevention and Control of Alcoholism and Grant AM 14180 from National Institutes of Health, National Institute of Arthritis and Metabolic Diseases.

characters Gargantua and Pantagruel which included excesses of wenching, humanism and ingestion.

The latter may be illustrated by the child Gargantua, or Great-gullet, who "never touched a drop without good reason; for whenever he happened to be out of sorts, vexed, angry or melancholy, if he stamped, wept or shouted, they brought him a drink. This invariably restored his native good humor. . . . Indeed, the mere clinking of pints and flagons sent him off into the ecstasy of one who tastes the joys of Paradise . . . they used to delight him every morning by making music on glasses with knives, on bottles with their stoppers, and on pots with their lids" (Rabelais, 1532, p. 25).

Such direct and conditioned sensory-hedonic aspects of ingestion were, for a time, denied by early versions of behaviorism, but were reinstated into the stream of behaviorism mainly through the persistent research of P. T. Young (1941, 1948, 1949). Current attention in physiological psychology has become focused not only upon the sensory determinants of ingestive behavior, but also, through the work of Jean Mayer (1955) and others, upon the interrelations among food-intake, body weight, and activity level. Recently, the relation of fluid intake and temperature regulation to all of the above factors has come under intensive investigation.

The measurement of food intake under various conditions of diet, activity, temperature, etc. is indispensable to the study of energy balance in organisms. Likewise, the measurement of fluid ingestion under various imposed conditions is necessary for an understanding of the regulation of an organism's fluid matrix volume and its composition. However, the relevance to scientific endeavours in the study of the phenomena of intake has only lately become appreciated. Distortions in food intake were formerly viewed as either gluttony or psychoneurotic manifestations, but in any case, beyond the purview of the biological sciences.

The current position of most water-electrolyte physiologists and those concerned with fluid therapy is that liquid and salt intakes are, at best, clinical signs and not really a part of the processes regulating the *milieu intérieur*. For example, Black (1952) states that "the wide normal range of dietary intake of salt suggests that this is determined largely by chance and custom, and that the fine biological regulation of the sodium content of the body must be sought elsewhere . . . the main regulation of body sodium seems to be by changes in excretion." Without deprecating the importance of renal regulation, it is well to remember that the kidney cannot make up for deficit states. It can only throw off excesses, operating on an economy of surplus. But affluent inputs of water and electrolytes cannot always be assumed to exist. Where they do not, certain compensatory intake mechanisms come into play (Falk, 1961).

The operation of compensatory intake regulation does not mean that various conditions of primary over- or under-indulgence will not occur. The classical assumption has been that all intake phenomena are essentially secondary manifestations of more basic internal changes. These changes are identified as losses, depletions, metabolic imbalances, circulatory and central nervous pathological changes. Those intake phenomena which are clearly not a direct function of such internal states are relegated to "social customs" or "emotional problems." While evolutionary processes have tied intake mechanisms to physiological need-state parameters, there are a multitude of conditions under which primary distortions in intake embarrass the physiological mechanisms of adjustment. A relative hyperphagia underlies most obesity, and this state is correlated with atherosclerosis. The over-indulgence of water in psychogenic polydipsia (Barlow and DeWardener, 1959; Falk, 1969) and of salt by the Northern Japanese (Dahl, 1960) and others can lead to the development of water intoxication on the one hand and essential hypertension on the other.

A. Rationale

Thus far, I have tried to indicate that the ingestive mechanisms can participate in the regulatory business of energy and water-electrolyte balance. As with any regulatory mechanism, they are subject to pathophysiological changes arising internally or from environmental circumstances. Let us now push this analysis one step further by asking what we are measuring when we measure ingestive behaviors.

Most investigators would agree that they are measuring the amount of certain commodities incorporated by the organism, and that they are interested in relating these amounts to other features thought to be involved in the regulatory processes: energy balance, nutritional status, the stimulus components of foods or fluids offered, such as their composition, concentrations and textures, the previous history of the organism, etc. But we must not forget an additional important point: we are measuring behavior, consummatory behavior, but behavior nonetheless. Since behaviorists sincerely hope that laws of behavior with wide generality can be developed, it would not do to have different laws for different "kinds" of behavior. Ingestive behavior, then, should vary as a function of variables which control a spectrum of behavior much broader than that classed as consummatory. It is not generally acknowledged that ingestive behaviors are operant responses, and as such are subject to the effects of CNS interventions, drugs, and other factors in complex ways. Ingestive behavior is not just a measure of some internal state called "hunger," "thirst," or "salt appetite." If the rate of some ingestive operant decreases, this does not necessarily mean that one of the above alleged internal states has been decreased.

There are a host of agents and means which suppress operant behavior, and relatively few of them are considered to interfere directly with the physiology of vegetative regulation. Some of these effects are classed as nonspecific side-effects, distracting stimuli, pain, etc. But more importantly, if the rate of some ingestive behavior increases, this does not mean necessarily that some state of "hunger" or "thirst," has increased. An increase in operant lever-pressing which, according to some intermittent schedule occasionally delivers food, cannot be uncritically accepted as an increase in "hunger." And what applies to operant responding on a schedule also applies to the operants called "feeding."

Food and fluid intake data are not simple measures of inputs into processes which are always in regulatory balance, nor are they affected only by variables participating in energy and water-electrolyte exchanges. They, of course, mirror energy and water-electrolyte requirements under a wide range of conditions. But this is correlation not, hopefully, dogma. They cannot be taken as unerring measures of metabolic requirements, nor even in some cases as responses to stimuli signalling any such requirement. Ingestion is an ongoing behavior subject to modulation by various stimuli, both interoceptive and exteroceptive.

When we look at intakes, we are not necessarily seeing (a) the operation of a regulatory balance process, or (b) a pure measure of a motivational state. For example, satiated animals which preferentially ingest non-nutritive sweet or saline solutions, will learn discriminations when these substances are utilized as reinforcing agents, and will perform under these conditions stably and persistently. Also, a marked polydipsia can be induced as a function of the food delivery schedule (Falk, 1969). None of these ingestive effects are explicable in terms of regulatory homeostasis. As a final example, we might note that certain drugs increase the intake of a $1 \cdot 5\%$ NaCl solution (Falk and Burnidge, 1970). From the results of other studies available on these compounds, it was concluded that the increased intake probably was due to the attenuation of the aversive effects of the solution rather than any increase in "thirst."

The ingestion of foodstuffs and fluids will therefore be regarded as

10 Determining Changes in Vital Functions: Ingestion

complex operant behaviors which are sometimes a function of vegetative regulatory processes. At other times, they are under the control of variables having little to do with regulation or traditional motivational conceptions of "hunger" and "thirst."

II. Mechanical Arrangements for Presenting Foods and Fluids

It is not my purpose here to attempt a comprehensive review of the various ways in which substances may be presented to organisms for ingestion. The individual investigator is advised to utilize methods tailored to his current objective, and consult certain journals which publish apparatus notes (see Preface). Since many companies that build animal cages also provide units for measuring intakes, the investigator dealing with common laboratory species encounters relatively few difficulties. However, the basic considerations, some conveniences, and a few pitfalls are certainly worth mentioning.

A. Basic Considerations

In some laboratories, food intake is measured in rats by placing several pieces of pelleted diet of known total weight on the cage floor of an individual animal; and then the remaining food is simply weighed after some fixed time period. This procedure has, however, certain undesirable features. Animals often foul their food so that it can become contaminated with a substance which confounds the results of a particular experiment. For example, if the animal is kept on a water-deprivation schedule, the urine fouling the food may be high in electrolytes and nitrogenous wastes. Again, drugs which have been injected may be excreted onto the food and be reingested. If the agent can be absorbed by this route, it can have, in effect, a rather prolonged action due to this chance recycling.

As an animal chews off pieces of a food pellet, variable amounts fall through the mesh floor. These crumbs and residue of the whole pellet are difficult to collect from the drop pan; weight is difficult to estimate in their soaked state. This problem is especially evident in animals with central nervous damage, particularly in the hypothalamus. Such animals often gnaw their food in such a fashion that large piles of powdered food collect in the drop pans, making estimates of actual intake using this method virtually impossible.

B. Food Intake

A better method for measuring food-intake is to present the diet as a powder in a feeding cup. A quite serviceable cup arrangement is manufactured by Acme Metal Co. It consists of an adjustable stainless-steel tunnel leading to the food cup. The unit attaches to the living cage by being slid into vertical tracks. The adjustable walls prevent the animal from turning around in the tunnel. The tunnel floor is slotted so that any food which may be raked out of the cup falls through these slots onto a removable pan. Food is placed into the cup, the weight recorded, and the cup attached to the feeder unit. Later, the cup is again weighed with any food which has fallen through the slots first being brushed back into the cup. The feeders come in various sizes which will accommodate all rat sizes except a large, hypothalamic static obese animal.

FIG. 1. Food magazine for delivering pellets. (Courtesy of Lehigh Valley Electronics.)

Where a continuous record of eating is desirable, other methods must be utilized. Fallon (1965) had adapted the Wahmann food cup so that the animal's snout operates a drinkometer circuit (see below) and feeding events can thus be recorded. Alternatively, by using a liquid food and a drinkometer circuit, bouts of licking at a drinking spout can be recorded (Teitelbaum and Campbell, 1958). Many investigators have used solenoid or motor-operated food magazines which deliver a food pellet upon the performance of a simple operant response. Such food magazines are available from most behavioral science suppliers (see Appendix). The pellets are available in various sizes and formulae. Since these pellet magazines are operated by the animal, the record of such operations has been taken as a record of the actual meal patterns. In those situations in which animals are noted to stockpile earned pellets, the contingency is changed so that a certain number of operant responses is required to deliver a pellet, or a short, minimum, mandatory time (5 sec) is imposed between the pellets (Kissileff, 1969).

While the above methods yield self-consistent data, there are reasons for not considering them as entirely comparable. First, there are acceptance differences when food texture is altered. Typically, rats eat more of the pelleted than the powdered form of the same food. However, less pelleted food is eaten when it is available from wire feeders hung in the cage than when the food is more readily available on the floor. Again, imposing an arbitrary operant response requirement for the availability of each food pellet may seem rather inconsequential, but it has some interesting results on ingestive functions.

Rats and pigeons will respond to obtain food pellets or brief access to grain when these same foods are freely available from cups within the experimental chamber (Neuringer, 1969). Why such responding is maintained at a high level and even learned *de novo* under nondeprived conditions is not readily explained by current notions concerning the major variables controlling food-related operant responses. However, this is another instance in which intermittently presented food has a major effect on both the ingestive functions and the operant behavior under their control. It is interesting to note that Flory (1969), using a fixed-interval 5 sec schedule for pellets with rats (cf. Kissileff, 1969 above), found that water intake was more than twice as high as in a home cage condition where a comparable amount of food had been available as a non-intermittent meal. Thus, even minimal intermittency in food presentation can produce a marked preference for the intermittent source or a state of relative polydipsia.

Aside from food-pellet magazines, there are other devices available for delivering limited quantities of food. As mentioned above, liquid foods can be dispensed by drinking-tubes. A tube can be moved into position for feeding by a motor-driven cam (BCS Machine and Manufacturing Co.). Most peristaltic and roller-type pumps using tygon tubing will dispense rather viscous slurries as well as fluids so that they can deliver various liquid diets. Such mechanisms have the advantage of not pumping such food through their own mechanisms, as do conventional pumps and automatic pipetting syringes. This circumvents most of the problems of jamming, cleaning and contamination. A solenoid-operated grain feeder (see Fig. 2) can present food for limited time periods to birds (Ralph Gerbrands Co.) and a cam-operated feeder can move a cup or tray of food into position for rats, guineapigs, etc. (BCS Machine and Manufacturing Co.). For larger pieces of food and special foods such as candies and meats, a Universal feeder is available (Ralph Gerbrands Co.).

FIG. 2. Solenoid-operated grain feeder. (Courtesy of Lehigh Valley Electronics.)

A variation of the operant response-pellet dispenser arrangement is available in which the response, instead of being a key peck or lever press, is a response to the food tray itself. A vertical, hinged baffle operates a microswitch whenever the animal places its head into a small chamber containing the food cup (Behavioral Controls, Inc.). The microswitch can indicate feeding time or be used to operate a pellet dispenser.

Another approach combines an operant lever-pressing schedule component with the response to the food cup to determine when the cup becomes available and for how long it remains available (George H. Collier, personal communication). For example, the animal can be required to complete a certain number of lever-pressing responses (fixed-ratio schedule) at which time a cam-operated feeder moves the food cup into an available position. The cup remains in this position as long as the animal's head interrupts a photobeam across the entrance to the cup. If the beam remains unbroken for some preset time period, the cup is withdrawn, and the fixed-ratio must again be completed before the cup once more is available.

The pattern of food intake within 24-hr periods can be measured by attaching, for example, six cups to a disc, so that every four hours a new cup is rotated into a position of availability by a motor-operated cam (George H. Collier, personal communication).

An interesting feeding device, the Selecto-feeder (Behavioral Controls, Inc.; Fig. 3), distributes pellets from a single pellet dispenser to up to twelve different cages by means of a rotating central arm which channels the pellets through tubes to the various locations. Each location can be controlled by a separate feeding-schedule clock.

C. Water Intake

The measurement of fluid intake is a simple procedure fraught with relatively few difficulties. An easily implemented method for measuring intake in small animals is the use of calibrated drinking tubes (Richter tubes) which may be clipped to the front of a cage. Although

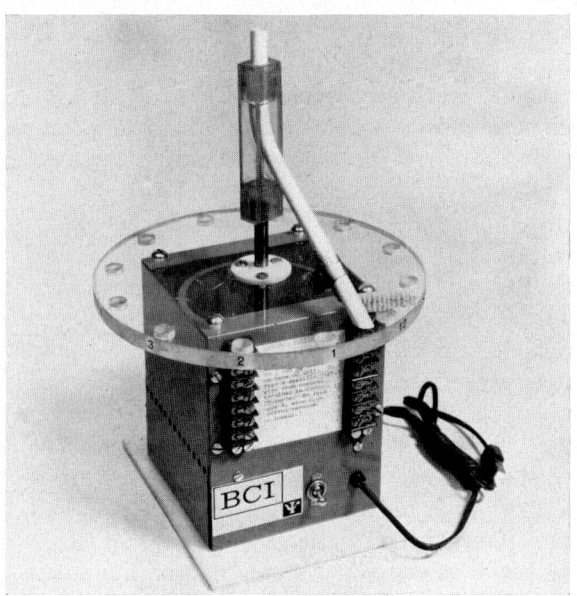

FIG. 3. Selecto-feeder device for distributing food pellets to 12 cages. (Courtesy of Behavior Controls, Inc.)

they are a little more difficult to fill and clean than a standard bottle, the 100 ml size affords a convenient and rapid measure of intakes in excess of 5 ml. When greater accuracy is required, such as in following the time course of drinking from minute to minute, a 100 ml gas eudiometer tube, calibrated in 0·1 ml units can be used if it is fitted with a drinking spout (O'Kelly, 1954). Owing to the height of these tubes, it is inconvenient to attach them to the usual animal living cages, and separate drinking boxes are usually constructed.

In order to obtain a record of the time course of drinking automatically, a device called a drinkometer is often employed (Hill and Stellar, 1951). These are available from several behavioral electronic companies. The system consists of a drinking spout, a metal-grid floor on which the animal stands, and a device which detects the passage of a minute DC current. When the animal's tongue contacts the spout, the circuit is completed and the lick may be counted, recorded, etc. The device is simple and reliable, but there are several considerations worth noting in the physical arrangements of the components and the interpretation of the licking records.

If the tube is positioned so that the animal's nose can contact it, or a paw can rest on it, false "licks" will be recorded in the first instance, and no licks will be recorded in the second case since the circuit has already been completed from paw to grid. If a hole or slot is cut in a panel so that the animal must lick the spout is through this aperture, these difficulties are avoided. Care must be exercised so that the spout orientation is constant from session to session, otherwise the animal may not be able to reach the tube properly through the aperture and the operant lick-rate changes from day to day, yielding inconsistent counts and records. The Acme Metal Co. manufactures stainless-steel drinking tubes which make serviceable spouts. We have fitted a metal flange onto these spouts near the bend and screwed the flange on to a plastic block so that the spout is projected through the block. The block can be drilled near the corners so that it can be bolted to the experimental chamber easily with wing-nuts. The block–spout assembly, then, slips into the identical location each time with respect to the aperture.

A plastic, 100 ml graduated cylinder is fitted to the spout and functions as a reservoir. If a larger reservoir is required, it is best to fashion a glass spout with a smaller hole at the end to prevent leakage. Bubbles within the spout can produce missed lick counts, since now the positive end of the drinkometer cannot be simply clipped to the drinking spout but must be led in to contact the drinking fluid. A simple solution to this problem consists of soldering several strands of wire to the tip of a hypodermic needle which has been occluded with solder and previously pushed through the rubber stopper bearing the glass spout. These wires reside within the cylinder and the electrical connection can be made to the other end of the needle. One or two wires can be brought out through the end of the spout and bent back along the outside of it. This prevents missed lick counts due to large bubbles within the spout.

The inside of the spout must be kept clean, otherwise bubbles do not form in the same way from day to day and different amounts of fluid are delivered per lick. Different fluids have different viscosities and surface tensions. Therefore, the licking records are difficult to compare quantitatively across different substances and across different concentrations of the same substance. Also, a spout-cylinder arrangement which is quite reliable under one circumstance may prove to leak easily when the surface tension is lowered.

There are also several simple electrical considerations worth noting in the use of drinkometers. Since these are electrically sensitive devices, the use of grounded, shielded cable is recommended. The grid on which the animal stands must be kept clean to ensure good contact. Finally, it is well to lead the output of the drinkometer relay through a pulse former in order to ensure positive operation of counters and recorders and also to avoid burning-out such devices if the drinkometer relay should remain operated due to accidental shorting between the spout and grid.

While the momentary licking rate has been found to remain rather constant under a variety of conditions (Stellar and Hill, 1952; Davis and Keehn, 1959; Corbit and Luschei, 1969), there is no assurance that the amount of fluid ingested per lick remains similarly constant. A lick as defined by a drinkometer is an electrical measure and not an actual record of ingestion. In our hands, different solutions yield different "licks per ml" values. This may be due to various physical factors (viscosity, surface tension) and also to the fine motor components of the lick topography varying with the taste (lick avidity) of the solution.

We have noticed that when water is taken from steel drinking spouts more is ingested by rats in a 24-hour period than when water is taken from Richter tubes. The difference is not large (about 5 ml), but quite consistent and is not due to leakage. This illustrates, in a simple way, that the operant behavior required for ingestion can determine the level of ingestion. Care must be exercised in the experimental design so that intakes are not compared across delivery devices, if these are confounded with experimental treatments.

Dipper magazines are available from several of the behavioral electronic companies. In these devices a dipper cup is raised from a pan containing a fluid by means of a solenoid or motor into a position where the animal can consume the contents (see Fig. 4). These work well mechanically, but again certain precautions should be observed.

What the cups are nominally supposed to deliver and what volumes they actually deliver do not always agree. The investigator should calibrate the actual delivery volumes or weights. Additional cups can easily be fashioned from steel-rod stock. If it is necessary to know how much fluid is actually consumed during a session, a measured volume is placed in the pan, the amount left at the termination of the session measured, the difference is taken and any disappearance due to evaporation subtracted. This last value can be estimated by running several blank sessions and measuring pre- and post-session pan volumes.

FIG. 4. Dipper magazine for delivering fluids. (Courtesy Lehigh Valley Electronics.)

As mentioned previously, many syringe, roller and peristaltic pumps are available. These work well if handled with care, but are relatively expensive. An inexpensive (approximately $35 (£15)) solenoid metering pump (SV-500, Valcor Engineering Corp.) can serve for many fluid and semi-fluid delivery requirements. It is adjustable from 0·01–1·5 ml per stroke and can deliver 60 strokes per minute in its standard configuration.

Other routes of administration are available besides delivering food or fluid into the animal's vicinity for possible oral consumption. Substances can be injected into the oral cavity by a cheek fistula, or directly into the stomach by fistula (Komarov *et al.*, 1963) or nasopharyngeal tube (see Fig. 3, Chapter 2, for gastric intubation procedure in the rat). (Epstein and Teitelbaum, 1962.) Nutrient solutions and other fluids can be delivered intravenously. All of these routes can be placed under the operant control of the animal by connecting a response device to the operation of a metering pump. Long-term venous cannulation techniques have been utilized for rodents (Weeks, 1962; Davis, 1966; Pickens, 1967; Popovic et al., 1963; Popovic et al., 1968), rabbits (Bazaral and Hamberger, 1970) and monkeys (Schuster and Thompson, 1963); Yanagita et al., 1963; Pickens et al., 1966; Trost et al., 1969; Craig et al., 1969). Helpful articles deal with cannula construction and connection (Epstein and Teitelbaum, 1962b; Heatley and Weeks, 1964; Robinson et al., 1969; Snow et al., 1969), as well as long-term pathological consequences (Hysell and Abrams, 1967).

III. Special Diets

In this section, I will discuss only a few points concerning dietary variables and their relation to behavioral research. The intake of various nutritional components has been studied as a set of dependent variables responsive to such factors as the range, concentration, and texture of components offered (palatability factors), the chemical condition of the organism (deprivation, altered metabolism), the previous history of the organism (feeding habits), and the current environmental circumstances (stimulus control factors). But dietary variables have been studied as independent variables as well. Such experiments have been concerned with diverse interests ranging from the effects of different incentive substances upon performance, to the relations between malnutrition and brain development (Winick, 1969), nutritional status and various biological responses (Friedman, 1966), and early malnutrition and learning (Scrimshaw, 1967; Eichenwald and Fry, 1969).

Richter et al. (1938) determined the survival times of rats given water and one other nutritional component consisting of various fat, carbohydrate, or protein substances. On the basis of the results, various components were chosen to be offered to animals in self-selection feeding experiments. These self-selection cafeteria studies stimulated much interest in the variables determining the quantities of such components accepted and the regulatory implications of these acceptance levels. Interest evolved not only in the proportions of components ingested, but also in "specific appetites" for the single components when these were temporarily removed from the diet and then offered to the specifically depleted animal as one choice among two or more food substances. Certain factors affecting such choices will be covered in the next section. Here, some basic considerations on special diets will be mentioned.

A. Solid Diets

The contemporary investigator is fortunate in being able to purchase a wide range of specialized diets commercially (Nutritional Biochemicals Corp., General Biochemicals). Diets can also be made up to the researcher's specifications. While this may seem expensive, the alternative of making up diets within the laboratory poses certain difficulties. Stocking a wide range of materials of variable shelf life which are usually available only in bulk quantities and are used in widely different proportions results in a high discard level. Only in a centralized shared diet-mixing facility or in a rather large research program is it practical to prepare a specific diet. The diet-mixing machines are also rather expensive. But for those occasions on which it is practical to prepare a diet within the laboratory, a small batch mixer is available. The series M-61 mixer from Kol, Inc. comes in several sizes with various special-purpose paddles.

The diet manuals from the above-mentioned companies provide a good deal of information on vitamin test diets, salt mixtures, mineral test diets, protein test diets, various purified components, etc. The National Academy of Sciences–National Research Council has published a series of rather complete pamphlets on the "Nutrient Requirements of Domestic Animals"; No. 10 in this series is particularly useful in that it covers laboratory animals. Standard laboratory chows are usually available from local suppliers (Purina laboratory chows, Wayne Lab-Blox) and specifications can be supplied by the manufacturers. Companies which make the pellets for electromechanical dispensers can also supply special sizes and formulae.

Many of the self-selection cafeteria arrangements and specialized test diets are poorly accepted by animals. This necessitates pair-fed control group feeding. While this satisfies the condition of comparing animals with equivalent food intakes, it cannot correct for the fact that neither group may grow at the normal growth rate. The resulting stress, stunting, and susceptibility to diseases may interact with the specific variables under investigation to vitiate the entire set of conclusions. The investigator should be aware of these considerations, know the growth potential of the population of animals utilized, and be willing to manipulate the composition of the test diet until he is satisfied that the level of acceptance is high enough so that he is mainly dealing with a specifiable depletion rather than a complex of depletions and their consequences.

It is worth noting that because a test diet disappears from the food cup does not necessarily mean that it is being utilized by the animal. The experimental variables imposed may have altered the animal's metabolic state. The diet taken into the gastro-intestinal tract may be poorly absorbed, so that as much as half of it may never be present in the animal in a functional sense. The diet may produce diarrhea, resulting in a set of depletions unplanned by the investigator. Finally, extreme care must be exercised to ensure complete mixing if the diet is prepared in the laboratory. For example, if a high-carbohydrate diet is mixed using granulated sucrose, rats can skillfully sort through the mixture, avoiding much of the sucrose, and thereby change the proportion of the components ingested. This situation can be avoided by using dextrinized starch or powdered sugar.

All foods, including standard chows, should be stored *away from heat*, since vitamins will be lost, proteins denatured, and fats turned rancid. We routinely refrigerate most foods, including pellets for dispensers.

The form in which the dietary component is offered is a major determinant of the amount ingested and the growth rate. The acceptance of many purified dietary components by rats is poor; growth rates are affected, and even serious depletions can develop. For example, Collier et al. (1969) found that animals selecting their diets from a protein fraction and a carbohydrate fraction keep the ratio of intakes constant. However, if the protein source was soy bean oil meal, intake and growth rate was higher than if the protein was presented in a purified form. In general, it is difficult to construct a balanced diet from purified components even though the specification of such components is desirable from the point of view of nutritional science. If offered as a self-selection diet, many such purified components are not accepted by animals.

B. *Liquid Diets*

Behavioral scientists are interested in caloric dilutents and non-nutritive substances for diverse reasons. Liquid foods can be simply diluted with water (Adolph, 1947), and solid diets with celluflour (Teitelbaum, 1955; Levitsky and Collier, 1968). Dilution allows caloric density, for example, to be varied without changing the ratios of the other dietary components. A diluted diet may become unacceptable because of the decreased caloric density, but other aspects of the diet are changed as well such as the texture, flavor, etc. An interesting solution to this confounding problem is provided by two diets described by Taylor and Bruning (1968). They contain 4·00k cal/g and 0·00k cal/g, respectively, and are quite similar in texture and taste. Both are well accepted by rats. Similarly, "non-nutritive" water can be presented in the form of an air-stream emerging from a spout. The licking of such placebo water varies as a function of factors which control water ingestion (Hendry and Rasche, 1961; Mendelson and Chillag, 1970).

Liquid diets have certain advantages and drawbacks. By using a drinkometer and a recorder, it is rather simple to obtain a record of meal number, meal size, and rate of ingestion. Liquid diets are more acceptable to animals recovering from operative procedures (Teitelbaum and Epstein, 1962) and to young animals. It is possible to have an animal both ingest the same diet and be stomach loaded with it via the esophagus. It is more feasible to deliver a liquid food via stomach fistula and by a chronic naso-pharyngeal tube than even a semi-solid food.

The main disadvantages of liquid diets are spoilage and settling. Diets spoil within about 12 hours at room temperature, necessitating a change in the reservoir at night. This can be avoided if the diet is kept cold. However, a cold diet delivered through a naso-pharyngeal tube produces sensory effects which may partially defeat the purpose of eliminating oropharyngeal sensations (Holman, 1968). Settling of the diet can be prevented by the addition of an emulsifier such as a viscarin (Marine Colloids, Inc.), Tween 80 (polysorbate), or sodium carboxymethylcellulose (Clark, 1965). The possible effects of these agents on digestive function or their interaction with drugs should be considered in the light of the investigator's purposes.

Several complete liquid diets have been described. Those fabricated in the laboratory are tedious to prepare and sometimes vary in consistency as a function of subtle variables, such as the order of combination and the thoroughness and speed of mixing (Epstein and Teitelbaum, 1962a; DeCarli and Lieber, 1967). I have found the diet described by Ellison and Riddle (1961) for monkeys to be suitable for rats. It is available from Nutritional Biochemicals Corp. in powdered form as Standard Monkey Diet (SKF). It is readily prepared in the laboratory by the addition of water and a little oil (Ellison and Riddle, 1961). Chemically defined liquid diets are available from General Biochemicals.

IV. Spatio-Temporal Arrangements: Their Influence on Intake and Choice

Some of the early self-selection diet studies were criticized for always offering a particular component in the same spatial location. The criticism is well taken, for animals do develop position preferences, often taking most of their food from a single location. If choices are being offered the animal, then some schedule of positional rotation must be instituted. This has been followed by psychologists for some time (Harlow, 1932; Young, 1941), but has only recently been adopted by physiologists.

A. Position

In a rather charming report, Gillespie and Lucas (1958) seem to have discovered the problem of position preference in the rat independently of the behavioral literature. Animals were offered 15% ethanol and water in different locations with respect to a food cup. "Too slavish an adherence to that fetish of many investigators, 'average' values and standard deviations, nearly let the most interesting fact escape notice . . . a careful study of the records of certain individual rats caused grave concern. Several of the 'alcoholic' rats suddenly appeared to have become 'teetotallers' and some of the others began to take considerable alcohol . . . the positions of the fountains seemed to affect the drinking pattern of certain rats to a remarkable extent." They go on to remark, perhaps a little wryly, that "most of the cases of 'alcoholism' observed in our 25 rats . . . cannot have had a genetic origin since the 'disease' was 'cured' by changing the positions of the dispensers."

In a two-tube choice situation using water and 10% ethanol, Myers and Holman (1966) also noted a strong position preference. When the fluid positions were alternated daily some animals simply continued to drink from one position. In order to disrupt this position-preference while retaining the advantage of a two-choice situation, a third empty Richter tube was introduced. The three tubes were rotated according to a randomly determined sequence. The empty tube apparently was sufficient to disrupt the position preference so that orderly ethanol preference thresholds were obtained.

B. Sequence

In determining the acceptability of a particular substance at some specified concentration, or its position in some preference hierarchy, the location of this determination within a series of tests is often important. For example, in preference tests between various NaCl solutions and distilled water, one group of rats was presented brief-taste preference tests in an ascending concentration series, while a second group was tested in a descending order (Young and Falk, 1956). In the first group (ascending order), all of the animals yielded significant preferences for 3·0% NaCl over distilled water, although with continued testing this marked preference gradually deteriorated. In the second group (descending order), the NaCl concentration had to be reduced to 0·75% before the majority of animals preferred the saline solution to distilled water. The experimenter must decide if such ordered series are to be studied so that any sequence effects may be evaluated, or whether he prefers to use a randomized presentation procedure which conceals, but probably does not eliminate, such effects.

Sequence effects can be used to induce animals to accept substances which they would reject under other circumstances. This was evident in the above experiment. Animals can be induced to drink concentrations of ethanol they would ordinary reject by slowly increasing the concentration offered. Other sequencing methods can also be used to acclimate animals to ethanol solutions (Myers and Veale, 1970). Among such methods, the procedure of simply allowing the choice between water and a 15% ethanol solution to be present for several months has been found effective with monkeys (Mello and Mendelson, 1966). This indicates the extreme caution which should be observed in the interpretation of experimental manipulations which are temporally far removed from the initial determination of the baseline level of intake behavior, especially where the intervening manipulations preclude the redetermination of the baseline level.

In working with a series of saline, quinine or sucrose solutions in brief-taste preference situations, the possibility exists that different generalization gradients are established by such differential histories. For example, the subsequent preference for tap water over distilled water following a history of saline tests contrasts with a preference for distilled water over tap water following a history of sucrose and quinine testing (Young, 1966). Most tap waters probably generalize to saline and quinine, while distilled water generalizes to sugars, if such experimental histories have been provided.

Another kind of sequence phenomenon needs serious consideration, insofar as many experimental situations have been shown to involve "bait shyness" effects. Garcia *et al.* (1961) showed that if the ingestion of a saccharin solution occurred during, or somewhat before, the administration of a small dose of ionizing radiation, the subsequent consumption of this solution was attenuated. They were able to show that this decrease was not the direct result of radiation injury (anorexia), but was related to the coupling of ingestion and radiation. Upon being followed by radiation-induced effects, a relative rejection of saccharin solution ensued. Since, then, other foods (Revusky and Bedarf, 1967), fluids (Peacock and Watson, 1964), and "poisoning" situations (Nachman, 1963) have yielded similar results. This points to the distinct possibility that whenever a noxious manipulation, such as the administration of a drug, coincides with or follows an ingestion test, subsequent ingestion determinations may yield decreased intakes due to a conditioned rejection of the test substance. On the other hand, an increase in the intake of a substance can be produced if such intake coincides or is followed closely by a beneficial effect (Garcia *et al.*, 1967).

Intermittent feeding is known to produce metabolic differences compared to meals which are undivided (Cohn and Joseph, 1968). However, food schedule intermittence has another effect on ingestion. Various schedules of intermittent food delivery to food-deprived animals result in a concurrent large increase in water intake (Falk, 1969). As I have already pointed out, any feature of an experiment which results in food intermittence, even of a few seconds, can induce marked polydipsia.

V. Extraneous Environmental Variables

There are numerous features of the environment which can affect ingestive functions. Some of these will be mentioned, but it is well to suspect all manner of environmental variation.

Noise should be held to a minimum. Individuals who delight in poking fingers, rubber ends of pencils, or other objects into a cage should be discouraged. A closed-door laboratory policy prevents unauthorized persons from feeding, teasing or freeing experimental animals.

The positioning of animals in a living rack should remain constant during an experimental series. All positioning should guard against placing animals in drafts. Temperature changes of more than a few degrees are to be avoided. If the room has a window, racks should be arranged so that sunlight does not strike them. However, a room without windows is more desirable for controlling lighting conditions. An explicit decision concerning the light cycle must be made. Lights can be left on continuously, or their on-off cycle can be controlled by an automatic timer. In any case, the decision should *not* be determined by the janitorial staff's schedule or by some chance activities.

Feeding and drinking bouts often become entrained with environmental changes. Sometimes, just the disturbance involved in observing an animal within its cage is sufficient to trigger a bout of ingestion. It is also not uncommon to observe such a bout when a food hopper or water bottle is changed. If a satiated animal is placed in another cage for an ingestion test, this disturbance can also result in a bout of feeding or drinking.

The circadian rhythm of a particular species affects how ingestive behavior is distributed across the 24-hr periods. Wayner and Peterson

(1965) studied the hourly distribution of drinking in rats in males and females in both colony and isolated conditions. On the basis of these results, the validity of certain assumptions concerning the water-balance state at specified times could be evaluated.

Some extraneous variables are occasionally introduced as a function of animal care operations. Certain insect sprays have effects on cholinesterase or upon enzyme induction which can interact with various experimental treatments such as drug administration. Under food deprivation conditions, some materials used for animal bedding or litter may be ingested.

VI. Acceptance, Rejection and Preference

In designing an experiment on ingestion and in evaluating the results, sets of terms and procedures are best agreed upon. In this section I will describe some of the terms, procedures, and the rationale underlying them. In the next section, interpretation and evaluation of the procedures will be discussed.

A. Concentration and Intake

When an investigator wishes to evaluate the effect of a particular manipulation upon the ingestion of a certain substance, several factors governing the selection of the form or particular concentration of the offered substance must be considered. One must be clear concerning the specification of concentration. Pfaffman *et al.* (1954) have described methods for the preparation of solutions. As they point out, there are at least three ways of preparing a "per cent" solution, and the researcher should specify which definition he is following.

Substances can be offered in acceptable or unacceptable concentration ranges and in vehicles of varying acceptability. Of course, any inference concerning the acceptability of the substance as affected by some manipulation can depend critically upon concentration and vehicle factors. Rats have been known to reject a vitamin solution until forced drinking procedures were instituted (Young, 1945). Many purified dietary components are low in acceptability. In adjusting the concentration of a substance to make it acceptable, however, the investigator can easily defeat his own purpose. For example, if a solution of NaCl is offered which is not fairly hypertonic, it will be more acceptable than water (Weiner and Stellar, 1951). If the purpose of the experiment is to ascertain the existence of an appetite for NaCl, the case is biased in favor of animals ingesting more NaCl solution than water. Stated another way, if the ingestive response rate is higher with respect to the NaCl solution than to water, then, other things being equal, any stimulus producing more drinking will increase the level of NaCl solution intake more than that of water. This consideration is also applicable when two different salts are compared to test for the specificity of NaCl appetite. If concentrations are chosen which are of unequal acceptability initially, then the test is biased (Falk, 1965). A conservative approach is simply to use a fairly unacceptable concentration which provides the animal with nothing other than the solute, i.e. it is too concentrated for the animal to extract body water increments from it, when ingested in quantity.

Since the intake of many substances varies as a function of the concentration offered, there is often no substitute for determining intakes at several concentrations and comparing these with the intakes following some experimental manipulation (Myers, 1968). Just as one must often explore a dose-response function in order to make inferences about drug action, one might, in the present case, be unwilling to draw conclusions from results gathered from but a single test concentration.

B. Terms and Methods

A confusing array of terms and methods are used in describing and investigating ingestion. It is of more than academic interest to clarify these, for when the same term is applied to different methods misunderstandings can occur in comparing outcomes. Most of the suggestions I would like to make have been explicitly put forward by P. T. Young already, or are implicit in his work.

There are obviously an infinite variety of ways in which combinations of foods and fluids may be presented for ingestion. The 24-hour intakes of self-selection components may be ascertained. Limited access to some component may be allowed. Various deprivation states may be imposed and the subsequent ingestion of an appropriate single component can be measured, or a choice among two or more alternatives investigated. Certain considerations are germane in guiding the selection of a method.

If the effect of some experimental variable upon the ingestion of a particular food or fluid is to be evaluated, it may be desirable to present the commodity of interest singly in a time-limited test. For example, if one were interested in water intake as a function of dosage of some drug and this drug affected food intake, it might be advisable to present the water for a limited-time test, without food being available. Since food and water intakes are usually positively correlated, the effect of the drug on food intake could itself alter water intake if food and water were presented together.

When the amount of a singly-presented food of fluid ingested is measured, this is usually referred to as the "single-stimulus method" (Weiner and Stellar, 1951). O'Kelly (1954) allowed rats to drink for $\frac{1}{2}$ hr per day in special drinking boxes. Since the animals' entire fluid ration is obtained in this particular single-stimulus situation, it has the advantage of yielding a single value for the major portion of the fluid input. Animals remain on this drinking schedule and readjust their fluid balance on the two or three days between experimental treatments. In experiments where it is desirable for animals to remain closer to a balance state each day, a drinking schedule allowing water intake to occur for a few hours a day some time after the single-stimulus test can be used (Weiner and Stellar, 1951). While this type of schedule is more difficult to maintain, it is useful in allowing animals with diabetes insipidus (Titlebaum et al., 1960) to maintain their water balance.

The volume or weight of a substance ingested on a single stimulus test is an acceptance measure, not a preference test. At one time, there was a hope that the single-stimulus method could be interpreted as a preference test among the fluids presented over sessions (Beebe-Center et al., 1948). However, the work of Young and Greene (1953) made it evident that the single-stimulus method yields results which differ from preference tests. When sucrose solutions were offered in one-hour, single-stimulus acceptance tests, more 9% sucrose was ingested than either 18% or 36%. However, a one-hour preference test between two simultaneously-presented fluids, 9% and 36% sucrose revealed a greater volumetric acceptance of the 36% solution. This agrees with the brief-exposure preference method in which the more concentrated sucrose solutions were preferred to less concentrated ones. In the brief-exposure preference method, a pair of solutions or foods is made available in two cups set close together. An animal is permitted to ingest from one or the other of the cups for only a few seconds at most. The cups are then made unavailable and presented again for another trial after the animal has returned to a start box. The spatial position of the cups can be altered from trial to trial.

Since there is no opportunity for a choice to occur in the single-stimulus method, no preference can be ascertained. The data obtained with sucrose solutions using different methods bears out this contention. Where the single-stimulus method is used and the resulting ingestion yields a range of concentration of greater acceptability than water and a more concentrated range less acceptable than water, the resulting function is often referred to as a "preference-aversion function" (Weiner and Stellar, 1951). Since I have indicated certain logical and empirical reasons for not using the term "preference" in connection with the single-stimulus method, P. T. Young's term "acceptance-rejection function" is preferable. Also the term "aversion" is typically used only in connection with stimuli proven to be negative reinforcers; this is perhaps the case with, for example, a concentrated NaCl solution, but the case has never been proven. It is more accurate, then, to refer to a relative level of rejection of a fluid or food component, rather than to affirm a certain theoretical notion which extends beyond current developments by using the term "aversive."

The investigator should, of course, evaluate the preference and acceptance methods available in terms of his experimental aims. In some cases, it is worthwhile automating some aspects of preference testing (Young, 1960), or a standard method can be improved upon short of automation (Falk and Herman, 1961). There are cases when a unique sort of test can be devised which has perhaps little general applicability, e.g. a consecutive fluids test (Falk and Titlebaum, 1963).

VII. Analysis and Interpretation of Food and Fluid Intake Patterns

The analysis of ingestion can be a simple matter of measuring food and fluid intakes once a day, or during some limited ingestion period. A more fine-grained analysis is provided by the temporal distribution of meals, and the relation of bouts of eating and drinking to each other. The interactions are quite complex and are functions of a host of environmental and physiological conditions. Level and patterning of ingestion are of interest under various dietary regimes, ambient temperature, and schedules of availability. Beyond the amount ingested within some time period, other simple indices are of interest, which include: the grams of solute ingested as a function of concentration, the number of meals taken, meal duration, and rate of ingestion.

Food/water ratios can be calculated, and where various separate dietary components are available, their intake ratios can also be calculated. Intake can be measured not only in grams ingested but also in terms of grams of solute ingested, which may not agree with the peak concentration measured as grams of solution ingested (Young and Greene, 1953). A standard method for both energy input and output analysis is in terms of calories (Mayer, 1959). Analyses relating dietary and behavioral variables have been reviewed by Lat (1967) and Le Magnen (1967).

In early research, the notions of sensory threshold and preferential threshold were not clearly differentiated. Sometimes a changed preference threshold was thought to indicate a change in sensory threshold (Richter, 1939). Bare (1949) distinguished between the preferential and sensory thresholds for NaCl solutions in adrenalectomized rats, noting a decrease in the preferential threshold but not in the electrophysiological sensory threshold (Pfaffman and Bare, 1951). Bare (1949) used various NaCl solutions paired with water in two-bottle tests with the bottles continuously available for a 48-hour period. Within this period, controls for food intake, light-cycle, bottle position, and particular bottle were observed. Somewhat similar methods were used by Richter (1939) and Richter and Clisby (1941) for obtaining preferential thresholds. Using a shock-avoidance method, Carr (1952) was able to obtain absolute NaCl discrimination thresholds which agreed well with the electrophysiological thresholds. This threshold of discrimination between water and NaCl solution did not change after adrenalectomy. Koh and Teitelbaum (1961) developed both shock-avoidance and food-acquisition procedures for determining absolute thresholds. They used a tracking procedure which enabled them to obtain thresholds rapidly.

In the investigation of preference thresholds, Pfaffmann (1952) has calculated the per cent of the total fluid intake (solution bottle plus water bottle) which is ingested from the solution bottle and plotted this as a function of concentration. Each of these points is then tested against the 50% point by a t-test for related measures. The first point differing at the 1% level is taken as the preferential threshold. Sometimes the absolute rather than the relative amounts ingested are tested statistically. Myers (1966) and Myers and Veale (1971) have described some of the methods and problems in obtaining preference thresholds for ethanol.

A persistent problem in the interpretation of intake changes involves the specificity of the change. It is not enough for the investigator to impose some experimental condition and note a change in the intake of some commodity. If a claim is made as to the specificity of the appetitive change, then alternate commodities should also be offered of equal initial acceptability (Falk, 1965). Tests of ethanol dependence made by measuring the preference for ethanol when it is paired with a sweet solution have been discouraging to those attempting to produce animal analogs of alcoholism (Lester and Greenberg, 1952). However, in this case, the initial acceptability difference may be so great that the case is biased against the maintenance of ethanol ingestion.

There are occasions when group mean data do not give a representative picture of what has occurred on a preference test. This is especially true when animals are not indiscriminate in their individual preferences but some members prefer A and others B. In such cases brief-test preference choices may be conveniently evaluated with Grant's (1946, 1947) tables. Individual two-bottle acceptance data can be evaluated by applying a chi-square statistic (Falk, 1965).

A. Theoretical Considerations

One of the central issues in the interpretation of food and fluid intake patterns is one which is seldom explicitly mentioned. Yet, it has important consequences, for at its heart, it maintains a distance among some investigators never to be bridged by significant citation of each others' work. I will try to outline this issue briefly, and in so doing reveal my own bias in the matter.

Some investigators in the area of ingestive processes, believe that the processes we refer to as "hunger," "thirst," "specific appetite," or "taste preference" are substantive states in the sense that the critical sensory integrating and executive motor control regions exist as areas and states able to be isolated in the central nervous system. An unstated corollary of this view is that the various behaviors, often involving ingestion, under the control of such states can be evaluated and assigned grades indicating their values as measures of these states.

The core interest is in making statements about the nature of these central states by integrating what we can learn from anatomy, physiology, pharmacology, and behavior. But the status of behavior within this scheme has usually been, to put it gently, plebian. Behavioral responses have been viewed as yielding rather degraded information. The most that the investigator can hope for in such a situation is to get the best behavioral "measure" of the internal state that he can. Therefore, in both food and fluid research considerable effort has been expended in comparing various behavioral measures of "hunger" and "thirst." With this approach, what is considered as a "good measure" is one which correlates well with an ingestive measure. In a particular situation, such a measure might be running speed, response latency, operant response rate, etc. If several measures thought to be good measures of an internal state correlate negatively with an increased level of ingestion, then the measures are accepted as valid and the increased ingestion is explained as a decrease in another internal state called "satiety" (Miller *et al.*, 1950).

The "measures" approach to the field of ingestive phenomena assumes that the internal states are causally prior to and independent of any measuring operation. The ideal measure, from this methodological vantage point, would be the attainment of some electrical or chemical signal which covaries with the drive state implied by such terms as "thirst" or "satiation." Such a breakthrough would allow us to abandon the measurement of behavior and have rather direct access to the central controlling events. Behavior research is sort of what you do until the real doctor comes. I am aware that this approach is not usually stated in so bald a manner. One is supposed to profess at least a perfunctory interest in relating behavior to internal events. But I have noticed colleagues become far more animated when displaying their neurophysiological gear than when discussing behavioral phenomena.

The situation is reminiscent of the status of "emotion" a few decades ago, when valid physiological indices and their intercorrelations were energetically sought. The problem now seems to involve less consideration of what physiological measures reflect "the emotional state," but rather what behavioral response units can be functionally dealt with and what are their dimensions. And as it has been with "emotion," just so is it likely to develop with the "drive" processes assumed to underlie various ingestive functions.

An alternate view regards behavioral processes as having no less honorific status than internal states. Behavior is more than just the obedient servant of a central motivational state or homeostatic process. It is, hopefully, not just a third-rate way to study the brain. Ingestive processes are complex behaviors controlled by many variables. Some of these variables are related to vegetative functions, while others are controlled by current behavior, social variables, the previous history of the organism, and the particular behavioral repertoire invoked by the environmental circumstance. This complex of variables is poorly denoted by common language terms fashioned to refer to introspective sensations of "hunger" and "thirst." More is involved than a quibble over terminology, for a methodology is embedded in the "measures" approach which precludes the control of ingestion by more than just a few central states played upon by outside and inside influences. The temptation is to try to "get a measure" of these states as one would read voltage with a voltmeter. But we have no units in the investigation of ingestion approaching the sophistication of "volts," nor can we, in my estimation, get the essentials of ingestive behavior between a pair of electrodes. The alternative is to delineate the variables of which ingestive behaviors are functions, without prejudging the convergence of these controlling variables into unitary, internal states, nameable by common-language words.

The position taken here is not that internal states do not exist, but that their commonalities with respect to behavior are not to be defined by considering only response topography. For example, it has been widely assumed that since water deprivation, NaCl loading, plasma volume decrement, centrally applied carbachol, and electrical stimulation of the hypothalamus all produce drinking, they are diverse operations inducing a common central state called "thirst." But upon closer inspection, the temporal characteristics, the range of fluids accepted, and response substitutability reveal that each such stimulus to drinking must produce a rather different central state. The control dynamics differ, and to assume that they can all be traced to "thirst" is analogous to saying that all verbal behavior serves communication, or that all biting is aggressive. Certainly the high intake levels in schedule-induced polydipsia have little to do with "thirst" (Falk, 1969). State variables cannot be reliably inferred from response topography alone; the stimuli must be critically considered, as well as the details of the functional relation.

REFERENCES

Adolph, E. F. (1947). *Am. J. Physiol.* **115**, 110–125.
Bare, J. K. (1949). *J. comp. physiol. Psychol.* **42**, 242–253.
Barlow, E. D. and De Wardener, H. E. (1959). *Q. J. Med.* **28**, 235–258.
Beebe-Center, J. G., Black, P., Hoffman, A. C. and Wade, M. (1948). *J. comp. physiol. Psychol.* **41**, 239–251.
Black, D. A. K. (1952). "Sodium Metabolism in Health and Disease." Blackwell, Oxford.
Carr, W. J. (1952). *J. comp. physiol. Psychol.* **45**, 377–380.
Clark, F. C. (1965). *J. exp. Anal. Behavior.* **8**, 16.
Cohn, C. and Joseph, D. (1968). *J. Nutrit.* **96**, 94–100.
Collier, G., Leshner, A. I. and Squibb, R. L. (1969). *Physiol. Behav.* **4**, 83–86.
Corbit, J. D. and Luschei, E. S. (1969). *J. comp. physiol. Psychol.* **69**, 119–125.
Craig, D. J., Frost, J. G. and Talley, W. (1969). *Lab Animal Care* **19**, 237–239.
Dahl, L. K. (1960). *Nutrit. Revs.* **18**, 97–99.
Davis, J. D. (1966). *J. exp. anal. Behav.* **9**, 385–387.
Davis, J. D. and Keehn, J. D. (1959). *Science, N.Y.* **130**, 269–271.
De Carli, L. M. and Lieber, C. S. (1967). *J. Nutrit.* **91**, 331–336.
Eichenwald, H. F. and Fry, P. C. (1969). *Science, N.Y.* **163**, 644–648.
Ellison, T. and Riddle, W. C. (1961). *J. exp. anal. Behavior.* **4**, 370.
Epstein, A. N. and Teitelbaum, P. (1962a). *J. comp. physiol. Psychol.* **55**, 753–759.
Epstein, A. N. and Teitelbaum, P. (1962b). *J. appl. Physiol.* **17**, 171–172.
Falk, J. L. (1961). *In* "Nebraska Symposium on Motivation" (M. R. Jones, ed.), pp. 1–33. University of Nebraska, Lincoln, Nebraska, U.S.A.
Falk, J. L. (1965). *J. comp. physiol. Psychol.* **60**, 393–396.
Falk, J. L. (1969). *Ann. N.Y. Acad. Sci.* **63**, 569–593.
Falk, J. L. and Burnidge, G. K. (1970). *Physiol. Behav.* **5**, 199–202.
Falk, J. L. and Herman, T. S. (1961). *J. comp. physiol. Psychol.* **54**, 405–408.

Falk, J. L. and Titlebaum, L. F. (1963). *J. comp. physiol. Psychol.* **56**, 337–342.
Fallon, D. (1965). *Science, N.Y.* **148**, 977–978.
Flory, R. K. (1969). "The control of schedule-induced polydipsia: frequency and magnitude of reinforcement." Ph.D. Dissertation. Arizona State University.
Friedman, L. (1966). *Fedn. Proc.* **25**, 137–144.
Garcia, J., Ervin, F. R., York, C. H., and Koelling, R. A. (1967). *Science, N.Y.* **155**, 716–718.
Garcia, J., Kimeldorf, D. J. and Hunt, E. L. (1961). *Psychol. Rev.* **68**, 383–395.
Gillespie, R. J. G. and Lucas, C. C. (1958). *Can. J. Biochem. Physiol.* **36**, 37–44.
Grant, D. A. (1946). *Psychol. Bull.* **43**, 272–282.
Grant, D. A. (1947). *Psychol. Bull.* **44**, 276–279.
Harlow, H. F. (1932). *J. genet. Psychol.* **41**, 430–438.
Heatley, N. G. and Weeks, J. R. (1964). *J. appl. Physiol.* **19**, 542–545.
Hendry, D. and Rasche, R. H. (1961). *J. comp. physiol. Psychol.* **54**, 477–483.
Hill, J. H. and Stellar, E. (1951). *Science, N.Y.* **114**, 43–44.
Holman, G. (1968). *J. comp. physiol. Psychol.* **69**, 432–441.
Hysell, D. K. and Abrams, G. D. (1967). *Lab Animal Care* **17**, 273–280.
Kissileff, H. R. (1969). *J. comp. physiol. Psychol.* **67**, 284–300.
Koh, S. D. and Teitelbaum, P. (1961). *J. comp. physiol. Psychol.* **54**, 223–229.
Komarov, S. A., Bralow, S. P. and Boyd, E. (1963). *Proc. Soc. exp. Biol. Med.* **112**, 451–453.
Lat, J. (1967). *In* "Alimentary Canal" (C. F. Code, ed.), Vol. 1, pp. 367–386. Williams and Wilkins, Baltimore, Md., U.S.A.
Le Magnen, J. (1967). *In* "Alimentary Canal" (C. F. Code, ed.), Vol. 1, pp. 11–30. Williams and Wilkins, Baltimore, Md., U.S.A.
Lester, D. and Greenberg, L. (1952). *Q. J. Stud. Alc.* **13**, 553–560.
Levitsky, D. A. and Collier, G. (1968). *Physiol. Behav.* **3**, 137–140.
Mayer, J. (1955). *Ann. N.Y. Acad. Sci.* **63**, 15–43.
Mayer, J. (1959). *Postgrad. Med.* **25**, 202–208.
Mello, N. K. and Mendelson, J. H. (1966). *Psychosomat. Med.* **28**, 529–550.
Mendelson, J. and Chillag, D. (1970). *Physiol. Behav.* **5**, 535–537.
Miller, N. E., Bailey, C. J. and Stevenson, J. A. F. (1950). *Science, N.Y.* **112**, 256–259.
Myers, R. D. (1966). *Psychosomat. Med.* **28**, 484–497.
Myers, R. D. (1968). *Science, N.Y.* **161**, 76–77.
Myers, R. D. and Holman, R. B. (1966). *Psychon. Sci.* **6**, 235–236.
Myers, R. D. and Veale, W. L. (1971). *In* "The Biology of Alcoholism" (H. Begleiter and B. Kissin, eds), Vol. II, pp. 131–168 Plenum press.
Nachman, M. (1963) *J. comp. physiol. Psychol.* **56**, 343–349.
Neuringer, A. J. (1969). *Science, N.Y.* **166**, 399–401.
O'Kelly, L. I. (1954). *J. comp. physiol. Psychol.* **47**, 7–13.
Pfaffman, C. (1952). *J. comp. physiol. Psychol.* **45**, 393–400.
Pfaffmann, C. and Bare, J. K. (1951). *J. comp. physiol. Psychol.* **44**, 320–324.
Pfaffman, C., Young, P. T., Dethier, V. G., Richter, C. P. and Stellar, E. (1954). *J. comp. physiol. Psychol.* **47**, 93–96.
Peacock, L. J. and Watson, J. A. (1964). *Science, N.Y.* **143**, 1462–1463.
Pickens, R. (1967). *Rep. Res. Labs. Dept. Psychiat. Univ. Minn.* No. PR–67–2.
Pickens, R., Hauck, R. C. and Bloom, W. (1966). *J. exp. anal. Behav.* **9**, 701–702.
Popovic, V., Kent, K. M., and Popovic, P. (1963). *Proc. Soc, exp. Biol. Med.* **113**, 599–602.

Popovic, P., Sybers, H. and Popovic, V. P. (1968). *J. appl. Physiol.* **25**, 626–627.
Rabelais, F. (*ca.* 1532). "Gargantua and Pantagruel." (Translation by Jacques Le Clercq. 1944. Modern Library, New York.)
Revusky, S. H. and Bedarf, E. W. (1967). *Science, N.Y.* **155**, 219–220.
Richter, C. P. (1939). *Am. J. Physiol.* **115**, 155–161.
Richter, C. P. and Clisby, K. H. (1941). *Am. J. Physiol.* **134**, 157–164.
Richter, C. P., Holt, L. E., and Barelare, B. (1938). *Am. J. Physiol.* **122**, 734–744.
Robinson, C. A., Hengeveld, C. A., Verster, F. De B. (1969). *Physiol. Behav.* **4**, 123–124.
Schuster, C. R. and Thompson, T. (1963). Committee on Drug. Addiction and Narcotics. NRC–NAS, Ann Arbor, Mich., U.S.A.
Scrimshaw, N. S. (1967). *Am. J. clin. Nutrit.* **20**, 493–502.
Snow, H. D., Steckel, R. J. and Collins, J. D. (1969). *Radiology* **93**, 1194–1196.
Stellar, E. and Hill, J. H. (1952). *J. comp. physiol. Psychol.* **45**, 96–102.
Taylor, C. and Bruning, J. L. (1968). *Behav. Res. Meth. Instru.* **1**, 32–33.
Teitelbaum, P. (1955). *J. comp. physiol. Psychol.* **48**, 156–163.
Teitelbaum, P. and Campbell, B. A. (1958). *J. comp. physiol. Psychol.* **51**, 135–141.
Teitelbaum, P. and Epstein, A. N. (1962). *Psychol. Rev.* **69**, 74–90.
Titlebaum, L. F., Falk, J. L. and Mayer, J. (1960). *Am. J. Physiol.* **199**, 22–24.
Trost, J. G., Talley, W. H. and Whitney, G. D. (1969). *Physiol. Behav.* **4**, 121–122.
Wayner, M. J. and Peterson, R. C. (1965). *Psychol. Rep.* **17**, 763–766.
Weeks, J. R. (1962). *Science, N.Y.* **138**, 143–144.
Weiner, I. H. and Stellar, E. (1951). *J. comp. physiol. Psychol.* **44**, 394–401.
Winick, M. (1969). *J. Pediat.* **74**, 667–679.
Yanagita, T., Deneau, G. A. and Seevers, M. H. (1963). Committee on Drug Addiction and Narcotics. NRC-NAS, Ann Arbor, Mich.
Young, P. T. (1941). *Psychol. Bull.* **38**, 129–164.
Young, P. T. (1945). *Comp. Psychol. Monogr.* **19**, 1–58.
Young, P. T. (1948). *Psychol. Bull.* **45**, 289–320.
Young, P. T. (1949). *Psychol. Rev.* **56**, 98–121.
Young, P. T. (1960). *Psychol. Rep.* **7**, 478.
Young, P. T. (1966). *Psychol. Rep.* **18**, 159–162.
Young, P. T. and Falk, J. L. (1956). *J. comp. physiol. Psychol.* **49**, 569–575.
Young, P. T. and Greene, J. T. (1953). *J. comp. physiol. Psychol.* **46**, 288–294.

Appendix

Suppliers and Manufacturers

Behavioral Equipment:
BCS Machine and Manufacturing Corp.
136 Market St.
Kenilworth, New Jersey, U.S.A.

Behavioral Controls, Inc.
1506 W. Pierce St.
Milwaukee, Wisconsin 53246, U.S.A.

BRS Foringer
5451 Holland Drive
Beltsville, Maryland 20705, U.S.A.

Davis Scientific Instruments
11116 Cumpston St.
North Hollywood,
California 91601, U.S.A.

Digital Equipment Corp.
146 Main St.
Maynard, Massachusetts 01754, U.S.A.

Ralph Gerbrands Co.
8 Beck Road
Arlington,
Massachusetts 02174, U.S.A.

Grason-Stadler
West Concord,
Massachusetts 01781, U.S.A.

Lafayette Instrument Co.
P.O. Box 1279
Lafayette Indiana 47902, U.S.A.

Lehigh Valley Electronics Inc.
Box 125
Fogelsville, Pennsylvania 18051, U.S.A.

Massey Dickinson Co.
9 Elm St.
Saxonville,
Massachusetts 01701, U.S.A.

Scientific Prototype
615 W. 131 St.
New York, New York 10027, U.S.A.

Animal Cages and Accessories
Acme Metal Co.
5500 Muddy Creek Rd.
Cincinnati, Ohio 45238, U.S.A.

Hoeltage
5242 Crookshank Rd.
Cincinnati, Ohio 45238, U.S.A.

Porter Mathews Scientific
Route 1
Princeton, New Jersey 08540, U.S.A.

Wahmann Manufacturing
Box 6883
Baltimore, Maryland 21204, U.S.A.

Foods and Food Processing
Allied Mills, Inc.
Chicago, Illinois, U.S.A.

General Biochemicals
Laboratory Park
Chagrin Falls, Ohio 44022, U.S.A.

Kol, Inc.
230 Eva St.
St. Paul, Minnesota 55107, U.S.A.

Marine Colloids, Inc.
P.O. Box 70
Springfield, New Jersey, U.S.A.

The P. J. Noyes Co.
Main St.
Lancaster, New Hampshire, U.S.A.

Nutritional Biochemicals Corp.
21010 Miles Ave.
Cleveland, Ohio, U.S.A.

Ralston Purina Co.
Checkerboard Square
St. Louis, Missouri 63199, U.S.A.

Pumps, Fluid and Infusion
Cole-Parmer Instrument
7425 N. Oak Park Ave.
Chicago, Illinois 60648, U.S.A.

Fluid Metering
48 Summit Street
Oyster Bay, New York 11771, U.S.A.

Harvard Apparatus
150 Dover Rd.
Millis, Massachusetts 02054, U.S.A.

Sage Instruments
230 Ferris Ave.
White Plains, New York 10603, U.S.A.

Sigmamotor
14 Elizabeth St.
Middleport, New York 14105, U.S.A.

Valcor Engineering Corp.
365 Carnegie Ave.
Kenilworth, New Jersey, 07033, U.S.A

AUTHOR INDEX

Numbers in italics refer to the pages on which the references appear

A

Abrahams, K., 159, 194, *201*
Abrams, G. D., 313, *328*
Adamson, R. H., 43, *60*
Adey, W. R., *87*, 177, 179, *203*, *243*
Adolph, E. F., 315, *327*
Aird, R. B., 159, 194, *202*

Ajmone-Marson, C., *88*, 159, 194, *201*
Akert, K., *87*
Albe-Fessard, D., *88*
Alcaraz, M., 146, *152*
Anderson, Barry F., *25*
Ankier, S. I., 250, *278*
Arbit, J., 194, *201*
Archibald, J., 28, *61*, *279*
Aronow, S., 136, *152*

B

Bailey, C. J., 325, *328*
Bak, A. F., *243*
Barclare, B., 313, *329*
Bare, J. K., 324, *327*, *328*
Barlow, E. D., 303, *327*
Barnes, C. D., 47, *60*
Barrera, E., 282, *299*
Barrow, M. V., 38, *60*
Baxter, B. L., 268, *278*
Baxter, C. F., 256, *278*
Bedarf, E. W., 318, *329*
Beebe-Center, J. G., 322, *327*
Bekkering, D. H., 201, *203*
Bell, R. E., 39, *61*
Ben, M., 43, *60*
Berman, A. L., *87*
Bernard, C. H., 79, *86*
Bernardis, L. L., *88*
Bettinger, L. A., *130*
Bickford, R. G., 157, 162, 166, 169, 170, *201*, *202*, 226, 227, *243*
Black, D. A. K., 302, *327*
Black, P., 322, *327*

Blackman, R. B., 196, *201*
Bleier, R., *87*
Blobel, R., *88*
Bloom, W., 313, *328*
Bodemer, Ch. N., *89*
Boegli, G., 39, 40, *60*, *61*
Bond, H. W., 171, *201*
Boretos, J. W., 43, *61*
Bourne, G. H., *87*
Bowman, R. E., *279*
Boyd, E., 312, *328*
Bradley, R. J., 161, *202*
Braitenberg, V., *89*
Bralow, S. P., 312, *328*
Braun, J. J., 152, *152*
Brazier, M. A. B., 157, 196, *201*, *243*
Breen, T. E., 136, *152*
Broca, P., *243*
Bromiley, R. B., *130*
Brumlik, J., 194, *201*
Bruning, J. L., 315, *329*
Buchwald, J. S., 158, *201*
Buchwald, N. A., 233, 234, 239, *243*
Bureš, J., 212, 213, *243*
Burnidge, G. K., 304, *327*

C

Campbell, B. A., 306, *329*
Campbell, Norman R., 6, *25*
Carpenter, M. B., *152*
Carr, W. J., 324, *327*
Casaday, G., 251, 256, *279*
Chan-Nao, L., *88*
Chapman, W. P., 157, *202*
Chatrian, G. E., 169, 170, *201*, *243*
Chávez-Ibarra, G., 269, *279*
Chillag, D., 316, *328*
Chusid, J. G., 162, *201*
Clark, F. C., 316, *327*
Clark, W. G., 256, *278*
Clarke, R. H., 68, *86*, 132, *153*
Clisby, K. H., 324, *329*

Clöetta, M., 247, *278*
Cobb, W., 200, *201*
Cohn, C., 319, *327*
Collias, J. C., 162, *201*
Collier, G., 315, *327*, *328*
Collins, J. D., 313, *329*
Comroe, J. H., Jr., 248, *278*
Conn, H. J., 282, *299*
Coons, E. E., 222, 223, *244*
Cooper, R., 159, 162, 163, 172, 173, 182, 184, 192, 194, 195, *201*, *202*
Cooper, R. M., 136, *153*
Corbit, J. D., 311, *327*
Coury, J. N., 250, 268, *278*
Craig, D. J., 313, *327*
Creutzfeldt, O. D., 158, *202*
Crow, H. J., 159, 162, 163, 194, *202*, *203*
Cushman, A. J., 73, 76, 77, 82, 85, *86*, *88*

D

Dahl, L. K., 303, *327*
Davis, J. D., 311, 313, *327*
Davis, R., *87*
De Carli, L. M., 316, *327*
Decima, E., 253, 254, *278*
Delgado, J. M. R., 157, 161, *202*, 212, 215, 220, 226, 229, 234, 235, *243*, *244*, 258, *278*
De Lucchi, M. R., *87*, 159, 194, *202*
Demole, V., 247, *278*
Deneau, G. A., 313, *329*
Dennis, B. J., *87*
De Quartel, F. W., 181, *202*
Dethier, V. G., 320, *328*
De Wardener, H. E., 303, *327*
Di Cara, L., 298, *299*
Dixon, R. L., 43, *60*
Dodge, H. W., 157, 159, 169, 170, *201*, *203*, *243*
Domino, E. F., 248, 265, *279*
Doty, R. W., 211, *243*
Downie, H. G., 28, *61*, *279*
Drury, R. A. B., 294, *299*

E

Eason, R. G., *244*
Ebbinghaus, H., *243*
Eddington, A. S., 13, *26*

Eichenwald, H. F., 313, *327*
Eidelberg, E., *87*
Eleftheriou, B. E., *88*
Ellison, T., 316, *327*
Eltherington, L. G., 47, *60*
Emmers, R., *87*
Epstein, A. N., 252, *278*, 312, 313, 316, *327*, *329*
Ervin, F. R., 233, 234, 239, *243*, 319, *328*
Essman, W. B., *88*
Everett, J. W., *89*

F

Falk, J. L., 303, 304, 317, 319, 321, 322, 323, 324, 325, *327*, *327*, *328*, *329*
Fallon, J. L., 306, *328*
Farris, E. J., 50, *60*
Fechner, T., *243*
Feldberg, W., 250, 255, *278*
Fernandez-Guardiola, A., 146, *152*
Ferrier, D., 132, *152*
Fifkova, E., *88*
Fischer, G., 162, 166, *202*, 226, 227, *243*
Fischer, H., 247, *278*
Fisher, A. E., 250, 268, 270, *278*
Flory, R. K., 307, *328*
Flourens, J. M., 208, *243*
Franz, S. I., *243*
Friedman, L., 313, *328*
Fritsch, G., 208, *243*
Frost, J. G., 313, *327*
Fry, P. C., 313, *327*
Fulton, J. F., 132, *152*

G

Gangloff, H., *89*
Garcia, J., 318, 319, *328*
Gardner, G. D., Jr., 60, *61*
Garoutte, B., 159, 194, *202*
Gavalas, R. J., *243*
Gay, W. I., 28, 34, *60*
Gengerelli, J. A., *243*
George, R., 253, 254, *278*
Gergen, J. A., *87*
Gillespie, R. J. G., 317, *328*
Gills, J. B., 268, *279*
Gilman, A., 28, *60*, *278*
Gloor, P., 157, *202*

Author Index

Goddard, G. V., 236, *243*
Gonzalo, L., *88*
Goodman, D. C., *130*
Goodman, L. S., 28, *60*, *278*
Goodrich, C. A., 256, *278*
Grahame, D. C., 174, *202*
Grant, D. A., 325, *328*
Greehey, B., 256, *278*
Green, J. D., *89*
Greenberg, L., 324, *328*
Greene, J. T., 322, 323, *329*
Groot, J. de, 73, 74, 77, 82, *86*, *88*, 265, *278*, *279*
Grossman, R. G., 171, *202*
Grossman, S. P., 268, 269, *278*, *279*
Grunden, L. R., 256, *279*
Gumnit, R. J., 171, *202*
Gurdjian, E. S., *130*
Guzman-Flores, C., 146, *152*

H

Halas, E. S., 158, *201*
Hamilton, P. B., 39, 40, *60*, *61*
Hamlin, H., 136, *153*, 157, *202*
Harlow, H. F., 317, *328*
Harris, R. J. C., 50, *61*
Hart, B. L., 69, 70, *86*
Harvey, J. A., 152, *152*, *153*
Hasama, B., 248, *279*
Hasenpusch, P. H., 49, *61*
Hauck, R. C., 313, *328*
Hawkins, K., 44, *61*
Hays, William L., *26*
Heatley, N. G., 313, *328*
Heller, A., 152, *152*
Hendry, D., 316, *328*
Hengeveld, C. A., 313, *329*
Herman, T. S., 323, *327*
Hernández-Peón, R., 269, *279*
Herrero, S., 136, *152*
Herz, M. J., *88*
Hess, W. R., 234, *243*
Hetherington, A. W., 132, *152*
Hill, D., 182, *202*
Hill, J. H., 310, 311, *328*, *329*
Hitzig, E., 208, *243*
Ho, P., 171, *201*
Hodos, W., *89*
Hoebel, B. G., 136, *152*
Hoffman, A. C., 322, *327*

Holman, C. B., 159, *203*
Holman, G., 316, *328*
Holman, R., 251, 256, *279*, 317, *328*
Holt, L. E., 313, *329*
Horel, J. A., *130*, 152, *153*
Horner, *243*
Horsley, V., 68, *86*, 132, *153*
Hubel, D. H., 260, *279*
Hudspeth, W. J., *88*
Huffman, R. D., *87*
Hughes, J. R., 171, *202*
Hunt, E. L., 318, *328*
Hysell, D. K., 313, *328*

I

Ingall, J. R. F., 49, *61*

J

Jacobsen, C. P., 132, *152*
Jasper, H. H., *88*, 158, *202*
Jenkins, G. M., 196, *202*
Jensen, D. H., 222, 223, *244*
Jensen, D. O., 222, 223, *244*
Jim, R. K., *88*
Jimenez-Castellanos, J., *88*
Johnson, D., *130*
Johnson, M. T., 162, *203*
Johnston, V. S., 161, *202*
Joseph, D., 319, *327*
Juhasz, L. P., *89*

K

Kado, R. T., *87*, 177, 179, *203*
Kamp, A., 181, *202*
Kapeloff, L. M., 162, *201*
Kapeloff, N., 162, *201*
Karten, H. J., *89*
Katzmann, R., 200, *202*
Kawa, A., 268, *279*
Keehn, J. D., 311, *327*
Kelley, J. W., 296, *299*
Kemali, M., *89*
Kennard, D. W., 248, *279*
Kent, K. M., 313, *328*
Kimeldorf, D. J., 318, *328*
King, F. A., 152, *153*
Kinnard, M. A., 218, *243*
Kissileff, H. R., 307, *328*
Klemm, W. R., *89*, 170, 191, *202*
Klippel, R. A., 73, 74, 75, 77, 82, *86*, 88

Klüver, H., 282, *299*
Knaggs, G. S., *89*
Koelling, R. A., 319, *328*
Koh, S. D., 324, *328*
Kok, M. L., 181, *202*
Komarov, S. A., 312, *328*
König, J. F. R., 73, 74, 75, 77, 82, *86*, *88*
Kottler, P. D., *279*
Kreig, W. J. S., *88*
Kunz, A. L., 39, *61*

L

Lashley, K. A., *244*
Lashley, K. S., 151, 152, *153*
Lat, J., 323, *328*
Lazarte, J. A., 159, *203*
Lee, A. J., 68, *86*
Lee, J. C., *87*, 143, *153*
Leech, C. K., 236, *243*
Le Magnen, J., 323, *328*
Leonard, E. P., 28, *61*
Leshner, A. I., 315, *327*
Lester, D., 324, *328*
Levitsky, D. A., 315, *328*
Levy, A., 68, *86*
Lewis, M., 222, 223, *244*
Lewis, R. E., 39, *61*
Libouban, S., *88*
Lieber, C. S., 316, *327*
Lillie, R. D., 294, *299*
Lilly, J. C., 229, 230, 237, *244*
Linburn, G. E., 256, *279*
Lindsley, D. B., *244*
Lints, C. E., 152, *153*
Livanov, M., 201, *202*
Long, C. J., 170, *202*
Loucks, R. B., 168, *202*, 215, 216, *244*
Lubar, J. F., 152, *153*
Lucas, C. C., 317, *328*
Lukaszewska, I., 150, *153*
Lumb, W. V., 28, 33, 34, 45, *61*
Luna, L. G., 286, *299*
Luparello, T. J., *89*
Lurie, M. B., 60, *61*
Luschei, E. S., 311, *327*
Lux, H. D., 158, *202*

M

McBride, R. L., *89*

McIntyre, D. C., 236, *243*
MacLean, P. D., *87*, 218, 222, 224, *243*, *244*, 248, 265, 268, *279*
McNew, B. R., 136, *153*
McNew, J. J., 150, *153*
Mahler, J., 215, 217, 231, *244*
Manley, R. G., 196, *202*
Mann, P. E. G., 43, *61*
Manocha, S. L., *87*
Manuelidis, E. E., 162, *201*
Mark, V. H., 136, *153*
Markowitz, J., 28, *61*
Markowitz, M. B. E., 260, *279*
Marks, M., 68, *86*
Marley, E., 253, *279*
Marsala, J., *88*
Masserman, J. H., 248, *279*
Massopust, L. C., *88*, 143, 145, *153*
Mayer, J., 302, 322, 323, *328*, *329*
Mazzuchelli, A. L., *87*
Mello, N. K., 318, *328*
Mendelson, J., 316, *328*
Mendelson, J. H., 318, *328*
Messen, H., *89*
Meyer, D. R., *130*, 152, *152*, *153*
Meyer, P. M., *130*, 152, *152*, *153*
Mickle, W. A., 229, *244*
Mihailovic, L., 234, 235, *244*
Miller, N. E., 222, 223, *244*, 275, *279*, 325, *328*
Miller, T. B., 256, *278*
Moffett, R. L., *88*
Molello, J. A., 44, *61*
Monnier, M., *89*
Moore, R. Y., 152, *152*
Morgan, C. T., *153*
Morgane, P. J., *88*, 152, *153*, 258, 269, *279*
Morocutti, C., 200, *201*
Moskalenko, Yu. E., 159, *202*
Muller, J., 208, *244*
Mullican, C. L., 60, *61*
Myers, A. K., 222, 223, *244*
Myers, R. D., 36, *61*, 249, 250, 251, 256, 257, 260, 265, 266, 267, 268, 270, 272, 273, 274, 275, 276, 277, 278, *279*, 317, 318, 321, 324, *328*

N

Nachman, M., 318, *328*

Author Index

Nashold, B. S., 268, *279*
Nastuk, W. L., *244*
Neuringer, A. J., 307, *328*
Newman, James R., *26*
Niemer, W. T., 69, *86*, *88*

O

O'Kelly, L. T., 310, 322, *328*
Olds, J., 248, 261, *279*
Olds, M. E., 248, 261, *279*
Olszewski, J., *87*, *89*
Osselton, J. W., 182, 192, 195, *202*
Oswaldo-Cruz, E., *89*

P

Pappenheimer, J. R., 256, *278*
Park, C. D., *89*
Parr, G., 182, *202*
Peacock, L. J., 318, *328*
Pecci Saavedra, J., *87*
Pellegrino, L. J., 73, 76, 77, 82, 85, *86*, *88*
Peters, M., 136, *153*
Petersen, M. C., 157, 159, 169, 170, *201*, *203*, *243*
Peterson, R. C., 319, *329*
Petraǔ, M., 212, 213, *243*
Petsche, H., 171, 201, *202*, *203*
Pfaffman, C., 320, 324, *328*
Phillips, D. G., 159, *202*
Phillips, G. B., 60, *61*
Pickens, R., 313, *328*
Plonsy, R., *244*
Pollack, C. S., 169, 170, *201*, *243*
Pool, R., 136, *153*
Popovic, P., 313, *328*, *329*
Popovic, V., 313, *328*
Popovic, V. P., 313, *329*
Porter, R., 177, 179, *203*

R

Rabelais, F., 301, 302, *329*
Ranson, S. W., 132, *152*
Rappelsberger, P., 171, 201, *202*
Rasche, R. H., 316, *328*
Ray, C. D., 168, *203*
Rech, R. H., 248, 265, *279*
Reitman, M., 60, *61*
Revusky, S. H., 318, *329*
Reynolds, R. W., 136, *153*

Rich, I., 136, *153*
Richeson, W. B., 194, *201*
Richter, C. P., 313, 320, 324, *328*, *329*
Riddle, W. C., 316, *327*
Riggs, Do. S., *26*
Robinson, C. A., 313, *329*
Robinson, D. A., *244*
Robinson, F. R., 162, *203*
Rocha-Miranda, C. E., *89*
Rose, J. E., *130*
Roth, J. G., 222, *244*
Roussy, G., *153*
Routtenberg, A., 268, *279*
Rowland, V., 171, *203*
Royce, G. J., *130*
Ruch, T. C., 50, *61*
Russell, G. V., *87*
Rutledge, J. H., 39, 40, *60*, *61*

S

Saladias, C. A., *87*
Sawyer, C. H., *89*
Sayre, G. P., 162, 166, *202*, 226, 227, *243*
Schramm, S., 158, *201*
Schuckardt, E., *88*
Schuster, C. R., 313, *329*
Schütz, J., 247, *279*
Schweigerdt, A., 150, *153*
Scrimshaw, N. S., 313, *329*
Sechenov, I. M., 209, *244*
Seevers, M. H., 313, *329*
Seifter, J., 269, *279*
Sem-Jacobsen, C. W., 157, 159, *201*, *203*, *244*
Shantha, T. R., *87*
Sharpe, L. G., 249, 257, 266, 274, 275, *279*
Shaw, S., 182, 192, 195, *202*
Sheatz, G. C., 221, *244*, 257, *279*
Sheer, D. E., 209, *244*
Sherrington, C. S., *244*
Short, D. J., 28, 33, 50, 60, *61*
Singer, M., *88*
Skelton, F. R., *88*
Slotnick, B. M., *88*
Smith, M., 168, *202*, 215, 216, *244*
Smith, O. A., *89*
Snider, R. S., 69, *86*, *87*, *88*, 143, *153*
Snow, H. D., 313, *329*

Sperry, R. W., 152, *153*
Spiegel, E. A., 68, *86*
Squibb, R. L., 315, *327*
Steckel, R. J., 313, *329*
Stein, L., 269, *279*
Stein, M., *89*
Stellar, E., 310, 311, 320, 322, *328*, *329*
Stephenson, J. D., 253, *279*
Stere, J., 201, *203*
Stevens, C. F., *244*
Stevens, S. S., *26*
Stevenson, J. A. F., 325, *328*
Stokes, L. D., 152, *153*
Storm van Leeuwen, W., 201, *203*
Strobel, G. E., 43, *61*
Stumpf, W. E., 268, 269, *279*
Stutinsky, F., *88*
Suckling, E. E., *244*
Sweet, W. H., 136, *153*
Sybers, H., 313, *329*

T

Talley, W. H., 313, *327*, *329*
Tapp, J. T., 170, *202*
Taylor, C., 315, *329*
Teitelbaum, P., 306, 312, 313, 315, 316, 324, *327*, *328*, *329*
Teuber, H. L., 152, *153*
Thompson, R., 136, 150, 152, *153*
Thompson, R. F., *244*
Thompson, T., 313, *329*
Thorndike, E. L., *244*
Tienhoven, A. van, *89*
Tigges, J. W., *87*
Timo-Iaria, C., 269, *279*
Titlebaum, L. F., 322, 323, *328*, *329*
Tindal, J. S., *89*
Tomka, I., 159, *202*
Toshio, K., *87*
Trust, J. G., 313, *329*
Tukey, J. W., 196, *201*
Turvey, A., *89*
Tyers, M. B., 250, *278*
Tytell, M., 268, *279*

V

Vanderwolf, C. H., 152, *153*
Van Manen, J., 68, *86*
Vaughn, D., *130*

Veale, W. L., 36, *61*, 318, 324, *328*
Verhaart, W. J. C., *88*
Verster, F. de B., 313, *329*
Villablanca, J., 256, *279*
Vivonia, C. A., 256, *278*

W

Wade, M., 322, *327*
Wagner, J. W., *279*
Wallace, J. D., 161, *202*
Wallington, E. A., 294, *299*
Walter, D. O., *243*
Walter, W. G., 159, 194, *202*, *203*
Warren, W. J., 184, *202*
Watanabe, S., 158, *202*
Watson, J. A., 318, *328*
Watts, D. G., 196, *202*
Wayner, M. J., 319, *329*
Weeks, J. R., 313, *328*, *329*
Weinberg, H., 159, 168, *202*, *203*, 215, 216, *244*
Weiner, I. H., 320, 322, *329*
Weinman, J., 215, 217, 231, *244*
Whitney, G. D., 313, *329*
Whittier, J. R., *152*
Winick, M., 313, *329*
Winter, A. L., 159, 194, *202*
Winters, W. D., *87*
Wolf, G., 298, *299*
Wollman, H., 43, *61*
Woolsey, 107
Woodnott, D. P., 28, 33, 50, 60, *61*
Woolsey, C. N., 107, *130*
Wundt, W., *244*
Wurtz, R. H., 171, *203*
Wycis, H. T., 68, *86*

Y

Yaksh, T. L., 249, 277, *279*
Yanagita, T., 313, *329*
York, C. H., 319, *328*
Young, P. T., 302, 317, 318, 320, 322, 323, *328*, *329*
Yum, C., 261, *279*
Yuwiler, A., 261, *279*

Z

Zachar, J., 212, 213, *243*
Zolovick, A. J., *88*

SUBJECT INDEX

A

Ablation (*see also* Lesion), 92, 129, 132
  cat-monkey, 125
  rat, 92
AC
  amplifier, 173
  bridge, 177, 179
  recording, 179
Acceptance-rejection function, 323
Acclimation period, 29
Acetic acid, 148, 149
Acetylcholine, 158, 209
"Action Commune", 208
Action potential, 157
Activity, 41
Adhesions, 123
After-discharge, 239
Age, 41
Albino rat, 74, 77
Alcohol, 99, 113, 117
Alpha rhythm, 197
Ambient temperature, 31
Amine, 273
Ammeter, 136
Amplification, 157
Amplifier, 171, 176, 181, 184
Amplitude, 209, 231, 233
  rate of, 157
Amygdala, 161, 236
Analeptic, 49
Anatomical
  code, 276
  control, 257
  details, 149
  landmark, 85
  locus, 276
  mapping, 277
Anchor screws, 221, 257, 260
Anesthesia, 43–49, 92, 128
  depth of, 47
  equipment for, 63
  excitable stage of, 114
  maintenance of, 97
  procedure for inducing, 43–49, 113, 114
  surgical stage of, 96
Anesthesia pack, 111
  sterilization of, 111
Anesthetic, 38, 40, 43–47, 60, 95, 140
  administration of, 41, 113, 114
  doses of, 40, 42, 46, 95
  injection of, 97
  mask, 43, 44
  overdose of, 48, 114
  volatile, 48
Anesthetist, 114
Angle calibrator, 72
Angular insertion, 72
Aniline stain, 295
Animal
  cages for, 62
  care of, 29–31
  handling of, 33
    monkey, 34
    mouse, 32
    rabbit, 34
    rat, 33
  identification of, 30
  resuscitation of, 49
  sacrificing of, 60
  sexing of, 30
  size of, 41
  sources of, 62
  surgery in, 48
  weight, 10, 32, 41, 95, 113
Animal behavior, 160, 161, 237, 241
Anion, 171
Anodal current, 133, 134
Anode, 133, 171
Anogenital distance, 30

Antagonist, 273
Anterior-Posterior (A.P.)
  coordinate, 81
  level, 86
  plane, 78, 80, 145
  scale, 79, 82, 139, 149
Antibiotic, 42, 56, 58
Anticholinergic action, 47
Antidromical response, 239
Antimycotic, 57
Antiseptic, 99, 111, 116
Anterior commissure, 79, 85
Application of crystals, 271
Applying a chemical, 260–270
Araldite, 166
Aramide, 52
Arbitrary horizontal zero plane, 79
Arecoline acetarsol, 57
Arecoline hydrobromide, 57
Artefact, 183, 191, 192, 194, 240
Arthritis in the mouse, 51
Artificial respiration, 48
Aseptic
  precaution, 110
  procedure, 140
Aspirator, 94, 103, 104, 109, 113, 124, 141
Asphyxiation, 113
Aspiration technique
  cat-monkey, 120–128
  rat, 103, 104, 107
Association areas, 160
Atlas coordinate, 79–82, 86
Atropine, 46, 47
Atropine sulfate, 43, 94, 97, 111, 113
Audiotransformer, 232
Auletta method, 282, 296, 297
Aureomycin, 56, 140, 141
Autoclaving, 111
Average reference
  point, 183
  recording, 182
  resistor, 183, 184
Aversion, 323
Axon, 157, 210

B

B-virus, 58
Bacterial diseases, 51, 53, 54, 56, 58
Bacteria, 50, 60

Bait-shyness, 318
Barbiturate, 40, 44, 45, 47, 95
  anesthetic, 47
  overdose of, 49
Batteries, 136
Bedding, 31
Behavior, 1, 2, 5, 6, 12, 25, 131, 136, 150, 325, 326
  animal, 4, 24, 25, 241
  change, 234
  consummatory, 303
  ingestive, 303
  operant, 307
Behavioral deficit, 132, 150, 152
  process, 326
  research, 211
  response, 214, 323, 325
  variable, 323
Bemegide, 49
Benzene hexachloride, 57
Benzyl benzoate, 57
Bicillin, 94, 107, 111, 128
  dose of, 106
Bilateral stimulation, 257
Binocular loupes, 94, 102, 112, 124
Biological measurement, 171
Bipolar
  electrode, 212–214, 219
  construction of, 218
  recording, 182, 184
Bladder worms, 55
Bleeding, 92, 99, 102, 103, 122, 126, 141, 144
  point, 108, 127
  stopping of, 108–110
Blocking, 285
Blood-brain barrier, 42, 250
Body temperature, 248
Bone
  chisel, 112, 121
  flap, 123, 124, 127
  removal, 102, 124
  wax, 108, 111, 120
Boric acid ointment, 94, 98, 111, 116
Bottle position, 324
Brain, 207, 208
  activity, 156
    malfunctioning, 160, 161
    normal, 160
  behavior relationship, 132

charts, 143
function, 150, 151, 155, 210
lesion, 298, 299
removal of, 284, 285
stimulation (*see* Stimulation of the brain)
Brain sections, 147
photographing of, 148
sketching of, 149
unstained, 146, 150
Bregma, 70, 77, 81, 82, 101, 145, 284
Body canker, 55
Body mange in the mouse, 52
Bordetella bronchiseptica, 56
Bromophenol blue, 266, 274, 275
Bur, 101, 112, 127, 221

C

Caesarean-derived breeders, 51, 53
Cage, 31, 62, 63
Calcium, 247, 248
Calomel electrode, 171
Calorie, 315, 323
Cam-operated feeder, 308
Candidate transmitter, 273
Cannula
array, 257, 258, 263
assembly, 254, 258
base, 250, 260
cap, 251
Collison, 255
construction of, 250
guide, 250, 253, 256–258, 275
implantation of, 259
inexpensive, 250
injection, 250, 258, 261, 264, 265, 269
intracerebral, 250–259
microinjection, 250
pedestal, 260
placement, 84
tip, localizing of, 297
Capacitor, 174
Cat, 34, 42, 46
Cathodal current, 134
Cathode, 133, 171
Cation, 171
Caudate nucleus, 143
Cautery, 136
Cell body, 151, 210

Cell group, 281
stain, 282, 290–292, 295–297
decolorizing of, 290
Celloidin, 288
Cellular depolarization, 158
Cellular-spike activity, 158
Central necrotic zone, 133
Central nervous system, 209
Central tegmentum, 144
Cephalic vein, 114
Cerebellar cortex, 132
Cerebellar nuclei, 68
Cerebellum, 78
Cerebral
activity, 156, 157
data processing system, 160
localization, 208
organization, 210
ventricle, 249, 255, 268
Cerebrospinal fluid, 126, 249, 268
Cerebrum, 209
Chattering, 51, 53
Chemical
"coding", 275
dose of, 276
irritation, 226
lesion, 136
methods of applying, 260–270
stimulation, 210, 248, 249, 260, 265, 268, 272, 276
anatomical aspects of, 274
interpretation of data, 270, 275
method, 270
pharmacological aspects of, 272
physiological aspects of, 275
stimulus, 274
substance, 264, 269
high dose, 272
injection of, 249
transmitter, 249
release and turnover, 278
Chemitrode, 258
Chimpanzee, 161
Chloral hydrate, 140
Chlorine, 171
Chloroform, 43, 60
Chloromycetin, 58
Chlortetracycline, 56
Cholinomimetic crystals, 248

Chronic implantation, 220, 224
  in rats, 222, 223
  in cats, 226
Chronic respiratory disease in the mouse, 51
Chronically implanted electrode, 214
Circadian rhythm, 319
Clippers, 94, 97
Closed circuit method, 45
Closing the wound, 104, 127
Coaxial electrode, 219
Coccidia, 53
Coccidiosis, 53, 54
Collison cannula, 225
Combined impedance, measurement of, 176, 179
Common effector pathway, 210
Common reference recording, 182, 184
Computer, 200, 201
  analysis, 159, 161
  techniques, 160
Concentration, 320
  test, 321
Concentric electrode, 213
  construction of, 219
Conditioning of the brain, 211
Conduction pathway, 151
Conical mask, 44
Conjunctivitis, 51, 56
Connector, 221–223
  suppliers of, 245
Consciousness, 160
Constant current, 232
  stimulator, 230
Constant voltage, 232
Consummatory behavior, 303
Convulsions, 236
Coordinate system, 68, 69, 77
Copper electrode, 134, 162, 166, 226
Coronal suture, 81, 101, 145
Corpus callosum, 85
Correlation analysis, 160, 194, 196
Cortex, 107, 157
  ablation, 103, 122, 125, 129
Cortical
  activity, 156
  electrodes, 166, 171, 201, 220
    construction of, 170
Cosine, 195, 197
Counterstaining method, 282, 295, 296

Cover slip, 288, 290
Cover slipping, 290
Covered chamber method, 45
Cranial cavity, 284
Cranioplast cement, 257–260
Craniotomy
  hole, 259
  techniques, 101, 122, 123
Cranium, 140
Cresyl violet
  acetate, 292, 296
  method, 292, 293
Cross contamination, 32
Cross-correlation
  coefficient, 185, 196, 197
  function, 197, 198
  technique, 185
Cross-infection, 32
Crystal, 248
  application of, 268, 271
  dose of, 269
Crystalline stimulation, 268
  technique, 270
Current, 231
  density, 215, 217
  sensitive paper, 212
Cysticerosis, 52
Cytolysis, 133

D

DC resistance, 175
  amplifier, 179, 180
  generator, 176
  measurement of, 175
Data sheets, 30
Decolorization, 291–296
Decolorizing solution, 291, 293, 294
Dektol developer, 148, 149
Delta activity, 189–191
Dendrite, 210
Dental
  bur, 112
  cement, 93, 220–222
  ejector, 101, 102, 112, 122
Deprivation, 313
Depth
  electrode, 156
  electroencephalography, 187, 191
  recording, 159, 168, 187
Desiccator jar, 36, 45

Diabetes insipidus, 322
Diarrhea, 51, 53, 54, 56–59
Dibutyl phthalate, 52
Diet, 313–316
  diluted, 315
  liquid, 315, 316
  manual, 314
  mixing, 314
  self-selection, 314, 315
  solid, 314, 315
  test, 314
Dietary
  components, 315
  regime, 323
  variable, 313, 323
Differentiated sinusoid, 229
Diffusion in brain tissue, 248, 249
  amount of, 267
  extent of, 261, 266
  of dye, 267
  problem of, 265
Dipper
  cup, 311
  magazine, 311, 312
Disease of laboratory animals, 49–59
  symptoms and treatment,
    cat, 56–57
    monkey, 58–59
    mouse, 51–52
    rabbit, 54–55
    rat, 53
Disinfectants, 60
Disposable
  needle, 37, 39, 42
  syringe, 42
Distemper, 56
Dose-response
  function, 321
  relationship, 270
"Double-dissociation", 152
Draping technique, 119
Dri-clave sterilizer, 138
Drill, 94, 101, 124
Drilling, 144
Drinking, 319, 320, 327
  bottles, 32
  schedule, 322
  spout, 310, 311
  tube, 307, 309
    stainless steel, 310

Drinkometer, 310, 311, 316
  circuit, 306
Drive state, 326
Drocarbil, 57
Drug, 152
  action of, 41
  administration, 11, 35
  calculation of amount, 42
  choice of, 41
  dose of, 40–42
  excretion of, 40
  response to, 40
  sensitivity to, 40
  suppliers of, 63
Dryer, 149
Dura, 81, 82, 141, 220, 224, 252
  elevator, 94, 112, 121, 124
  flap, 124, 125
  hook, 112
Dura mater, 102
  puncture of, 102
Duration, 233
  of stimulus, 209, 217
Duties of the circulating nurse, 110, 115, 116, 117, 120, 124
Dye, 274
  diffusion of, 268
Dysentery, 58
Dyskinesia, 158
Dyspnea, 51, 56

E

Ear
  bar, 73, 78, 79, 82–84, 98, 115, 116, 139, 141
  canker, 55, 57
  mange in the mouse, 52
  plug, 82–84
Eating, continuous record of, 306
Ectoparasites, 52, 53, 55, 57, 59
Ectromelia virus, 51
Edema, 109, 126, 127
Effector event, 241
Electrical
  activity, 156, 160, 168, 169, 201
    abnormal, 162, 187
  charge, 172
  double layer, 172–174, 181
  evoked response, 160
  interface, 230

recording, 211
signal, 157
stimulation, 159, 161, 208, 209, 248, 249, 258, 270
 effect of, 210
 interpretation of, 238–242
 usefulness of, 211
Electroanatomy, 211
Electrocautery, 109
Electro-convulsive therapy, 191
Electrode, 68, 69, 72, 78–82, 86, 132–152, 156–161, 166, 210, 232
 anatomy, 211
 angle calibrator, 72, 73
 array, 212, 236
 bipolar, 213, 214
 calomel, 171
 carrier, 69, 72, 138, 213, 219, 220
  adjustment of, 139
  driving mechanism, 73
 chronically implanted, 214
 coaxial, 219
 concentric, 213, 214, 219
 construction of, 137, 170, 215–220
 cortical, 161, 166, 168, 171–201, 220
 distribution board, 183
 EEG, construction of, 162
 exploring, 212
 extracellular stimulation, 212
 flexible, 224
 holder, 72, 222
 impedance, 179, 181, 217
 implantation, 170
 insulation, 78, 137, 139, 166, 167, 218
 intracerebral, 168, 185, 194, 198, 224
 length, 168
 localization, 297
 metallic, dangers of, 162
 midbrain, 161
 monopolar, 133, 137, 213
 montage, 184
 multilead, 218
 multipolar, 214
 nonpolarized, 156, 171, 173
 placement, 84
 polarized, 173, 176, 179, 180, 183, 192
 potential, 172–174, 176
 resistance, 175, 180, 181
 reversible, 173, 176

scalp, 192
sheaves, 169, 171, 182
subdural, 192
suppliers of, 154, 245
testing of, 219, 221
types of, 212, 213
wire, 166, 216, 219
 coating of, 167
 coding of, 170
 diameter, 167
Electroencephalogram (EEG), 156, 157, 162
 activity, 158, 160, 166–169, 182, 187, 197
 analysis, 194
 correlates of learning, 160
 correlates of stress, 160
 electrodes, 161–171
 machine, 175, 179
 record, 160, 162, 163, 169, 185
 recording, 156, 161, 173, 175, 181, 239
  interpretation of, 185
  of psychiatric patient, 186
 rhythm, 237
 types of, 182
Electroencephalograph, manufacturers of, 204
Electrolysis, 133, 219
Electrolytic damage, 228–230
 etching, 216, 218
 lesion, 168
 polishing, 217, 218
Electron, 171
 conduction of, 171
 flow, 210
 flux, 210
Electrophysiology, 156, 210
Embedding, 285
 in gelatin, 286
Enamel insulation, 167, 169
Encephalography, 158, 162
 clinical application, 158
Endotracheal catheter, 45
Environmental variable, 319
Epidemic murine pneumonia, E.M.P., 53
Epileptic
 seizures, 160, 208, 239
 zones, 161

Epileptogenic lesion, 161
Epoxylite, 137, 138, 218
Equivalent circuit, 173, 175
Error variance, 31
Ether, 43, 97
Ethyl chloride, 44
Ethylene oxide machine, 60
Euthanasia, 60
Evans blue, 266, 274, 275
Evoked
  potentials, 237, 239
  response, 159, 200, 201, 239
Excitatory post-synaptic potentials (EPSP), 158
Exploring guide cannula, 269
Exposed cortical area, 156, 157
Exposure of the brain, 99
External auditory meatus, 83, 93, 97, 98, 116
Extirpation, 103, 104, 106, 132
Extracellular
  recording, 219
  stimulation, 219
Extraneuronal space, 210
Eye speculum, 100

F

Fascia, removal of, 100, 101
Fear reaction, 41
Feed, 41–61
Feeder, 306
Feeding, 304, 319
  control group, 314
  cup, 305
  habit, 313
  intermittent, 319
Feline
  enteritis, 56
  panleukopenia, 56
  pneumonitis, 56
Femoral vein, 38
Fever, 40, 56
Fiber
  bundles, 151
  stain, 282, 291–293, 297
    differentiation of, 293
  tract, 281, 295, 297
Filter paper, 289
Final instrument coordinate, 79, 80

Fistula
  cheek, 312
  stomach, 312
Fixer, 148, 149
Flatworm, 57
Flea, 57
Flexible electrode, 224
Fluid, 311
  balance, 322
  intake, 302, 304, 323, 325
  measurement of, 309
  presentation of, 305–313
Fluothane, 44
Focal stimulation, 207, 239
Food, 31
  acquisition procedure, 324
  cup, 306, 308, 314
  deprivation of, 106, 113
  hopper, 32
  intake, 31, 302, 305, 309, 314, 321, 323–325
  measurement of, 305, 309
  liquid, 315
  magazine, 306
  pellet, 307
    dispenser, 308
    magazine, 307
  presentation of, 305–313
  storage, 315
  supplement, 31
  water ratio, 323
Forceps, 94, 95, 97, 100, 101, 106, 110, 112, 119, 120, 141, 142
Formalin, 147, 148
  buffered, 283–285, 291
Formvar, 166, 219
Fornix, 80–82, 86
Fourier analysis, 195, 197
Freezing microtome, 146, 147, 286
Frequency, 22, 233
  analysis, 194, 195
  distribution, 15–19
  of stimulus, 209
  ratio, 20, 22
Frontal
  base plane, 77
  bone, 101
  lobe, 158
  plane, 68, 145
  pole, 77

section, 290
  zero plane, 77
Frozen sectioning, 286, 288
"Functional map", 276
Fungal disease, 52, 54, 57
Fungus, 52, 54, 57

G

Galvanometers, 156, 157
Gamma-benzene-hexachloride, 55
Gastro-intestinal route of administration, 36
Gelatin embedding, 286
Gelatin solution, 288, 289
Gelfoam, 94, 108, 111, 120, 259
General anesthetic, 43–44
Gentian violet, 59
Germicidal ultraviolet irradiation, 60
Germicide, 113
Gigli saw, 113, 123
Glia, 210
Gliosis, 133
Gliotic field, 150
Gloving technique, 118
Gold electrode, 162, 167, 168, 173, 176, 177, 179, 180, 186, 191, 193, 226
Gown pack, 111
  technique, 117
Grain feeder, 308
Granny-knot, 106
Griseofulvin, 57
Guide
  cannula, 250–253, 256–258, 275
  tube, 259, 265, 268
Gyrus, 126

H

Habenula, 108
Habituation, 160, 201
Halothane (fluothane), 43
Head-holder, 93, 139, 141, 144
  technique for placement
    rat, 97–98
    cat and monkey, 115–116
Heisenberg's principle of uncertainty, 13
Helminths, 52, 55, 57, 59
Hematoxylin staining solution, 294
Hemorrhage, 38, 92, 102, 108, 109, 159

Hemostasis techniques, 48, 108, 110, 120, 122, 125, 126
Hemostatic agents, 108, 110
Hexa-germ, 113
High-amplitude low-frequency activity, 163–166
High-frequency stimulus, 234
Hippocampus, 85
Histological
  localization, 252
  material, 282
  procedure, 147, 148
  section, 73, 85, 276, 297
    unstained, 146
  study, 225, 275
  verification, 259
Homeostasis, 304
Horizontal (H)
  coordinate, 81
  plane, 68, 139, 146
  scale, 79
  zero, 72, 77, 79–81, 139
Hormone implants, 248
House-Rosen needle, 94, 103, 112
Humidity, 31
Hunger, 304, 305, 325
Hunter timer, 263
Hydrogen electrode, 173, 174
Hyperpnoea, 159
Hyperphagia, 303
Hyperthermia, 277
Hypodermic needle, 96, 112
Hypoglycaemia, 159, 160
Hypothalamic
  area, 152
  hyperphagia, 136
Hypothalamus, 132, 143, 152, 234, 248
  anterior-posterior level, 73
Hypothermia, 48
Hypoxia, 160

I

Impedance, 179, 183, 231
Implantation, 73, 78
  procedure, 220, 224
Incision, 99, 106, 108, 121, 125, 133
Incubator, 110, 128
India ink, 274, 275
Induction coil, 208

Subject Index

Infantile diarrhea in the mouse, 51
Infection, 98, 159
Inferior colliculus, 143
Infraorbital ridge, 116
Infusion, 266
Ingestion, 302, 304, 318, 320, 321
  analysis of, 323
  test, 319
Ingestive
  behavior, 303, 304, 319
  function, 301, 326
  measure, 325
  mechanisms, 303
  processes, 325
Inhalant anesthetic, 45
Inhalation, 43
  of a drug, 35
Inhibitory post-synaptic potentials (IPSP), 158
Injection, 42, 95, 97, 265
  intradermal, 36
  intramuscular, 36, 42
  intrathecal, 36
  intraperitoneal, 39, 40
  parenteral, 37
  site, 42
    histological localization of, 252
  technique for, 96
Injector
  cannulae, 250, 251, 253, 258, 259, 261, 263–265, 269
  needle, 252, 254–257, 264, 265
  tube, 268
Insl-X, 138, 218
Instrument
  tray, 93
    cat-monkey, 111–112
    rat, 94
  zero coordinate, 79
Insulating material, 227
Insulation, 137–139
  of electrodes, 166, 167
Intake behavior, 318
Interaural line (IAL), 73, 77, 79, 81, 82
Interface, 230, 231
Internal state, measure of, 325
Interpeduncular nucleus, 144
Interval data, 31
Intracellular potential change, 157
Intracerebral electrode, 224

Intracerebral
  cannula, 250–259
    construction of, 250
    recording, 161, 163
  sheaves, 169
Intradermal administration, 36
Intragastric
  intubation, 36, 44
  tube, 36
Intralaminar nuclei, 108
Intramuscular injection, 36, 42, 46, 107
Intraperitoneal injection, 39, 40, 46, 95, 97, 113
  technique for, 96
Intraperitoneal route, 46, 60
Intrathecal injection, 36
Intravenous injection, 39, 46, 113
  technique for, 113
Intravenous route, 38, 46
Intraventricular
  infusion, 256, 257
  injection, 255, 257
    cannula for, 255
  route, 249, 250, 268
Ion, 171, 172, 209, 248
  flow, 210, 230
  flux, 210
Ionic
  conduction, 171
  stimulation, 248
Iontophoretic application, 261
Iris
  forceps, 260
  scissors, 94, 97, 99, 125
Iron electrode, 134
Iron-hematoxylin method, 282, 292, 293, 295
Irradiation, 60
Ischemia, 160
Isolation, 29
  unit, 232, 238

K

Kaopectate, 58
Klüver-Barrera method, 282, 295–297
Knife, 99
  blade, 94, 111, 119, 123, 125
  handle, 94, 119
Kodabromide paper, 148

L

Laboratory equipment, 62, 63
Labyrinthitis, 53
Lambda, 70, 101, 145
Lateral (L)
  hypothalamus, 266
  plane, 80
  scale, 79, 81, 139
Leptazol, 49
Lesion, 68, 80, 92, 129, 132–152, 159, 270, 281, 297
  accuracy of placement, 143
  analysis of, 150
  cat, 125
  chemical, 136
  control of size, 142
  damage, determination of, 298
  direct current, 136
  electrolytic, 133–152, 168
  epileptogenic, 161
  evaluation of, 150
  how to make, 136–143
  makers, 136, 137, 154
  mechanical, 136
  metals, 162
  monkey, 125
  method, weakness of, 151–152
  one stage vs two stage, 143
  organic, 158, 188, 191
  placement, 84
  radio frequency, 136, 137
  rat, 92, 125
  skin, 54, 57, 58
  suction, 136
  surgical procedure for, 141
  symmetrical, 144
  test, 142
  thermoregulative, 136, 137
  verification of, 146
  volumetric analyses of, 298
Lethal dose, 95
Lick, 311
  count, 311
  rate, 310, 311
  record, 311
Lighting conditions, control of, 319
Line drawing, 73, 150
Liquid food, 315
Litter, 31
Litter products, 31

Lobectomy, 159
"Localized response", 160
Longitudinal suture, 145
Loss of consciousness, 44
Louse, 57
Luxol blue, 292, 295–297

M

Macroelectrode, 158
Macrotome, 68
Magnesium, 247, 248
Maintenance of surgical equipment, 95
Malathion, 52, 53
Mange, 57
"Mapping" study, 257
Marking ink, 275
Mayo stand, 119
  tray, 111, 113, 117
Mean, 16–20, 23
Measurable property, 6, 8–10
Measurement, 3, 5–7, 11–13, 15, 16, 23
  derived, 10
  errors in, 14
  fundamental, 9
  original units of, 19
  practical aspect of, 10
  scientific theory, 3
  squared units of, 18
  qualitative, 6
  quantitative, 11, 18
Measuring instrument, 11, 18
Mechanical
  lesion, 136
  trauma, 225
Medial
  mammilary nuclei, 144
  septal nuclei, 144
Median, 16
Membrane potential, 158
Meninges, 166
Meperidine, 46
Mephenesin, 47
Merthiolate, 140, 141
Mesencephalic reticular formation, 161
Metabolic rate, 41
Metachromasy, 282
Metachromatic reaction, 296, 297
Metal electrodes, toxicity of, 215, 216, 226, 227

Metallic
  ions, 133–135
  plates, 133
Methodology, 4
Methoxyflurane, 44, 47, 94, 96, 97
Metrazol, 114
Micro
  dot, 238
  electrode, 158
Micro-infusion, 252
Micro-injection, 250, 253, 255, 264–267, 275–277
  accuracy of delivery, 262
  by hand, 262
  cannula for, 250
  marking of, 274
  pump motor, 263
  site, verification of, 274
  of a solution, 261, 262, 271
  syringe, 262
Microliter droplet, 264–266, 274
Microliter syringe, 253, 261, 275
Micro-manipulator, 73
Microprojector, 297
Microscope, 297
  slides, 288
Microtome, 146, 148
  freezing, 286
  knife, 287
Midbrain, 143
  reticular formation, 209
Midline thalamic nuclei, 144
Mites, 52, 53, 55, 57, 59
Monitoring of behavioral and physiological parameters, 35
Monkey, 32, 34, 42, 46, 161, 234, 238
Monopolar electrode, 213, 215
Montage, 184
Mortality, 56
Mosquito forceps, 94, 95, 100, 113, 121
Motivational state, 304, 326
Motor cortex, 158
Mounting, 288, 289
Mouse, 32, 46
  pox, 51
  typhoid, 51
Multichannel recorder, 181
Multi-lead electrode, 218, 222
  construction of, 218
Multiple amplification, 157

Multipolar electrode, 214
Muscle retraction,
  cat-monkey, 121
  rat, 101
Mycobacterium tuberculosis, 58
Myelinated fiber, 282
Myelin stain, 293
Myothesid, 47
Myxomatosis, 54

N

Narrow pulse, 157
Naso-pharyngeal tube, 312, 316
Natural number, 7
Naturalistic observation, 3–5
Neck-lead mange, in the mouse, 52
Necropsy, 50
Necrosis, 150
Necrotic
  material, 127
  tissue, 162
  zone, 142, 150
Needle, 37, 40
  holder, 94, 95, 105, 106, 112, 113
  hypodermic, 96, 112, 114
  lesion, 137–139, 141, 143
  marking with, 141, 143
  stop, 39, 40
  suture, 105, 106, 112
  tubing, 250
    for cannulae, 280
Negative
  lead, 137
  number, 7
  potential, 158
Nematode, 52, 57, 59
Nembutal, 46
Neocortical ablation, 92–108
  cat-monkey, 120–128
  rat, 92, 94, 100, 103, 104
Neodecortication, 125
Neosalvarsan, 54
Nerve,
  action potential, 157
  impulse, 209
Nervous propagation, 208
Neural lesion, 133, 134, 136
Neuroanatomical study, 208
Neuroanatomist, 225
Neuroanatomy, 67

Neuroglia, 108
Neurohumoral substance, 270, 276
Neuron, 157, 158, 249
Neuronal,
 action potential, 157, 158
 activity, 272
 membrane, 210
 organization, 210
Neuropathology, 132
Neurophysiologist, 24
Neuropsychologist, 69
Neuropsychology, 28, 132, 150
Neurosurgical procedure, 92–130
Neurotransmitter, 249
 code, 276
 substance, 276
Nitrous oxide, 43
Non-polarizing electrical stimulation, 236
Non-polarizable electrode, 156, 173–176
Norepinephrine, 152, 209, 276
Normal
 brain, 160
 distribution, 16, 17, 20
 saline, 94
Nose cone—rat, 94–97
Number, 8, 12, 13, 15
 basis, 13
 exact, 11
 experimental, 11
 meaning of, 7
 system, 7
Numerical law, 10
Nutritional disease, 53

O

Observation, 3, 4, 14
 controlled, 4
 independent, 15, 16
 naturalistic, 3–5
 reliable, 19
Obturator, 252, 259
Occipital cortex, 132
Ohmmeter, 219
Ohm resister, 136
Ohms law, 172
Open-drop method, 44
Operant
 behavior, 307
 response, 304, 307

Operating room set-up,
 cat-monkey, 110
 rat, 93, 94
Operative procedure, 28
Optic
 chiasm, 108
 tract, 86
Optimal frequency, 234
Oral administration of a drug, 36, 46
Organic lesion, 158
Organizing concept, 23
Orienting reflex, 160
Oscilloscope, 181, 200
Overdose of nembutal, 60
Oxyacel, 108, 111, 120

P

Paraffin, 288
Parameter of the population, 17
Parasitic protozoa, 54
Parenteral administration, 36, 37
Parietal bone, 101, 108
Parkinson's syndrome, 68
Pathogenic organism, 50
Pedestal, 221
 base, 252, 258
 suppliers of, 280
Pellet magazine, 307
 dispenser, 308, 309
Penicillin, 54, 56, 58
Penthrane, 44
Pentobarbitone sodium, 46, 47
Pentothal, 46, 47
Percent solution, preparation of, 320
Perfusion, 283
 needle, 284
Peripheral
 nerve, 233
 sense organ, 156
Peristaltic pump, 312
Peritoneal
 cavity, 40
 space, 39
Permount, 290
Pharmacological
 dose, 40
 specificity, 273
Phenothiazine, 47, 59
Phisohex, 113

Physica
  condition, 40
  science, 14
Phosphate buffered
  formalin, 284, 285, 291
  solution, 288
Photographic
  enlarger, 146, 148, 150
  equipment, 146, 147
Photographing brain sections, 148
Photomicrograph, 73, 75
Physiological
  mechanism, 275
  psychology, 2, 4, 5, 12, 24, 28
  saline, 101, 284
  stress, 159
Pia-arachnoid membrane, 102–104, 106, 125
Piperazine
  acid citrate, 52, 57
  hydrate, 59
Pipette, 100, 103, 104, 126
Platinum electrode, 134, 162, 168, 173, 215, 226
Pleuropneumonia-like organism (PPLO), 51, 53
Pneumonia, 54, 56, 58
Polarization, 230
Polarized electrode, 173, 174, 176, 179, 180, 183, 194
Polydipsia, 319, 327
Polyethylene (PE)
  collar, 252
  sleeve, 253
  tube, 253
  tubing, 251, 255, 257, 261
Polyvinyl chloride (PVC) tubing, 257
Population distribution, 17, 19, 20
Porcelain crucible, 290
Position preference, 316, 317
Positive
  integer, 7
  lead, 137
  potential, 157
  rational fraction, 7
Posterior commissure, 79
Post-mortem examination, 50
Post-operative
  care, 106, 128
  death, 48

Post-synaptic
  membrane, 272
  potential, 158
Potassium, 209, 248
  hydroxide, 52–54
  nitrate, 217
Potentiometer, 136, 137
Pre-anesthetic, 46, 47
Preference, 317, 320, 323
  tests, 322, 325
  threshold, 324
    for alcohol, 324
Preference-aversion function, 322
Prefrontal cortex, 132
Preparing the animal for surgery, 95, 113
Primate, 34
Principle
  of Indeterminacy, 13
  of Research, 1
Probability, 13, 20, 21, 23
  of occurrence, 16, 22
Protocol sheet, 30
Protozoa, 53, 54
  disease, 53, 54
Psychomotor epilepsy, 157, 187
Pulmonary acariasis, 59
Pulse, 157
  duration, 215, 235
  rate modulation system, 157
  stimulation, 232
Pump-syringe system, 263
Pure theory, 24
Purified protein derivative (PPD) test, 29, 58
Purse-string suture, 260
Pyrethrin dust, 57
Pyronin, 274, 292, 295

Q

Quantity, 9
Quantitative
  measurement, 6
  statement, 6

R

Rabbit, 33, 46
  pox, 54
Radiation, 318
Radioactive tracer method, 269
Radio frequency isolation unit, 232

Random
  error, 16
  experiment, 22
  observation, 22
  series, 21
  variables, 16
Range, 17, 18
Rat, 33, 46, 148
  albino, 74, 77
  hooded, 77
Rebreathing
  bag, 45
  valve, 45
Receptor, 272
  site, 272
Recruiting response, 239, 242
Rectal administration, 36
Recycling stimulator, 238
Regulatory balance, 304
Reliability, 14, 19
Removal of brain, 284, 285
Repetitive stimulation, 234
Repetitive stimulus, 233
Research, 4
  in animals, 159, 191
  in humans, 159
Resistance, 157, 174
Resistor, 183
Respiration, during anesthesia, 114, 115
Respiratory
  acidosis, 44
  arrest, 113
  blockade, 141
Response, 25
  antidromic, 239
  evoked, 239
  measure, 25
  recruiting, 239
Resting membrane potential, 157
Restraining
  box, 34
  chair, 34, 238
Restraint of the rat, 33
Resuscitator, 49
Retaining screw, 260
Reticular
  formation, 233, 239, 240
  nuclei, 108
Retraction of the skin, 99, 100, 121

Reversible electrode, 173, 174
Rhesus monkey, 34, 68, 135, 222
Richter tube, 32, 309, 311, 317
Ringworm, 52, 54, 57
Rongeurs, 94, 112, 122, 284
  technique, 95, 100, 102, 109, 122
Round worm, 52, 57, 59
Rules for counting, 8

S

Sacrificing an animal, 60
Sage pump, 264
Sagittal
  plane, 68
  section, 78
  suture, 81, 123
Saline, 94, 104, 106, 113, 120, 121, 123–125
  bath, 133, 134
Salmonella bacteria, 51, 58
Sample distribution, 17, 19, 20, 22
  of the mean, 19
Sanitation, 52, 54
Saphenous vein, 38
Scale, 10, 11
Scalp,
  depth relationship, 194
  electroencephalogram, 157
  incision, 99, 121
  recording, 159
  retraction, 120, 121
Scalpel, 141
Scientific
  community, 7
  fact, 3
  inquiry, 5
  instrument, 15
  measurement, 3
  observation, 3
  study, 2
  thinking, 23
Scissors, 95, 111
Scrub pack, 111, 116
Scrubbing techniques,
  for the animal, 116
  for the surgeon, 116
Secobarbital sodium, 47
Seconal, 46, 47
Sections, 289
  frozen, 288

Subject Index

mounting of, 288, 289, 294
  preparation of, 283, 286
  shrinkage of, 288
Sectioning, 285, 286
  frozen, 286
Securing an animal in a head-holder, 97–98, 115–116
Seizure, 237
Selecto-feeder, 309
Self-inject, 248
Self-selection, 313, 315, 316, 321
  cafeteria arrangement, 314
Self-stimulation, 241
Septal region, 236
Septicemia
  in the mouse, 51
  in the cat, 56
Sequence effect, 318
Sernyl, 46
Serotonin (5-HT), 152, 272
Set, 7, 8
  of a series, 7
  observed, 7
Sex, 40
Sexing animals, 30
Shaving the animal, 114
Sheatz pedestal, 221, 222
Shigella bacteria, 58
Shim, 254, 255
Shope fibroma virus, 54
Signal/noise enhancement, 195, 200
Significant figure, 11, 12
Silk thread, 95
Silver
  electrode, 162, 166, 226
  silver chloride electrode, 174, 176, 177, 179, 180
Sine, 195, 197
  wave, 237
Single-pulse electrical stimulation, 159
Single shock stimuli, 233
Site of injection, 264
Site-specificity, 276
Sinusoidal alternating current, 230
Single-stimulus method, 322
Size, 41
Skin
  flap and retraction, 141
    cat-monkey, 121
    rat, 100

incision, 100
suturing technique, 105
Skull, 99, 141, 144, 168, 224
Slides, preparation of, 287
Small animal resuscitator, 49
Snuffles, 54
Socket, 221
Sodium, 171, 209, 248
Sodium chloride, 171
Sodium pentobarbital, 94–97
  dose of, 113
Solution, 261
  micro-injection of, 262
Spacer, 254
Spatial and temporal analysis, 195, 201
Spatiotemporal patterning, 242
Spike
  activity, 158, 185
  discharge, 157
Spindle wave, 158
Sponges, 106, 113, 116, 123–125
Spout-cylinder arrangement, 311
Squamosal bone, 102
Square
  knot, 106
  wave, 229, 231, 232, 236
Squirrel-monkey, 224
Stain, 292–297
Staining,
  method of, 282
  procedure of, 290–293
  solution, 290, 292, 293, 295
  time, 287
  uniformity of, 287
Stainless steel electrode, 162, 167, 173, 175, 180, 215, 216, 218, 226, 231
Standard
  deviation, 17, 18, 20
  error, 23
    of measurement, 20
    of the mean, 20, 22
  series, 8
  set, 9, 15
  unit, 6
  volume, 15
Standards, 9
Statistical
  inference, 19
  regularity, 22
Statistics, 13, 23

Stencil, 150
Stereotaxic
  adaptor, 69
  angle, 73
  atlas, 73–82, 86, 139, 143, 145, 150, 214, 224, 285, 297
    for the cat, 69, 87
    for the dog, 87
    for the primate, 87
    for the rodent, 73, 74, 83, 88
    for other species, 88
  coordinate, 75, 79, 80, 139, 143, 145, 146
  electrode holder, 78
  implantation, 73, 78
    error of, 1
  instrument, 68, 69, 73, 77, 78, 82, 83, 132, 133, 139, 143, 219, 220, 285
    calibration of, 78
    for small animals, 69, 70
    suppliers of, 89, 246
  placement, 73
  plane, 73
  procedure, 93, 259
  surgery, 68, 69, 73, 83
  technique, 67–90, 132, 133, 139
    for the cat, 71
    for the monkey, 72
    for the rat, 70, 71, 78
  zero, 79, 80, 139, 145
Sterile surgical techniques, 99, 110–120
  gloving, 118
  gowning, 117
  positioning instruments, 117
  preparation of the animal, 113
  "scrub-in", 116, 117
  towels, folding of, 119
Sterilization, 60, 110, 225, 226
  by autoclaving, 111
  by solution, 111
  of cages, equipment, and bedding, 51, 52, 54
Sterilizer, 63
Sterilizing, 150
  solution, 50
Stimulation of brain tissue,
  chemical, 210, 248, 265
  crystalline, 268
  electrical, 209, 248, 249
  experimental, 209
  ionic, 248
  repetitive, 234
  solutions *vs* crystals, 271
  subcortical, 211
  of the conscious animal, 237
Stimulation-evoked response, 209
Stimulator, 231, 232
  recycling, 238
  suppliers of, 245
Stimulus, 25, 160, 321, 323
  dimensions of, 209
  duration of, 232
  effect of, 238
  exteroceptive, 304
  high frequency, 234, 237
  interoceptive, 304
  parameters, 233
  pulse, 236, 237
  repetitive, 233
  single shock, 233
Streptobacillus moniliformis, 51, 53
Strongyloides, 59
Study
  of animals, 131, 151, 159
  of humans, 131, 151
Stylet, 137, 138, 252, 256, 258, 259, 262, 264, 265, 268
  tube, 264
Subcortical brain stimulation, 211
Subcutaneous
  injection, 40, 46
  route, 40
Subpial aspiration, 92
Suction
  hose, 113
  lesion, 136
  pump, 103
  tubing, 142
Sulcus, 126
Sulphadimidine, 54
Superior sagittal sinus, 144
Surface negativity, 158
Surgery, 92
Surgical
  anesthesia, 44, 45
  gloves, 99, 111, 116
  gloving, 117, 118
  gowns, 111, 117
    how to fold, 111, 114

instruments, 94
  care of, 95
  positioning of, 117–119
knot, 29, 105, 106, 127, 128
  how to tie, 105
pack, 94
procedure, 99–103, 141
shock, 48
Suture, 104
  buried, 127, 128
  interrupted, 127
    technique, 105, 127, 128
  needle, 105, 106, 111, 127, 128
  thread, 94, 105, 106, 111
Swivel-connector, 238
Syphilis, 54
Syringe, 37, 38, 40, 94, 120, 261
  barrel, 38
  disposable, 261
  micro-injection, 262
  microliter, 261
  needle, 38, 39, 262
  plunger, 261
Systems approach, 24

T

Tamping needle, 269
Tantulum electrode, 162
Tapeworm, 55, 57
Tap, 269
Taste preference situation, 318
Teflon, 227–228
Telestimulation, 238
Temperature, 31, 48, 248
  change, 319
Temporal
  lobectomy, 157
  lobe epilepsy, 159
  muscle retraction, 101, 104
  spatial patterning, 209
Terramycin, 56, 58
Tetracycline, 56, 58
Tetraethylthurium monosulphide, 55
Thalamus, 143, 158, 239
Theoretical
  frequency distribution, 20
  probability, 21
    distribution, 22
Thermal damage, 228, 230
Thermistor, 48, 63

Thermobond, 227
Thiopental sodium, 47
Thirst, 304, 305, 325, 327
Threshold
  effect, 234
  of discrimination, 324
Thrombin, 109, 111, 113, 120
Tick and flea powder, 29
Tissue damage, 227, 228
Tolerance, 12, 13
Topical, 36
Towel, 112
  clamp, 113, 119, 124
  folding of, 119
Toxicity, 43
  of enamel tint, 167
  of metal electrode, 162, 215, 226, 227
Train duration, 234
Tranquilizer, 47
Transmitter, 209, 260
  substance, 249, 273
  system, 270
Transverse
  sinus, 102, 104
  suture, 102, 145
Trauma, 109, 122
  of insertion, 159, 162, 166–168, 191
  mechanical, 225, 226
Treatment of animals, 29
Trephine, 101, 112, 122, 123, 144
  hole, 220
  technique, 102, 122–124
Trilene, 43
Tuberculin syringe, 94
Tuberculosis, 29, 58
Tubing,
  polyethylene (PE), 251, 255, 257, 261
  polyvinyl chloride (PVC), 257
Tungsten electrode, 162, 215–217, 226
Two-bottle test, 324
  acceptance data, 325
Tygon, 227
Tylocin, 53
Tyzzer's Disease, 51

U

Unidirectional pulsating DC, 229
Unipolar (common reference) recording, 182

Units, 6, 9
Upper incisor bar, 73, 77, 84
  calibration of, 82

V

Vaccination, 54, 56
Vaccinia virus, 51, 54
Vacuum pump, 93, 103, 124, 128
Validity, 13, 14
Vapor anesthetic, 47
Variability, 15, 17–19
Variance, 18, 19
Varying duration, 235
Vector field, 215
Velocity, 10, 13
Venipuncture, 38
Ventricle, 256, 268, 275
Ventricular lumen, 256
Ventromedial hypothalamus, 136
Vernier scale, 79, 81
Vertical zero plane, 77, 81
Viral disease, 51, 53, 54, 56, 58
Virus, 51, 53, 54, 56
Visual
  cortex, 160
  response, 241
Vitamin E, 53
Volatile anesthetic, 43–45, 48
  administration of, 44
Voltage, 179, 231
Voltmeter, 174
Volume, 9, 10
  problem of, 265
Volumetric analysis of lesions, 298

W

Warburg impedance, 174
Washing procedure, 99
Water
  balance, 303, 322
  deprivation, 106, 113, 140
  electrolyte balance, 303
  ingestion, 316
  intake, 31, 309, 321
Watering devices, 32
Wave form, 195–197, 229–231, 236
Weighing animal, 10, 32, 95, 113, 143
Weight, 6, 8–11, 41
Weil-Weigert method, 293, 294
Whole-brain assay, 249
Wire
  electrode, 166, 167, 170
  gauge, 205
Worksheet, 150
Wound clip, 112, 113, 121, 141
Wullstein fine knife, 112, 125

X

X-ray,
  of electrode, 225
  photograph, 162
Xylene, 293

Y

Yolk-sac-virus-vaccine, 56

Z

Zero, 12
  reference, 81, 82
Zephiran chloride, 110, 113, 116

QP
360
M 38
v. 1

MAY 6 1974